PIMLICO

559

BRITONS

Linda Colley has taught and written history on both sides of the Atlantic. Formerly Richard M. Colgate Professor of History at Yale University, she is currently Leverhulme Research Professor and School Professor of History at the London School of Economics. She is a Fellow of the British Academy, and a regular commentator on current events as well as past cultures. When *Britons* was first published in 1992 it won the Wolfson Prize and provoked a major debate on national identities in Britain and elsewhere. Her most recent book is *Captives: Britain, Empire and the World 1600–1850* (2002).

Praise for *Britons*

'A triumph, bold in scope and intellectual range, executed with skill, clarity and understanding.' Jeremy Black, *Times Educational Supplement*

'Dashingly readable . . . lively and stimulating. She makes excellent use of artistic evidence.' Keith Thomas, *New York Review of Books*

'Witty and original' Antonia Fraser, *Sunday Times*, Books of the Year

'Linda Colley writes with clarity and grace . . . She also has a capacity for historical generalization that puts her into the front rank of her contemporaries . . . Her purpose is to mark out firmly the boundaries of national consensus . . . She does this superbly well, with controlled judgements and with abundant information. Her stimulating book will be, and deserves to be, influential.' E.P. Thompson, *Dissent*

'A major contribution to our understanding of Britain's past and of the contemporary debate about the shape and identity of Britain in the future.' Colin Dobson, *Oxford Times*

'Lavishly researched and illustrated . . . a remarkable amount of light is shed upon current and coming events.' Enoch Powell, *Spectator*

'The most original, penetrating and readable volume on the eighteenth-century published for many a long year.' Tim Blanning, *Independent*, Books of the Year

'Richly varied . . . a bold and exciting book.' John Derry, *Times Higher Educational Supplement*

'Magnificent . . . a brilliant account of how those elements which went into the making of the British, and which still grip the British imagination, are rapidly losing relevance.' John Osmond, *Western Mail*

'*Britons* offers one of the most persuasive and broad-ranging analyses of loyalism in the eighteenth and early nineteenth centuries. Its analysis of how a ruling elite reconstituted itself in the face of threats from without and within is outstanding. Colley's account of the effects of war in transforming the scope and character of the British state is also unsurpassed.' John Brewer, *Times Literary Supplement*

'An excellent subject and Colley's book does it full justice.' David Papineau, *Independent on Sunday*

'Very original . . . The general reader cannot fail to enjoy it and the professional historian will be stimulated by it.' J.H. Plumb, *Financial Times*

'Resonates insistently with today's headlines . . . a sweeping survey of an important period.' Harriet Ritvo, *New York Times*

'Powerful and absorbing' Blair Worden, *Sunday Telegraph*

'Extremely learned and penetrating. It is also most entertaining . . . a brilliant use of iconography.' Conor Cruise O'Brien, *New Republic*

'Piquantly germane to present concerns . . . Time and again, the arresting connection or the startling detail makes one see familiar ground from a new perspective.' Hugo Young, *Guardian*

BRITONS

Forging the Nation 1707–1837

LINDA COLLEY

With a New Preface by the Author

PIMLICO

Published by Pimlico 2003

2 4 6 8 10 9 7 5 3

First published by Yale University Press 1992
Pimlico edition 1994
New Pimlico edition 2003

Pimlico
Random House, 20 Vauxhall Bridge Road,
London SW1V 2SA

Random House Australia (Pty) Limited
20 Alfred Street, Milsons Point, Sydney,
New South Wales 2061, Australia

Random House New Zealand Limited
18 Poland Road, Glenfield,
Auckland 10, New Zealand

Random House (Pty) Limited
Endulini, 5a Jubilee Road, Parktown 2193, South Africa

The Random House Group Limited Reg. No. 954009
www.randomhouse.co.uk

A CIP catalogue record for this book
is available from the British Library

ISBN 0–7126–9785–3

Papers used by Random House are natural,
recyclable products made from wood grown in sustainable forests;
the manufacturing processes conform to the environmental
regulations of the country of origin

Printed and bound in Great Britain by
Biddles Ltd, Guildford & Kings Lynn

For David

Contents

Acknowledgements

BRITONS TOOK ME A LONG time to write, and I accumulated a proportionately large number of debts. I first approached this topic amidst the palladian splendours of Christ's College, Cambridge, and I must repeat my thanks to its Fellows for their many kindnesses to me, and record my gratitude for the aid and inspiration lent me over the years by the late Sir John Plumb, its then Master. More than anything else, though, this was a Yale book. I worked in that University's history department from 1982 to 1998, and profited beyond measure from the wisdom of colleagues there, especially Ivo Banac, John Blum, Jon Butler, David Brion Davis, John Demos, Peter Gay, Michael Howard, Paul Kennedy, Edmund Morgan, Peter Sahlins and David Underdown. Yale also allowed me to plunder its range of remarkable archives and libraries, especially the wonderful Lewis Walpole Library at Farmington, Connecticut, and the Yale Center for British Art in New Haven, an institution that transformed my approach to the past. Duncan Robinson, its then Director, Betty Muirden, Elizabeth Fairman, Julie Lavorgna, and the staff of its sister organization, the Paul Mellon Centre for Studies in British Art in London, supplied me with tremendous help and tremendous pleasure both. Finally, *Britons* was originally a Yale University Press volume. Like so many other writers, I found in John Nicoll a quite remarkable publisher, unvaryingly enthusiastic and incisive, and extraordinarily patient. I benefited enormously from working with him, and with my impeccably attentive and creative editor Gillian Malpass.

The ideas in these pages evolved over many years and were honed by contact and argument with many other scholars. The Past & Present Society of Oxford allowed me to work out some of my initial thoughts in the pages of its journal, and various chapters were much improved by comments from seminar and conference groups at Cambridge University, the Institute of Historical Research in London, the Dutch Graduate School for Cultural History in Amsterdam, the Center for European Studies at Harvard University, and the Davis Center at Princeton University. Prys Morgan, Alexander Murdoch and Christopher Smout helped save me from some of my errors in Welsh and Scottish history. Chris Bayly enhanced my understanding of Britain's empire. Bruce Smith proved an indefatigable research assistant during the book's final stages. Will Sulkin oversaw its transition from hardback to Pimlico paperback with characteristic verve and commitment; while my agent, Mike Shaw, was a fund of encouragement and good advice throughout.

But my best thanks, now, as back in 1992, as always, go to my husband and comrade-in-arms David Cannadine.

L.J.C.
London, 2002

Preface to the Second Pimlico Edition

THIS BOOK HAD ITS GENESIS IN THE 1980s when I was teaching at Yale University and uncertain whether I would ever again live for any length of time in Britain, which is where I was born and grew up. It took me almost a decade to complete and my motives for writing expanded as I went along.

Britons remains primarily, however, what it was initially projected as: a work of eighteenth- and early nineteenth-century history. It deals with multitudes of long-dead men and women, and with a small island that came over this period to matter hugely. Like most books, *Britons* also reflects the particularities of its author's own past. At one level, I was reacting as I wrote it against the tendency of many of the best and brightest historians of Britain active in the 1960s and '70s to focus overwhelmingly on episodes of riot, radicalism, rebellion and revolution – repression on the one hand and resistance on the other. This appetite for charting division and contest in the British past was in part healthy and legitimate, but it made me as a (then) young historian on the make curious about the other side of the picture. This book was never intended as a comprehensive vision of early modern Britain. I did not set out to make a case in its pages for an unvarying consensus in this society, which would have been absurd, or to deny the manifold fissures and failures within it. But I was concerned to investigate what I saw – and still see – as a profoundly significant shift over time.

After 1707, the 'one united kingdom by the name of Great Britain' proclaimed by the Treaty of Union remained divided in all kinds of ways. Nonetheless, over the next 130 years, it acquired sufficient cohesiveness for a series of domestic insurrections to fail (as they had not invariably failed before 1707), for successive dangerous invasion attempts from abroad to falter and be resisted, and for a string of evermore demanding and geographically ambitious wars to be embarked upon and – with one exception – won. Moreover, there developed in this period both a language of Britishness and a widespread though never uncontested or exclusive belief that the unit called Britain constituted, as one late eighteenth-century Scot put it, an umbrella, a shelter under which various groupings and identities could plausibly and even advantageously congregate. Great Britain became a workmanlike nation of sorts, albeit one that encompassed other, smaller nations. I wanted to explore how and why this came to be so.

This curiosity derived in the main from what I had read in books and archives and from discussions with other historians, but it was also prompted by my own upbringing. Like many others born in Britain I am a mongrel (part Welsh, part Irish and part English), and my education crossed borders. Consequently I have never found resolutely single-stranded histories of my birthplace all that convincing or resonant with my own experience. As a sixth-former in Cardiff I remember feeling perplexed and irritated that lessons in Welsh history were pressed upon me on some days, and lessons in English history on others, with little attempt being made to link these histories or suggest how they might both be part of something bigger. The fact that English, Welsh, and Scottish history have more often than not been taught and interpreted separately is of course politically and culturally significant. But it is equally significant that quarentining these societies from each other, and concentrating only on what is distinctive about their respective pasts, quickly results in distorted and shrunken history. There are important separate stories that need prising open, to be sure, but there are also shared, interlinked and over-arching stories. Without ignoring the former, *Britons* focuses on the latter.

Its format and content reflect my beliefs about how history should be pursued and presented in other respects.

Over the years, there have been many distinguished books on nation-making by theorists of nationalism and historians of political thought, and I have learnt much from them. But purely abstract analyses and a concentration on the ideas of intellectual elites can lead to the rich, messy and discordant – but scarcely unimportant – views of the vast majority of human beings in the past being glossed over or tidied into excessive uniformity and rationality. In this book, as in its companion volume *Captives: Britain, Empire and the World 1600–1850* (Jonathan Cape, 2002), I tried very hard to elicit the opinions and experiences of women as well as men, and to excavate testimonies on the part of the poor and the unsophisticated, not just the prosperous, educated, and powerful. I also made extensive use of visual images, prints, paintings, murals, sculptures and more, employing them as an integral part of, and added dimension to my text. Britishness (like Britain's empire), was imagined, communicated, debated and memorialised in stone and on canvas, in maps, sketch-books, and embroidery, as well as through the spoken, written and printed word. Britishness was also fashioned in reaction to external and not simply internal stimuli. *Britons*, like *Captives*, situates Britain in a wider European, Transatlantic and global context. Without such a broad-angled vision, British history cannot be adequately understood. Nor can the very recent British past and the present, which also have a bearing on this work.

Books that take a long time to write are inevitably at the mercy of change and serendipity: and this was the (largely) happy fate of *Britons*. In some respects, the transformations that occurred as I was writing it were personal ones. What had been projected purely as a history book became inflected at a minor level, I am sure, by my own consciousness of identity under pressure while working as a resident alien in the United States. Far more importantly, however, the book's conclusions were sharpened, though not I believe distorted, by events in Britain and elsewhere during the course of its completion. By the time *Britons* was first published in 1992, the Falklands War, Margaret Thatcher's long tenure of power, the increased grip and contentiousness of what is now the European Union, growing support for devolution in Wales and Scotland, fierce debates about the future of Northern Ireland and immigration, and a besetting and excessively self-flagellatory obsession with British decline, had all served to make questions of identity and patriotism, the cements and corrosives of nationhood, current and contentious to a degree that had not obtained when I first embarked upon the project. Partly as a result of this, *Britons* secured a level of review attention, media comment, political notice – and sales – not normally available to scholarly analyses of the Georgian past. This is manifestly not a complaint. Historians are bound by their profession to unpack and interpret the past. They are privileged indeed if their writings penetrate beyond the academy and influence and inspire contemporary debate.

If there was a downside to the attention lavished on *Britons*, it was that a degree of political and even prophetic purpose was occasionally attributed to it quite beyond its author's intention or capacity. On one occasion, a celebrated periodical published two different critiques of this book adjacent to each other. One of them, by a Scottish nationalist, claimed that I was covertly seeking to perpetuate the Union; the other, by an evident Tory, accused me of plotting the break-up of Britain. As this exchange underlines, there is in fact no single, monolithic conclusion to be drawn from this book about Great Britain's future survival (or not) as a political unit and comparatively recent and hybrid nation. As a citizen, I naturally have my own opinions and preferences.[1] And I still adhere to this book's conclusion: 'that a substantial rethinking of what it means to be British can no longer be evaded', and to the view that the events and developments set out in these pages help to explain why that is the case. But *Britons* is a history book, not prophecy or polemic. It aspires to help interested readers understand aspects of the British present as well as a vital portion of the British past. Britain's future, however, like the future of its three component countries, can only be a matter for their varied peoples, for the politicians, and for chance.

This said, a better, and more nuanced understanding of the past could contribute a useful measure of clarity and depth to current debates on these issues.

An otherwise stimulating book by Richard Weight has recently suggested that Great Britain and subsequently the United Kingdom were disreputable and violent creations from the start: 'founded on greed, religious and racial bigotry, fear and contempt', and '. . . primarily established to further the quest for Empire'.[2] This strikes me as a historian not so much as untrue as beside the point. As *Britons* makes abundantly clear, the post-1707 invention that was Great Britain was indeed a markedly aggressive and predatory state, though no more bigoted in religious terms than most Western and non-Western polities at that point. As happened with other made-up, composite nations, fifteenth-century Spain for instance, or the republic forged out of the thirteen American colonies after 1776, a political union embracing different peoples and cultures was followed and fostered in Britain's case by recurrent war against external enemies and persistent prejudice as well against internal 'others'. The Roman Catholic was often feared and despised in Britain (and of course in Ireland) in this period and after; just as the Native American was harassed in the early American Republic, and Muslims were hated and enslaved in Ferdinand and Isabella's Spain. In each case, attacking an internal minority that was perceived as alien, dangerous, and inferior helped foster a sense of nationhood and common purpose.

As this suggests, however, the aggression that accompanied Britain's forging was scarcely unique, though for a while it was uniquely world-wide. To label Great Britain, and later the United Kingdom, as somehow peculiarly nasty entities from their inception is to lend credence to the idea that there are other nations which are inherently natural and benign. In historical fact, all nations that have ever existed have been man-made constructions, and as such impure, imperfect, intolerant at times of various minorities, and prone to violence. Great Britain may or may not implode in the near or distant future. But if it does, this will not be because it is uniquely malign and synthetic, but rather because it can no longer function adequately as a unit or command sufficient support or belief from its varied peoples.

Britons' sub-title was carefully chosen and designed to be understood at various levels. 'Forging the Nation' was intended to convey both a process of making and that element of counterfeit and invention that has characterised all nations at some point, but was striking and recent in Britain's own case. I was also thinking of an epigram by the American poet Chester Kallman:

To *forge a style*. Does that mean *fraudulently ape*
Or *work out a garment you never can escape?*
It well could mean instead
A way to get ahead.[3]

Post-1707 Britain cohered and grew powerful in part by way of varieties of internal and external violence. But it also worked and prospered because for a long while it was able to convince many (never remotely all) within its boundaries that it offered ways for them to get ahead, whether in terms of commercial opportunity, or enhanced religious security and constitutional freedoms, or greater domestic stability and safety from invasion, or access to improved job opportunities at home and abroad, or less tangible forms of betterment. By the same token, if Great Britain fissures in the future into autonomous Welsh, Scottish and English nations – and it may – this will in part be because its different peoples have decided that they can get ahead better without it.

There is another respect in which thinking more carefully and more coolly about the past might contribute to the current debate about Britain's future. In recent years, much of this debate has been couched in terms of real and imaginary cultural traditions and essences. Writings and speeches of varying quality on 'Scottishness', 'Englishness', 'Welshness' and 'Britishness' now abound, so much so that the impression is sometimes conveyed that these are purely domestic phenomena nurtured by and dependent upon internal circumstances only. Yet in reality national identity and identities within the island of Great Britain have always been influenced by events and forces beyond it, and this continues to be the case today.

It is a major argument of *Britons* that, in all kinds of ways, Britishness was constructed and contested after 1707 in response to overseas developments. On the one hand, the existence from the 1600s of flourishing colonies in North America and the Caribbean meant that there came into being what David Hancock calls a 'British Atlantic community'.[4] As a result, and as Chapter 4 of *Britons* describes, the loss after 1776 of the most populous sector of this Transatlantic community, the Thirteen Colonies, provoked both trauma at home and an unavoidable reappraisal of how Britain could be renovated and its rulers re-legitimise themselves.

Overseas empire impacted in other ways too. The commercial, investment and employment opportunities it afforded helped reconcile previously refractory individuals, lobbies and regions to British union, most conspicuously, and as Chapter 3 sets out, in Scotland. The imperatives of empire also compelled the rulers of Britain themselves to adapt and compromise. The decision to break the official link between Britishness and Protestantism and pass the Catholic Emancipation Act in 1829, a theme of Chapter 8, was scarcely unconnected to the fact that – by that stage – Catholic Irishmen made up over a half of the empire's white soldiery in India.[5] This was only one respect in which expanding empire had the effect of making Great Britain an even more hybrid entity than it was to begin with. Imperial aggression and slave trading may have served at one level to make some white Britons more racially self-conscious and arrogant. But empire and slavery also served to expand the number of black Britons. And it was some of these men and women, as well as white abolitionists, who led the campaign against the slave trade: a crucial component – as the final chapter of this book describes – of the Victorian conception of what Britain was all about.

It needs stressing however that, in this period as in others, Continental connections were always as influential and as multifarious as Transatlantic ties and other imperial networks. One of the recurrent arguments of *Britons* is that the overwhelming Catholicism of large parts of Continental Europe, and especially France and Spain, provided a newly-invented Britain with a formidable 'other' against which it could usefully define itself. The real and imaginary threat represented by French and, to a lesser extent after 1707, Spanish forms of government, religion, and military power allowed the different Protestant traditions of Scotland, Wales, and England to come together in a common union of self-preservation, anxiety, and defiance.

This did not mean however – as some have suggested – that Continental Europe always functioned or was regarded as Britain's antithesis. Militant but nervous Protestantism also provided in the period covered by this book for important and persistent British alliances with co-religionists in various German states. From 1714, until the end of the timespan covered by this volume, 1837, Britain was regnally joined with the Protestant German electorate of Hanover. It was ruled by successive Hanoverian monarchs; individual Hanoverians filled various of its state offices; and it regularly went to war on the Continent whenever Hanoverian interests were threatened. Hanoverian soldiers, as well as troops from other Protestant German states, also provided invaluable additional cannon fodder for British military purposes. At least a third of all 'British' troops employed in the American Revolutionary War were in fact German Protestant warriors. More positively, it was the aid and armies of Protestant Prussia that allowed Britain to emerge so victorious in the Seven Years War (1756–1763), and to win the Battle of Waterloo in 1815, the very foundation – as outlined in Chapter 8 of this book – of its nineteenth-century European and global hegemony. Right up to 1914, and even after that in some quarters, Britain's 'natural ally' was not generally viewed as being the United States of America, but rather Germany.

Why is all this historical detail significant now? Because it helps to explain why current debates about Britain's identity and future can appear so tortured and intractable. This is not simply due to domestic factors, fissures and frictions. From its very invention as a unitary state and would-be nation in 1707, Great Britain has pushed and been pulled in many and different overseas directions. It was part of a Transatlantic community. Imperial greed gave it interests and investments in every other ocean and continent as well. And it was an integral part of Europe quite as much as it fought in Europe. What has changed over the last half century and more, is that Britain's freedom to balance and choose between these different alignments and attachments has radically diminished.

At its eighteenth-, nineteenth-, and early twentieth-century peak, being at once Transatlantic, global and European was a function and an emblem of British power. Now these self-same multiple alignments often seem only to contribute to British division and disarray. On the one hand, American global hegemony vitally determines, and arguably sometimes distorts, Britain's foreign policy, defence procurement, culture and economy. On the other, Brussels and the European Union interfere progressively with Britain's laws and internal government. More perhaps than by any other issue, Britain's political classes – and especially the English – are riven between the claims of its partners in Continental Europe and the claims and power of the United States, neither of which in truth can be substantially or plausibly resisted by a small offshore island. In addition, Britain's own growing non-white population, in large part the legacy of its past imperial ventures, functions as a vivid source of domestic change, and – in the eyes of some – as an encroaching challenge. Britain, that one-time presumptuous and promiscuous global player, has become – *or so it can appear* – a plaything of others.

But there are other ways of looking at things.

'The importance of the idea of identity can scarcely be doubted', Amartya Sen has recently written, yet neglecting 'our plural identities in favour of one "principal" identity can greatly impoverish our lives and our practical reason.'[6] Given the unprecedented level of change we are all now living through (and this is emphatically not just a challenge felt by the British), it is understandable that many people hunger for some kind of renewed anchorage, and often for a narrower, more traditional, and seemingly more secure sense of who they are. As far as this small island is concerned, the current interest in learning Cornish and arguing for Cornish autonomy, or in exploring some of the more uncompromising versions of Islam, are both examples of a much more widespread yearning for roots and a kind of imagined ancestral purity. It is important that such yearnings, however sincere and deeply-felt they may be, do not lead to an embracing of a single, *exclusive* identity. It is important, too, that the natural human desire for a sense of belonging should not be accompanied, in Britain or anywhere else, by a recoiling from overseas influences which in reality offer myriad opportunities as well as (sometimes) shocks and dangers.

Under pressure from without as well as within, Britain's capacity to function as an efficient umbrella over different peoples and cultures may – or may not – continue long into this new millennium. But whether it does continue or no, we should not panic; and we should not allow obsessive navel-gazing to distract us from evolving a broad-angled view of the world and a better and more generous sense of citizenship. Sen's vision of a 'unitary but freedom-centred conception of Britain as a society of persons, with various backgrounds, who are free to choose their own identities and priorities', and who are also at ease with an ever-more inter-connected world in which they are no longer paramount, but must collaborate with others, will never command universal support.[7] But neither should it too easily be given up.

L.J.C.
London, 2002

Notes

1. Christopher Harvie, 'Uncool Britannia: Linda Colley's *Britons* reconsidered', and Michael Gove, 'The Flight from History', *Times Literary Supplement*, 8 January 1999. For my thoughts about identities and nationhood as a British citizen rather than as a historian, see my Millennium Lecture, 'Britishness in the 21st Century', 10 Downing Street website.
2. Richard Weight, *Patriots: National Identity in Britain 1940–2000* (London, 2002), pp. 1 and 727.
3. Chester Kallman, *Absent and Present* (Middletown, CT., 1963), p. 70. The emphases are the poet's own. I am grateful to David Underdown for drawing my attention to this verse.
4. See David Hancock, *Citizens of the World: London Merchants and the Integration of the British Atlantic Community, 1735–1785* (Cambridge, 1995).
5. For more on this, see Chapters 10 and 11 of my *Captives: Britain, Empire and the World 1600–1850* (London, 2002).
6. Amartya Sen, 'Beyond Identity. Other People', *The New Republic*, 18 December 2000, pp. 23 and 25.
7. *ibid.*, p. 29.

Introduction

THIS BOOK IS ABOUT THE FORGING of the British nation between the Act of Union joining Scotland to England and Wales in 1707 and the formal beginning of the Victorian age in 1837. I have written it with two linked intentions in mind. The first is to uncover the identity, actions and ideas of those men and women who were willing to support the existing order against the major threats their nation faced from without, to establish exactly what it was these Britons thought they were being loyal to, and what they expected to gain from their commitment. The second is to show that it was during this period that a sense of British national identity was forged, and that the manner in which it was forged has shaped the quality of this particular sense of nationhood and belonging ever since, both in terms of its remarkable strengths and resilience, and in terms of its considerable and increasingly evident weaknesses.

What made these themes, mass allegiance on the one hand and the invention of Britishness on the other, so central during this 130-year long period was a succession of wars between Britain and France. Prime powers on sea and on land respectively, the whale and the elephant as Paul Kennedy styles them, they were at war between 1689 and 1697, and on a larger scale and for higher stakes between 1702 and 1713, 1743 and 1748, 1756 and 1763, 1778 and 1783, 1793 and 1802, and, finally, between 1803 and the Battle of Waterloo in 1815. And these were only the most violent expressions of a much longer and many-layered rivalry.[1] Even in the interludes of token peace, the two powers repeatedly plotted against and spied on each other. Their settlers and armed forces jostled for space and dominance in North America, the West Indies, Africa, Asia and Europe. French clerics, intellectuals and tourists scrutinised Britain's political system, moral fibre and cultural achievements, and their British counterparts did the same with regard to France, in both cases with a manic obsessiveness that betrayed their mutual antagonism and anxiety.[2] Like another famously unhappy couple, the British and the French had their teeth so sunk into each other in these years (and long after) that

1. *The Gallic Cock and English Lyon*, anonymous print, 1739.

2. The British Lion and the French Cock: a sketch by Philippe de Loutherbourg, *c.*1797.

they could neither live together peacefully, nor ignore each other and live neutrally apart. The result was less a series of separate and conventional wars, than one peculiarly pervasive and long-drawn out conflict which rarely had time to become a cold war in the twentieth-century sense.

It is a commonplace that this prolonged struggle tested and transformed state power on both sides of the Channel. In Great Britain, it led directly to the founding of the Bank of England and to the creation of the City, to the evolution of a more efficient and nationwide fiscal system, and to the emergence of a massive military machine which has only begun to be seriously dismantled since the Second World War.[3] Yet to read most history books is to gain the impression that these organisational changes took place within a human vacuum. We know extraordinarily little about how the majority of British civilians responded to this succession of wars, and to the innovations, conquests and dangers that accompanied them.[4] In part, but only in part, this is because – unlike almost every other European nation in this period – Great Britain never experienced a major invasion from without. As a result, it never had to resort (though it came close to it) to implementing mass conscription. Consequently, the impression has persisted that what has been mis-called Britain's second hundred years war with France took place largely outside the thought-world of its civilian population: that in these conflicts – in contrast to the Civil War of the mid-seventeenth century or the World Wars of the twentieth – the politicians, bureaucrats and professional soldiers remained an active minority surrounded by an indifferent multitude.

Yet this is quite wrong. The fact that Britain escaped a substantial invasion did not make the prolonged conflict with France seem irrelevent to the mass of its inhabitants. It merely made responses to the wars more unabashedly chauvinistic. Unlike most of their European neighbours, Britons at this time – like Americans in the twentieth century – were able to savour military glory without ever having to pay the price in terms of civilian casualties and large-scale domestic destruction. Singularly free from these more brutal imperatives, they were able to focus, many of them, on the broader, less material characteristics of the struggle with France, a struggle that played a crucial part in defining Great Britain through the very process of exposing it to persistent danger from without.

At one level, these were religious wars, and perceived as such by both sides. One of France's primary objectives in the Nine Years War (1689–97), in the War of Spanish Succession (1702–13) and in the War of Austrian Succession (1739–48) was an invasion of

Britain in support of the Stuart claimants to the throne, first the exiled James II, then his son, James Edward Stuart, and finally his grandson, Charles Edward Stuart, alias Bonnie Prince Charlie. Since these princes were Roman Catholics, all of these wars were bound to raise the issue of the security of the Protestant settlement within Great Britain itself, as well as the spectre of another civil war on its shores. Even in the Seven Years War (1756–63), there was a slight, vestigial threat of a French-sponsored Jacobite invasion.

By then, though, Jacobitism throughout Britain was plainly dust and ashes. The main ideological threat posed by the next two wars with France was not religious but overwhelmingly political. By allying with the Americans after 1778, France succeeded in stripping Britain of the most valuable sector of its first empire, and the part with which the bulk of its population felt the closest emotional ties. A territory once governed from London was converted into a republic which raucously proclaimed itself not just independent, but freer, better and more genuinely Protestant than the mother country. In other words, this war, too, forced the British to look anxiously and inquiringly inwards, even though the bulk of the action took place three thousand miles away on the other side of the Atlantic. The French Revolutionary and Napoleonic Wars (1793–1802 and 1803–15) would prove still more corrosive to British constitutional complacency, as well as lasting longer, extending over a larger geographical area and posing a much greater threat of invasion.

All of these major wars, then, challenged the political and/or religious foundations upon which Great Britain was based, and threatened its internal security and its commercial and colonial power. Consequently, its rulers were obliged, over and over again, to mobilise not just the consent, but increasingly the active co-operation of large numbers of Britons in order to repel this recurrent danger from without. Of course, not everyone responded positively. In recent years, we have learned a great deal about those men and women who defied the authorities and persisted in supporting a Jacobite invasion of Britain in the first half of the eighteenth century, or who opposed Britain's war with America after 1775, or who supported peace with Republican and Napoleonic France after 1793.[5]

There were always dissenting voices: and it is right and proper that they should emerge loud and clear from the historical record and that we acknowledge them. But we should not let them drown out the other, *apparently* more conventional voices of those far greater numbers of Britons who, for many different reasons, supported these successive war efforts. What follows is partly an attempt to rescue these people, the seeming conformists, from the condescension of posterity (I had more appropriately said from the ignorance of historians). Their behaviour badly needs reconstructing because it usually represented much more than visceral chauvinism, or simple-minded deference, or blinkered conservatism. For all classes and for both sexes, patriotism was more often than not a highly rational response and a creative one as well. Patriotism in the sense of identification with Britain served, as we shall see, as a bandwagon on which different groups and interests leaped so as to steer it in a direction that would benefit them. Being a patriot was a way of claiming the right to participate in British political life, and ultimately a means of demanding a much broader access to citizenship.

Looking critically and comprehensively at patriotism in this period is also vital if we are to understand the evolution of what must be called British nationalism. I am aware that in referring to Great Britain as a nation, I may bewilder, and even offend those who are accustomed to thinking of nations only as historic phenomena characterised by cultural and ethnic homogeneity. My reply would be that, if we confine our use of the term 'nation' to such pure, organic growths, we shall find precious few of them available in the world either to study or to live in. By contrast, if we accept Benedict Anderson's admittedly loose, but for that reason invaluable definition of a nation as 'an imagined political community', and if we accept also that, historically speaking, most nations have always been culturally and ethnically diverse, problematic, protean and artificial constructs that take shape very quickly and come apart just as fast, then we can plausibly regard Great Britain as an invented nation superimposed, if only for a while, onto much older alignments and loyalties.[6]

It was an invention forged above all by war. Time and time again, war with France brought Britons, whether they hailed from Wales or Scotland or England, into confrontation with an obviously hostile Other and encouraged them to define themselves collectively against it. They defined themselves as Protestants struggling for survival against the world's foremost Catholic power. They defined themselves against the French as they imagined them to be, superstitious, militarist, decadent and unfree. And, increasingly as the wars went on, they defined themselves in contrast to the colonial peoples they conquered, peoples who were manifestly alien in terms of culture, religion and colour. National identity, Peter Sahlins has written, 'like ethnic or communal identity, is contingent and relational: it is defined by the social or territorial boundaries drawn to distinguish the collective self and its implicit negation, the other'.[7] In other words, men and women decide who they are by reference to who and what they are not. Once confronted with an obviously alien 'Them', an otherwise diverse community can become a reassuring or merely desperate 'Us'. This was how it was with the British after 1707. They came to define themselves as a single people not because of any political or cultural consensus at home, but rather in reaction to the Other beyond their shores.[8]

I am not suggesting for one moment that the growing sense of Britishness in this period supplanted and obliterated other loyalties. It did not. Identities are not like hats. Human beings can and do put on several at a time. Great Britain did not emerge by way of a 'blending' of the different regional or older national cultures contained within its boundaries as is sometimes maintained, nor is its genesis to be explained primarily in terms of an English 'core' imposing its cultural and political hegemony on a helpless and defrauded Celtic periphery.[9] As even the briefest acquaintance with Great Britain will confirm, the Welsh, the Scottish and the English remain in many ways distinct peoples in cultural terms, just as all three countries continue to be conspicuously sub-divided into different regions. The sense of a common identity here did not come into being, then, because of an integration and homogenisation of disparate cultures. Instead, Britishness was superimposed over an array of internal differences in response to contact with the Other, and above all in response to conflict with the Other.

Recognising this helps to explain some of Britain's current difficulties. As an invented nation heavily dependent for its *raison d'être* on a broadly Protestant culture, on the threat and tonic of recurrent war, particularly war with France, and on the triumphs, profits and Otherness represented by a massive overseas empire, Britain is bound now to be under immense pressure. It is not just that it has had to adjust to the loss of its empire, though that is obviously part of the problem. It is also that Protestantism is now only a residual part of its culture, so it can no longer define itself against a predominantly Catholic Europe. Indeed, now that it is part of the European Economic Community, Great Britain can no longer comfortably define itself against the European powers at all. Whether it likes it or not, it is fast becoming part of an increasingly federal Europe, though the agonies that British politicians and voters of all partisan persuasions so plainly experience in coming to terms with Brussels and its dictates show just how rooted the perception of Continental Europe as the Other still is. In these circumstances, the re-emergence of Welsh, Scottish and indeed

English nationalism which has been so marked in recent decades can be seen not just as the natural outcome of cultural diversity, but as a response to a broader loss of national, in the sense of British, identity. The Other in the shape of militant Catholicism, or a hostile Continental European power, or an exotic overseas empire is no longer available to make Britons feel that – by contrast – they have an identity in common. The predictable result has been a revival of internal divisions among them. The manner in which Great Britain was made out of that remarkable succession of wars with France in the past is a root cause of its uncertain identity in the present, and may well be the means of its unmaking in the future.

This book, then, deals both with a specific problem – why did Britons in the eighteenth and early nineteenth centuries become patriots and with what results? – and with a process that continues to have broad-ranging repercussions to this day: the invention of a nation. I have cast the book chronologically, focussing on different themes and groups according to the time when they became most prominent. The first three chapters explore the main cements in Great Britain from its creation as a nominally united kingdom in 1707 to the outbreak of the American Revolution some seventy years later: the overwhelming influence of Protestantism, the contribution made by trade, and the growing connexions between Scotland and the rest of the island and its empire. Chapters four to seven focus on the half-century after the Declaration of Independence in 1776, one of the most formative periods in the making of the modern world and – not accidentally – in the forging of British identity. These were the years in which the monarchy and the governing class became authentically and very effectively British, and both ordinary working men and unprecedented numbers of women were drawn into national affairs and especially national defence as never before. The final chapter takes the story from Waterloo to the accession of Queen Victoria in 1837, years when the shock of peace after so many major wars forced a re-examination of the connexions between Britishness and active citizenship.

In adopting this structure, I am aware that much has had to be glossed over and some things have had to be left out altogether. I have concentrated on civilian responses, rather than on attitudes in the armed forces, which desperately need separate and detailed attention. I have tried to bring together in one book the experiences and mental furniture of Britons from different social backgrounds and from different parts of the island, and in particular to bring out the myriad voices of those who have often and wrongly been deemed too conventional to be listened to; but I have not attempted a history of high culture. There is nothing here on political theory. And although I have drawn heavily on visual evidence as well as on written sources in reconstructing what Britishness involved, I have not discussed in detail what fine art, or the theatre, or literature, or music can tell us about this subject. I hope that in the future others will. Finally, I have chosen to look at Wales, Scotland and England, and at how their inhabitants defined themselves in relation to the rest of Europe and to the British empire. But although I occasionally refer to those Irishmen and women who lived on the British mainland, I have deliberately not written about Ireland itself. The invention of Britishness was so closely bound up with Protestantism, with war with France and with the acquisition of empire, that Ireland was never able or willing to play a satisfactory part in it. Its population was more Catholic than Protestant. It was the ideal jumping-off spot for a French invasion of Britain, and both its Catholic and its Protestant dissidents traditionally looked to France for aid. And although Irishmen were (and still are) an important component of Britain's armed forces, and individual Irishmen played leading imperial roles as generals, diplomatists and pro-consuls, Ireland's relationship with the empire was always a deeply ambiguous one. How could it not be, when London treated it as a colony, and when Irishmen of all kinds partook, as Roy Foster has written, 'psychologically and pragmatically . . . of attitudes best called colonial'?[10] Ireland was cut off from Great Britain by the sea; but it was cut off still more effectively by the prejudices of the English, Welsh and Scots, and by the self-image of the bulk of the Irish themselves, both Protestants and Catholics.

One last point: this book is about patriotism and nationalism, but I have tried to ensure that neither its content nor its approach is insular. The evolution of Britishness as I understand it cannot, in fact, be understood without reference to both European and world history, and one of my wider aims in tackling this subject was to get away from the highly introverted and specialised mode of historical writing to which post-war British historians have been so prone. I wanted to integrate the domains of military and imperial history with the broad political and social history of Great Britain as a whole. Doing this seems to me to be the only appropriate way to make sense of this nation's past and of its present. For, contrary to received wisdom, the British are not an insular people in the conventional sense – far from it. For most of their early modern and modern history, they have had more contact with more parts of the world than almost any other nation – it is just that this contact has regularly taken the form of aggressive military and commercial enterprise. As I have said and as I shall continue to argue, this is a culture that is used to fighting and has largely defined itself through fighting. Indeed, if a recent trans-European survey is correct, over two-thirds of Britons remain only too willing to fight for their country. By contrast, less than a half of their European neighbours indicate a similar willingness to express their patriotism in this fashion.[11] Perhaps someone who is part Welsh, part English, Transatlantic in lifestyle and European by choice – as well as British – may be allowed to express the hope that, if Britishness survives (and it may not), it will in the future find a more pragmatic and more generous form.

3. God Land: Benjamin West, *Allegory of Britannia*, 1812.

1 *Protestants*

When Britain first at heaven's command,
Arose from out the azure main,
This was the charter of the land.
And guardian angels sung this strain:

'Rule Britannia, rule the waves,
Britons never will be slaves'.[1]

JAMES THOMSON'S WORDS HAVE BECOME so familiar since they were composed in 1740, have been roared out so often in concert halls, at football matches or church services, in a mood of jingoistic pride or, more recently, self-indulgent nostalgia, that we hardly bother anymore to think about what they mean or what they fail to say. We barely notice that opening all-important reference to Britain's divine origins, even though for Thomson – a minister's son from the Scottish Lowlands – it would have meant a great deal. And the chorus is so rousing that it scarcely seems to matter that it is Britain's supremacy *offshore* that is being celebrated, not its internal unity. Or that the British are defined less by what they have in common, than negatively – whatever these people are, we are told, they are not slaves. Yet Thomson's emphases, like his silences, are suggestive. It is almost as if God is being invoked and bombast is being deployed to deter more searching questions. For just who were the British? Did they even exist?

A LESS THAN UNITED KINGDOM

As a would-be nation, rather than a name, Great Britain was invented in 1707 when the Parliament of Westminster passed the Act of Union linking Scotland to England and Wales. From now on, this document proclaimed, there would be 'one united kingdom by the name of Great Britain', with one Protestant ruler, one legislature and one system of free trade. Like the earlier Act of Union between England and Wales in 1536, this was very much a union of policy, as the novelist and journalist Daniel Defoe called it, not a union of affection. The politicians in London had feared that unless a formal, political union with Scotland was cemented, as distinct from the existing dynastic union, the country might opt on the death of poor childless Queen Anne (1702–14) for James Edward Stuart, her exiled Roman Catholic half-brother, instead of agreeing, as the English and Welsh had already done, to import a new Protestant dynasty from Hanover. A full, legislative union was the only solution London was prepared to consider.[2] But few pretended at the time or later that a union on paper would automatically forge a united people.

Of course, Scotland and England had been drawing increasingly together since the Reformation in the sixteenth century. Since 1603, the two countries had been ruled by the same Stuart dynasty. They shared the same King James version of the Bible. And long before the Act of Union, a cognate language with English called Scots had spread throughout the Scottish Lowlands and beyond, so that men and women on one side of the border could – usually – communicate with their neighbours on the other side. In commercial terms, too, Scotland and England had a long history of interdependence, the latter taking easily a half of Scottish exports by 1700.[3] None the less, a thoroughgoing political union between Scotland and the rest of Britain had by no means been a foregone conclusion, and even the Act of Union only partially achieved it. Scots were now represented in the same Parliament as the English and the Welsh; they paid the same taxes and customs duties, and competed for the same government and administrative appointments. But they still retained their distinctive religious organisation and social structure, as well as their own legal and educational systems. And in the first half of the eighteenth century, especially, poor transport, inadequate maps and the sheer distance separating Scotland from London enabled them to remain largely self-governing in practice.[4]

For the majority of Scots at this early stage, the Union was of only marginal relevance to their lives. As for the wealthy or ambitious minority, they were torn between anger at the loss of Scotland's ancient independence and a natural desire for a wider stage than their own homeland could afford them. At one and the same time, they resented the South and craved its bounty and opportunities, kicking against the Union when it proved uncomfortable, yet demanding full parity with the English inside it. On the other side of the border, ambiguity and reluctance were just as marked. It is sometimes supposed that the Act of Union was a piece of cultural and political imperialism foisted on the hapless Scots by their stronger southern neighbour. But this was not how many eighteenth-century Englishmen regarded it. To some of them, union with Scotland seemed a blatant affront to older identities. They bitterly disapproved of 'English' and 'England' giving way to 'British' and 'Great Britain', as they were in both official and everyday vocabulary by the 1750s.[5] And many regarded the Scots as poor and pushy relations, unwilling to pay their full share of taxation, yet constantly demanding access to English resources in terms of trade and jobs. There was also an element of fear. The fact that in 1715 and 1745, hostile Jacobite armies marched into England from Scotland ensured that older memories of cross-border hostilities remained alive. 'Scotland . . . is certainly the sink of the earth', a Whig grandee would write to the Duke of Newcastle after the Battle of Culloden in 1746. 'As to Scotland,' replied Newcastle, who was then Secretary of State as well as the Prime Minister's brother, 'I am as little partial to it as any man alive.' 'However,' he added, in a rare fit of generosity, 'we must consider that they are within our island.'[6]

English nationalists were much less repelled by their union with Wales, partly because this connexion was so much older, but primarily because the Welsh seemed so much less threatening than the more numerous and militarily minded Scots. Yet in some respects, Wales was a more aloof and distinctive country even than Scotland. True, its separate identity was not rooted in institutions. It had lost its own legal system, its religious organisation was modelled on England's own, and it had no universities or capital city like Edinburgh to serve as a focus for its cultural life. What distinguished the Welsh was their language, a language that three out of four of them still spoke out of choice as late as the 1880s.[7] In the eighteenth century, English was largely confined to Radnor, Monmouthshire, Glamorgan and parts of Pembroke, to the few well-established towns like Conwy in North Wales, and to emerging urban centres like Neath and Cowbridge in South Wales.[8] Some Welsh-speakers were bilingual. Even in the mountains and remote villages of central Wales, travellers and traders from England could usually find a few individuals to understand them. But amongst themselves, most Welshmen and women below gentry level spoke only their own language. And for much of the time – though not for all of the time – they seem to have regarded the English as a different people. In 1751, a Welshman living in London would claim that his poorer countrymen back home knew 'no other name for Englishmen at this day, than *saison*, or saxons'.[9]

At one level, then, Great Britain at the beginning of the eighteenth century was like the Christian doctrine of the Trinity, both three and one, and altogether something of a mystery. The inhabitants of

Wales, of Scotland and of England were separated from each other by history and in some cases by language. And until the end of the century, when better transport, together with a greater supply of mass-produced goods and English-language books and newspapers, began to reduce local peculiarities somewhat, they were also separated from each other and among themselves by different folklores, different sports, different costumes, different building styles, different agricultural practices, different weights and measures, and different cuisines. Yet acknowledging that England, Wales and Scotland in 1707 differed sharply from each other is not the same as saying that ordinary men and women in each of these three countries were invariably possessed by a single and overwhelming sense of their own distinctive identity as Englishmen, or Welshmen, or Scots. Most of them were not.

The Welsh and the Scots, for example, rarely defined themselves against the English by reference to the kind of rich Celtic nationalism that certain Irish patriots would make so much of after the 1840s. Nor did they usually see themselves as fellow Celts, and for good reason. Wales and Scotland had no frontier in common, and precious little culture in common either. The Gaelic spoken by Scottish Highlanders was very different from the Celtic language spoken by many of the Welsh, far more different in fact than English was from French or German. And the majority of Lowland Scots and a substantial minority of Welshmen were not even Celtic in ethnic origin, but Anglo-Saxon or Norse. So while it is highly convenient to use the term 'Celtic fringe' as a piece of shorthand for Wales and Scotland as well as for Ireland – and the phrase is sometimes used in that fashion in this book – doing so tells us very little about how the inhabitants of these countries actually saw themselves.[10]

Moreover, attachment to Wales, to Scotland and even to England was always complicated by the fact that these three countries were neither united in themselves nor distinct from each other. 'Different as English-speaking Scotland was from its southern neighbour', as Tom Nairn writes, 'it actually contained a much greater internal differentiation within its own historical frontiers'.[11] In terms of language, religion, levels of literacy, social organisation and ethnicity, Scottish Lowlanders had far more in common with the inhabitants of northern England than they did with their own Highland countrymen. This was reflected in the vocabulary of the time. Sassenach (in the original Gaelic, *sasunnach*) means a Saxon, and the word is now used as one of the kinder Scottish epithets for someone who is English born and bred. But in the eighteenth century, it was used overwhelmingly by Scottish

Highlanders as a blanket term to cover English-speaking Scottish Lowlanders as well as the English themselves. In Highland eyes, these two peoples were virtually indistinguishable, and both were equally alien. In turn, Lowland Scots traditionally regarded their Highland countrymen as members of a different and inferior race, violent, treacherous, poverty-stricken and backward. They called them savages or aborigines, labels that some Lowlanders continued to use well into the 1830s, despite Sir Walter Scott's literary efforts to romanticise and sanitise the glens, clans and tartans of the far north.[12]

The degree to which the Welsh were able to see themselves as one people was also limited by an acute north–south divide, the country's central range of mountains making trade, communications and ordinary human contact between counties in South Wales, like Glamorgan, Carmarthen and Pembroke, and northern counties, such as Flint, Merioneth and Caernarfon, very difficult indeed. No Glamorgan landed family, for example, intermarried with a family from North Wales during the eighteenth century – because people from these two regions simply did not encounter each other, unless, that is, they happened to meet up in England.[13]

And what of that 'heterogeneous thing, an Englishman', as Defoe called him?

> In eager rapes, and furious lust begot,
> Betwixt a painted *Briton* and a *Scot*:
> Whose gend'ring offspring quickly learnt to bow,
> And yoke their heifers to the *Roman* plough:
> From whence a mongrel half-bred race there came,
> With neither name nor nation, speech or fame
> In whose hot veins now mixtures quickly ran,
> Infus'd betwixt a *Saxon* and a *Dane*.
> While their rank daughters, to their parents just,
> Receiv'd all nations with promiscuous lust.
> This nauseous brood directly did contain
> The well-extracted blood of Englishmen . . .[14]

Defoe's uncompromising insistence on the ethnic diversity of England, its early exposure to successive invasions from Continental Europe, and the constant intermingling of its people with the Welsh and the Scots, was fully justified in historical terms. Yet the sheer mocking savagery of *The True-Born Englishman* is less straightforward than it seems. Defoe was deflating English conceit to be sure, but the fact that he – an Englishman – was prepared to do so in such remorselessly satirical language was in itself a powerful demonstration of English confidence. Far more than the

Welsh and Scots felt able to do, the English could–occasionally–ridicule themselves because they had a strong sense of who they were and of their own importance. England's population was four times that of Wales and Scotland put together, and its economy much richer. Unlike its two neighbours, it had long possessed a strong and highly centralised state, it contained only one major language, and its internal communications were more advanced and much less disrupted by geography.

Yet in England, too–as Defoe was concerned to point out–there was only limited uniformity in terms of culture, custom or outlook. Northumberland, for instance, in the way that its people looked and lived and thought, was much closer to being a Scottish than an English county. Here, as in the Scottish Lowlands, the poor consumed oatmeal as a matter of course, a cereal that–as Samuel Johnson remarked in his famous dictionary–more affluent southerners dismissed as animal fodder. Here, too, over a third of all adults may have been able to read by the early 1700s. This was virtually the same level of literacy as existed in Lowland Scotland, but a much higher level than, say, in the English Midlands where Johnson himself hailed from.[15] Books and newspapers from Scottish printing presses were far more common in Northumberland than London-produced reading matter, and Scots and their accents were infinitely more familiar than visitors from the south. Northumbrians and Lowland Scots even tended to look alike, with the same raw, high-boned faces and the same thin, angular physiques. 'To pass from the borders of Scotland into Northumberland', a Scottish clergyman would write at the end of the eighteenth century, 'was rather like going into another parish than into another kingdom.'[16]

Much the same could be said of Shropshire and Herefordshire with relation to Wales. Here, as in Northumberland, centuries of cross-border trade, migration and marriage had forged a distinctive but mongrel regional culture. 'The manners of the people', noted one early nineteenth-century antiquarian of this region, 'are half English, half Welsh'.[17] My own surname, 'Colley', is a common one in this part of the world. It means black, and is probably a testament to all those dark-haired Celts who, like my own ancestors, crossed over from Wales and settled on the English side of the border. But even in those parts of England that were not directly exposed to Welsh or Scottish influences in this way, there was still massive diversity. How could there not be, when scenery and soil types varied enormously even over short distances, when the bulk of roads and people were too poor for long-distance travel to be common, and when no one–however rich–could journey faster on land than a horse, that is at ten miles an hour at the most? 'I had never been above eight miles from home in my life', the labouring poet John Clare would write of his youth in Northamptonshire, 'and I could not fancy England much larger than the part I know.'[18]

Looked at in this way, Great Britain in 1707 was much less a trinity of three self-contained and self-conscious nations than a patchwork in which uncertain areas of Welshness, Scottishness and Englishness were cut across by strong regional attachments, and scored over again by loyalties to village, town, family and landscape. In other words, like virtually every other part of Europe in this period, Great Britain was infinitely diverse in terms of the customs and cultures of its inhabitants.

Some of these internal disparities would be smoothed out as this period progressed, by the advance in road and postal communications, by the proliferation of print, and by the operation of free trade throughout the island. But it was not primarily this limited process of cultural integration that made possible an emerging sense of Britishness. Instead, men and women came to define themselves as Britons – in addition to defining themselves in many other ways – because circumstances impressed them with the belief that they were different from those beyond their shores, and in particular different from their prime enemy, the French. Not so much consensus or homogeneity or centralisation at home, as a strong sense of dissimilarity from those without proved to be the essential cement.

It was partly geography that underlay this marked sense of difference, the simple fact that Great Britain was an island. The encompassing sea was a vital defence and a highly effective frontier, keeping Britons enclosed and together, as well as keeping enemies out. But the sea could also be imagined as a telling symbol of identity. In France, as in most Continental European states, national boundaries would fluctuate throughout the 1700s and long after:

> Not only did the idea of territorial sovereignty remain undeveloped, in theory as in practice, but the political boundary in the north and east was largely undelimited. France's frontiers were riddled with enclaves, exclaves, overlapping and contested jurisdictions, and other administrative nightmares.[19]

By contrast, British boundaries after 1707 seemed settled once and for all, marked out by the sea, clear, incontrovertible, apparently pre-ordained. As one clergyman put it in a sermon delivered in celebration of the Act of Union: 'We are fenced in with a wall which knows no master but God only.'[20]

This conviction that Britain's physical identity, its very shape and place on the map, had been laid down by God points to the much more profound sense in which its inhabitants saw themselves, particularly in times of emergency, as a people apart. At odds in so much of their culture and secular history, the English, the Welsh and the Scots could be drawn together – and made to feel separate from much of the rest of Europe – by their common commitment to Protestantism. To a very limited extent, this had been the case since the Reformation. But throughout the eighteenth and nineteenth centuries, and even after, external pressures and imperatives made the fact that this was an overwhelmingly Protestant culture relevant and compelling in a quite unprecedented way.

From the Act of Union to the Battle of Waterloo in 1815, Great Britain was involved in successive, very dangerous wars with Catholic France. At the same time and long after, it was increasingly concerned to carve out a massive empire in foreign lands that were not even Christian. In these circumstances of regular *and violent* contact with peoples who could so easily be seen as representing the Other, Protestantism was able to become a unifying and distinguishing bond as never before. More than anything else, it was this shared religious allegiance combined with recurrent wars that permitted a sense of British national identity to emerge alongside of, and not necessarily in competition with older, more organic attachments to England, Wales or Scotland, or to county or village. Protestantism was the dominant component of British religious life. Protestantism coloured the way that Britons approached and interpreted their material life. Protestantism determined how most Britons viewed their politics. And an uncompromising Protestantism was the foundation on which their state was explicitly and unapologetically based.

THE STRUGGLES OF GOD'S ELECT

The absolute centrality of Protestantism to British religious experience in the 1700s and long after is so obvious that it has proved easy to pass over. Always reluctant to be seen to be addressing the obvious, historians have preferred to concentrate on the divisions that existed within the Protestant community itself, on the tensions between Anglicans and Protestant non-conformists in England and Wales, between Presbyterians and Episcopalians in Scotland, and between the older forms of dissent that emerged in the seventeenth century, Congregationalists, Baptists, Quakers and the like, and newer versions such as Methodism. These internal rivalries were abundant and serious. But they should not obscure what was still the most striking feature in the religious landscape, the gulf between Protestant and Catholic.

At its most formal, the division was enshrined in the law. From the late seventeenth century until 1829, British Catholics were not allowed to vote and were excluded from all state offices and from both houses of Parliament. For much of the eighteenth century they were subject to punitive taxation, forbidden to possess weapons and discriminated against in terms of access to education, property rights and freedom of worship. In other words, in law–if not always in fact–they were treated as potential traitors, as un-British.[21] The legal position of Protestant non-conformists, however, was utterly different. As 'an effectual means to unite their Majesties' Protestant subjects', the Toleration Act of 1689 had permitted dissenters who accepted the doctrine of the Holy Trinity the right to worship freely.[22] They could vote providing they met the relevant property qualifications, they could build their own churches, they could set up their own academies to educate their children, and they could carry arms. By law they still had to conform at least occasionally to Anglican worship in order to be eligible for state or local office, and some Tory politicians would have liked to exclude them from official life altogether. But in practice, English and Welsh Protestant dissenters were able to penetrate almost all levels of the political system up to and including Parliament itself, and so too were Scottish Presbyterians.

Great Britain, then, was not a confessional state in any narrow sense. Instead, its laws proclaimed it to be a pluralist yet aggressively Protestant polity. It was not primarily the law that made Protestantism and anti-Catholicism such powerful and pervasive emotions, however. Official intolerance, like mass intolerance, was rooted in something far more intangible, in fear most of all, and in the way that Britons chose to remember and interpret their own past. For large numbers of them, as David Cressy has shown, time past was a soap opera written by God, a succession of warning disasters and providential escapes which they acted out afresh every year as a way of reminding themselves who they were.[23] Every 30 January until 1859, Protestant worshippers throughout England and Wales fasted and prayed in memory of Charles I's execution in 1649. By contrast, 29 May, the anniversary of the restoration of the monarchy in 1660, was a jubilee day marked out by bonfires and bells, a time for celebrating the end of political instability and martial rule. The first day of August marked the accession in 1714 of the first Hanoverian king, the securing of the Protestant Succession. And 5 November was doubly sacred, not just the anniversary of the landing in England in 1688 of

William of Orange, come to do battle with the Catholic James II, but also the day when in 1605 Parliament and James I had been rescued from the gunpowder plotting of Guido Fawkes, yet another Roman Catholic.

The prayer laid down to be used on the latter occasion set out the moral that devout Protestants were expected to draw from all of these red-letter dates in the patriotic calendar: 'From this unnatural conspiracy not our merit, but *thy* mercy; not our foresight, but *thy* providence delivered us.'[24] God, Britons were encouraged to believe, watched over them with a particular concern. Nothing in their troubled past had escaped his notice or eluded his influence, for they were special. They had a mission, a distinctive purpose. But they also had, this version of their history taught them, an unvarying enemy. It had been a Catholic who had plotted to blow up James I and his parliament. A Catholic queen, Henrietta Maria, together with her interfering priests had led Charles I astray and the whole island into war. The would-be tyrant James II had been Catholic, just as those responsible for the St Bartholomew's Day massacre in 1572, or the Irish 'massacres' of 1641, or the Great Fire of London in 1666 had, they were assured, been Catholic also. That much of this Protestant version of the past was grossly inaccurate was immaterial. As Ernest Renan once remarked: 'Getting its history wrong is part of being a nation.'[25]

Men and women believed these pious lies not just because of what they were told in church, but also because of the cheap printed matter that flooded from Britain's abundant printing presses. The yellowing copies of *Old Moore's Almanac* that can still be seen on the shelves of many British newsagents' shops today are a reminder of the time when this kind of publication made up the heart of popular literature, the contemporary equivalent of the tabloid press, both in tone and popularity.[26] An almanac published in Aberdeen in the 1680s sold an astonishing 50,000 copies every year. In Great Britain as a whole, more than half a million copies of different kinds of almanacs were sold every year, a circulation figure far in excess of any other kind of book, including the Bible. And, since farmers used them as guides to when to plant and harvest, almanacs were as common in rural areas as in urban. The majority were crude and intolerant productions, offering a jumble of useful and sensational information, combined with 'an endlessly popular diet of jingoism, abuse of Catholics, and predictions of the downfall of the Pope and the French'.[27] But together with patriotic sermons on 30 January, 29 May, 5 November and the king's accession day, and the official fast-day services observed annually throughout England, Wales *and* Scotland during all of Britain's

The PROTESTANT

ALMANACK,

For the Year 1700.

Since		
	The Creation of the World	5706
	The Incarnation of Jesus Christ	1700
	England received the Christian Faith	1510
	Martin Luther wrote against the Pope	184
	Our first Deliverance from Popery by K. *Edward* VI.	152
	Our second deliverance from Popery by Q. *Elizabeth*	141
	The horrid design of the Gun-Powder Plot	95
	The Burning of the City of *London*	34
	Our Third Deliverance from Popery, by K. *Will.* & Q. *Mary*	12

Being the

BISSEXTILE or LEAP-YEAR.

WHEREIN

The Bloody Aspects, Fatal Oppositions, Diabolical Conjunctions, and Pernicious Revolutions of the Papacy against the Lord and his Anointed, are described.

With the Change of the Moon, some probable Conjectures of the VVeather, the Eclipses, the Moons place in the Zodiack, and an account of some principal Martyrs in each Month.

Calculated according to Art, for the Meridian of *Babylon*, where the Pope is elevated a hundred and fifty degrees above all Right and Religion; above Kings, Canons, Councils, Conscience, and every thing therein called God. 2 *Thess.* 2. And may without sensible Errour, indifferently serve the whole Papacy.

By *Philoprotest*, a well-willer to the Mathematicks.

London, Printed by *John Richardson* for the Company of STATIONERS. 1700.

4. Frontispiece to *The Protestant Almanack*, London, 1700.

major wars, almanacs constituted the only history lessons the majority of Britons received.

As far as English almanacs were concerned, readers were usually supplied with a list of all the monarchs since the Norman Conquest, plus a highly selective and imaginative resumé of world history: the dates of the Creation, of the birth of Christ, of England's conversion to Christianity and of Luther's rebellion against the Pope. Then came the date of Elizabeth I's accession in 1558, of the destruction of the Armada in 1588, of the Gunpowder Plot, of the Irish 'massacres', of the Great Fire of London, of the Glorious Revolution and of any other event that seemed to the compiler to demonstrate the country's centrality and 'miraculous deliverance from popery'. Scottish almanacs sometimes celebrated different historical events and myths, but the bulk of them seem to have been just as militantly Protestant and just as anti-Catholic as their English equivalents. As for Wales, over eighty different Welsh-language almanacs are known to have circulated there in the late seventeenth and early eighteenth centuries, and hundreds more were published thereafter: all of them, Geraint H. Jenkins remarks, 'shot through with the most vigorous anti-Roman animus'.[28]

The continuing resonance of anti-Catholicism throughout Great Britain after 1707 and far into the nineteenth century needs stressing because it is often supposed that intolerance of this kind receded rapidly in the face of growing rationalism and literacy. Among the well-educated and the political élite, religious toleration *did* increase, especially after the final defeat of the Jacobite cause at Culloden in 1746. With the Stuarts now well and truly out of the picture, London became far more willing to relax the laws against Britain's own Catholic population.[29] Moreover, in communities where they were known and trusted, individual Catholics were often able to live tranquil and respected lives even before 1746, socialising with their Protestant neighbours, entering the professions and in some towns, even attending mass openly.[30]

But Catholics could still encounter personal abuse and physical injury at the hands of Protestants, particularly in time of war when the enemy was a Catholic state. Britain was at war with France, for example, when major anti-Catholic riots broke out in the Scottish Lowlands in 1778. It was still at war two years later, when the most destructive and intolerantly Protestant of all British riots, the Gordon Riots, erupted in London. At such times, vulnerable Catholics might see their property smashed or even be assaulted themselves. Very often, they were ducked in some nearby pool or river or water-butt until they came close to drowning.[31] This was exactly the same kind of treatment as reputed witches had received in earlier centuries, and it was meted out to Catholics in the 1700s for much the same reasons. In time of danger or insecurity, Catholics – like witches – became scapegoats, easy targets on which their neighbours could vent fear and anger. The slang adjective most commonly applied to Catholics was 'outlandish', and this was meant quite literally. Catholics were not just strange, they were out of bounds. They did not belong, and were therefore suspect.[32]

Repellent though this kind of behaviour was, we miss the point entirely if we simply dismiss it as an atavistic survival of an earlier age, an embarrassing and peripheral aspect of British plebeian culture perhaps, but as otherwise unimportant because so plainly irrational. Intolerant Protestantism represented far more in this society than paranoid thuggishness. To begin with, it served as a powerful cement between the English, the Welsh and the Scots, particularly lower down the social scale. It was no accident that the first major protest in which English and Scottish artisans openly collaborated was the anti-Catholic campaign culminating in the Gordon Riots, named, of course, after a Scottish figurehead, Lord George Gordon. By the same token, the first genuinely nationwide petitioning campaign that involved Welshmen and women on a massive scale was that organised against Catholic emancipation in 1829. What David Bebbington has written of nineteenth-century Britain is also true of the eighteenth century: 'Outside England popular Protestantism was emphatically British in flavour rather than Welsh or Scottish, for Britain as a whole seemed a Protestant bastion against Roman ambitions.'[33]

Nor was this Protestant world-view as irrational as it seems. Eighteenth- and nineteenth-century Britons reminded themselves of their embattled Protestantism in what often seems a wearyingly repetitive fashion precisely because they had good cause to feel uncertain about its security and about their own. In 1707, the Counter-Reformation was still very much in progress in parts of Continental Europe. France had attempted to expel its Protestant population in 1685, and many of these Huguenot refugees had settled in Britain, living reminders to their new countrymen of the enduring threat of Catholic persecution. In Spain, the Inquisition continued to take action against Protestants throughout the eighteenth century. While in some of the German states, and in parts of the Austrian empire, such as Hungary, pressure on Protestant communities was actually fiercer in the early 1700s than it had been earlier.[34] These and other examples of militant Catholicism abroad were extensively referred to in British sermons and newspapers, as in this extract from the *Weekly Medley* in 1729:

> Our letters from Paris make mention of the renewing of the persecution of our Protestant brethren, which they pursue with such warmth, that their children are forc'd from them, and some put to nunneries, and others to monasteries, there to be brought up in the Romish religion, and everyone forbid, upon pain of death, to follow the light of his conscience; all marriages celebrated by Protestant clergymen, within these four years, to be dissolved, and the children to be declared bastards, unless these marriages are a second time solemniz'd according to the rites of the Romish Church.[35]

But such (usually exaggerated) reports of Catholic iniquities abroad would not have made the impact they did had there not also been danger much closer to home.

In 1708, 1715 and again in 1745, expeditionary forces in support of the Stuart claimants to the throne landed in Scotland with the intention of marching south to capture London and thereby the entire island. There were other Jacobite invasion scares in 1717, 1719, 1720–1, 1743–4 and even 1759 which never came to anything but were still unsettling. A successful Stuart restoration would have meant the replacement of a Protestant monarchy with a devoutly Roman Catholic dynasty. Moreover, since the Stuarts could never hope to get back without substantial French or Spanish military and financial aid, it seemed more than likely that their restoration would be accompanied by a foreign army of occupation, and not just a foreign army but a Catholic army. The prospect of all this, though it never came to pass in fact, made the sufferings of other European Protestants seem frighteningly relevant. 'The miseries of which we have been witness in the distressed condition of the poor French refugees; the exiles of the principality of Orange; the Palatines heretofore; and now lately the half-starved Saltzburgers, driven from their native country in the depth of winter', all these horrors, argued a dissenting minister in 1735, were a poignant reminder of Britain's own blessings, and a warning of how easily they could be snuffed out.[36]

Even after Jacobitism had dwindled into nostalgia, there remained the challenge posed by France. Because we know now that Great Britain and its allies won the Battle of Waterloo, it is easy to assume that its protracted duel with France between 1689 and 1815 was somehow always destined for ultimate success. But, of course, those living at the time did not and could not view it in this light. Right until the end of the nineteenth century, in fact, most politicians, military experts and popular pundits continued to see France as Britain's most dangerous and obvious enemy, and for good reason.[37] France had a larger population and a much bigger land mass than Great Britain. It was its greatest commercial and imperial rival. It possessed a more powerful army which regularly showed itself able to conquer large tracts of Europe. And it was a Catholic state. This last point was the crucial one in shaping responses throughout Great Britain *as a whole*. Gerald Newman has supplied us with a highly skilful dissection of the secular lineaments of English Francophobia, but, because of their close alliance with France in the sixteenth century and earlier, the inhabitants of Scotland were far less likely to view it as the natural enemy merely because it was France.[38] But since France was also Catholic, a majority of Scots, like the English, and like the Welsh, were able to feel an emotional and ideological stake in the consequences of this protracted cross-Channel feud.

To summarise then: the prospect in the first half of the eighteenth century of a Catholic monarchy being restored in Britain by force, together with recurrent wars with Catholic states, and especially with France, ensured that the vision that so many Britons cherished of their own history became fused in an extraordinary way with their current experience. To many of them, it seemed that the old popish enemy was still at the gates, more threatening than ever before. The struggles of the Protestant Reformation had not ended, but were to be fought out over and over again. How could Britons hope to survive? How were they to snatch victory out of peril? And what did this incessant battle with Catholicism tell them about who they were and what purpose they served? For answers to these questions, they turned to the Bible, to sermons and homilies, and to a vast popular literature which was taken for granted then but has barely been investigated for this period since.

One of the most influential volumes, John Foxe's *Book of Martyrs, containing an account of the sufferings and death of the Protestants in the reign of Queen Mary*, had first appeared in 1563. Its immediate religious impact had been enormous, not just in England but in Scotland, too, where John Knox was deeply influenced by it; and copies had been chained alongside the Bible in every cathedral, set reading for every attentive Protestant.[39] What is seldom realised, however, is that this ageing classic went through a new and much wider period of fame and was interpreted in a far more aggressively patriotic fashion in the eighteenth century and after. In 1732, a printer in Smithfield, London – close by where so many Protestant martyrs had perished under Mary Tudor – produced a new edition adjusted to the very different and much wider reading public that had come into being since Foxe wrote:

5. Woodcut from a seventeenth-century edition of John Foxe, *Book of Martyrs*.

6 (facing page). The martyrdom of Katherine Cawches, in John Foxe, *Book of Martyrs*, London, 1761.

> The purchase of so voluminous a work cannot be reached by everyone's purse at once; and therefore this expedient was resolved on, of publishing a certain number of sheets weekly, by subscription, that the common people might be also enabled, by degrees to procure it.[40]

His edition appeared in thirty-one installments, and this publishing device proved so successful that subsequent editions took it even further. New editions in 1761 and 1776 were each issued in sixty cheap installments; while further editions in 1784 and 1795 were sold by 'all . . . booksellers and newsmen' in eighty even cheaper installments. *The Book of Martyrs* was thus re-packaged so that, together with the Bible and a handful of almanacs, it came to be one of the few books that one might plausibly expect to find in even a working-class household.

The work's patriotic importance was twofold. First, Foxe linked

brutal religious persecution with Roman Catholicism *and* with foreign intervention. Mary Tudor–as he made clear–had been married to Philip II of Spain when most of the burnings and heresy hunts had taken place. But second, and still more tellingly, Foxe's martyrs could stand for Everyman. They included women as well as men, the poor and insignificant as well as the eminent and prosperous, and all ages from the venerably old to the most vulnerably young. One of Foxe's most grisly fables, for example, was of Katherine Cawches, 'a poor widow' who was burnt together with her two grown-up daughters, Perotine and Guillemine, in St Peter's Port in Guernsey in 1556. Perotine had been heavily pregnant at the time, and when her 'belly . . . burst asunder by the vehemancy of the flame', her baby was miraculously flung clear and rescued by the crowd, only to be tossed back into the fire by order of the bailiff:

> And so the infant baptised in his own blood to fill up the number of God's innocent saints, was both born and died a martyr, leaving behind to the world, which it never saw, a spectacle wherein the whole world may see the Herodian cruelty of this

graceless generation of popish tormentors, to their perpetual shame and infamy.[41]

The pathos of such tales, together with the horribly graphic illustrations which kept so many readers glued to the book, did much more than feed anti-Catholicism, though they obviously did that. The crucial point, as far as successive generations of British readers were concerned, was that Mary's victims had indeed been martyrs. Their agony had been for a purpose, to demonstrate their own resolute faith and to bear witness to their countrymen's Protestant destiny. The weak and miscellaneous had gone through bitter trials to the stake and the torch, but out of the flames had come forth both a common steadfastness and triumphant confirmation that their land was blessed.

A very similar lesson could be drawn from that other Protestant classic, John Bunyan's *The Pilgrim's Progress.* Published first in London between 1678 and 1684, it had reached its fifty-seventh edition there by 1789. Every self-respecting Scottish press issued its own editions as well, and there were Welsh-language editions in 1688, 1699, 1713, 1722, 1744, 1770 and 1790. Here, then, was another canonical text that was authentically British in its impact, and that appealed particularly to the subordinate classes. For Christian's and Christiana's companions on their perilous journey are in the main ordinary folk. Those who seek to prevent them from reaching the Heavenly City include – it is explicitly stated – Catholics. The cave in the valley of the shadow of death is guarded by two giants, Pope and Pagan, grim equivalents as far as Bunyan is concerned: 'by whose power and tyranny the men whose bones, blood, ashes etc. lay there, were cruelly put to death'.[42] But though these fearsome opponents often make our heroes suffer, they do not make them fail. Instead, *The Pilgrim's Progress* is a celebration of the importance of willed activity, a paean to individual commitment and indomitable struggle, and an assurance that they will indeed win through. As such, and as Christopher Hill and Edward Thompson have shown, the book inspired generations of British radicals.[43] But it also contributed to a more conventional mass patriotism.

Through reading or hearing others read Protestant publicists like Bunyan and Foxe, through studying the Bible, or listening to sermons, or leafing through the dog-eared pages of almanacs and homily books, Protestant Britons learnt that particular kinds of trials, at the hands of particular kinds of enemies, were the necessary fate and the eventual salvation of a chosen people. Suffering and recurrent exposure to danger were a sign of grace;

and, if met with fortitude and faith, the indispensable prelude to victory under God.

This way of making sense of adversity, and of comforting themselves in the face of it, would persist subliminally into the twentieth century. During the First World War, British soldiers in the trenches regularly turned to *The Pilgrim's Progress*, some even comparing themselves in their letters and diaries to Christian himself. This was partly because they, like Bunyan's hero, were weighed down by a heavy burden, in their case a knapsack. But identifying themselves with Christian was clearly also a way of steeling themselves against danger and suffering, and a way, too, of reassuring themselves that their cause was just.[44] Britons drew on the self-same Protestant culture during the Second World War. When the Germans drove the British expeditionary army back through France in 1940, for instance, and the survivors were rescued in only a haphazard and partial fashion by flotillas of brave, civilian boats, this near-fiasco was speedily converted by the British themselves into an auspicious deliverance. Instinctively and under pressure, they incorporated this event within the Protestant interpretation of their history and drew the customary moral: civic exertion among miscellaneous and humble Britons had, under Providence, won out against a powerful and malignant enemy.[45] Not for nothing, did they but know it, do the British still refer to the Dunkirk *spirit*. It is striking, too, that the best-known photograph of the London Blitz during the Second World War is one that shows the dome of St Paul's cathedral – the parish church of the empire as it was then called – rising unscathed from amidst the smoke and destruction surrounding it. What better image could there be of a Protestant citadel being safeguarded amidst Armageddon by the watchful eye of Providence? Even after the religious power of Protestantism dwindled, its grip on the British imagination remained.

In the eighteenth and nineteenth centuries, though, Britons held to this system of beliefs both devoutly and consciously, and drew on it for courage and dignity in the face of recurrent wars and threatened invasions. Like the Swedes, in their wars against Poland and the Catholic German states in the sixteenth and seventeenth centuries, and like the Dutch in their struggle for independence against Catholic Spain, Protestant Britons believed they were in God's special care.[46] They knew that they were bound to be regularly tested by periods of extreme sin and suffering, and they took it for granted that struggle – especially struggle with those who were not Protestants – was their birthright. But they also believed that under Providence they would secure deliverance and achieve distinction. In short, they believed, many of them, that their land was nothing less than another and a better Israel.

JERUSALEM THE GOLDEN

Bring me my bow of burning gold:
Bring me my arrows of desire:
Bring me my spear: O clouds unfold!
Bring me my Chariot of fire!

I will not cease from Mental Fight
Nor shall my Sword sleep in my hand:
Till we have built Jerusalem,
In England's green and pleasant land.

When William Blake wrote these lines in the early 1800s, he was employing for his own mystical and political purposes a set of images that had been at the centre of Protestant thought in Britain since the early seventeenth century.[47] That they were a chosen people struggling towards the light, a bulwark against the depredations of Antichrist, had proved as compelling an idea for English puritans, as it did for the Scottish Covenanters. Superimposing the language of the Bible on their own countrymen's progress through life and towards redemption had seemed to these earlier generations of Protestants both natural and instructive, and in the eyes of many clergymen this continued to be the case throughout the eighteenth century and long after.

When the Hampshire-born dissenting minister Isaac Watts compiled his best-selling translation of the psalms in 1719, he thought nothing of replacing references to 'Israel' in the original text with the words 'Great Britain'. Such parallels between their own island and the Promised Land became even more precious in times of danger. In 1745, when Charles Edward Stuart and his Highlanders were on the march, Presbyterian ministers in the Scottish Lowlands rallied the faithful by taking as their favourite text Ezekiel's prophecy of the coming of Antichrist:

> Thus saith the Lord God . . . thou shalt come from thy place *out of the north parts*, thou, and many people with thee, all of them riding upon horses, a great company and a mighty army: and thou shalt come up against my people of Israel, as a cloud to cover the land.[48]

Another favourite parallel, among clergymen from all parts of Great Britain, was that between the Jacobites (or whoever the enemy happened to be at the time) and the Assyrians and their allies. Adam Ferguson sent the King's Highland regiments off to do battle with what was left of the Jacobite army in December 1745, with a Gaelic sermon based on Joab's speech to the army of Israel in advance of its battle with the Ammonites. Victory sermons, too, drew heavily on very similar analogies. Alexander Webster, the staunchly pro-government minister of Tolbooth church in Edinburgh, dedicated his sermons on Culloden to those filled with 'concern for the welfare of our Jerusalem, and zeal for the British Israel'.[49] While another clergyman, an Englishman this time, trumpeted the cosmic significance of the Seven Years War in the title of his sermon in celebration of the Peace of Paris in 1763: *The triumph of Israelites over Moabites, or Protestants over Papists.*[50]

There are innumerable other examples of this kind of clerical language. But to quote even a fraction of them would be superfluous as well as wearisome, for the crucial point is a very simple one. An apocalyptic interpretation of history, in which Britain stood in for Israel and its opponents were represented as Satan's accomplices, did not fade away in the face of rationalism in the late seventeenth century, but remained part of the thinking of many devout Protestants long after. Acknowledging that this was so does not mean, however, that we should regard Britons in this period as being invariably pious, or as particularly assiduous in terms of their attendance at formal worship. Church attendance was actually in decline here as it was in other parts of western Europe. But the Protestant world-view was so ingrained in this culture that it influenced people's thinking irrespective of whether they went to church or not, whether they read the Bible or not, or whether, indeed, they were capable of reading anything at all.

One of the most powerful transmitters of the idea of Britain as Israel, for instance, took the form of the sung rather than the printed word. From the moment he settled in London, George Frederick Handel flattered his new surroundings, and especially his patrons at court, by inserting into his music regular comparisons between events in British history and the endeavours of the prophets and heroes of the Old Testament.[51] The anthem he composed for George II's coronation in 1727, which has been played at every subsequent coronation, is a case in point: 'And Zadok the priest and Nathan the prophet anointed Solomon King'. But it was in the oratorios that he exploited the parallel between Britain and Israel to the full. *Esther*, *Deborah*, *Athalia*, *Judas Maccabaeus* (which was composed in honour of the Duke of Cumberland's victory over the Jacobites at Culloden), *Joshua*, *Susannah*, *Jephtha*, and self-evidently, *Israel in Egypt* all have as their theme the deliverance of Israel from danger by leaders inspired by God. The moral Handel wanted his listeners to draw was an obvious one. In Great Britain, second and better Israel, a violent and uncertain past was to be redeemed by the new and stoutly Protestant Hanoverian dynasty, resulting in an age of unparalleled abundance:

> He bids the circling seasons shine,
> Recalls the olive and the vine,
> With blooming plenty loads the plain,
> And crowds the field with golden grain.

It was because he celebrated Britain in this glowing fashion, that Handel became such a national institution. As the eighteenth century progressed, his oratorios were performed at Westminster Abbey, at cathedral concerts like the annual Three Choirs Festival at Worcester, Gloucester and Hereford, in northern dissenting chapels, in Welsh assembly rooms and in Scottish cities and towns eager to advertise their fashionability. The first Edinburgh Musical Festival in 1815, for example, was dominated by Handel's music. Richard Wagner caught a glimpse of why it appealed so much when he attended a concert in London during the 1850s, and noticed

> the feeling among the audience that an evening spent in listening to an oratorio may be regarded as a sort of service, and is almost as good as going to church. Every one in the audience holds a Handel piano score in the same way as one holds a prayer book in church.[52]

It was an extremely shrewd observation, for the men and women Wagner saw listening so intently were indeed engaged in an act of faith. Only what many of them were worshipping was Great Britain, and indirectly themselves.

Summoning up the example of Israel could be a way, as it was for William Blake, of calling for radical change. But most of those who saw Britain in this light were giving expression to at least some element of complacency. As members of the chosen land, they might, were indeed virtually bound to have their lapses and their periods of failure. But almost by definition, they were blessed, and these blessings had a material as well as a spiritual form. An extraordinarily large number of Britons seem to have believed that, under God, they were peculiarly free and peculiarly prosperous.

Yet why should this have been? Britons were more heavily taxed in this period than many of their Continental counterparts. Large numbers of them were subject to an extremely harsh and often arbitrary criminal code. Even Defoe, committed publicist for Great Britain as the Protestant Israel though he was, conceded that 'notwithstanding we are a nation of liberty', there were more prisons in London than in 'any city in Europe, perhaps as many as in all the capital cities of Europe put together'.[53] And most Britons were very poor. In Wales, between a half and a third of the population at this time lived out their unknown lives at subsistence level. Knowing all this, it is tempting to believe – and some historians have actually argued – that the sublime confidence running through Handel's oratorios or Defoe's political and economic writings was little more than the propaganda of an affluent and atypical minority.[54] After all, why should men and women living lives of no promise whatsoever believe that Britain was in any sense a promised land?

Doubtless a great many of them did not believe it for all, or even for most of the time. Some certainly made it clear that they rejected the idea out of hand. None the less, the conviction that Great Britain was peculiarly blessed was not confined to the prosperous. Nor was it confined to the inhabitants of England. Nor, emphatically, was it confined to Whigs. Like all sustaining national myths, the idea that Britain was a chosen land and therefore fruitful, did not depend for its effectiveness upon its being true. Poor or not, large numbers of Protestant Britons believed – believed precisely because they *were* Protestant, and because it was comforting to believe it – that they were richer in every sense than other peoples, particularly Catholic peoples, and particularly the French.

William Hogarth's brilliant *Calais Gate, or the Roast Beef of Old England* shows just how savage this complacency could be, and just how much it was relied upon to define and demean the enemy. The fat monk salivating over a newly roasted joint of imported English beef; the singularly unattractive nuns, bare-footed and fatuously pleased because they think they have found Christ's image in the features of a skate fish; the French soldiers, at once scrawny and ragged and curiously effeminate; even the forlorn Scottish Highlander, forced into exile and garlic-eating because he has rebelled against his Protestant sovereign George II: all these are rather ritualised figures of fun, an array of centuries-old Protestant stereotypes. Only after a time do we notice the really deadly and innovative part of Hogarth's satire. By the mere act of looking at the print we have come within the arch of a French prison. All of a sudden, we – the spectators – have become unfree, just like the French. And just like Hogarth, who intended this print as an act of revenge for what had happened to him during a visit to Calais in 1747.

Sketching the ancient fortifications, Hogarth had been arrested and temporarily imprisoned as a British spy.[55] Even as he applies

7. William Hogarth, *Calais Gate*, engraving, 1749.

pencil to paper in the background of this scene, we can see the heavy hand falling on his shoulder, the soldier's pike looming over his head. For Hogarth, this petty incident pointed to the heart of French disadvantages: lacking real liberty, their wealth was bound to be superficial and grossly ill-distributed, their religion entangled forever in superstition:

> Let France grow proud, beneath the tyrant's lust,
> While the rack'd people crawl, and lick the dust:
> The manly genius of this isle disdains
> All tinsel slavery, or golden chains.[56]

In the print, the sunlight falls only on the old city gates of Calais, a last stout relic of the English occupation. It illumines the English royal coat of arms. But above all, it shines on the cross surmounting the gate, symbol of that true religion that we–Hogarth's audience–are supposed to connect with the succulent roast beef and the prosperity it represents.

At just how deep a level this kind of propaganda convinced even its makers is unclear, but its utility is obvious. Particularly in the first half of the eighteenth century, this way of seeing France enabled the British to exorcise some of the deep insecurity they felt in the face of its military might and cultural splendour. Asserting that the millions of Frenchmen massed against them on the other side of the Channel were in reality impoverished, downtrodden, credulous, even somehow unmanly, was a panacea for nagging anxieties and a way of coping with envy.[57]

But characterising the French and other predominantly Catholic states as poverty-ridden was also a way of claiming that only Protestants could enjoy a true and lasting prosperity, that those who lacked fervour and clear vision in serving the Lord were likely to be slothful, misguided and ineffective in the more mundane aspects of life as well. The crowd of artisans roaming the streets of Bristol in 1754 who reputedly shouted out 'No French . . . No lowering wages of labouring men to four pence a day and garlic', were subscribing to this belief pattern, just as much as was the elegantly bisexual Lord Hervey who dashed off this poem as he was touring Italy in 1729:

> Throughout all Italy beside,
> What does one find, but want and pride?
> Farces of superstitious folly,
> Decay, distress and melancholy:
> The havoc of despotic power,
> A country rich, its owners poor;
> Unpeopled towns, and lands untilled,
> Bodies unclothed, and mouths unfilled.[58]

To be Catholic, according to this view, was to be economically inept: wasteful, indolent and oppressive if powerful, poor and exploited if not.

As the English acknowledged at the time, Scottish responses to Catholic Europe could sometimes take a different and markedly more generous form. A long tradition of supplementing limited incomes at home by selling their swords to whichever Continental army was most in need of them, encouraged members of Scotland's male élite in particular to be more relaxed in the face of European differences, less censorious in the presence of religious practices other than their own. But Scots at all social levels were by no means invariably better Europeans than their southern neighbours, particularly when they were staunch Presbyterians. Robert Wodrow, minister of a parish near Glasgow, gleefully recorded how a fellow Scot journeying 'in Spain or Italy' (for Wodrow, evidently, one Catholic country was much the same as another) expressed his contempt for a holy relic in a nearby Catholic church:

> He prepared himself by taking somewhat laxative, and came in on a solemn day, thrumbled in to the very altar, and there voided himself. Very soon, we may be sure, a cry arose; and he only desired liberty to tell the occasion. He had his story ready for delivering: that for many days he had been under a violent consumption, that he believed nothing would relieve him but this; that as soon as he came to the relic . . . this cure was wrought. And, upon this, the priests presently took it as a miracle, and published it to the people, and he was the happiest that could get some of the excrements![59]

It is a repulsive story, and probably a false one. But it illustrates very well the extreme Protestant conviction that Catholic values were completely upside down. That here were people who were so ignorant and credulous, so poor and so lacking in a sense of the real worth of things, that they would even chase after filth.

There existed, then, a vast superstructure of prejudice throughout eighteenth-century Britain, a way of seeing (or rather misseeing) Catholics and Catholic states which had grown up since the Reformation if not before, which was fostered by successive wars with France and Spain, and which encouraged many Britons, irrespective of their real income, to regard themselves as peculiarly fortunate. Yet it would be condescending to dismiss this raucous complacency as nothing more than ignorant xenophobia. Even if it had been nothing more than that, its impact would still have been important. But, as it happened, it was something more. Britons were manifestly wrong in believing that their experience was utterly and invariably different from and better than that of other Europeans. But those historians who have suggested that the British experience in the past was essentially no different from that of Continental Europe are no less mistaken.[60] To reach the truth, we have to sail between the Scylla of complacent British exceptionality and the Charybdis of assuming that Britons were part and parcel of an homogenised European-wide *ancien régime*, and recognise that there were some respects in which Britons *were* markedly different from and more fortunate than many of their Continental neighbours.

To begin with, proportionately fewer of them starved. The famine that devastated parts of Scotland between 1697 and 1699 was the last to occur on the British mainland, and had itself been an exceptional misfortune. Thereafter, there were certainly periods of savage dearth, like the late 1730s and early '40s, when a combination of terrible harvests, bitter weather and cattle disease seems to have driven up the level of mortality throughout Britain. And there was always hunger, which was why the poor succumbed so easily to respiratory diseases and the more dramatic killers, typhus and smallpox and the like. None the less, the experience of much of Continental Europe with regard to food shortages was grimmer than this, and grimmer for very much longer. The Scandinavian countries remained liable to famine into the nineteenth century. So did France. This, indeed, was the other side of its enormous advantage over Britain in terms of population: it simply could not feed its people very well. And sometimes it could not feed them at all. Between 1700 and the Revolution of 1789, France suffered no fewer than sixteen *nationwide* famines, as well as local famines which occurred almost every year, in one place or another.[61] So the stereotype cherished by the British of the starving French peasant was by no means simply the product of prejudice and ignorance. French peasants did starve: a great many of them.

Most Britons, however, did not starve, and this proved doubly advantageous to their rulers. On the domestic front, the relative absence of famine was a powerful aid to social stability. Rioting when food prices rose too sharply was common enough. But since this was usually caused by a temporary local shortage rather than by uncompromising, all-pervasive dearth, the authorities were more often than not able to defuse trouble by shipping in additional supplies from elsewhere. And comparative agricultural self-sufficiency (plus the availability of Ireland as a captive granary) bestowed another, vitally important advantage. It enabled Britain to compensate for the disadvantages it laboured under in military terms from having a smaller population than its European rivals. By the end of the century only a third of the labour force in England, the most highly populated and productive part of Great Britain, was engaged in agriculture. In France, by contrast, the proportion of the labour force tied down to the land was twice as large, and recruiting efforts always had to contend with the resistance of millions of peasant farmers. Britain's fruitfulness, then, that 'rural reign' that James Thomson celebrated in 'Rule Britannia', fed its war machine, as well as its complacency and its people.[62]

Pride in abundance as the token of an elect nation rested not just on agriculture but, even more stridently, on commerce. And here, too, there was more to pride than prejudice. In terms of the freedom of its trade, the rate of its urban expansion, the geographical mobility of its inhabitants and the range of its communications, Great Britain's experience was genuinely distinctive.

8. Roads, trade, and mobility: the title-page of John Ogilvie, *Britannia: or an Illustration of the Kingdom of England and dominion of Wales*, London, 1675.

One of the most significant clauses in the Act of Union of 1707 had been that which did away with all internal customs duties and trade barriers. Whereas Austria would retain its internal customs barriers until 1775, and France would do the same until 1790, in Great Britain the 800 miles between northern Scotland and the south coast of England could from now on be crossed and re-crossed by domestic traders duty free. Slowly and grudgingly up to the 1730s, but far more rapidly thereafter, this was what happened. The surviving and imperfect trade figures illustrate the growing volume and complexity of internal trade, so too does the pressure on Parliament to allow turnpike roads to snake through England, and by the second half of the century through Wales and Scotland as well.[63] But perhaps the most powerful testaments to an emerging British-wide market are the numerous complaints from vested interest groups who felt that they were losing out in the process. In 1748, the English-dominated House of Commons tried to pass legislation limiting the large number of Scots peddling their country's manufactures south of the border. Four years later, 150 Edinburgh merchants issued a stern declaration that they would no longer purchase or commission goods from visiting English salesmen.[64] Not surprisingly, these attempts to preserve English trade for the English, and Scottish commerce for the Scots proved totally futile, like trying to plug a hole in a dike after the flood had already overwhelmed it.

The movement in goods between different parts of Great Britain was accompanied by an incessant movement of people. England and Scotland, though not Wales, experienced a much faster rate of urban growth in the eighteenth century than did any other part of Europe. On the Continent, the degree of urbanisation would barely rise at all until after the 1770s; and in Holland, where town life had once been so splendidly and creatively affluent, the urban population actually shrank in this period.[65] But across the Channel, things were very different. Not just in London, but in Plymouth, Norwich, Birmingham, Bristol, Liverpool, Leeds, Halifax, Manchester, Newcastle, Edinburgh, Glasgow, Paisley and scores of other, lesser towns economic growth was visibly a matter of here and now, marked out for all to see by an explosion of new buildings, streets, shops, houses, taverns, inns and civic amenities, and by the stream of new immigrants arriving every day from the countryside.[66]

Most of these men and women had not travelled far, no further than ten or fifteen miles in the majority of cases. None the less, Britons at all social levels, and particularly the poor, seem to have travelled in much larger numbers and far more frequently than their more stay-at-home contemporaries in France, or Spain, or Germany, or Italy.[67] Here, it was the exception, not the rule, to spend all one's days in the same village or isolated hovel in which one was born. And even those who were able to resist the temptation and the pressure to leave home, rarely lived completely self-contained and isolated lives. The outside world came to them by way of the hawkers who made a living penetrating the more distant parts of the land, peddling finished goods, small luxuries, ballads and gossip, or in the shape perhaps of cattle drovers, like the men who braved the Roman roads and faltering bridle paths of Caernarfonshire and of Anglesey (one of the more remote regions in Great Britain at this time) to purchase meat cattle for Chester, Liverpool and London. In turn, country dwellers were drawn out of their seclusion to trade, farmers and their servants turning out regularly to visit some kind of town so as to sell produce and purchase essential goods.

The idea, then, that Great Britain at this time was a land of small, inward-looking communities, frozen in custom and cut off from trade and communications, is at best only a half-truth. The majority of men and women simply could not afford entirely self-contained lives. The business of earning a livelihood drove them, whether they wanted it or not, to towns, to markets, to pedlars, and at some stage, to travel. Trade, and what one journalist referred to in 1716 as 'those other encouragements which naturally bring people together, and keep 'em together',[68] were not the preserve of a few, but a necessity for the many, tying the different regions together in networks of economic self-interest, credit and human contact. And there was something else that brought Britons of all ranks into contact with each other, namely the printed word.

Printing presses had flourished in Scotland since the early sixteenth century, and Edinburgh in particular was one of the world's great centres of print, producing books, pamphlets and sermons for readers throughout Britain, Continental Europe, and the American colonies. South of the border, however, government legislation had worked to confine printing to London. Only with the lapsing of the Licensing Act in 1695 did provincial printing houses begin to establish themselves successfully. Wales acquired its first printing shop in 1718, when a man named Isaac Carter set up a small business in a village in Carmarthenshire, while in England, just under sixty printing houses were established in the first half of the eighteenth century (thereafter, their number expanded at a much faster rate).[69] All this is well known, of course; but the importance of print in unifying Great Britain and in shaping its inhabitants' view of themselves as peculiarly privileged has been much less understood.

For the prosperous, the most dramatic aspect of the new availability of print was undoubtedly the newspapers. Whereas the French had to wait for a daily newspaper until the last quarter of the eighteenth century, Londoners acquired one is 1702 and were supporting half a dozen dailies plus various tri-weekly papers by the 1730s. Half a century later, the English provinces were generating fifty different newspapers. A further nine newspapers existed in Scotland, as did periodicals such as the monthly *Scots Magazine* which could be purchased, so its publishers boasted, from most of the country's seventy-odd booksellers.[70] Wales had no successful, home-produced newspaper until the nineteenth century. Instead, its landed gentry and more prosperous tradesmen obtained their copies of English papers by mail; or purchased them from the pedlars and chapmen whom every printer employed to sell his (sometimes her) publications in more distant regions.

Although many people read them primarily for private reasons, to scan the advertisements or to savour the more horrific and prurient accounts of crime and sexual adventures, newspapers could make the process of reaching out between the various cultures and regions of Britain easier and more common. To pad out his slim quota of local news, every provincial editor borrowed heavily from the London press, filling his closely printed columns with accounts of the content of parliamentary debates, the vicissitudes of the stock market, the latest court gossip, the chances of war with foreign states or the prospects of peace. Scottish newspapers were no different from the English in this respect. They, too, reprinted swathes of south-of-the-border news culled from the metropolitan press, grimly substituting the words 'Great Britain' in place of the more parochial references to 'England'.[71] For the minority who could afford them, or who had the chance to pore over free copies in coffee houses and taverns, newspapers must have made it easier to imagine Great Britain as a whole. Reading them, they would be constantly reminded that their private lives were bounded by a wider context, that whether they liked it or not they were caught up in decisions taken by men in London, or in battles fought out on the other side of the world.

Yet for most Britons, it was not the newspapers, or the grammar books, or the dictionaries, or all the other autodidactic material flooding from the presses at this time, that did most to teach them who they were. Striking though this secular material is, the fact remains that religious works formed easily the bulk of what every British printing press was producing in this period. For proof of this, one has only to look at the contemporary lists of published books issued as a service to their readers by the more up-market periodicals, the *Gentleman's Magazine*, the *London Magazine*, or the *Scots Magazine*. In 1750, the first of these journals listed 430 new books, categorising them under a wide variety of different headings: novels, plays, atlases, travel books, cookery books, gardening books, translations from the classics and so forth. With over 130 titles listed, religion was overwhelmingly the dominant category.[72] Its real dominance, however, becomes apparent only when one remembers that the *Gentleman's Magazine*'s coverage was far from exhaustive. It ignored the productions of most of the English provincial and Scottish presses – which were even more heavily weighted towards religious matters than was the London press – just as it nearly always omitted religious chapbooks, almanacs, ballads and new editions of the Bible.

For the subordinate classes, this must have been the aspect of the explosion in printed material that affected them the most generally: the fact that Protestant theology and polemics, be it the authorised version of the Bible, or the works of Bunyan and Foxe and the like, or the more popular sermons, were now broadly accessible in geographical terms, and far more accessible, too, in terms of price. In this sense, the freeing of the printing presses in 1695 can be seen as completing the popularisation of the Protestant Reformation. As Geraint H. Jenkins writes: 'One of the salient features of this period is that the central doctrines of the Reformation were disseminated intensively in print, in intelligible and popular forms, for the first time in Wales.'[73] The same was true, though to a less dramatic degree, in Scotland and in England. Throughout Great Britain, ordinary men and women now had increased access to religious material in their own language. They had opportunities, on a scale that had never existed before, to listen while others read the Protestant classics out aloud, or to read and possibly purchase them for themselves. This enormously enhanced access to print was a vital part of the conviction that Protestant Britons were peculiarly privileged. However poor or unimportant or ill-educated they might be, they still had direct access to the word of God in a way (they believed) that Roman Catholics did not, and for this reason, if for no other, Protestants, even the poorest of them, were free men. Catholicism, declared a society of journeymen in Edinburgh towards the end of the century, meant 'The denying to the common people the free use of the holy scriptures.' Catholics, wrote an English private soldier stationed in Spain, 'do not read the Bible; the priests have entire control over the masses . . . Oh, Britons! let us prize our privileges.'[74]

This outburst, from a poor man, brings us back to the belief that Protestant Britons were peculiarly blessed, blessed in this case with superior religious freedom, but in other contexts, as we have seen, blessed with a deeper and more substantial prosperity. All too often, economic growth in this society has been seen as a modernising agent *and therefore as antipathetic to religion.* But there is no need to adopt this either/or view of the past. In practice, economic growth co-existed very comfortably with a profoundly Protestant patriotism and complacency. Today, this outlook invites unease and scepticism. Yet, if we want to understand how eighteenth- and early nineteenth-century Britons saw themselves and their world, their enormous conceit has to be recognised and taken seriously. It was not just ignorant insularity, though some of it certainly was. It was bound up with a Protestant world-view which helped men and women make sense of their lives and gave comfort and dignity in the face of difficulty and dangers. And it was more than prejudice.

In terms of its agricultural productivity, the range and volume of its commerce, the geographical mobility of its people, the vibrancy of its towns, and the ubiquity of print, Britain's economic experience in this period *was* markedly different from that enjoyed by much of Continental Europe. The relative sophistication of its economic networks played an important part in keeping this culturally diverse land together. But even those Britons who scarcely benefited at all from these networks, even the very poor, could be caught up in the conviction that Great Britain was somehow richer and freer than its neighbours, Jerusalem the Golden. As Georges Duby has written of a very different people, at a very different time: 'The attitudes of individuals and groups of individuals to their own situation in society and the conduct these attitudes dictate are determined not so much by actual economic conditions as by the image in the minds of the individuals and groups'.[75] The image that many Britons nurtured of their land was coloured and made more roseate by their overwhelming Protestantism. And it was on this strong substratum of Protestant bias from below that the British state after 1707 was unapologetically founded.

A POLITY BY FORCE OF FAITH

God save our noble King
God save great George our King,
God save the King.
Send him victorious
Happy and glorious,
Long to reign over us,
God save the King.

O Lord our God arise,
Scatter his enemies
And make them fall:
Confound their politicks,
Frustrate their knavish tricks.
On him our hopes are fix'd
O save us all.

It was in a London theatre in September 1745 that these words were first sung publicly, and the men and women present received them rapturously, rising clammily to their feet in the warm autumn evening and calling repeatedly for encores.[76] Ironically, different versions of the song had been in circulation for well over half a century, mainly, it seems, among supporters of the exiled Stuart dynasty. That it should have been seized on now by loyalists was owing to its sentiments, and above all to the political and military context. Because of London's mismanagement, Charles Edward Stuart's inadequate army had been able to march through Scotland and was now heading southwards. Originally contemptuous of this threat to their security, those in the path of the invasion had begun to panic and found in 'God Save the King' a comforting and blessedly familiar lifeline to lay hold of. Its words offered them what their Protestant culture had taught them to demand: yet another assurance that – although surrounded by enemies – they were in God's particular care. Exactly like 'Rule Britannia', and like William Blake's lines – which would not be set to music as 'Jerusalem' until a very different scale of national emergency in 1916 – 'God Save the King' summoned up a people exposed to struggle but redeemed through faith.

Not until the early 1800s would this song come to be called the national *anthem*, a term that the British invented, and that confirms just how closely patriotic identity in Great Britain was yoked to religion.[77] In 1745, the song's status was much less formal, but it was disseminated effectively enough through being sung in church services and by way of the print network. Newspapers and monthly magazines quickly supplied their readers with the words and music; even the *Scots Magazine* printed it, despite the fact that Scotland was still technically under Jacobite occupation. And it was spread among the poor by way of broadsheets and by the ballad singers, who would sing the words to those who could not read them in return for half a penny or less. Hogarth painted one of these women in his *March to Finchley*, a tumultuous evocation of the king's forces assembling in one of the poorer London districts in readiness for their march north to do battle with Charles Edward

. William Hogarth, *The March to Finchley*, engraving, 1750.

Stuart and his men. George II is supposed to have found the painting subversive, because it showed the chaos of a not all that well-planned mobilisation: the bewildered common soldiery, with their stiff new uniforms, their provisions bundled haphazardly into carts, and their camp-followers and wailing bastards tagging along behind them.[78] Yet, like so much of Hogarth's work, this is, in fact, a profoundly patriotic image.

Its central figure, a particularly harassed-looking guardsman, being fought over by two women who may or may not be his two wives, is actually Britain itself. Clinging devotedly to his right arm is a ballad-singer dressed in rags but none the less all in white, fair of face and heavily pregnant. Attacking him from the left (the wrong side by artistic convention) is a much older and viciously ugly newsvendor, draped in black like a monk, a crucifix swinging from her neck, her sack full of virulently opposition newspapers. What we are being shown in microcosm is a crisis of political decision-making taking place on a much wider scale. Was Great Britain to remain true to the Hanoverian dynasty represented here in the person of the woman in white, the ballad-singer, with the words of 'God Save the King' hanging conspicuously from her basket? Or would it succumb to the Stuarts in the person of the newsvendor? In the light of the painting, there can be no doubting as to what is the right decision. The woman in white is fertile as well as fair, her belly, like the basket she carries on her arm, filled with the future. By contrast, the Stuarts' representative is old and therefore barren. She threatens violence, and she is unmistakably Roman Catholic. Such characterisations plainly reflect Hogarth's own bias, but underlying them is a valid and important point. The politics of Great Britain at this time, the way in which the state was organised and the ideas men and women held about it, were inextricably linked with perceptions of Catholicism and Protestantism.

The most dramatic evidence that this was so lay, of course, in its brutally reconstructed monarchy. In 1688, and again in 1714, the strict rules of dynastic succession were ostentatiously broken so that the evil – which was how most Britons regarded it – of a Roman Catholic monarch could be avoided. In the first case, the openly Catholic James II and his male heir were coerced by force of arms into fleeing to France, so that the crown could pass to his elder, Protestant daughter, Mary, and in reality to her Dutch, Calvinist husband, William of Orange. And when Anne, Mary's sister and successor as queen, failed to keep any of her huge and sickly brood of children alive, a Parliament dominated by Tory country gentlemen passed the Act of Settlement in 1701 confirming that anyone who was Catholic or married to a Catholic was 'forever uncapable to inherit, possess, or enjoy the crown and government of this realm', a law that still stands.[79] To make sure of obtaining a Protestant successor, Parliament had to sweep away considerations of hereditary right not just once but many times over. It passed over more than fifty individuals who were closer as blood relations to Queen Anne but ineligible because of their Catholic faith, in order to arrive at the man who eventually became king in 1714, George Lewis of Hanover, a German with only a smattering of the English language, a plain, middle-aged, uncharismatic man, with no great appeal except the essential one. He was Lutheran, not Catholic.[80]

The significance of these successive acts of iconoclasm was set out most clearly by Henry St. John, Viscount Bolingbroke, a disappointed, brilliant individual who had once been a Tory cabinet minister. In his *Idea of a Patriot King* (1738), a tract written for the benefit of George I's grandson, then Prince of Wales, he argued that a British monarch could still make himself the vital centre of politics, the father of his people. But he also told the heir to the throne in no uncertain terms that the basis of loyalty to the ruling monarch had of necessity shifted: 'The spring from which this legal reverence . . . arises is *national*, not *personal*.'[81] The Hanoverian kings were still powerful. But they did not rule primarily because of who they were. Nor because of who their ancestors had been. Parliament had brought them to the throne, and Protestantism kept them there. They were essentially serviceable kings, occupying their office because they catered to the religious bias of the bulk of their subjects, as the Stuarts had so often refused to do. 'A Protestant country can never have stable times under a Popish Prince' was how one English bishop put it, 'any more than a flock of sheep can have quiet when a wolf is their shepherd.'[82]

It took time to gloss over this pragmatic arrangement, time to make a convenient and functional dynasty an attractive and ceremonious one as well. And the task was made harder by the continuing appeal of the Stuart princes in exile, James II's son James Edward Stuart, and his grandson Charles Edward Stuart. In their propaganda images – which were all that most Britons ever saw of them – they were both physically attractive men in a way that the early Hanoverians were not. They enjoyed wide, though by no means unanimous support in Scotland, especially in the early 1700s when the Union was profoundly unpopular. And even outside Scotland, their misfortunes and bravery made them seem endlessly romantic, as the stolid, successful and equally courageous Hanoverians had no desire to be. Moreover, like all leaders who are absent, the Stuarts seemed to promise much, because they were not there in the flesh, in the intrigue and amidst the practicalities of government to disillusion and disappoint.[83] But for all this, the Stuart cause operated under an overwhelming handicap. Its representatives would not abandon the Catholicism that had cost their dynasty the throne in the first place. Steadfastly, admirably, but in political terms, lethally, the Stuarts would not embrace Protestantism, and this proved decisive.

Those who had replaced them on the British throne knew that religion was their strongest card and they played it to the full. The coronation ceremony undergone by William and Mary in 1689, for instance, was deliberately remodelled so as to highlight the asset and indispensability of their faith. For the first time, a copy of the English Bible, the key text of the Reformation, was carried in the coronation procession to Westminster Abbey. The joint monarchs had to swear to rule – as none of their predecessors had been asked to do – according to the 'true profession of the gospel, and the Protestant reformed religion established by law'. Once crowned, Bibles were handed to each of them: 'To put you in mind of this rule and that you may follow it'.[84] All of these innovations were retained in subsequent coronations, and if anything, the anxiety to remind the monarchs at this, the most crucial ceremony in their lives, that they held their office on account of what they were in religious terms, and what they were not, only increased. When Queen Anne was crowned in 1702, she was required to make a lengthy declaration against the doctrine of transubstantiation before she could proceed to the oath.[85]

To legitimise the rule of these new, assertively Protestant monarchs, apologists abandoned appeals to the divine right of kings, a doctrine that had always posed enormous problems, and took their stand instead on both divine providence and the people's will. They argued that William of Orange had vanquished James II in 1688, and that the Hanoverian dynasty had succeeded to the British throne in 1714, because divine providence had willed it. Yet again, a Protestant deity was watching over his chosen people. But God favoured the Protestant kings in this manner only because they had agreed to carry out their responsibilities to their subjects, as the Stuarts had so lamentably failed to do. A religious foundation of monarchy and the idea of a contract between ruler and ruled were thus, at least in theory, satisfactorily squared.[86] George I owed his crown to his lineal descent 'from the royal blood in the Protestant line', argued one clergyman in 1714, but equally important was the fact that he was 'of the nation's own choice' and would rule in accordance with the laws of the land.[87] The last verse of 'God Save the King' made the same point:

The choicest gifts in store
On him be pleased to pour,
Long may he reign.
May he defend our laws,
And ever give us cause,
With heart and voice to sing,
God Save the King.

Their re-ordered monarchy, Britons were repeatedly told, was one reason why they were peculiarly free. Not only was succession to the throne conditional on the monarch belonging to the Protestant faith, but the people's allegiance was conditional on his abiding by the constitution. Both of these things – Protestantism and the laws of the constitution – would be shattered if the Stuarts were restored.

This was perhaps more of an appeal to the mind than to the emotions, a recognition that the new regime was founded on utility and religious bias rather than on personal loyalty. Written and spoken propaganda in support of the early Hanoverian kings has none of the poetry, and little of the rich, folkloric quality that characterises some of the best Jacobite polemic. It was often better at urging caution with regard to Britain's present, than at summoning up golden images of an ideal future when all things would be well. Yet for all its limitations it won. It won because it was able to draw, as Jacobitism never could, on mass Protestantism. But it won also because a reconstructed monarchy was only one half of what the post-Revolution political settlement had to offer Britons. The other, equally vital and powerfully attractive half was Parliament, which now met – as it had never been able to do before 1688 – for several months at a time every year.

The immediate effect of this had been to sharpen party conflict and electoral strife.[88] But the way that Parliament functioned and the myths that gathered around it also fostered national unity. After 1707, virtually every part of the island had a nearby peer who sat in the House of Lords and/or sent representatives to the House of Commons. And though Wales, Scotland and northern England were badly under-represented in comparison with the south, in practice the system worked more equitably than it appeared. Wealthy and influential men from the less favoured regions frequently got themselves elected for seats in the more abundantly represented regions, and in this indirect way their localities obtained a voice at Westminster. In 1761, for example, more than half of the forty-four Members of Parliament elected by Cornwall, then as now a culturally distinct and fairly isolated county, were men born and based outside its boundaries. So were half the MPs elected by two other over-represented counties, Devon and Wiltshire. As so often happened, supposedly rotten boroughs served a practical purpose, in this case enabling men from the less well-represented parts of Britain to gain admission to Westminister and its law-making machinery.[89]

This was quite different from the situation in the sixteenth and seventeenth centuries, when local gentry élites had usually taken great care to keep local seats for local men. The fact that outsiders were increasingly able to get elected in the 1700s showed how much more volatile the electorate now was, but also how much more English-minded, and increasingly British-minded local élites were now prepared to be. Providing a man had money, contacts and preferably ability, it was no longer so important that he be Cornish, or Devonian or Wiltshire born. Or even, by the second half of the eighteenth century, that he be English. For whereas few Scotsmen had represented Welsh or English constituencies before 1750, Scottish – and to a lesser extent Welsh – penetration of English constituencies subsequently became far more common. Between 1760 and 1790, 60 Scots were elected for seats outside their own country. Over the next thirty years, over 130 Scots sat for seats south of the border.[90] This was one indicator, and there would be many more, that by the end of the century Britain's ruling class was British indeed.

A reverence for Parliament became an increasingly important part of élite attitudes, and a vital part of élite patriotism. It was not just that Parliament provided peers and MPs with an unparalleled vehicle for advancing their own sectional interests, though it obviously did that. And it was not just that Parliament became a vital forum for career advancement and for securing appropriate legislation. Serving (and the fact that this word was so often used is surely significant) in Parliament provided a male élite drenched in the classics with the chance to play the Roman senator. It drew on whatever rhetorical ability they possessed, and it catered to their sense of civic worth. Moreover, as men who were likely to have gone on the Grand Tour knew very well, Parliament's importance in Britain distinguished its government from that existing in almost every other European state. By the early 1700s, most comparable institutions had ceased to meet, as the Estates General had in France, or had been emasculated, like the diets in most German states, or had come to be regarded – as the Polish diet was – as little more than archaic and tiresome defenders of class and regional privileges, obstacles to good and effective government.[91]

The knowledge that the institution they served was different, that it was efficient by the standards of the time not obstructive, and that its scope and importance were actually increasing, reassured British patricians of their polity's superiority and by implication their own. Peers and MPs regularly disagreed over the executive's influence in the House of Commons, or over the frequency of general elections, or over the conduct of an individual minister. But these conflicts stemmed from real or assumed anxiety that the beauty of the system was being adulterated, not from doubt about the validity of the system as a whole. As a glance at the recorded debates will very quickly show, there was an almost embarrassing consensus in the eighteenth and nineteenth centuries that Parliament was unique, splendid and sovereign, the hard-won prerogative of a free and Protestant people.

But the cult of Parliament was not confined to the landed classes who manned it, though it does seem to have been restricted for much of the early 1700s to the English. In part, this was because the bulk of the Welsh and the Scots received so little direct benefit from the institution. Very little public or private legislation was passed specifically affecting Wales until the end of the eighteenth century, and what laws were passed would not have been understood by the mass of its inhabitants. A far-sighted proposal by Lord Raymond in 1730 that all of Parliament's proceedings should be translated into Welsh so as to deepen his people's attachment to it was dismissed in the House of Lords as ludicrous by the Scottish Duke of Argyll.[92] Yet for all this, Wales, with its sizeable electorate, was far more closely entangled in the parliamentary system than Scotland was. Even its own Edinburgh Parliament had played only a minor part in Scottish patriotism before 1707, so the Westminster Parliament was scarcely likely to provoke broad enthusiasm north of the border, particularly during the first three or four decades after the Union. It was far away. Before 1745, it passed only occasional pieces of legislation for Scotland's benefit. And, crucially, only a minority of Scots–fewer than 3,000–had the vote.[93]

The situation in England and even in Wales was quite different. There, the proportion of the adult male population in possession of the franchise was never less than 14 per cent, and in the years immediately after the Union it was almost 25 per cent.[94] Moreover, from the Revolution of 1688 until 1716, general elections occurred at least every three years, and sometimes more frequently still. This is often seen as a cause of acute instability. Yet I suspect that the recurrent opportunities this glut of elections provided for men and women to see, cheer and jeer at their gentry representatives may well have helped the new political order to become more deeply entrenched. Tensions could be released, and anger expressed in an acceptable and ritualised fashion. And, in this early period and after, elections served as a form of patriotic and Protestant, not just political education.

Whether there was a pitched battle between rival candidates for a constituency, or whether–as in the majority of cases–the Member of Parliament was in effect nominated by the most influential local landowners, an election was still a civic occasion. The Union Jack was flown, bands played patriotic tunes, the Pope might be burned in effigy, and free beer encouraged loyal toasts as well as the occasional disloyal demonstration. If a man's right to vote was disputed, he might well have to take a public oath of allegiance in the village or town square, thereby reminding spectators of who the reigning monarch was, and reminding them, too, that only Protestants could be citizens. Even those who could not vote were encouraged, by the language and the rites of the election process, to believe that their representatives' power was conditional, that Parliament had somehow a bounden duty to them.[95] It was because they believed this, that unenfranchised men and on occasions women, who were always voteless, so often took part in petitions to Parliament on matters to do with trade, roads, bridges and local government. In the 1730s, for example, Parliament received over 100 petitions from shopkeepers in England and Wales wanting tighter regulation of itinerant pedlars who were taking away some of their business.[96] Many of these petitioners must have had no direct say in the choice of Parliament. Yet, as their actions showed, they still felt they were represented there, that they had a claim.

And there is evidence that even lower down the social scale, Parliament inspired respect. In 1757, a Lincolnshire magistrate called Lawrence Monck was confronted with an angry crowd of farmers, labourers and farm servants protesting about the provisions of the recently passed Militia Act. The culmination of their dialogue – which had begun with threats of violence against Monck and the local gentry – is deeply revealing:

> They [the crowd] were told in reply that an Act of Parliament never had deceived them, nor was likely ever to do so. They agreed *that if Parliament was not to be trusted there would be an end of all things*, so desired Mr Monck would turn back and give them some ale, and promised to do him no mischief.[97]

A cult of Parliament is not the invention of the Whig historians of the nineteenth century. Its social depth in England and parts of Wales much earlier than that – and its growing popularity in Scotland by the second half of the eighteenth century – helps to explain why parliamentary reformers found it so difficult for so long to gain committed support on a large scale. Parliament was part of the Protestant inheritance, venerated more often than it was cold-bloodedly analysed. Moreover, within its very limited terms of reference, it worked.

For in the end, nothing succeeds like success. And success, above all success in war, was what the men who governed Great Britain were able to hold out as a legitimisation of their rule to the millions below them. The Nine Years War with France, the War of Spanish Succession, the wars of Jenkins's Ear and Austrian Succession, the Seven Years War and the wars against Revolutionary and Napoleonic France, all brought enough military and naval victories in their train to flatter British pride, and in most of these conflicts the victories were not only massive but durable in terms of empire won and trade routes gained. Only the War of American Independence was emphatically a defeat, and in the minds of contemporaries it was scarcely coincidental that this was also the only major war of the period in which the initial enemy confronting the British was Protestant rather than Catholic.

Apart from this one, telling débâcle, there was victory. And, as I have suggested, the fact that this was so provided a powerful justification for a united Great Britain, and a Protestant Great Britain. From the fifteenth century to 1688, England and Wales, like Scotland, had been peripheral kingdoms in the European power game, more often at war with each other than with the Continental powers, and – except under Oliver Cromwell – scarcely very successful on those occasions when they did engage with the Dutch, or the French, or the Spanish.[98] It was easy, therefore, for Protestant polemicists to argue, and tempting for the mass of men and women to believe, that it was the expulsion of those Stuart princes who had inclined towards Catholicism, and the uniting of the island under a Protestant dynasty that had transformed Britain's position in the world. Now this second Israel had the rulers it deserved and God required, was it to be wondered at that it reaped victory and dominion?

Reconstructing this way of thinking has been a complex and sometimes uncongenial business. Self-evidently, the Protestant construction of British identity involved the unprivileging of minorities who would not conform: the Catholic community, most Highland Scots before 1745, and the supporters of the exiled Stuart dynasty, those men and women who were not allowed to be British so that others could be. Self-evidently, too, this way of viewing the world fostered and relied on war. There are few more effective ways of bonding together a highly disparate people than by encouraging it to unite against its own and other outsiders. A fundamental reason why Britain was not torn apart by civil war after 1688 was that its inhabitants' aggression was channelled so regularly and so remorselessly into war and imperial expansion abroad.

But, as I have also tried to show, Protestantism meant much more in this society than just bombast, intolerance and chauvinism. It gave the majority of men and women a sense of their place in history and a sense of worth. It allowed them to feel pride in such advantages as they genuinely did enjoy, and helped them endure when hardship and danger threatened. It gave them identity. There were other powerful identities at work, of course. A sense of Protestant unity did not always override social class, anymore than it overwhelmed the profound cultural and historical divisions between the English, the Scottish and the Welsh. But to the questions: Who were the British, and did they even exist? Protestantism could supply a potent and effective answer, perhaps the only satisfactory answer possible. Great Britain might be made up of three separate nations, but under God it could also be one, united nation. And as long as a sense of mission and providential destiny could be kept alive, by means of maintaining prosperity at home, by means of recurrent wars with the Catholic states of Europe, and by means of a frenetic and for a long time highly successful pursuit of empire, the Union flourished, sustained not just by convenience and profit but by belief as well. Protestantism was the foundation that made the invention of Great Britain possible.

2 *Profits*

PROTESTANTISM, BROADLY UNDERSTOOD, PROVIDED the majority of Britons with a framework for their lives. It shaped their interpretation of the past and enabled them to make sense of the present. It helped them identify and confront their enemies. It gave them confidence and even hope. It made it easier for them to think of themselves as a people apart. But if religion underpinned national identity here as in so many other states – France, or Holland, or Sweden, or Russia or the United States of America – it was also the case that an active commitment to nation was often intimately bound up with an element of self-interest. This, too, was and is a widespread tendency. As the Czech historian Miroslav Hroch puts it: 'National ideology is effective where it reflects (even though in a merely illusory fashion) the interests of the groups to which it makes its appeal, or contains at least in part the kind of programme which is close to their interests.'[1] And though in translation Hroch's prose scarcely dances, his insight is still an acute one. Great Britain was forged in the way that it was after 1707, and to the extent that it was, in part because different classes and interest groups came to see this newly invented nation as a usable resource, as a focus of loyalty which would also cater to their own needs and ambitions. From patriotism, men and women were able to anticipate profits of some kind.

This point needs stressing because it has sometimes been argued that the regime established by the Act of Union in 1707, and by the accession of the Hanoverian dynasty seven years later, rested on a very narrow social and political base and relied for its continuance almost exclusively on military force.[2] That the men who governed Britain for much of the eighteenth century were a set of rapacious Whig banditti appealing to the 'baser instincts of the political class' and little more.[3] That from the viewpoint of the ordinary man or woman, there was little to choose between the 'close-knit élite' oppressing them at home, and the 'absolutism of Bourbon France'.[4] That the ruling order in this society was lucky to survive and should never have done so, in fact.[5] Such characterisations capture very well how different opposition groups sometimes perceived the structures of authority in Britain. But for precisely this reason, they scarcely provide a balanced and comprehensive appraisal of why those structures endured. And they fail to convey the degree to which this artificial nation, governed at the highest level by a predominantly landed and – in the early decades especially – an aggressively Anglocentric oligarchy, was none the less able to attract support from much broader sectors of the population.

Traders of different kinds were always prominent among these supporters, in part because of their sheer number. Perhaps one in every five families in eighteenth-century Britain drew its livelihood from trade and distribution: and this was on top of those farmers and manufacturers who relied on domestic and external trading networks for their profits.[6] But it was also the case that, more than most British civilians, traders needed the state. Domestic traders, even the small fry, relied on it for the good order that made commercial and credit transactions feasible and safe. Overseas merchants required its naval protection on the more dangerous sea routes, especially in time of war. And almost all of those engaged in trade benefited in some way from Britain's ruthless pursuit of colonial markets and from its intermittent struggle with the other main contender for imperial and commercial primacy, France. Not all traders were patriots, of course. And not all of those who were invariably supported the government of the day. Even so, for much of the time – and especially in time of emergency – this broad occupational group had one of the best and most compelling reasons for loyalty. Quite simply, it paid. Especially in the first half century of Great Britain's existence as a united kingdom, when both the Act of Union and the Hanoverian dynasty were still recent and controversial, this close and surprisingly harmonious relationship between a landed ruling class and a broad commercial community was a vital source of stability. It was also creative, in that a cult of commerce became an increasingly important part of being British.

LAND, TRADE, WAR AND EMPIRE

In 1740, William Hogarth painted not only one of his best portraits, but also one of the most powerful evocations of the pretensions of commerce in this culture. His subject was Thomas Coram, the man responsible for organising Britain's first hospital for foundling children. Broad, downright and ruddy, he poses confidently, his back against a massive pillar, his hair a benignant white and his own, not covered by a looped or pig-tailed wig as it should have been for fashionable society. His clothes, too, are comfortable but

10. William Hogarth, *Thomas Coram*, 1740.

plain, the coat cuffs turned well back so as to free his hands for business. At first glance, this might almost be the figure of some bucolic patriarch, a no-nonsense Squire Allworthy exuding solid worth and rural integrity. But closer inspection reveals something very different.

No country estate adorns the background of this picture; no sporting dog, or thoroughbred horse, or decorative agricultural implement. Emphatically a state portrait, in the sense that it is clearly intended to be viewed by an admiring public, its subject is neither royal nor patrician. Instead, to one side of Coram is the open sea and a sailing-ship, and by his stoutly buckled shoes is a globe – an emblem of dominion – turned to show the Atlantic Ocean which he had crossed and re-crossed as a young man plying his trade as a shipwright. Not inherited rank or broad acres, but commerce and enterprise are visibly the foundations of this man's civic virtue. Coram, as Hogarth paints him, is the self-made man of trade as hero; and something more than a hero. The portrait hung in the Foundling Hospital's chapel, and legend has it that some of the children, their eyes wandering during prayers to the painted gaze of their benefactor, came to confuse Our Father with plain Tom Coram. In their *naïveté*, they glimpsed what Hogarth almost certainly wanted to convey to more sophisticated spectators: that Coram, and men like Coram, were the source of Great Britain's material blessings and of its moral worth, that stout-hearted commercial activity and ideal patriotism were one and the same.[7]

Superficially, Coram's life and work provided eloquent and irresistible testimony that this was indeed the case. The son of a Dorset ship's captain, he had crossed over to Boston in 1694 as an agent for some London merchants. After ten years in the American colonies as a ship-builder and salesman, he came home and embarked on a remarkable career as a lobbyist for a wide range of secular charities. Initially, he tried to interest the Board of Trade in a project for settling demobilised sailors and soldiers in the colonies. Failing at this, he turned his attention to the hundreds of infants, most of them illegitimate and many of them dying, abandoned in the streets and doorways of London. Other European nations already possessed institutions to look after *enfants trouvés*, usually funded by the state or by the Catholic Church. In Great Britain, by contrast, the creation of a foundling hospital had to wait on private enterprise. Coram's initial approaches to George I on behalf of the foundlings got nowhere. Urging bishops or members of the nobility to speak on his and the children's behalf, he once exploded, was about as easy as persuading them to exhibit their bare backsides at court. Not until the next reign did he secure powerful patrician backing, and even then it was limited. The list of 375 hospital governors approved by George II in 1737 contained some very illustrious names, but the majority of active governors were merchants and men of Coram's own type.

From the outset, the charity was run in their commercial image. As a voluntary corporate body with its own directors and legal identity, it was modelled on London's joint-stock companies, the first time an organisation of this kind had been extended to the work of philanthropy. The hospital's avowed aim was mercantilist as well as humanitarian: to rescue young lives that would otherwise be wasted and render them useful to the state. Once grown, the girls were sent out as servants; the boys went to sea or worked in husbandry. To raise the necessary funds, publicity techniques were employed that were both inventive and unabashedly commercial. Hogarth, who was one of the governors, designed a distinctive uniform for the foundlings as well as an affecting coat of arms: a new-born child flanked by the figures of Nature and Britannia, with the plaintive motto 'Help'.[8] He also came up with a strategy that promoted the charity's work alongside his own. Together with other enterprising artists, Francis Hayman, Allan Ramsay, Thomas Hudson and Joseph Highmore, he began exhibiting his most recent paintings in the hospital's public rooms. The rich and the leisured came to gape and stayed to give; while Hogarth furthered his private agenda, to increase the respectability and marketability of British as distinct from Continental art. The annual meetings of the Foundling artists, as they came to be called, held at the hospital every 5 November in honour of the Revolution of 1688, of liberty and of Protestantism, led in time–though in much slower time than Hogarth wanted–to the creation of the Royal Academy of Art.[9]

At first glance, then, Thomas Coram's philanthropic monument triumphantly confirmed the moral of his portrait. Here was a pioneering charity, founded by self-made men and run by others of the same kind, a venture of national importance publicising (apparently) the superior public spirit of commercial men. And the claim that trade was the muscle and the soul of Great Britain, both the source of its greatness and the nursery of patriots, was abundantly echoed in the poetry, drama, novels, newspapers, tracts, parliamentary speeches, private correspondence, even the sermons of the time. In 1718, the chapter on 'Trade' in the annual directory *The Present State of Great Britain*, read by virtually everyone who mattered, opened with the ringing assertion that 'Next to the purity of our religion we are the most considerable of any nation in the world for the vastness and extensiveness of our trade.'

Some forty years later, the same chapter omitted any reference to religion and simply told the reader that 'Our trade is the most considerable of the whole world. And, indeed, Great Britain is, of all other countries, the most proper for trade.'[10] Abundant trade was not just materially desirable: for Britons in this period it was also proof positive of their status as the freest and most distinctively Protestant of nations.

This cult of trade crossed party divisions, just as it crossed social boundaries. 'Whenever our trade perishes', a government pamphleteer would warn in 1731, 'so must our public dignity and strength.' 'Be commerce then thy sole design', urged the opposition poet John Gay, 'Keep that, and all the world is thine.'[11] 'Our trade is our chief support', Lord Carteret told his fellow peers in 1739, 'and therefore we must sacrifice every other view to the preservation of our trade.' And though he spoke on behalf of the Opposition, the ministerialists who answered him were just as insistent that Britain was pre-eminently 'a trading nation'.[12] 'You turn your thoughts a little upon trade and commerce', wrote the exquisite Lord Chesterfield to his bastard son in the 1750s, '. . . I am very glad you do'.[13] 'Commerce', said the historian Thomas Mortimer in 1762, with the weary conviction of a man uttering a necessary platitude, 'the great idol of this nation, and to which she sacrifices every other consideration'. 'To the instrumentality of commerce *alone*', pronounced the Aberdeen-born economist, Adam Anderson, in his *Historical and Chronological Deduction of the Origin of Commerce* (1764), 'the Britannic empire is most peculiarly indebted.'[14] It would be easy to find hundreds, even thousands of other comments to the same effect.

Yet in some respects this din of acclamation was deceptive. In the eyes of almost all of the political class, trade was the mainspring of Britain's economy and a vital part of its identity, yes. But in terms of wealth, status and power, men of trade in this society came a long way behind men of land, and continued to do so for a very long time. Even in the mid-nineteenth century, landed millionaires would be more numerous than millionaires who had built their fortune out of commerce.[15] Intermarriage between the wealthier landowners and families still active in trade was rare, and even penurious younger sons were more likely to seek refuge in the armed forces, in the law or in government office than in trade.[16] So while broad-acred Members of Parliament virtually always spoke approvingly of commerce, they spoke of it as a worthy occupation indispensable to the well-being of the nation, not as *their* occupation, and not as their children's occupation if they could help it.

Left unspoken, but often there, was the conviction that trade was admirable as long as its exponents knew their place. When William Pitt the Elder ripped through this polite convention and told the House of Commons in 1758 that he would be prouder of being an alderman of London than a peer of the realm, he caused an outcry. As far as their lordships were concerned, this compliment to the fat bourgeoisie who packed the aldermanic bench was plutolatry run mad, sheer class treason, and they were outraged.[17] They need not have worried, however. Pitt's own social ambitions turned out in the end to be deeply conventional. He purchased a landed estate in Kent and accepted not just one peerage but two, a title for his clever and long-suffering wife as well as an earldom for himself.

For land-ownership still provided the best and most reliable means of admission to power at the top as it did to social status. Whereas fewer than sixty mercantile MPs were elected to the House of Commons at each general election between 1714 and 1770, members of the landed élite made up over 75 per cent of the Commons' membership as late as 1867. Peers of the realm, who formed the bulk of almost every British cabinet until the early twentieth century, were also, usually, men with landed estates to their name. Until the end of Queen Victoria's reign, landed men virtually monopolised high office at the royal court and were massively over-represented in the upper ranks of the army and navy, in the diplomatic and colonial service, in the hierarchy of the Church of England and in the administration of justice.[18] Wealth, status and power, then, both formal power in the state and informal power over opinion and over the lives of ordinary men and women: on all these the grip of the titled and territorial élites was enormously strong. No one knew this better than Hogarth's tradesman hero, Thomas Coram. To win approval for his Foundling Hospital, he danced attendance on the court, on Parliament and on individual patricians and their bored and elegant wives. To give his project cachet as well as supporters in high places, he included men of rank among the hospital's governors, even though it was rarely they who did the real work. So if Coram's life illustrated the pretensions of trade in this culture, it also suggested the social and political constraints under which men of trade often had to operate. Even the most energetic and successful of them were likely to require the aid, custom and patronage of the traditionally landed at some point. Some degree of clientage and deference on their part was almost inescapable.

How are we to understand, then, this society's noisy cult of commerce? What did the widespread conviction that trade was the foundation of Britain's greatness and identity mean, when land was still the main source of power and prestige within it? In reality this seeming paradox was no paradox at all. It was partly because the status of land and landed men was so great and so secure, that peers, Members of Parliament, ministers of state and even monarchs were prepared to adopt such an approving attitude towards the contribution made by trade. During the War of Spanish Succession in the early 1700s, when the land tax was abrading the incomes of the lesser gentry, and in the last third of the eighteenth century, when landed authority came under attack at home and in the American colonies, in both cases from sectors of the trading community, this complacency occasionally and understandably wavered.[19] But from the signing of the Union to the 1760s, British patricians were usually powerful enough and confident enough to be able to regard trade with serene approval.

This was one reason, I suspect, why the Venetian artist Canaletto proved such a runaway success with his British patrons. The views of Venice purchased in such numbers and at such high prices by Whig grandees like the Duke of Richmond, the Earl of Carlisle, and the Duke of Bedford (who designed a whole room around his twenty-four Canalettos at Woburn), and by Tory landowners like Sir William Morice and the Egertons of Tatton, were all idealised. The crumbling stucco, dank canals and tattered beggars that characterised the real Venice of this time, and that Canaletto's early works faithfully represented, were not what these titled buyers wanted to see on their walls. What they wanted when they began to buy up the Venetian master's works in bulk from the late 1720s onwards, and what Canaletto gave them if they paid enough, were views of Venice painted as if it were still in its fifteenth-century prime, the perfect maritime republic, with turquoise lagoons, golden masonry, bustling harbours and well-dressed inhabitants: Venice as the Queen of the Adriatic, a trading empire, proud of its freedom, *yet securely controlled by an oligarchy*.[20] Venice, or rather the legend of Venetian power and prosperity, exerted a powerful attraction, because it suggested that commercial energy, imperial dominion, a taste for liberty, and stable rule by an exclusive élite could all be painlessly combined. Most British patricians were sufficiently assured in their status to believe that these things were fully compatible in their own island also, and they were right.

Most of them believed also that commerce, especially foreign commerce, was the engine that drove a state's power and wealth, just as they took it for granted that the world's supply of raw materials and markets was strictly finite, that competition to win access to them was bound to be intense, and that if British traders were to succeed in the struggle, they must be vigorously supported

11. London in Venice and Venice in London: William Marlow, *Capriccio: St Paul's and a Venetian Canal*, *c.*1795.

abroad and protected at home. This brand of mercantilism was common to virtually all European élites at this time, but for two reasons Britain's rulers were particularly receptive to it. First of all, most of them spent at least part of the year in the only city other than Venice that Canaletto painted repeatedly, the city that was Britain's chief port, financial centre and trading metropolis: namely, London. Home to at least one in every dozen Britons, visited at some point in their lives by perhaps as many as one in six, London was in a league apart from every other European capital.[21] Only one in forty Frenchmen lived in Paris in the eighteenth century, and a mere one in eighty Spaniards made their home in Madrid. Neither city was a major port. Berlin, Vienna and St Petersburg were socially, ceremonially and culturally resplendent but of little commercial importance. Of all the major European powers, only Great Britain – and to a less concentrated degree the Dutch Republic – possessed a metropolis of trade and population that was also its centre of power.

London was not just the hub of British commerce, but the home of the court, the arena in which ministers and bureaucrats did much of their work, and the meeting place of Parliament. All of these lures ensured that there was a huge annual influx of country squires and noblemen into the city, plus their wives, families, friends and hangers-on. By the 1750s indeed, virtually all English, Welsh and Scottish peers and Members of Parliament either owned a residence in London or rented one.[22] Naturally, these men inhabited very different parts of this sprawling metropolis from the bulk of its mercantile and trading population. But there were still abundant opportunities for contact between the two groups, and no one, however reclusive and well-bred, was likely to spend a substantial time in London without being impressed by the ubiquity of commerce. The Thames that flowed through it, carrying every kind of craft from royal barges, private pleasure boats, naval gunships and merchantmen loaded with the world's goods, was a constant reminder of the city's unique diversity and of the foundation of its and the nation's wealth.[23]

The second reason why the British élite was peculiarly responsive to the demands of trade was far more important, however. Trade was simply much too valuable for them to do otherwise. The great trading companies like the East India Company, the Levant Company and the Russia Company, together with London's mercantile community in general, supplied successive governments with their most substantial creditors. The long-term loans that funded on average some 30 per cent of wartime expenditure after 1688, and just under 40 per cent of the cost of the American war, came in the main not from landed investers who might have only a limited amount of liquid capital at their disposal, but from merchants, financiers, businessmen and women, and even minor shopkeepers and traders.[24] More important still, it was domestic and foreign trade that supplied the bulk of taxation. After the War of Spanish Succession ended in 1713, as Patrick O'Brien and others have shown, the rate at which taxes were levied on land was allowed to decline during peacetime. The resulting fiscal slack was taken up by customs dues levied on imports, and by excise taxes on selected commodities produced or distributed in Britain, beer, salt, malt, candles, leather, paper, silk, soap, leather, starch and so forth. The land tax remained an important part of the state's fiscal armoury, especially in time of war. None the less, until the end of the eighteenth century, customs and excise levies together supplied over 60 per cent of government revenue, and sometimes more than 70 per cent.[25]

If this were not enough to endear commerce and manufacturing to Britain's landed classes, relieved now of some of the weight of direct taxation, there was also the matter of the Royal Navy. This had been expanding in size and firepower since the 1650s, and by the middle of the eighteenth century needed a shipboard population of more than 40,000 men in time of war.[26] To raise them, it relied on the mercantile marine. Many of the navy's volunteers first learnt their seacraft there, and so, too, did virtually all of the men it pressed into service. Despite the black legends that have gathered around press gangs, they rarely in fact preyed on just any poor man they encountered on shore. Both the law and the practical demands of shipboard life demanded that they confine their attentions to 'seamen, seafaring men, and persons whose occupations or callings are to work in vessels and boats upon rivers'. In wartime, the Royal Navy needed experienced seamen, not reluctant tyros who were all too likely to get their shipmates as well as themselves killed. The peacetime training and employment supplied by Britain's merchant service were thus indispensable for the operation of its naval power, a point Lord Haversham set out in a speech to the House of Lords in 1707:

> Your fleet and your trade have so near a relation, and such a mutual influence upon each other they cannot be well separated; your trade is the mother and nurse of your seamen; your seamen are the life of your fleet, and your fleet is the security and protection of your trade, and both together are the wealth, strength, security and glory of Britain.[27]

Haversham's stress on the intimate connexions between trade on the one hand, and the imperatives of a British state dominated by landed men on the other, is important. Forever on the alert for signs of an emerging and autonomous middle-class identity, historians have tended to concentrate on the causes and occasions of conflict between the landed and commercial sectors. Conflict and dissatisfaction there often was, of course, over taxation, over foreign policy and over the government's commercial policy at home.[28] But while acknowledging these disagreements, we should not forget the background of mutual dependence. For if Britain's landed politicians had a vested interest in advancing trade, it was also the case that the majority of men and women of trade needed what the nation state had to offer.

Whether he was a gilded merchant, a substantial middleman, a humble shopkeeper or even an itinerant pedlar, the quality of a trader's livelihood was bound to be closely linked to the preservation of law, order and domestic peace. Any threatened invasion from abroad or any prospect of insurrection at home was almost certain to disrupt business and endanger money supply and credit. Because of the Mint's incapacity to produce enough silver and copper coin, credit played a more vital part in Britain's economy than in that of almost any its competitors.[29] Shopkeepers in Britain – and there were some 140,000 of them in England and Wales alone – purchased a substantial part of their merchandise on credit. And since many of their customers had no regular income, and even prosperous farmers and landed gentry might only settle their bills once a year when rents came in, they in turn had little choice but to sell goods on credit. More often than not, shopkeepers also acted as informal bankers to their more dependable customers, giving out small loans in return for a fixed rate of interest. The more substantial wholesale merchants who operated from London and the major outports also allowed generous credit arrangements, long-term credit for export traders who might take a year or more before repaying what they owed, as well as short-term credit for retail traders in the region and outside it. Between 1711 and 1715, 154 bankrupts from forty-one English and Welsh counties, almost all of them retailers, were sued by Londoners, mainly wholesale distributors, for whom the business of extending credit on a nationwide basis had badly misfired.[30]

Easy credit, then, meant that traders had to undertake considerable economic risks. The men and women who benefited from it found themselves caught fast in a complex web of dependency and obligation:

> Inland bills of exchange passed between the provincial shopkeeper and the London wholesaler; small masters, craftsmen

> and farmers raised money by signing short-term bonds or mortgaging their property; local attornies encouraged widows to lend to those in need of capital; shopkeepers allowed their customers to pay 'on tick'; tradesmen extended credit to one another; even labourers' pay was sometimes given in the form of credit rather than cash.[31]

For some, the need to be involved in these transactions was a profound source of irritation, a reason for opposing a governmental system that conspicuously failed to provide sufficient hard currency for Britain's developing economy. But credit's contribution to political stability also needs to be recognised. All credit systems rely on confidence, confidence that interest payments will be made at the correct level and at the correct time, and confidence that debts will ultimately be repaid. So however much they disliked particular administrations, creditors and many of their clients were likely to regard any serious breach of the peace with alarm. As far as borrowers were concerned, widespread civil unrest would probably lead to a rise in interest rates; while a full-scale domestic rebellion or an invasion from abroad might mean that lenders would never recover what was owed to them.

This was the point of the famous parable that Joseph Addison wrote for the *Spectator* in 1711, in which he imagined public credit as a beautiful virgin enthroned in a great hall hung about with those acts of Parliament that sustained the existing order, the Toleration Act of 1689 and the Act of Settlement of 1701:

> The lady seemed to set an unspeakable value upon these several pieces of furniture, insomuch that she often refreshed her eye with them, and often smiled with a secret pleasure, as she looked upon them; but, at the same time, showed a very particular uneasiness, if she saw any thing approaching that might hurt them.[32]

This was Whig, partisan argument, but it was still valid for all that. Severe political or military disruption *was* likely to undo public credit, just as it was certain to upset the myriad private credit arrangements that fuelled British trade. In time of crisis, those possessed by a strong opposition ideology of some kind might be willing to disregard these material considerations. But for those who wavered or were neutral, the economic advantages of loyalty or at the very least of quiescence could, as we shall see, appear overwhelming.

Not least because the Protestant ruling order established by the Revolution of 1688, and ensured by the Hanoverian Succession of 1714, supplied traders with positive advantages. One of its foremost innovations, after all, was annual sessions of Parliament, and this was of considerable value to men and women hungry for parliamentary intervention and sympathetic legislation. The papers of virtually every Member of Parliament and peer from this time show just how large initiatives to do with trade–petitions for new bridges, new roads, new market places or better street lighting, plans for improvements to ports and lighthouses, requests for new duties on imports, or demands for an end to old monopolies–loomed in the political business of the day.[33] Lesser tradesmen would band together to petition their local magnate or MP for what they wanted. More powerful men lobbied directly, or employed agents to do so for them. In 1739, for example, the prosperous merchants who ran the Convention of the Royal Burghs in Edinburgh paid a London-based solicitor called Thomas White the sum of £100 to lobby in support of legislation for Scotland's linen industry. Over the next dozen years, this same body petitioned Parliament on the state of the coinage, on the problem of smuggling, in support of convoy protection for merchantmen in time of war, in favour of a standardisation of weights and measures, and on behalf of legislation changing the bankruptcy laws.[34]

For men such as these, the machinery of the state was scarcely alien or parasitic. It was something that opened up opportunities, something that could, occasionally and with luck, be used to their own profit. And if the state's civil wing could be seen in these utilitarian terms by trading groups, the same was even more true as far as its military power was concerned. For it was the British government's huge investment in the navy, together with the imperial reach that this increasingly made possible, that allowed overseas trade to grow in the way that it did, and with the speed that it did. It this sense, it was actually trade that was parasitic on the resources of the nation state.

Like much that is real and important, the value of the empire to British traders at this time can actually be obscured by the relevent statistics. These show that at the time of the Union in 1707, and at the outset of the Seven Years War some half a century later, it was still Continental Europe that was easily Britain's most important market, absorbing some four-fifths of its domestic exports and re-exports, and supplying most of its imports.[35] Yet for at least three reasons, this is less conclusive than it seems. First, Continental markets for British goods were growing only slowly after 1700, in large part because European states were just as aggressively protectionist as Great Britain was itself. By contrast, the commercial dynamism of the imperial sector–Britain's colonies in North

America and the West Indies, and its trading outposts in India – seemed almost boundless. Imports from North America increased almost fourfold in value in the first half of the century, West Indian imports more than doubled in the same period, while the amount of tea shipped into the country by the East Indian Company (as distinct from by the smugglers who brought in a great deal more) increased more than forty-fold from some 67,000 pounds weight in 1701 to close to three million pounds fifty years later.[36] Exports to the colonies grew just as dramatically. In 1713, British merchants shipped out some £32,400-worth of exports to the Carolinas. By 1739, exports to these same colonies were worth seven times more than this.[37] In all, 95 per cent of *the increase* in Britain's commodity exports that occurred in the six decades after the Act of Union was sold to captive and colonial markets outside Europe.

But, secondly, colonial imports into Britain came to play an increasingly important part in what can be called its balance of payments as far as European trade was concerned. By the 1750s, re-exports of colonial goods made up almost 40 per cent of total British exports, and a still higher proportion just of Scottish exports.[38] Much of these re-exports went to Continental markets. Naturally, however, a great deal of colonial goods was retained for the domestic market, and this was the third and perhaps most far-reaching consequence of imperial trade: the impact it had on perceptions of commerce and empire at home. Exotic goods which had previously been imported only in small quantities for a cosseted élite – silk, rice, dyestuffs, coffee, tobacco and, above all, tea and sugar – now became far more abundantly and broadly available. By the 1740s, moralists like John Wesley and Jonas Hanway were complaining that travelling salesmen were even selling tea by the cup to haymakers at harvest-time, and that the 'very chambermaids have lost their bloom by drinking tea'.[39] This was an exaggeration as far as the bulk of the poor were concerned. But it was the case that colonial consumer goods had by now become sufficiently widespread to bring the spoils of empire to the level of every village shop, and the attractions of empire to the minds of many more Britons than ever before:

> The British navy thro the ocean vast
> Shall weave her double cross, th'extremest climes,
> Terrific, and return with odorous spoils
> Of Araby well fraught, or Indus' wealth,
> Pearl, and barbaric gold . . .[40]

As these lines suggest, there was a real sense in which this

12. *Britannia receiving the riches of the East.* Spiridione Roma's ceiling painting for East India House, London, 1778.

commercial bonanza was dependent on government investment in naval power and imperialism. The population of British North America quintupled between 1675 and 1740, a phenomenal rate of growth unequalled in any other European empire. And most traders – like most Britons in general – took it for granted that they could maintain their dominance in this, the western world's fastest growing market, only so long as Americans remained subject to the crown. As it turned out, American dependence on British manufactured goods persisted long after the winning of independence. None the less, if the imperial embrace proved less indispensable for British commercial success in this part of the world than many people anticipated, war and empire indisputably played a vital part in breaking into and securing markets elsewhere. In return for its participation in the War of Spanish Succession, for example, Britain won Gibraltar, Minorca, Nova Scotia, Newfoundland, Hudson's Bay, and trading concessions in Spanish America. It was the memory of this booty that led merchants throughout Britain to push for another war against Spain in the late 1730s. The resulting War of Jenkins's Ear proved, in fact, a fiasco. But the Seven Years War, with its huge gains in North America, the West Indies, Africa and India, seemed to confirm, more dramatically than any previous conflict had done, that commerce could, in Edmund Burke's words, be 'united with, and made to flourish by war', that British power and commercial profit went hand in hand.[41]

Once won, of course, trade routes, colonies and monopolies had to be defended. And in an extremely aggressive world system, this meant having constant recourse to the Royal Navy. During wartime, naval protection was indispensable if British merchantmen were to be safeguarded from enemy warships, and from the privateers operating out of French ports like St Malo and Brest. In peacetime, the navy worked to keep foreign merchantmen out of British territories overseas, and to provide an escort for British ships plying the more hazardous trade routes.[42]

In short, the relationship between the trading interest on the one hand, and the landed interest that dominated the legislature and policy-making on the other, though by no means an equal or an invariably tranquil one, was for much of the eighteenth century and after mutually beneficial. Trade was not only an indispensable part of the British economy, but also vital for the state's revenue and naval power. In return, traders depended on the state for the maintenance of civil order, for sympathetic legislation, for protection in peace and war, and for access to captive markets overseas. The political and patriotic responses of those engaged in trade were never monolithic. There were simply too many of them, with too many conflicting incomes, needs and aspirations, for that ever to be likely. But traders of all kinds did have a stake in Great Britain's survival, in its independence and in its unity which made it the West's largest free market. Especially in the half century or so after the Act of Union, men and women of trade played a vital part in preserving the nation from invasion from without and in supporting its world-wide aggression.

JACOBITISM AND THE ECONOMICS OF LOYALTY

Was a nation with a large commercial sector more likely to produce mass resistance to invasion from without? Writing in 1755 – but with an eye to events ten years earlier – an obscure Cambridge don called Benjamin Newton decided that it was:

> National courage will be proportional to the share of property which each individual possesses, or hopes to possess. And as

> trade naturally leads to an equal division of property, it follows that the people of a trading nation will (other things being equal) exert more courage and more strenuously defend their country.[43]

The debate over whether a commercial culture caused civic vigilance to blossom as never before, or whether instead it led to a decline in martial virtue, was a familiar one throughout western Europe at this time. But in Great Britain, the question acquired a particular urgency. Not just because trade was so important here, but also because danger from without threatened so often and threatened so much.

During the first half-century after the Union, Great Britain was faced with recurrent invasion threats from abroad and insurrections at home on behalf of the Stuart claimants to the throne. In 1708, there was a small-scale invasion of Scotland. In 1715, a major rising in support of James Edward Stuart, James III to his supporters, broke out in parts of Scotland and the north of England. Three years later, the Spanish government sponsored another abortive invasion of Scotland. And in 1745, Charles Edward Stuart launched the last and most serious of these invasion attempts, managing to come within 140 miles of London. In addition, there was a succession of invasion plots which were never translated into action, in 1720–21, in 1743–44, in 1750 and finally in 1759.[44]

To understand why the bulk of Britain's trading sector – like the majority of Britons – reacted to these emergencies as they did, we need to consider what a Stuart restoration would have entailed in terms of violence, disruption and political change. This might seem an obvious enough strategy, yet in practice it is rarely adopted. A cynic might argue that this is because a disproportionate number of those who write about Jacobitism are themselves Jacobites who shut their eyes to the less attractive aspects of their cause.[45] But I suspect that what has most distorted our understanding of the response to Jacobitism is the fact that British historians are a sheltered species where large-scale political violence is concerned. Since no political revolution, or full-scale civil war, or successful invasion from overseas has occurred in their island since the seventeenth century, and since few writing today have ever fired a shot in anger, they are always in danger of approaching these phenomena too wistfully and idealistically, of looking avidly for signs of turmoil and convulsion without considering what they would have meant for the men and women living at the time. Yet, as most Irishmen and Continental Europeans could tell them, civil wars and invasions and occupations by foreign armies tear countries apart and people apart. There is always a price.

The more serious Jacobite conspirators always recognised this. They took it for granted, as all historians now admit, that their only real chance of victory after the Hanoverian Succession had been accomplished in 1714 lay in securing substantial military aid from a foreign power.[46] Even in 1688, William of Orange had felt obliged to provide himself with a force of well over 15,000 men before embarking on his successful invasion of England. Military developments since then meant that a would-be invader ideally required a still more substantial force. James II's army had been 40,000 strong.[47] But many of his troops had possessed little or no battle experience, and some – as events showed – had been too bitterly alienated from his religious policies to be reliable. By contrast, the British army in the first half of the eighteenth century averaged over 70,000 men in time of war. Its officers and men had been tested time and time again on European battlefields, and though its training was still defective, its professionalism was improving rapidly. In peacetime, of course, the army was much smaller, no more than 17,000 men as far as regiments based in Britain were concerned.[48] But this was of small advantage to the Jacobites, since foreign governments were unlikely to launch a massive invasion of Britain on behalf of the Stuarts in time of peace. Therefore, Jacobites had little choice but to wait for Britain to go to war – and for much of its army to be deployed abroad – and hope that one or more of the states opposing it would then be interested in pouring men and money into an invasion attempt on behalf of the Stuarts.

The problem with this strategy was that it was almost certain to lead to a considerable loss of British lives, a large-scale destruction of property, widespread disorder *and* the disruption of trade. Some Jacobites tried to believe otherwise. They hoped that the Stuart claimant might return by way of a bloodless coup, as Charles II had done in 1660, or that the Hanoverian kings and their forces might lose their nerve and retreat painlessly in the face of their enemies, as James II and his supporters had done in 1688. But these were pipe dreams. Whatever their faults, George I and George II were both physically courageous men, ambitious, resilient and tough. Both kings had led troops into battle many times in Germany. Both were guarded in London by a huge concentration of household cavalry and foot guards, and both had additional regiments in Ireland, Europe and Britain to call on in time of danger. A Jacobite or foreign army might easily land in North Wales or northern Scotland, where few British troops were quartered. But to win the kingdom it would have to penetrate its centre. It would have to be prepared to fight pitched battles against substantial numbers of

British troops and their allies, and it would have to kill on a very large scale.

That committed Jacobites understood this is suggested by Joseph Enzer's superb stucco decorations in the House of Dun, a modest but profoundly elegant country house near Montrose on the eastern coast of Scotland.[49] A splendid, almost shocking mixture of chaste classicism and gloating violence, Enzer's plasterwork was commissioned some five years before the Battle of Culloden by David Erskine of Dun. Erskine was an episcopalian, a Jacobite and a relation of the Earl of Mar, the leading figure of the 'Fifteen rising, who had advised him on the design of his house. At one end of its graciously proportioned William Adam saloon there is a relief of Neptune, the god of the sea who was to bring the exiled Stuart Pretender back to his kingdom. The facing wall is given over to Mars, god of war. In helmet and breastplate he tramples on the royal crown and the Union Jack, the British lion reduced to cringing humility beneath his feet. Above Mars, in a massive and still more explicit relief, a goddess sits among the paraphernalia of battle, cannons, mortars, pikes, guns and human captives in chains.

To say that this was how Erskine anticipated the triumph of his cause is no criticism of him. He desperately wanted to replace the Hanoverian dynasty with the Stuarts; he almost certainly wanted to break the Act of Union and resurrect Scottish independence, and he was realistic enough to know what the price of such violent alterations was likely to be. My point is that, in the last resort, Jacobitism cannot just be understood in terms of ideologies, folk myths and picturesque anecdotes, golden-haired princes, loyal Highlanders, clandestine toasts and the like. This is a sentimentalised vision of the movement coloured by the retrospective knowledge that it failed. At the time, the Jacobite cause was essentially about access to military power. The price of its victory would almost certainly have been prolonged civil war. And given the kind of armies and the kind of hardware available, a British civil war in the mid-eighteenth century might well have been more destructive even than the War between the Three Kingdoms a hundred years before which had killed some 50,000 men and women in England, Wales and Scotland.[50] The tendency of so many Jacobites to express their allegiance only in harmless ways, by drinking healths to the Stuarts, or by joining secret societies of like-minded sympathisers, or by collecting souvenirs of the exiled dynasty, or (more dangerous this) by cursing the reigning monarch, easily lends itself to mockery. Theirs was scarcely a heroic brand of protest. Yet the motives behind this kind of diffidence were often impeccable. However much they hated the

13a and b. Details from Joseph Enzer's plaster-work at the House of Dun.

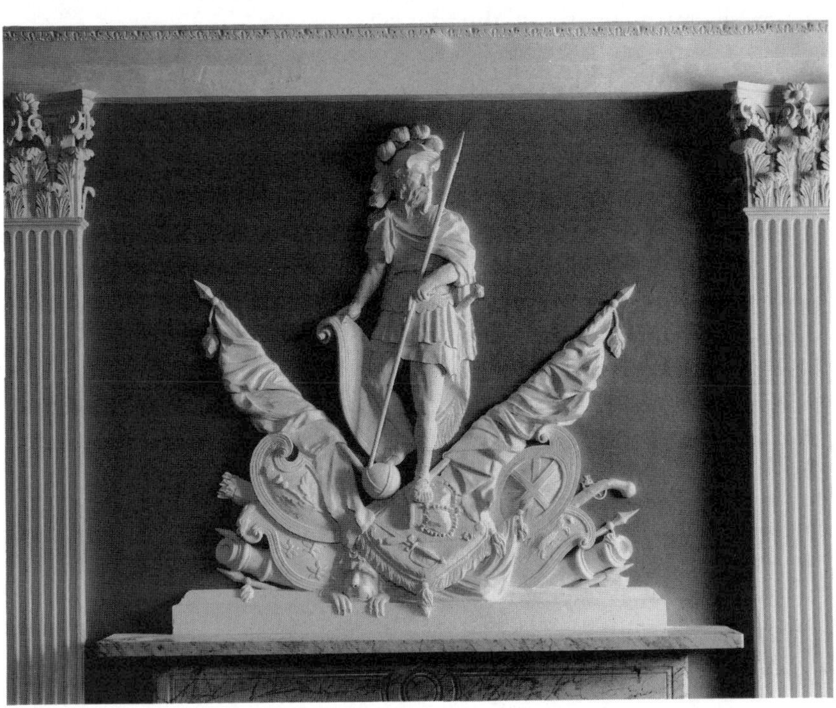

Hanoverians, these people had no stomach for engineering civil war and the death of fellow Britons, nor perhaps for putting their own property and lives at risk. As Samuel Johnson, a Tory who sometimes leaned towards emotional Jacobitism, put it: 'People were afraid of a change, even though they think it right.'[51]

But it was conventional patriots and waverers who were most affected by the knowledge that the Stuart dynasty was only likely to be restored at the cost of massive violence on home territory. For most of them, Protestantism provided the positive, most fundamental reason for coming down in support of the existing order. But fear of invasion and civil war certainly played a part in hardening opinion against the Stuart cause. There was a real sense indeed in which their necessary reliance on violence emptied the Jacobites' propaganda of much of the appeal it might otherwise have had.[52] Jacobite ideologues summoned up highly attractive visions of peace, yet Jacobite conspirators were obliged to yearn for war and exploit it when it happened. They spoke of order and plenty, yet had no choice in practice but to incite armed destruction. They claimed to be fighting on behalf of a more united Britain, and doubtless many of them believed it. But to their opponents it was the Jacobites themselves who were the insidious agents of division, while the ruling dynasty was the best guarantee of a measure of quiet and abundance:

> Under our vines we'll sit and sing,
> May God be praised, bless George our King;
> Being happy made in every thing
> Both religious and civil:
> Our fatal discords soon shall cease,
> Composed by George, our prince of peace;
> We shall in plenty live at ease,
> In spite of popish envy.[53]

Many Presbyterian and Anglican clergymen, as we have already seen, saw Jacobites–and encouraged their congregations to see them–as the agents of Antichrist, or as the Assyrian hordes of the Old Testament, savage and warlike aliens threatening God's people Israel.

All social classes could be affected by anxiety in the face of the Jacobite threat. Both Whig and Tory landowners worried about the security of their estates, and about the prospect of civil commotion leading to the same kind of social and political upsets as had occurred in the 1640s. Government creditors, and those embroiled in the nets of private credit arrangements, worried about the security of their investments and about recovering what was owed to them in the event of a civil war. And when invasion loomed, the poor, who had no money, no influential friends and no easy means of escape, worried most of all. 'Those who look closely at the eighteenth-century poor', Olwen Hufton has written, 'cannot but be struck by their aggressive independence and their desire to be left alone to live out their lives without intrusion.'[54] And this went for intrusion by the state's enemies, as well as by the state itself.

Nothing showed this better than the sullen response the Jacobite army encountered when it marched into England in 1745. Although its route took it through a succession of towns, hardly any civilians who were not Roman Catholics joined it. True, very few civilians acting on their own initiative attempted physically to stop it either. But those historians who put this inaction down to indifference need to think again. English civilians at this time had no adequate militia training and only limited and usually obsolete firearms. Unless they were very brave or very stupid, therefore, they were hardly likely to take pot shots at an army of Highlanders and risk reprisals against their homes and families.[55] Instead, the English poor seem to have responded to the invasion with seething passivity, until, that is, the army broke up and retreated. Then they struck. As one Jacobite commander subsequently complained, all of his men 'that were left sick on the road were either killed, abused or jailed'. One young, exhausted Scotsman sleeping on the roadside had his throat cut by a vagrant woman and her child. This was hardly cowardice as Frank McLynn calls it.[56] This was hate, hate by the poor and the vulnerable for outsiders who had dared to shatter the peace of their communities.

The reactions of Britain's trading sector were usually less savage than this, but just as unambiguous. For them, the anxiety was not just that a violent change of dynasty would almost certainly damage internal trade and credit networks, but that a Jacobite victory was likely to redound to the advantage of Britain's foremost competitor in overseas trade and colonialism, namely France. Both the Nine Years War (1689–97) and the War of Spanish Succession (1702–13) had been fought, as far as Britain was concerned, in large part because the French monarch at that time, Louis XIV, had insisted on recognising the exiled James II and his son as the only rightful kings. The rising of 1715 had taken place on the expectation of a French invasion (which never actually ensued). It was Louis XV of France who allowed James Edward Stuart asylum in France for most of his life; and in 1743 ordered a huge invasion fleet to transport 10,000 troops to Britain on his behalf, a project that was only undermined by the Jacobites' own

14. *The Highlanders Medley, or the Duke Triumphant.* George Bickham's pastiche of different anti-Jacobite propaganda prints, 1746.

inefficiency.[57] France, in short, was the Stuarts' most devoted ally. Britons had every reason to suppose, therefore, that a restored Stuart dynasty would operate, whether it wanted to or not, under the shadow of French power and in support of French interests. France had paid the Pretenders and would surely try to call their tune.

This carried with it serious implications for Britain's commercial sector. Since the War of Spanish Succession, French trade had expanded at a faster rate than any other country's, including Great Britain's. It had won the European re-export market with its cheaper sugar and coffee. In Turkey, its success had undermined the operations of Britain's own Levant Company. In Persia and India, French cloth had a reputation that the East India Company still found difficult to challenge. And French mercantile and military power was constantly pressing on British interests in the West Indies and North America.[58] In other words, British merchants and traders already faced intense competition from the French. If a Jacobite invasion of Britain were to lead to protracted civil war, if the country were to suffer military occupation, or if France were to demand from a restored Stuart sovereign colonial and commercial concessions in the New World in return for past favours, or a reduction of the Royal Navy perhaps, what would happen to British commerce then? Jacobite agents were not above suggesting to French politicians that invading Britain would be the best way to take it out of the colonial and commercial race. 'The English project', wrote George Flint from Paris in 1732,

> is effectually to ruin the French woollen manufactury, and it is likely they may proceed to destroy every other valuable branch of the French foreign trade; and so to ruin France. This, I told the Cardinal de Fleury face to face in the King's antichamber . . . the English would do sooner or later, if the French took not care to prevent it.[59]

The French, of course, were fully able to work this out for themselves, and so were the British.

In practice, then, Jacobitism involved much more than a debate about the merits of a particular dynasty. Men and women were well aware that its success was almost certain to involve them in civil war. And the more politically educated knew that the Stuart Pretender was a pawn in a worldwide struggle for commercial and imperial primacy between France and Britain, a struggle in which the trading community had quite as much at stake as its ruling élite.

I am not suggesting that material considerations determined the defeat of Jacobitism. The overwhelming strength of Protestantism throughout Great Britain did that, if anything did. But material factors, and especially the size and importance of the trading sector, certainly influenced the way in which it was defeated, and the extent of its defeat. The point is driven home not so much by civilian responses to the rising in 1715, which was over too quickly to have much impact on the majority of men and women, but by the much more prolonged and geographically extensive reactions to the 'Forty-Five.

Charles Edward Stuart, eldest son and heir of the Old Pretender, landed in the Hebrides late in July 1745. By September, he had rallied some 2,500 Highlanders, forced his way into the Lowlands, taken the city of Edinburgh and defeated a small British force at the Battle of Prestonpans. By December, his motley army, which now numbered some 5,000 men, had penetrated England as far south as Derby, but this was the apex of his fortunes. Retreating into Scotland, his men were cut apart at Culloden near Inverness in April 1746. He himself fled back to France, alcoholism, tawdry affairs and disillusionment.[60] But the romantic aura that still hovers around his memory should not obscure the seriousness of his invasion. That it had achieved so much with such minimal resources was a testament to the Jacobite army's mettle and leadership, and to the ineptitude of much of the formal machinery of the British state.

George II was away in Hanover when his rival invaded, and he casually lingered there until the end of August. The bulk of the British army, at this time some 62,000 strong, was also absent, on active service in Flanders and Germany. Fewer than 4,000 men had been left behind to defend Scotland, many of them raw recruits. The cabinet was currently split by ministers struggling for influence and patronage. And Parliament did not assemble until mid-October, almost three months after the Young Pretender landed.[61] The cumulative result of all these lapses was logistical chaos. The government failed to provide loyal Scottish strongholds such as Glasgow with sufficient arms to defend themselves, nor did it send appropriate supplies to the frontline towns in the north of England. Carlisle surrendered to the Jacobites in November because the city's militia had received no pay from the government or from anyone else for two months. Despite the ever-present danger of a Stuart invasion attempt, little had been done to keep the wheels of civil defence well oiled. At this stage, the Scottish counties had no Lords Lieutenant to co-ordinate their defence, and the performance of the great landowners who held that office in England and Wales was too often clogged with inefficiency. The Lord Lieutenant of Cornwall informed the government that his county's militia had been in abeyance for so long that he no longer knew how to summon it. Cheshire's Lord Lieutenant reported that the lists of men eligible to serve in the militia had disappeared together with their weapons.[62]

If large numbers of Britons had really wanted to throw in their lot with the Jacobite cause, it is hard to see in these circumstances how they could have been stopped. Yet only the poorer Highland clans, a handful of Welshmen and some 300 Englishmen rallied to the Young Pretender.[63] The vast majority of men and women remained stolidly at home, and a substantial minority committed their time, money or armed service in support of the established order. Typically, but also with a measure of calculation, the government combined serious mobilisation of its regular troops with informal, even amateurish, expedients for civil defence. Several peers of the realm were promised state funds in return for raising regiments in their respective areas of influence. And, as in 1715, men of property were urged to associate under their Lord Lieutenant, and to recruit and arm any volunteers willing to take the oath of allegiance. Local activism was called upon to redress the organisational failings of the nation state, and to serve a propaganda function as well. In the words of the Earl of Hardwicke, the Lord Chancellor, the 'evidence and éclat' of these armed associations of loyal citizens were designed to show that the Hanoverian dynasty rested on the active consent of its subjects.[64] Between September and December 1745 alone, fifty-seven associations are known to have been founded in almost three-quarters of the fifty-two English and Welsh counties (see Appendix 1).[65]

It is clear that the men who joined them, who came from all social and occupational backgrounds, did not necessarily think in terms of defending Great Britain as a whole or even just England or Wales. Cornwall's Lord Lieutenant managed to get 6,300 Cornishmen to commit themselves to an armed association. But while these stalwarts expected London to pay for their weapons, they had – like their ancestors in the civil wars a century earlier – their own priorities: 'They all express great readiness to defend their country, but they mean their county.'[66] Even less remote southern counties, Surrey, Sussex and Kent, were reluctant to establish associations for the defence of the country at large. And ten of the Welsh counties, together with Dorset, Somerset and Herefordshire, failed to establish them at all. Residual Jacobitism in these areas may have contributed to this, and so did limited funds, especially in Wales. But the main obstacle to concerted action in the south and west was geography. Scotland, to most of the men and women living in these regions, seemed a long way off and so even did northern England. 'The rebellion was begun in the North', one particularly sluggish loyalist grumbled to the Lord Lieutenant of Somerset, 'and was likely to be determined there.'[67] Only in the ten northern English counties, in fact, wide open as they were to the Young Pretender's army, did county society *at gentry level* combine to make the associations effective weapons of home defence.

Below gentry level, however, the pattern of active loyalty was markedly different. Commerce, in all its different forms, forged its own resilient alignments. After the Lord Mayor of London had organised a subscription among the city's merchants to purchase comforts for British soldiers in Scotland, the orders for the necessary goods – 1,000 blankets, 15,000 pairs of breeches, 16,500 pairs of stockings, 12,000 woollen shirts and the like – were deliberately placed with manufacturers and traders in the north of England and Lowland Scotland. The subscription committee's report was quite frank about its motives. Increasing job opportunities in these vulnerable regions, 'at a time when our common enemies are using every art and contrivance to destroy both our trade and our credit', was good for business and would help ensure that the local working man was less inclined to treason.[68] The soundness of such reasoning was demonstrated in the case of Manchester, the only place in England to give the Young Pretender more than ten recruits. Some two hundred men, many of them unemployed weavers, threw in their lot with him there (and later suffered appallingly for their decision). Those Mancunians who had a job but none the less risked rebellion seem in the main to have been Catholic, Irish or apprentices, outsiders in some way or beginners, but only rarely men who were securely established in their trade.[69]

Those who had their own shop or business or substantial investments in the businesses of others were also more likely than not to be staidly disinclined to Jacobite adventure. 'Blessed be God the silk mill is safe', a non-conformist doctor scribbled shudderingly in his diary, as the Young Pretender's army marched out of Stockport leaving his wife's small but precious stock of capital intact.[70] In Trowbridge and Bradford in Wiltshire, the local clothiers and substantial tradesmen grew so impatient at the landed gentry's delay in forming an armed association, that they broke social ranks and initiated their own defence force. The more urbanised areas of Somerset also seem to have formed their own impromptu defence forces, again in defiance of the local gentry's refusal to associate.[71] Men with considerable landed estates, particularly those far removed from the scene of battle, might feel able to survive a major invasion. But individuals whose entire fortune

15. *The Highland Visitors.* Jacobites as despoilers of peace and property: an anonymous print, 1746.

was tied up in just one manufacturing outlet or shop or warehouse were far more vulnerable and acted accordingly.

The more one studies the map of resistance to Charles Edward Stuart, the more it is clear that commercial and manufacturing centres played a substantial part in his defeat. Virtually all of the major Scottish towns occupied by the Jacobite army exhibited active or passive pro-Hanoverianism, which was why Charles had to impose governors on them as he marched triumphantly southwards rather than run the risk of holding new burgh elections. Edinburgh failed to provide him with the regiment of volunteers that he had expected. In Glasgow, the Presbyterian clergy preached loyalist sermons even when the city was occupied by armed Highlanders.[72] In Dumfries, the local postmaster did his best to keep the government informed of events throughout the rebellion. And the Jacobite governors of Perth and Dundee were both attacked by loyalists on 30 October, George II's birthday.[73] The only major exception to this urban trend in Scotland seems to have been Montrose, and it was perhaps the exception that proved the rule.

In 1706, this burgh had petitioned its MP to support an act of union with England, out of fear that London would otherwise impose sanctions on cross-border trade: 'the only valuable branch of our trade, the only trade by which the balance is on our side'.[74] Yet the economy of Montrose was rather more mixed than this initiative implied. Close to the Jacobite stronghold, the House of Dun, and surrounded by other landowners with the same politics, it was the base of a powerful and entrepreneurial Jacobite smuggling gang. The gang's members enjoyed illicit but highly profitable connexions with sympathetic merchants and bankers on both sides of the North Sea, and thereby created a lucrative commercial network vital to the local economy. In other words, this town's brand of economic enterprise was not threatened by the prospect of a Stuart restoration: rather the reverse.[75] Commercial enterprise and Stuart legitimism here went profitably together. But other Scottish towns, by now beginning to benefit from the free-trade clauses of the Act of Union and from increasingly lucrative access to British colonies, could not be so certain that their interests lay in a violent change of dynasty.[76] Nor, emphatically, could the major English cities. Liverpool, which had been propelled into riches only since the Revolution of 1688, reacted to the invasion by forming its own highly efficient volunteer corps, and in just one meeting its merchants raised £3,000 to pay for it. In Bristol, where the economy also rested heavily on overseas trade with North America and the West Indies, the citizens collected ten times that amount to fund its armed association. Further south, the major cloth manufacturing centre of Exeter, in fierce competition as all such centres were with the French textile industry, also raised an armed association of local men between the ages of 18 and 55, and dispatched a loyal address to London, blotted and crumpled, as the mayor breathlessly explained, because it 'was impossible to restrain the impetuous and eager zeal of our citizens. Every one pressing forward to give the earliest marks of his duty and loyalty.'[77]

There were many other local initiatives, hurried, uneven, ramshackle, and almost always a mixture of panic, self-interest and public spirit; yet, because of these very qualities, more widely revealing than any systematic defence measures ordered and imposed by the state could have been. By no means all of those who earned their livelihood from trade sided actively with the government in this crisis. Those who did might not all have continued resolute had the Jacobite army succeeded in coming closer to London. We shall never know. What is revealing, though, is that in those six months between July and December 1745 in which the Jacobite army was advancing, and when a Stuart restoration might–just–have been on the cards, large numbers of men from commercial as well as landed backgrounds took an active part in raising money and in taking up arms on behalf of the existing order. By contrast, the vast majority of people in Scotland, as well as in Wales and England, neither supported the Young Pretender with arms nor with voluntary donations of cash. To the unbiased eye, this is suggestive. It was even suggestive to Samuel Johnson, who had little love for the Hanoverian dynasty. He once remarked that, 'If England were fairly polled, the present king would be sent away to-night'. But then he added, more realistically as well as sorrowfully perhaps, that the people 'would not . . . risk any thing to restore the exiled family. *They would not give twenty shillings a piece to bring it about*'.[78] And so it proved.

Johnson's reduction of Jacobitism's chances to hard considerations of money is important, because although material considerations by themselves do not explain the Stuarts' failure, they certainly contributed to it. The centrality of trade in the British economy helped to ensure that the rejection of the Jacobite option was decisive. In 1745, especially, negligible civilian support for Charles Edward Stuart's cause, and conspicuous support for the existing order especially in the more affluent and urban areas, proved critical. It was the Jacobites' own perception that 'the counties through which [their] army had passed had seemed much more enemies than friends', which shaped the decision to retreat from Derby rather than to try to push on to London.[79] Had civilian responses been different, more obviously sympathetic, Louis XV might have committed himself to a French invasion of Britain, a project he had already attempted in 1743–44.[80] As it was, deprived both of widespread domestic support and of substantial foreign aid, the Jacobites were defeated long before Culloden. Defeated not because their own supporters looked to the past, but rather because so many Britons had too much to lose in the present.

INVESTING IN THE NATION

The two decades that followed the Battle of Culloden were an intensely creative period in terms of patriotic initiatives and discussion of national identities both in Great Britain and in other parts of Europe: in France to a conspicuous degree, but also in Spain, Russia, Holland and in many parts of Germany. In all of these states, a much broader debate took place than ever before about the boundaries and meanings of citizenship. There was a marked increase in the number of voluntary societies established for patriotic purposes. And there was a more conscious attempt to enshrine and glorify national culture. In France, this was the period in which exhibitions of assertively nationalistic art began in the Louvre. In Britain, the British Museum was founded and so was the *Encyclopaedia Britannica*. (One must add that these explicitly *British* initiatives were accompanied by an increased interest in purely English, Welsh or Scottish culture. This was, after all, the era when James Macpherson invented the romantic Celtic hero Ossian.[81]) Since all Europeans still write history in an intensely nationalistic fashion, it remains unclear why this resurgence of interest in matters patriotic occurred in so many different countries at the same time. The coming of war on a hitherto unprecedented scale, the growth of towns, the spread of printing and the increasing importance of that class that we have to call the bourgeoisie must all have contributed something to this widespread mood of national awakening. But in the case of all of the countries involved, there were also influences at work specific to them.

In Great Britain, the initial stimulus was the shock administered by the Jacobite revolt. For an island power, accustomed for a century to fighting its battles at sea, abroad or at the very least on its own distant peripheries, it was profoundly unnerving that a hostile army, drawn from its own population, had been able to penetrate so close to its pampered centre. Particularly as the army in question had been small, badly equipped and composed largely of Highlanders, an essentially backward people in the eyes of Lowland Scottish, Welsh and English loyalists. The subscription ticket for Hogarth's invasion print *The March to Finchley* had been typically complacent in contrasting the bagpipes, shields, axes and maces supposedly wielded by the Highlanders with the hard-gloss modernity of the British army's cannon and guns.[82] This confidence in superior technology, which was rooted in a sense of racial superiority, only deepened the humiliation of the Jacobites' initial triumphant advance. The often dishevelled fashion in which the rebellion had been suppressed also unnerved. Patriotic endeavour had been widespread and in the end decisive. But too many individuals had stayed at home, not joining the rebellion but not leaping to the defence of the Hanoverian dynasty either. And until the Duke of Cumberland's final march into Scotland, too many of the agencies of the state had seemed less than effective.

All this prompted fears about Britain's security and the adequacy of its manpower. Charles Edward Stuart had landed under French naval protection and with the expectation of further military assistance. It never materialised, but the episode was a forcible reminder of just how easy it might be for France, with its superior army and much bigger population, to subvert British domestic affairs. It was scarcely an accident that the late 1740s and '50s saw the foundation in London of a spate of maternity hospitals designed to cut the mortality rate among the childbearing and infant poor, or that in 1753 the House of Commons passed a bill implementing a nationwide census (the House of Lords vetoed it on libertarian grounds), or that in 1756, after the outbreak of another war with France, Parliament began to subsidise the work of Coram's Foundling Hospital.[83] One year later, demands for a more effective civil defence force were finally answered by the passing of a new Militia Act.

But for many patriots, these practical measures designed to enhance the nation's cannon-fodder came nowhere near to resolving the heart of the problem. Writers like the Perthshire-born James Burgh, whose aptly titled *Britain's Remembrancer, or the danger not over* sold over 10,000 copies in 1746, or the Anglican cleric, John Brown, whose lengthy jeremiad *An Estimate of the Manners and Principles of the Times* proved an even greater success in 1757, argued that the real danger lay not so much in the power of France, as in Britain's own internal divisions and moral corruption. Britain was vulnerable because it lacked adequate reserves of public spirit: 'there is no cement or cohesion between the parts'.[84] Pessimists pointed to a major cattle plague which had sent the price of roast beef, the archetypal food of patriots, soaring. And to the fact that the capital itself had been seen to shudder – quite literally. In 1750, five years before the Lisbon earthquake caused a tremor in European sensibilities, London experienced two minor earthquakes of its own.[85]

But reaching agreement on the source of Britain's disease proved more difficult than identifying its symptoms. One theory, much favoured by John Brown, was that commerce itself was to blame. Too much devotion to the penny-pinching practicalities of trade had fostered self-interest and led to a neglect of public spirit and martial prowess: 'We think if we get more *money* we secure all things.' The loyal subscriptions to which so many traders had contributed in 1745 impressed Brown not at all:

> It hath been urged indeed, as a proof that the national spirit of defence is not yet extinguished, that we raised such large sums during that rebellion . . . This is weak reasoning: for will not cowardice, at least as soon as courage, part with a shilling or a pound to avoid danger? The capital question therefore still remains, 'Not who shall pay, but who shall fight?'[86]

Far more common than this argument, however, was one that placed the blame squarely on the silken shoulders of the fashionable and governing classes. Gerald Newman has shown just how furiously they were attacked from the late 1740s onwards, how repeatedly poets, playwrights and pamphleteers accused them of corrupting the nation from within by their indolence, luxury and rampant Francophilia.[87] As long as British patricians spoke French among themselves, the claim went, as long as they favoured French clothes, employed French hairdressers and valets, and haunted Parisian salons on the Grand Tour, as long as the taste for French cultural and luxury imports was allowed to put native artists, traders and manufacturers out of business, national distinction would be eroded and national fibre relaxed:

> Trulls, toupees, trinkets, bags, brocades, and lace;
> A flaunting form, and a fictitious face.
> Rouse! Re-assume! Refuse a gallic reign,
> Nor let their arts win that their arms could never gain.[88]

Anxiety that Britain laboured under a malaise and must be regenerated from within lay behind a development that would have far-reaching social and political repercussions, the foundation – primarily by men of commerce – of a succession of patriotic societies. Voluntary associations of different kinds were breaking out like measles over the face of Britain and the rest of Europe at this time, especially in towns, and almost exclusively among men. There were street clubs, patronised by the leading inhabitants of a particular district, clubs devoted to hobbies, everything from rose-growing to cruel sports and idiosyncratic sex, innumerable masonic and quasi-masonic societies catering to the male delight in secret rituals and dressing-up, box clubs, which poorer men joined to provide themselves with a modicum of insurance, clubs devoted to party politics or food, discussion clubs where blue-chinned autodidacts pondered the mysteries of science and philosophy, and more genteel associations where responsible citizens met to dine well and discuss the local poor.[89] In terms of organisation, the new patriotic societies had much in common with these other clubs. Yet in one crucial respect, they were different. Then, as now, the average British men's club was both democratic and rigidly exclusive, treating its own members as equals but shutting out the rest of the public from its business. By contrast, the declared business of the patriotic societies *was* the public. They looked deliberately outwards – to the reformation of the nation state.

The first and most shadowy of these organisations was the Laudable Association of Anti-Gallicans, founded by a group of tradesmen in London during the invasion crisis in 1745.[90] A particularly splendid version of its badge is still on display in the

16. *Britain's Rights maintained, or French Ambition dismantled.* Anti-Gallican propaganda, 1755.

British Museum today, topped with sprightly British merchantmen ploughing the waves to profit, and at its centre St George spearing the arms of France and trampling them underfoot. The club's motto was 'For our country', and its declared aim was crudely mercantilist: 'to discourage by precept and example, the importation and consumption of French produce and manufactures, and to encourage, on the contrary, the produce and manufactures of Great Britain'. In practice, this meant that members raised money to reward acts of patriotic enterprise and advertised these prizes in the press as a way of publicising their work. A lace-maker whose work was judged fine enough to compete with that of the French received their bounty, as did a sea-captain in recognition for a bumper catch of whales, and a cartographer who had mapped out the ideal boundaries of Britain's possessions in North America. But the association, which soon spread to the major provincial cities as well as to colonial Massachusetts, also saw itself as a kind of think tank. Four times a year, its members commissioned a clergyman to preach a sermon on the need for civic exertion against the iniquities of France. This was then published at the association's expense, so that the public at large could be informed of just how much was at stake.

The message put out was paranoid but consistent: French contamination had been an evil since the Norman Conquest and could be thrown off now only by Britons becoming more moral and more united. John Free, for example, who preached before the association in 1756, argued that Englishmen, Lowland Scots and the Hanoverian kings were all descended from the same Saxon race, and should therefore live in harmony with each other and with the Welsh, who were only Ancient Britons after all.[91] To be at odds with each other, as in the rebellion, was to play France's game and to squander Britain's destiny. As another clergyman, John Butley, explained:

> The kingdom was formed to stand forth alone, and be distinguished from the nations: And its separation from the continent points out and advises a disjunction also from their manners . . . We are at peace, it is true, with the power; but it would be well for us if we were at war with the manners of France.[92]

Allowing Frenchisms to infiltrate the English language, importing French manufactured goods, polishing themselves 'into a refined insincerity' merely because it was fashionable were nothing less than cultural treason, a vicious squandering of true identity.

The Society of Arts, or to give its full name, the Society for the Encouragement of Arts, Commerce, and Manufactures in Great Britain, was less xenophobic but just as preoccupied with national trade and national culture. It started in 1754 with only seventeen members and was the brainchild of William Shipley, the son of a London stationer who earned an undistinguished living as a provincial drawing-master. By 1764, it had over 2,100 supporters as well as correspondents in different parts of Britain and in the American colonies.[93] Like the Anti-Gallicans, but on a far more systematic basis, the society awarded premiums to men and women whose work and discoveries seemed likely to benefit the economy. Its minute books, for example, reveal an obsession with encouraging the discovery of cobalt and the growing of madder, which seems incomprehensible until one remembers that cobalt dyes a brilliant blue and that madder was the principal source of all red dyes until the nineteenth century. Quite simply, the society wanted to enable Britain's most important industry, its textile manufacturers, to be able to dye their cloth at home rather than having to send it abroad.[94] Another of the society's preoccupations was the need for more native timber for merchant and naval shipping. In 1757, it established prizes for the growing of oaks, chestnuts and elms. The following year, it extended its bounty to fir trees, so that the Scots, too, could play their part in the work of national refurbishment.[95]

This was the mundane, improving side of the society's work, the side that earnest visitors from abroad, like Benjamin Franklin, never failed to comment on approvingly. But there was another, seemingly more ambitious side. Every year, prizes were set aside for the most promising child artists and sculptors, and in 1761 the society opened up its premises in London to the first large-scale public exhibition of domestic art ever organised in Britain. Samuel Johnson wrote the preface to the catalogue and more than 20,000 people reputedly attended.[96] For once, the staid and sturdily pragmatic members of the Society of Arts seemed to hover on the brink of the chic and the creative. Yet for Shipley and his fellow patriots, their work was all of a piece. If Great Britain was to compete successfully with France, it needed to be able to match that country's luxury exports and cultural reputation. In this sense, investing time and money in cultivating British art was essentially no different from encouraging the growth of madder or the planting of turnips. As Shipley wrote, his aim was 'to render Great Britain the school of instruction as it is already the centre of traffic to the greatest part of the known world'.[97] Britain must command the arts as it commanded the seas, in both cases as a means of competing with the French.

This brand of economic and cultural nationalism became only more strident with the outbreak of war in 1756. In June of that year, Jonas Hanway, a member of the Russia Company, met with twenty-two other merchants at the King's Arms tavern in Cornhill and decided to establish the Marine Society. The aim this time was to raise money so that unemployed and vagrant men and orphaned and pauper boys could be rounded up, clothed and sent into the Royal Navy. The success achieved was stunning. By the end of the war, the society had well over 1,500 subscribers, and some 10,000 men and boys had been sent to sea.[98] Yet for Hanway and many of the other organisers, it was the existence of the society and the way that it operated that mattered, not just its end-product:

> British benevolence being thus united with native British fire, will diffuse the genuine spirit of patriotism through these realms . . . If we instruct these young persons in the fear of God, and at the same time teach their hands to war, and their fingers to fight in the cause of their country, in the cause of real and substantial virtue, we may hope such a conduct will draw down the mercies of heaven on this nation.[99]

Charity, in other words, was meant to regenerate the donors as well as their beneficiaries. Giving money to a patriotic cause would root out the apathy and division that had sometimes been evident in 1745. Men and women would be redeemed and reunited in philanthropy, and victory over the French would naturally follow. This same broad ambition lay behind yet another patriotic association initiated by Hanway, the Troop Society, founded in 1759 to assist British soldiers fighting in North America and the German states, and their dependents.[100]

Many other societies sprang up around this time, both in London and outside it, societies to advance commerce and manufactures, societies to assist servicemen, societies to promote the national birth-rate, societies to convert bedraggled prostitutes into the decent mothers of a new generation of useful and vigorous Britons. Clearly all of these initiatives stemmed from a certain perception of the nation's problems and possibilities, but some contemporaries also claimed what has often been argued since: that such associations represented nothing less than the scaffolding of middle-class ambition.[101] That, at a time when the patrician classes were coming under fierce attack for being rather less than wholeheartedly British, the commercial classes had seized the initiative and were giving ostentatiously to public causes so that in the future they might better control the public sphere. 'The public spirit of persons in the middling rank of this kingdom', declared the MP for York in 1753, 'and the depravity and selfishness of those in a higher class, was never more remarkable than at present.'[102] This is an attractive interpretation of what was happening, but it is far from being altogether true. In some respects, the patriotic societies represented not a bid for autonomy on the part of the middling classes, but a further demonstration of the close links that existed between the trading community and the people above.

The two largest contributors to the Marine Society, for example, were George II, who gave £1,000, and his grandson, the Prince of Wales, who donated £400.[103] The Society of Arts was founded by a mere drawing-master, to be sure, but its long-time president was a peer of the realm, Lord Romney, and among its members in 1760 were scores of aristocrats and politicians, including the Duke of Newcastle, First Lord of the Treasury, William Pitt the Elder, Secretary of State, the Earl of Bute, the future premier, and virtually all of the senior ministers of the Board of Trade.[104] The Anti-Gallicans were less gentrified, but even they took care to make the Countess of Middlesex an honorary sister of their organisation in recognition of her efforts to ban the wearing of

French fashions at the royal court and encourage clothes and materials made in Britain instead.

For many merchants, the fact that these patriotic societies offered occasional opportunities for mingling socially with people of rank and influence, with all the prospects this opened up for making useful contacts and a good impression, was one of the more concrete attractions of membership. To this extent, the societies did not challenge the existing social and political order, they mirrored and endorsed it. The generous donations that the Russia Company, the East India Company and hundreds of individual traders made to the Marine Society after 1756, for example, were due in part to their desperate need to curry government favour in time of war. Not only were various lucrative contracts being given out, but all overseas traders were dependent on the Admiralty for convoy protection against enemy warships and privateers. Doing one's bit for the manning of the Royal Navy was one way of impressing the authorities, a public-spirited gesture that might just ensure some kind of reward.

It would be wrong then to see the patriotic societies crudely and simply as a piece of bourgeois assertiveness. But they do illustrate how easily active patriotism in this society, as in any society, blends into a demand for wider citizenship and political change.

Merely by existing, the societies challenged the way that the British state was currently organised. To begin with, by taking on certain tasks, they underlined just how much the state itself left undone. In 1756, William Shipley's Society of Arts set up special prizes as a means of encouraging the making of new and accurate maps of the English and Welsh counties. Its minutes noted, meekly enough, that a cartographic survey of the whole of France had been ordered by its government, but that no such action had yet been taken by Britain's rulers despite the obvious advantages an up-to-date and comprehensive map would have for the economy.[105] The anonymous writer of an essay contributed to the society in 1761 was much more forthright in demanding an interventionist state closely attuned to the needs of traders and entrepreneurs. Why, he argued, did Britain's rulers not confer honours on 'inventers of any improvement in any manufacture, as in our rival nation has been done with success'? And why was there no standing parliamentary committee in existence that could reform the statute law in the interests of commerce?[106]

The patriotic societies also encouraged an alternative and much broader interpretation of what it was to be an active patriot. Whereas the existing order made access to political rights dependent on rank, property and adherence to the correct religion, the way that the societies worked suggested that it was the willingness to participate that marked out the true Briton. The quality of an individual's exertion, they implied, not conformity to legal qualifications was what really mattered. Believing that, in Hanway's words, 'charity is the great bond of union, and the surest cement of society', all of the societies went out of their way to invite contributions from as many people as possible, irrespective of class, location, religion, party or gender.[107] William Shipley refused ever to declare his own religious affiliation because, as secretary to an all-embracing patriotic society, he felt it important to appear non-sectarian. By the same token, he made sure that some of the Society of Arts's prizes were open to the poor, and that room was made for women. Initially, he wanted the latter to be eligible for full membership, 'as there is no reason to imagine they will be behindhand in a generous and sincere regard for the good of their country'.[108] His fellow members resisted this suggestion, but the society's premiums were conscientiously awarded to women as well as men. 'Exulting thought', wrote one female prize-winner, clearly amazed at her transition from the private sphere to recognition for performing a public good, 'that my poor endeavours may one day prove beneficial to my country.' And women were invited to give as well as to receive. All of the patriotic societies had female subscribers: 120 women are known to have subscribed to the Troop Society's collection for British soldiers in 1760, for instance, as against forty clergymen and just ten peers of the realm.[109]

In this sense, then, the patriotic societies were spectacularly open institutions, a standing affront to oligarchy in terms of the range of their participants and, indeed, in the scrupulousness with which they conducted their affairs. As Hanway boasted, they recruited the nation, calling forth an active citizenry that was very different in size and composition from that formally recognised by the state. But in terms of the men who actually created them and determined their brief, the societies were much more restrictive. Almost without exception their leading activists came from the middling classes, and the majority of them were men of trade.

The Society of Arts certainly attracted a large number of titled and ministerial subscribers, but only very rarely did these glittering figures attend regularly or do the work of organisation. It was the 'people of no account in life', as Arthur Young would later style them, the merchants, tradesmen and craftsmen who made up almost half of its 2,000 members, that gave the society its direction.[110] Only one peer of the realm, Lord Romney, played a prominent part in the Marine and Troop societies. By contrast, commercial men dominated their committees and subscription lists. Hanway's own Russia Company donated £100 to the Marine Society, the East India merchants in London contributed £200, and their brother traders in Bombay raised over 1,300 rupees. Of the 1,500 individuals who subscribed to the Troop Society in 1760, 267 were merchants prominent enough to appear in London's city directories.[111] The rest were mainly small traders, grocers, apothecaries, innkeepers, tailors and the like, from the provinces as well as the capital, shopkeepers claiming their nation.

What did men of this kind hope to gain from their investment in patriotism? For some of them, the material attractions are clear enough. Take the case of Thomas Johnson, for instance, a brilliant wood-carver and enthusiastic member of the Anti-Gallican Association. Johnson specialised in carving marvellous rococo frames for mirrors and pictures, delicate and time-consuming work that commanded high prices. In 1758, he published a collection of his designs, with a frontispiece showing a rather skittish Britannia flourishing the Anti-Gallican arms and a cupid torching a piece of French *papier mâché*. Why? Because *papier mâché*, that concoction of pulp and glue which my generation at least learned stickily to make at school, was a French invention increasingly being used for making mirror frames. It was quick and easy to mould and much cheaper than finely carved wood. Exactly why Johnson felt attracted to an association opposed to French imports is therefore clear. The French, from whom he had so unashamedly borrowed his flamboyant rococo designs, were now threatening to undercut his business.[112] Stephen Theodore Janssen, a London alderman who was one of the founders of the Anti-Gallicans, had a very similar private motive for his doubtless very genuine public patriotism. He ran an enamels factory in Battersea which produced exquisite and expensive jewel cases and the like, but faced stiff competition from French luxury imports of a similar kind.[113]

It is not hard to detect a similar element of material self-interest in the work of the other societies. The bulk of the money collected for the benefit of British soldiers by the Troop Society, for instance, was spent on home-produced consumer goods: 14,000 pairs of shoes, 6,000 waistcoats, 3,000 pairs of gloves, 400 gross of horn buttons and, to sew them on with, 9,000 needles at four pence apiece.[114] Providing Britons fighting abroad with their due measure of comforts was thus nicely combined with providing business orders for fellow traders at home. But the profits of trading patriotism were never just or even primarily economic. Participation in these societies and subscriptions was a highly visible activity. The

French Paper Machees
To the Right Hon.ble
LORD BLAKENEY,
Grand President of the
Antigallican Associations,
(and therest of the Bretheren
of that most Honourable Order,
This Book
is most humbly Dedicated
by his Lordships,
most Obedient
humble Serv.t
and Brother,
Tho.s Johnson
Sold by
T. Johnson Carver.
At the Golden Boy.
in Grafton Street, St. Ann's
Westminster.
Publish'd by Act of Parliament
April 23.d 1758.

17. Dedication page to Thomas Johnson's furniture designs, 1758.

societies made certain of this by advertising their meetings widely in the press and by issuing lists of subscribers in pamphlet form. The regular appearance in print of a trading patriot's name and address must often have been good for business, and still better for his own sense of worth and importance in the community.

For it was hunger for recognition that drove many of these men. Take Jonas Hanway, who is remembered today, if he is remembered at all, only for being a well-meaning bore and as the first British male regularly to use an umbrella. No one thinks to ask why Hanway was so anxious to keep his clothes dry when it rained. Yet his concern to do so surely derived from the same kind of social anxiety that made him always wear a sword and adopt an entirely bogus coat of arms. Here was a man who desperately needed to impress and to be taken seriously. Founding the Marine Society gave him status, made him a someone and, in the end, earned him burial at Westminster Abbey.[115] In the same way, for thousands of lesser men, clubbing together in patriotic associations was a means of acquiring a degree of influence and importance which they could never have commanded as individuals. And it was a means, too, of making Great Britain a nation even more adjusted to the needs and preferences of traders than it was already.

The patriotic societies, as we have seen, accepted donations from anyone. But the money was spent in accordance with commercial imperatives, to foster an orderly and industrious as well as a more powerful Britain. The Society of Arts used its premiums to reward hard-working, entrepreneurial individuals. The more blatantly chauvinist societies tried to encourage good conduct among ordinary soldiers and sailors. Each boy recruited by the Marine Society was supplied with a new set of clothes and with a new set of ideas:

> You are the sons of freemen. Though poor, you are the sons of Britons, who are born to liberty; but remember that true liberty consists in doing well; in defending each other, in obeying your superiors and in fighting for your King and Country to the last drop of your blood.[116]

True liberty consists in doing well. This is the authentic voice of the bourgeois patriot who believes that his individual prosperity and the country's good are forever twinned. Just how many of the boy-sailors were able to read and understand these words is unclear. What *is* certain is that many of the Marine Society's more affluent supporters – like the blind London magistrate John Fielding – advocated recruiting orphans and unemployed men for the Royal Navy as a sterling solution to crime, disorder and

18. Frontispiece to *Motives for the Encouragement of the Marine Society*, London, 1757. Engraving by Samuel Wale.

poverty. Stronger national defence was to go hand in hand with clearing the streets of potential thieves, beggars and disturbers of trade. And perhaps it worked. Of the 4,787 boys recruited by the Marine Society during the Seven Years War, only 295 could be accounted for at its end.[117] Whether the rest had indeed been reformed, whether they had found in the navy a lifelong commitment, or whether the war had simply ensured that their lives were short, would never be known. For many trading patriots, it may have been enough that the boys were no longer idle or obstructing other people's industry.

THE PRICE OF IT ALL

We come back full-circle to Thomas Coram, that other man of trade who wanted to redeem stray children for the sake of humanity, for the sake of Great Britain and for the sake, too, of good order and a more abundant labour supply. Coram, like William Hogarth, like William Shipley, like Jonas Hanway, like the thousands of men and women who supported patriotic societies, and the myriad other Britons who owned shops and businesses, or simply bought and sold, believed that the interests of trade were fully compatible with the interests of the national state. This was a smug attitude, perhaps, but it was not an unrealistic one, and for the first six, even seven decades of the eighteenth century especially, it seemed in the main to be justified.

Although men of land dominated the polity, they took the demands of trade seriously. In part this was because it was in their interests to do so, but many of them were also quite as convinced as any mercantile publicist could be that Britain's prosperity was a testament to its peculiar grace. War remained a game of kings, engaged in primarily for dynastic and strategic reasons. None the less, particularly before 1775, Britain's wars helped to fill the pockets of a multitude of commercial pawns. The Nine Years War with France (1689–97) had provoked a serious economic crisis and a string of mercantile protests, but the three major conflicts that followed, the War of Spanish Succession, the War of Austrian Succession and, above all, the Seven Years War seemed to many traders abundantly worthwhile. This last war, which saw British exports reach a record level and vast areas of the world taken captive, was the high point of the interplay between commercial interests and British imperial aggression:

> The trade of the whole world centred in this island; she was the mart of all nations: the merchants engrossed the riches of the universe, and lived like princes; and the manufacturers were enabled to live in credit and reputation, being supplied with many things necessary for their use from our conquests, at an easy rate for which they had been obliged to pay dear before.[118]

This was bombast in the sense that, as in every war, certain businesses and industries suffered, individuals went bankrupt, ships were lost to enemy privateers, credit became a problem, and a measure of weariness and disillusionment eventually set in. But for the traders who survived, there was at least an illusion and often the reality of profits. Profits from servicing the war machine; profits as more and more colonies were won; profits from new markets forced open by naval power and treaties; profits from cheaper raw materials and exotic commodities; and a sense of profit, too, because the enemy in all of these wars was France, Britain's prime commercial competitor. The fact that Britain's foremost enemy was also perceived, quite correctly, as its chief rival in terms of overseas and internal trade, meant that those who governed Great Britain could usually rely on substantial commercial support in time of war and invasion threats.

Trade followed the flag, then, but it also helped to keep the flag flying. The mechanisms of trade helped to bring together the different regions of Great Britain. The business of trade helped to stock the Exchequer. The merchant marine was the Royal Navy's training ground. And men and women of trade played a signal part in preserving the Hanoverian dynasty.

For all these reasons, there is little point in debating whether eighteenth-century Britain (or indeed nineteenth-century Britain) was essentially a landed society or a commercial society. It was neither of these things alone, because it was both of these things together. It is the *relationship* between land and trade that is the important issue; and before 1775, that relationship was widely and correctly believed to be a mutually beneficial one. If it subsequently became more adversarial, this was due in part to the quickening pace of economic and social change, but also to the changing experience of war. Both the war with the American colonies and the protracted struggle with Revolutionary and Napoleonic France damaged British commerce as conflicts earlier in the century had not done. Once this was noticed, commercial tolerance of the landed classes' predominance in central government was likely to become rather more frayed.

Yet even before 1775, it was possible to detect ambiguities and tensions. There were clear signs that some British traders were becoming impatient with their existing, indirect influence in the state. The rise of voluntary associations like the Anti-Gallicans, the Society of Arts and the Marine Society had a double significance. They supplied additional proof of the willingness of men (and women) of commerce to invest in Great Britain, to preach and practice patriotism, in part because it brought them profit. But at a deeper level, these private organisations also bore witness to dissatisfaction with the more formal institutions of the state, to a growing belief that they were too hidebound and too exclusive to carry out all the changes that traders wanted. In the 1760s, many of these societies would swing over to support John Wilkes and parliamentary reform.[119] And logically so. All that was happening was the working out in public politics of the private pretensions that Hogarth had observed in Thomas Coram long before. Since trade shone on Great Britain, then surely those who promoted it had a right to a more prominent place in the sun?

3 *Peripheries*

THE SEVEN YEARS WAR WAS THE MOST dramatically successful war the British ever fought. They conquered Canada. They drove the French out of most of their Indian, West African and West Indian possessions. They tore Manila and Havana from the Spanish. Their navy devastated its European rivals. And they assumed for themselves the reputation of being the most aggressive, the most affluent and the most swiftly expanding power in the world. 'Look around', declared the young and still conventionally chauvinistic Charles James Fox to his fellow MPs: '. . . Observe the magnificence of our metropolis – the extent of our empire – the immensity of our commerce and the opulence of our people'.[1]

Yet the euphoria soon soured. In part, this was because of the hangover that always follows excessive indulgence in major war. There was the predictable social strain of absorbing more than 200,000 demobilised men, most of them poor, some of them mutilated, all of them trained to violence. There was the hard, unpleasant fact of a massively inflated National Debt which led inexorably to a rise in taxation. And there were the unpalatable diplomacies of the Treaty of Paris in 1763, in which Britain restored some of its winnings to France and Spain in the vain hope that they would refrain from going to war in the future to regain the rest. Yet significant though these irritants were, the root cause of post-war uncertainty and division was more profound and long-lasting. More than anything else, it was the quality and extent of the victory itself that subsequently inflamed the peace. The success had been too great, the territory won was at once too vast and too alien. The British had enormously inflated their national prestige and imperial power. But, rather like the frog in the Aesop fable which exploded in trying to compete with the ox, at the end of the day they were left wondering if they had overstretched themselves, made nervous and insecure by their colossal new dimensions.

NEW LANDMARKS

Before the Seven Years War, Britain's empire had been small

enough and homogeneous enough to seem reasonably compatible with the values that the British, and above all the English, believed they uniquely epitomised. But the post-war empire was simply too large to cater to these insular prejudices. The pre-war empire had been predominantly Protestant and Anglophone, hingeing on the thirteen American colonies. But the post-war empire included Quebec with its 70,000 French Catholic inhabitants, as well as large stretches of Asia which were manifestly neither Christian nor white. The military component of the pre-war empire had in practice been considerable, but it had none the less been popularly perceived as a trading empire, as the beneficent creation of a liberty-loving and commercial people, and thus quite different from the Roman and Spanish empires, bloodily and insecurely raised on conquest. The spoils of the Seven Years War made it far more difficult to sustain this flattering contrast between the failed empires of the past and the British empire of the present. And this made for problems of morale as well as practical difficulties. Now that Britain's empire no longer pivoted on commerce but was sustained by force of arms like earlier empires, what guarantee could there be that it would not in turn decay and destroy the mother country in the process? The question nagged at a whole generation of British intellectuals, most profitably Edward Gibbon who made the decision to chronicle the decline and fall of the Roman empire just one year after the signing of the Treaty of Paris.[2]

Most Britons, though, were more worried about the immediate challenges of extended empire. The pre-war empire had been sufficiently informal and sufficiently cheap for Parliament to claim authority over it without having to concern itself too much about what this authority entailed. The post-war empire necessitated a much greater investment in administrative machinery and military force. This build-up of control had to be paid for, either by British taxpayers or by their colonists. But new levels of control also had to be legitimised. In what terms could a people who claimed to be uniquely free justify their massively extended dominion to others and to themselves? As Edmund Burke inquired, how was 'the strong presiding power, that is so useful towards the conservation of a vast, disconnected, infinitely diversified empire' to be reconciled with the preservation of traditional British liberties?[3] The entirely realistic fear that adapting to their new responsibilities would involve a sacrifice of their own intrinsic and insular qualities was particularly acute in the face of the empire's Asiatic and Roman Catholic subjects, since Asia, like Catholicism, was for many Britons synonymous with arbitrary power. 'The riches of Asia have been poured in upon us', warned one peer in 1770, 'and have brought with them not only Asiatic luxury, but I fear Asiatic principles of government.'[4]

The spoils of unprecedented victory unsettled, then, in part because they challenged longstanding British mythologies: Britain as a pre-eminently Protestant nation; Britain as a polity built on commerce; Britain as the land of liberty because founded on Protestantism and commerce. All of these premises seemed to be put in question by the scope and nature of the post-war British empire. In the last quarter of the twentieth century, Britons have been understandably obsessed with the problem of having too little power in the world. In the third quarter of the eighteenth century, by contrast, their forbears were perplexed by the problem of having acquired too much power too quickly over too many people. They had been plunged dramatically and very profitably into the midst of the Great Game, but most of them had still to learn and accept its rules. The adjustment was made only harder by simultaneous changes in the rules of the power game at home.

Support for the Seven Years War had been remarkably and deceptively unanimous. In contrast with every previous war with France since 1689, there had been no French-sponsored invasion of the British mainland on behalf of the Stuart claimants to the throne, and no even halfway serious plot for an internal rising on their behalf.[5] By 1763, it had become clear to even the most paranoid Whig politician that–in England and Wales at least–Jacobitism was now too marginal to influence the course of events. Tories, both within and outside Parliament, had been as satisfyingly belligerent during the war as their Whig counterparts. The Hanoverian dynasty was once and for all securely entrenched. So, apparently, was Scotland's union with the rest of Great Britain. For the first time ever, the British army had been able to recruit men on a massive scale from the Scottish Highlands. Those clans that had taken up arms against the Union in 1715 and in 1745 had been wooed to the British cause by way of favours and promotions for their former chieftains, and transformed into the cannon-fodder of imperial war. 'I sought for merit wherever it was to be found', as William Pitt the Elder boasted: 'I found it in the mountains of the North . . . a hardy and intrepid race of men . . . They served with fidelity as they fought with valour, and conquered for you in every part of the world.'[6]

But to whom would these spoils of victory belong? Now that Tory loyalty had been proved beyond a shadow of a doubt, now that Jacobitism was ashes and now that Scotland as a whole, and not just the Lowlands, had invested in British patriotism, what justification could there possibly be for any longer confining high

19. *The Highland Hero: James Campbell.* An anonymous print celebrating a member of the British Army's earliest Highland regiment, 1745.

office and opportunities to Whigs and Englishmen? As far as Tories, Scotsmen and, most importantly, the new king, George III, were concerned, the answer was no justification at all.

To those used to being at the centre of things, then, but also to those below them, the prospects in 1763 were exhilarating but also frighteningly wide open. Indeed, it is not too much to say that from this point on until the American Revolution and beyond, the British were in the grip of collective agoraphobia, captivated by, but also adrift and at odds in a vast empire abroad and a new political world at home which few of them properly understood. It was a time of raised expectations, disorientation and anxiety in which demands for change on the one hand, and denunciations of change on the other, came from the peripheries of the political nation, from the peripheries of Great Britain itself and from the peripheries of the empire as well. At home, John Wilkes and his supporters launched a turbulent campaign for old English liberties and new English rights, while English patriots more generally felt themselves under threat from Scottish ambition and Scottish constructions of Great Britain. Abroad, those American colonists whom many Englishmen and women had been accustomed to viewing as mirror images of themselves, rejected both the authority of the British Parliament and in the end their own residual British identity. Reacting to these pressures would force a major reassessment of the meanings of Britishness and of the implications of empire.

JOHN WILKES AND ENGLISHNESS

On 15 August 1763, a Scotsman challenged an Englishman to a duel in the streets of Paris.[7] The Englishman was John Wilkes, holidaying in France so as to escape his creditors back home, and to recover his poise after his brush with the government over a matter of seditious libel. His would-be assailant was a brash young man called John Forbes, son of an Aberdeenshire Jacobite who had fled to France in the wake of the 'Forty-Five. He had recognised Wilkes from Hogarth's portrait of him, that brilliant cartoon in which the patriot's slim elegance and journalistic pretensions are utterly offset by his cynical leer, obvious squint and a bogus cap of liberty suspended over his fashionably bewigged head like an inverted chamber-pot. But Forbes was not in pursuit of the real or even the false prophet of liberty: he wanted to kill the hammer of the Scots. Back in Wilkes's lodgings, he told him that his life was forfeit for his scandalous attacks on North Britain and its inhabitants. Wilkes extricated himself with his customary blend of wit, pomposity, impudence and intelligence. He pleaded a previous duel with an English Secretary of State. He declared himself too useful a subject of the crown to risk his life. He called Forbes a rebel not worth fighting. Then, once the young man had stormed off in a rage, he put himself swiftly under the protection of the French magistrates.

This was not the only Scottish attempt on Wilkes's life. Later that same year, an insane Scottish marine was caught creeping into his London apartments, armed with a penknife. He told the authorities that he and twelve other Scots had sworn an oath to assassinate their national enemy.[8] Other irate Scots excoriated Wilkes in private letters, in public pamphlets and even in Gaelic songs. In Edinburgh, and other Scottish towns, apprentice boys burnt effigies of him on the sovereign's birthday, a practice that would continue into Queen Victoria's reign.[9] These expressions of Scottish anger are usually omitted from English history books, just as Wilkes's forthright hostility to Scotland is often marginalised as a regrettable vulgarity of no real relevance to the movement that gathered around him. Yet in viewing Wilkes as the personification of arrogant English chauvinism, the Scots had, in fact, identified the essence of what his movement was about–a celebration of a certain kind of Englishness and an assertion of English rights.

If this swaggering and intolerantly Little English patriotism has subsequently been downplayed, it is because Wilkes can so easily seem a purely dissident figure. A born Londoner with a background in trade, a dissenter who was educated in Holland and dabbled in freethinking, a lecher who cheerfully abandoned his wife, joined a Hell Fire club and attempted a sexual autobiography in the manner of Rousseau, a man who stood out against the smoke-filled rooms of Westminster and Whitehall and became a folk hero in the process, a household name throughout the length and breadth of England: Wilkes was undeniably the joker in the pack, an unabashed outsider in terms of origins, temperament, and behaviour.[10] As such, he still brings out the prig in British historians to an excessive degree. They linger on his cynicism, his opportunism and his delight in women, as though politicians in general are invariably possessed of sincerity, principled consistency and tight-lipped moral probity, and as though self-indulgence is necessarily incompatible with the possession of significant ideas. Yet John Wilkes and the arguments associated with him deserve to be taken seriously. The man himself was indisputably a rake on the make. He told outrageous lies, relished mischief and was often frivolous. But he was also a popularist who made his fortune by knowing how to tap mainstream opinions and prejudices, and in one vital respect at least his actions were remarkably consistent.

20. William Hogarth, *John Wilkes*, aquatint, 1763.

Even before he entered Parliament in 1757, Wilkes had attached himself to precisely those ginger groups that other middle-class Londoners of a patriotic disposition liked to patronise – the Anti-Gallican Association and the Society of Arts. Once elected MP for Aylesbury in Buckinghamshire, he became an enthusiastic colonel in the county militia and displayed a proper anxiety for maintaining the plebeian birth-rate by serving as Treasurer to the local branch of the Foundling Hospital. (Honesty compels the admission that he also embezzled its funds.)[11] The two furores that made his name, his arrest in 1763 for libelling the king and his minister in the forty-fifth number of the *North Briton*, the newspaper he edited with the poet and playwright Charles Churchill, and his election – while still an outlaw – for the county of Middlesex in 1768, were each converted by his supporters and his own public statements into contests over what was owing to Englishmen. When finally allowed to take his seat in Parliament in 1774, his less-than-distinguished speeches included pleas for a national art gallery and for a more splendid capital city, as well as his much better-known proposal for universal manhood suffrage.[12] Ten years later, he was campaigning on behalf of William Pitt the Younger and 'his patriotic plans to . . . recover the faded glory of our country'.[13] And almost his last public action before his death in 1797 was to award the Freedom of London to a successful naval commander called Horatio Nelson.

Looked at this way, the shift from the younger, more popularist Wilkes of the 1760s and early '70s to the City bigwig of his later years, becomes rather less stark. Although its political significance certainly changed over time, an ostentatious patriotism characterised his career throughout. So did a cult of *England*, which emerges from his private correspondence just as much as from his public writings and speeches. On trial before Lord Chief Justice Pratt in 1763, he told the court that its verdict would determine 'whether ENGLISH LIBERTY be a reality or a shadow'. Once acquitted, he told the jury that thanks were due to them 'from the whole English nation, and from all the subjects of the English crown'.[14] In exile the following year, he committed himself to writing a three-volume history of England since the Glorious Revolution, and actually went on to complete one volume of it. Immured in King's Bench in 1768, he assured his supporters that 'In this prison, in any other, in every place, my ruling passion will be the love of England.' And much later, in a strange and strictly private argument with the law reformer Samuel Romilly in the 1780s, he would defend frequent death sentences and public executions on the grounds that they accustomed Englishmen to a contempt for death. Out of an English gallows came forth English courage.[15]

John Wilkes, Esqr.
G. Bock – fecit
Member of Parliament for the County of Middlesex, Alderman of the Ward of Farringdon Without
Friend to Liberty, a Lover of his King, Opposer of Ministerial Tyranny, and Defender of his Country.

21. A mezzotint of John Wilkes after his disputed election for Middlesex, by G. Bock, 1769.

Why did Wilkes, so supremely conscious of his audience, choose to present himself in this fashion? One obvious answer, of course, is that cloaking attacks on the government of the day in patriotic slogans and gestures was a well-established way of making them acceptable. Or as Samuel Johnson famously pronounced in the 1775 edition of his dictionary (with Wilkes very much in mind): patriotism was the last refuge of the scoundrel. Like many previous opposition groups in England, Wilkes and his supporters argued that it was not they who were deviating from right, constitutional behaviour, but rather the court and its minions. They, the Wilkites, were the authentic Englishmen: it was their enemies in high office who were alien by birth and by conduct.[16] If the Wilkites employed this style of polemic more extensively and more successfully than earlier dissidents, it was partly because the circumstances allowed them to do so. It was a sheer gift to them that the Prime Minister in 1763 was a Scot, the hapless John Stuart, 3rd Earl of Bute, not an Englishman like all his predecessors. It was a further bonus that one of the judges Wilkes had to grapple with in 1768 was yet another Scot, William Murray, 1st Earl of Mansfield. Here, the Wilkites claimed, was concrete proof that Englishness was being eroded from above.

And those who governed Britain after 1760 could be portrayed as alien in another and more substantial respect. Ever since the establishment of the Hanoverian dynasty in 1714, high political office had been confined to men calling themselves Whigs. Tories, the traditional supporters of Anglican supremacy, had been proscribed. As a result, Protestant dissenters had felt secure in their religious rights and had been almost excessively loyalist. Then came George III. By admitting a very few Tories back to government office and by expressing a more overt enthusiasm for the Established Church, the new king broke with the conventions of forty-six years of Hanoverian rule. However good his intentions, however sound the precedents for his actions were in fact, he still shattered assumptions, outraged vested interests and added to the mood of post-war anxiety and disorientation.[17] Those who felt threatened by these changes–and most leading Wilkites were Whigs and a large proportion of them were dissenters–maintained that English history had gone into reverse. Wilkes's own collisions with the authorities, like the widening rift with the American colonists, merely confirmed that the country's 'glorious inheritance', the achievements of the Protestant Succession, the Revolution of 1688, the Civil War, even the Saxon struggle against the Norman Yoke, had been laid open to attack.

In response, and as a way of vindicating their own pretensions to patriotism, the Wilkites championed an aggressively Whig interpretation of English history. In the case of Wilkes himself, this meant literally composing a history book, *The History of England from the Revolution to the Accession of the Brunswick Line* (1768), a highly conventional if rather well-written celebration of 1688. More importantly, much of the public symbolism of his movement was a celebration of Whig constitutionalism. The pressure group formed to pay his debts and educate the public about the need for reform called itself the Society of the Supporters of the Bill of Rights (the S.S.B.R. for short), deliberately invoking the anodyne charter of English liberties passed by Parliament in 1689 to buttress its own more radical intentions. The hundreds of prints published championing Wilkes linked him time and time again with those earlier martyrs in the Whig pantheon who had suffered in the struggle against arbitrary power: John Hampden, John Pym, John Lilburne and Algernon Sydney.[18] And it was in the context of this same heroic and quasi-mythical past that his grass-roots supporters were encouraged to see him. In Middlesex in 1768, for example, a typical procession of Wilkite voters assembled at a tavern named after William of Orange, before setting out to vote for their hero, under banners of Magna Carta and the Bill of Rights.[19] Similar demonstrations occurred throughout England and in some parts of Wales.

Seizing control of an important and emotive part of the *English* national memory in this way was one of Wilkes's greatest strengths. He and his supporters were able to portray his personal dilemmas, his trial for sedition, his expulsion from Parliament after being elected for Middlesex by a large majority, and his subsequent imprisonment as but a continuation of the Englishman's centuries-old struggle for liberty, another vital stage in his distinctive pilgrimage towards habeas corpus, trial by jury, freedom of election and the liberty of the press. Wilkes became the personification of liberty, and liberty was the hallmark of Englishness. One great advantage of this position was that Wilkes in his gut probably believed it. Cynical, mannered and lax though he so obviously was, it should always be remembered that he was bred a Protestant dissenter. The idea that England was an elect nation, marked out by God with the possession of a peculiar degree of freedom, would almost certainly have been familiar to him from an early age. How could it not have been, when both his father and his brother were called Israel? But this approach to Englishness had a much wider advantage. It could be understood and appreciated at two very different levels, and utilised for two very different purposes: as an argument for change, and as an affirmation of existing identity.

For hard-line supporters of Wilkes, those lawyers, professionals, retail tradesmen and would-be gentlemen who joined the S.S.B.R., or organised his power base in London and Middlesex, or manned its outposts in the great provincial cities, this version of the English past and the English present was chiefly valuable as a means of validating their radical aspirations for the future. To them, Wilkes himself was little more than an attractive symbol for a campaign aimed at transforming the social distribution of political power and the theory on which it rested. In the words of William Beckford, the London MP whose fortune rested on West Indian trade, Wilkite activists rejected the belief that a man's patriotism was to be measured 'by the number of his acres'.[20] Instead, by stressing their supreme solicitude for liberty and by arguing that liberty was synonymous with Englishness, they advanced their own superior claims as patriots. Individuals like themselves, men of movable property, whether dissenting or Anglican, not only had an equal right with the landed classes to active citizenship. They had a better right, for they were better Englishmen.

For these activists, the affair of John Wilkes was just part of their political education, only a step on the way to a more protracted commitment to parliamentary reform and policy change, annual parliaments, an extension of the franchise, a crack-down on bribery and a repeal of the measures that were alienating the Americans. For the mass of Wilkes's supporters, though, those who were too poor, too conventional, too uninformed or too ground down with the business of keeping alive to read radical newspapers and pamphlets or to concern themselves with the S.S.B.R.'s political programme, the issues at stake were at once less specific and more short-term. For them, the movement turned on Wilkes himself, not on his real personality or even on his proclaimed ideas, so much as on his totem-like value as the personification of a certain version of English freedom and identity. This was why so many Wilkite songs were sung to the tunes of 'Rule Britannia' or 'God Save the King', why toasts in Wilkes's honour at prosperous dinners, or slogans in his support roared out in the street so often linked his name with that of the king, why the predominant tone of the movement was, as John Brewer has commented, 'remarkably loyalist'.[21]

In the confused aftermath of the Seven Years War, as men and women struggled to come to terms with unprecedented and expensive victory and new imperial responsibilities, Wilkes affirmed the traditional canons of Englishness. Through his own words and exploits, he offered boisterous reassurance that the English *were* a uniquely free and distinctive people who could keep alien and arbitrary rule at bay, a reassurance that was all the more potent because he himself–and this is sometimes forgotten–was able to win so many of his battles. Arrested in 1763, he outfaced his judges and was triumphantly discharged. Elected MP for the most important county in England, with minimal personal wealth and the penalty for outlawry hanging over him, he was none the less able in the end to take his seat in Parliament. True, he suffered imprisonment in 1768. But when he left the King's Bench in April 1770, it was as a celebrity snowed under with presents and applause. Four years later, he even emulated that earlier folk hero, Dick Whittington, by becoming Lord Mayor of London, achieving like him a place in the sun against formidable odds. In spite of debt, profound ugliness, religious non-conformity and the opposition of the law, the king and his ministers, Wilkes had clambered up the greasy pole and made himself the first citizen of the capital of the British empire.

By achieving so much, so outrageously, he made his opponents in the upper echelons of British society and government appear both helpless and ridiculous, and this gave enormous vicarious satisfaction to his supporters. But precisely because Wilkes succeeded, the message he communicated was as likely to foster complacency as alienation. 'Wilkes and Liberty' became a slogan expressive of triumph, celebration and relief, rather than a war-cry stimulating further protest. This, I suspect, was one reason why neither the man nor the slogan was much referred to by subsequent generations of radicals.[22] Wilkes–so deceptively disruptive as a personality–was in practice just too easy to incorporate into a conventional, approving English patriotism. That was one reason why his movement attracted such wide support south of the Scottish border. But the extent to which he appealed to and incited complacency also made him too ambiguous a figure to be comfortably accommodated in a later, more uncompromising and more *British* radical canon:

> Triumphant they bore him along throughout the crowd,
> From true English voices joy echo'd aloud,
> A fig then for Sawney, his malice is vain,
> We have Wilkes–aye and Wilkes has his freedom again.
> O sweet liberty! Wilkes and Liberty!
> Old English Liberty, O![23]

If we see Wilkes in this light–as a man offering reassurance that plucky Englishmen could win through and maintain their identity amidst the confusions and challenges of the post-war world–his noisy Scottophobia becomes far more comprehensible. Scots, so the Wilkite argument went, were inherently, unchangeably alien, never

22. *Famine.* Wilkite propaganda in 1763: Scotland as Poverty.

ever to be confused or integrated with the English. In Wilkite prints they were invariably (and inauthentically) portrayed as wearing tartan kilts, garments banned by Parliament after the 'Forty-Five. Highlanders and Lowlanders, cultivated patricians, like the Earl of Bute, and the poorest, most illiterate clansmen were all conflated

ARMS designed for the PEOPLE of ENGLAND.

By PHILO-SERVITUDINIS.

SCOTCH KING AT ARMS.

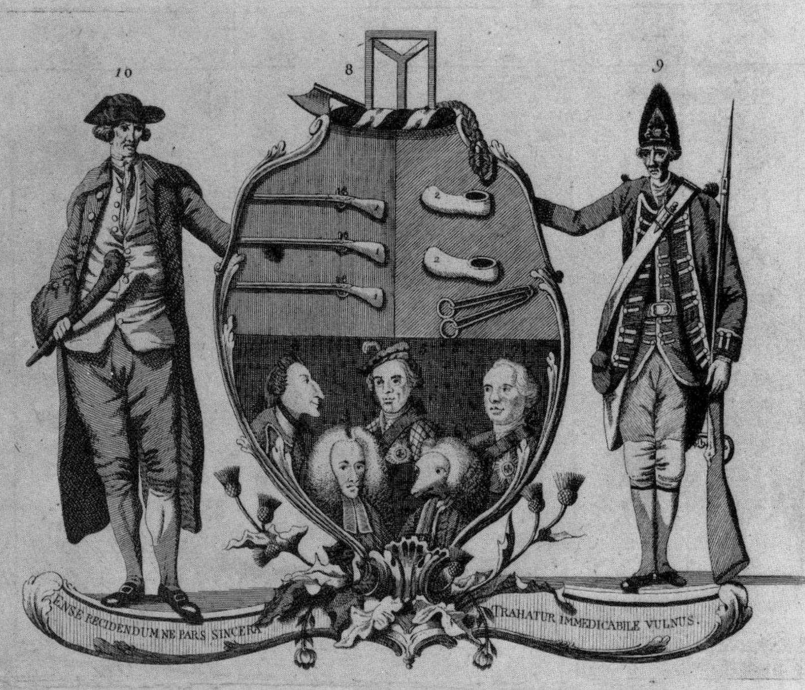

EXPLANATION.

ARMS.

1. Weighty and convincing Arguments for the obstinate and refractory.

2. Wooden Shoes and Fetters, blessings sincerely designed for the Protestant Subjects of Great Britain, by the worthy Company in the lower Department, consisting of

3. A white Scotch Lawyer. Mansfield.

4. A black English Duke. Grafton.

5. A Scotch Earl. —— Bute.

6. A public Defaulter, and Holland.

7. An insignificant, peace-making Duke. Bedford.

CREST.

8. The Ax, Gallows and Halter, the sure Fate of inferior Culprits; one or other of which, is unfeignedly recommended to each of the worthy Company just mentioned, according to the Motto.

"*Ense recidendum ne pars sincera trahatur immedicabile vulnus.*"

SUPPORTERS.

9. A Scotch Peace-officer.

10. An Irish, Middlesex Freeholder.

23. *Arms designed for the People of England.* The Scots as agents of arbitrary rule.

in a common sartorial foreign-ness.[24] By the same token, Wilkes used the pages of his newspaper, the *North Briton*, to remind his readers of the linguistic divisions between the two countries ('I will endeavour to write plain English, and to avoid . . . Scotticisms'), and to protest against the growing popularity of the term 'Great Britain'. His preference for using 'England' as a word to describe the entire island, and for 'Englishman' over 'Briton', was taken up by many of his more committed supporters. John Horne Tooke, for instance, a leading figure in the S.S.B.R., used his *Petition of an Englishman* (1765) to warn the likes of Bute and Mansfield – and indeed George III himself – against melting 'the English name . . . down to Briton'.[25]

But the prime difference that the Wilkites claimed to detect between the English and the Scots was one of political temperament. By this they did not mean the split that some commentators argue for today: between the 'natural' conservatism of the English and the ingrained radicalism of their northern neighbours. Quite the reverse. For Wilkes himself, and for many other more conventional Whigs on both sides of the Atlantic, the fact that the Stuart dynasty came from Scotland was proof positive that the country harboured a taste for arbitrary power on the one hand, and a willingness to cringe before it on the other. 'The principal part of the Scottish nobility are tyrants and the whole of the common people are slaves', declared Wilkes dismissively in 1763.[26] It was the misfortune of the Scots, one of his supporters agreed six years later, 'that those of the highest rank have been born and nurtured in arbitrary principles, and those of the lowest orders in the most abject slavery, and passive obedience'. This line of attack reached its logical conclusion in Wilkite accusations that it was the Scots who finally precipitated war with America after 1775: 'The ruin of the British empire is merely a SCOTCH QUARREL with English liberty, a SCOTCH SCRAMBLE for English property.'[27] Alien men and alien attitudes from North Britain had finally succeeded in infecting the seat of power in London, forcing those other Englishmen across the Atlantic into righteous rebellion.

That many of these accusations were arrant prejudice of the most unpleasant kind is obvious enough. When a Welshman called Thomas Pennant, a highly civilised gentleman tourist, journeyed around Scotland in the late 1760s, he was appalled to discover just how bitter more informed Scots felt at being so constantly and crudely misrepresented in the south. His best-selling *Tour in Scotland* (1771) was in large part an attempt – as he admitted – 'to conciliate the affections of the two nations, so wickedly and studiously set at variance by evil-designing people'.[28] Such well-meaning moderation remains heartwarming. Yet to adopt Pennant's line and dismiss the Wilkites' Scottophobia as nothing more than the irresponsible indulgence of a group of small-minded chauvinist thugs would be utterly wrong. The accusations they levelled against the Scots need to be taken seriously in two senses at least. First of all, they show once again how John Wilkes functioned as an English nationalist administering comfort to a people in flux. By dwelling on how irreversibly alien the Scots were, he offered a reassurance to his more intolerant and worried countrymen that they would not be absorbed into an all-embracing and non-Anglocentric Great Britain. Scottish difference, he implied, was a guarantee that traditional Englishness *and* English primacy within the Union would remain intact. This was exactly what large numbers of English men and women wanted to hear. Yet, in practice, it was a deeply misleading reassurance. For – and this is the second point – the real significance of Wilkite complaints that Scots were invading the British polity to an unprecedented extent is, quite simply, that they were true.

A SCOTTISH EMPIRE?

Runaway Scottophobia in England after 1760 was not the product of a traditional antipathy between two peoples, but a response to something much more recent. There was, of course, a very long history of mutual hatred, mistrust and armed conflict. Englishmen had been regularly swarming into Scotland, and Scots had been just as regularly invading northern England since the eleventh century at least. Memories of rape, slaughter and pillage ran deep on both sides of the border and were kept alive in folklore and children's games. Well into the nineteenth century, boys in the Scottish Lowlands played at 'English and Scotch', a tug-of-war in which one team tried to drag the other across a line, the victors snatching up the losers' coats and hats in the process.[29] But for men and women living in the 1760s, there were much grimmer legacies of recurrent invasion and plunder. To remind themselves of Scottish depredations, Englishmen had only to think back to the Highlanders' march on Derby in 1745, or glance at the beacon towers still strung along the hills of Cumberland and Westmorland, erected over the centuries so as to give warning of impending Scottish raiders. As for Scotsmen, the genocide that had reputedly followed the Battle of Culloden was reminder enough of the English capacity for racialism and hate.

Joined together by a common Protestantism, by trade and by the Act of Union, Scots and Englishmen could still succumb to fear, contempt or even open violence when they encountered each other. Peter Kerr and Helen Halliday, poor Lowlanders who together manned the toll-bar at Ravenshaugh on the border between East Lothian and Mid-Lothian, discovered this one evening in October 1760.[30] It may have been that Lieutenant-Colonel John Hale and his party of fellow English dragoon officers tried to get round the toll-bar without paying, or it may have been – as the officers subsequently claimed – that the Scottish couple insulted them (perhaps on their Englishness). Whatever the reason, the Englishmen reacted ferociously. They beat up the toll-keeper, and when his wife rushed to aid him, they flung her to the ground and pistol-whipped her as well. She was pregnant at the time. The couple's relations and neighbours met with similar treatment when they tried to intervene, and Kerr and Halliday were left unconscious and near to death. Hale and his fellow heroes were drunk, but this was not the root cause of their behaviour. Hale had been stationed in Scotland in the immediate aftermath of the 'Forty-Five, and one of his men apparently yelled out at the toll-keeper, 'God damn him for a Scotch rebel bugger!' With their discipline slackened by alcohol,

24. *Sawney Scot and John Bull.* A satire published in London in 1792. Note the shift by this time from simple English anti-Scottishness to English self-mockery.

and their nerves on edge perhaps from riding at dusk through an alien landscape, these men had simply and instinctively reverted to seeing Scotland as enemy territory, and its people – particularly its plebeian people – as fair game.

English aggression, however, was not the most illuminating aspect of this episode, but what came after. The local gentry clubbed together to fund a public prosecution against Hale and his men, and they were put on trial in Edinburgh. Sober now, and horribly aware of what they had done, their apologies and offers of private compensation were brushed aside. Nor did London intervene to save their honour and their faces. Instead, George III himself insisted they should submit to the Scottish courts, ordering them to be severely reprimanded as well: 'to regain the good opinion and confidence of their *fellow* citizens'. It was this reaction on the part of the authorities in the south that was the most remarkable part of the Ravenshaugh toll affair. It showed that in official eyes, Scotland was no longer the old enemy, and no longer either an alien province to be left gingerly alone or viewed with unrelenting suspicion, the standard ministerial responses to it in the first half of the eighteenth century. Instead, Scotland was coming to be seen by those in power as useful, loyal and *British*, just as entitled as any other part of the island to have its civilian law upheld against arbitrary attack by members of the regular army.

This shift in official attitude had only come about since the 'Forty-Five. Having suppressed the rising, Parliament did what it had largely failed to do after the Act of Union, or after 1715. It devised legislation to undermine the cultural, political and economic distinctiveness of the Scottish Highlands. The wearing of tartan was banned on pain of imprisonment, except, indicatively, for Highland regiments serving with the British army. Episcopalian clergymen, often proponents of Jacobitism in the past, were required to take new oaths of allegiance and to pray from now on publicly and explicitly for the Hanoverian royal family. Most notably, the Heritable Jurisdictions Act of 1747 substituted royal jurisdiction for the private jurisdictions previously exercised by clan chieftains. The intention being, as one MP succinctly put it, to 'carry off the King into every part of the United Kingdom'.[31] These were the sticks designed to beat down Highland autonomy. But an attempt was made to create some meagre carrots as well.

As far as the Highlands were concerned, this meant ploughing money from confiscated Jacobite estates back into the economy. Basic industries like tanning, whaling and paper-making were subsidised. Schools were established to instruct adults in the mechanics of linen production and to teach Gaelic-speaking children English.

Yet again, the rulers of the British state betrayed their absolute conviction that trade and patriotism were inseparably linked.[32] If more Scottish Highlanders could be hooked into the commercial system, the argument went, their loyalty would be bound to blossom. And once that happened, they could be safely absorbed into the imperial war machine. For ministers had no wish to destroy all of the Highlanders' ancestral values. Their obedience and bravery when their chieftains summoned them to war were entirely admirable characteristics in Whitehall's view, so long as from now on they were channelled exclusively into British military service. As the Secretary at War, Lord Barrington, told Parliament in 1751:

> I am for having always in our army as many Scottish soldiers as possible; not that I think them more brave than those of any other country we can recruit from, but because they are generally more hardy and less mutinous: and of all Scottish soldiers I should choose to have and keep in our army as many Highlanders as possible.[33]

Here was a *volte face* of striking proportions. Scotland – including its Highlands – was no longer an expensive nuisance. It had become the arsenal of the empire.

As shrewder English politicians recognised, however, substantial changes in the running of the state and in the thinking behind it were needed if this asset was to be exploited to the full. Scotland's loyalty to the Union and Scotland's manpower would have to be paid for by giving its titled and talented males increased access to London and its plums. Just one year after the slaughter of Culloden, the then Prime Minister, Henry Pelham, conceded that 'Every Scotch man who had zeal and abilities to serve the King should have the same admission with the administration as the subject of England had.'[34] This was to be the other side of forcible integration: allowing Scots to compete for advancement in the state on a wider scale and on more favourable terms than ever before. And it was the recognition that this was what was happening, in fact, that made English outsiders like John Wilkes and his followers so furious. In their prejudiced but not unperceptive eyes, more opportunities for Scots meant fewer perks for Englishmen:

> Into our places, states, and beds they creep;
> They've sense to get what we want sense to keep . . .[35]

Wilkes himself, it needs to be remembered, went into opposition journalism in the first place only because his frantic lobbying to be the first governor of newly conquered Quebec failed. Instead, the

25. *The Caledonians Arrival in Money-land.* A satire on Scottish ambitions in England, 1762.

job was given to Brigadier James Murray, who was, of course, a Scot.

Wilkite virulence against the Scots, then, was deeply felt but also profoundly ironic. So often interpreted at the time and since as evidence of the deep divisions between south and north Britain, in reality its extremism was testimony to the fact that the barriers between England and Scotland were coming down, savage proof that Scots were acquiring power and influence within Great Britain to a degree previously unknown.

English insecurity in the face of this new Scottish leverage helps to explain the obsession in so much written and visual polemic at this time with Scottish sexual potency.[36] The most extreme expression of this was the claim that Lord Bute was bedding George III's mother, the Princess Dowager. In one ribald print after another, the elegant and almost certainly entirely innocent Scottish minister was shown flaunting his long legs (of which he was intensely proud) before the swooning princess, or mounted provocatively on a broomstick, or with a set of rampant bagpipes placed as suggestively close to his body as the artist could conceivably devise.[37] Crowds rioting in support of Wilkes regularly made the same none-too-subtle point by brandishing a woman's petticoat to represent the princess, together with a boot (in other words, Bute). This was not an attack on immorality in high places. The accusation that one Scottish minister was penetrating the mother of the King of England was symbolic shorthand for the real anxiety: namely, that large numbers of Scots were penetrating England itself, compromising its identity, winning access to its riches and cutting out English men. As the princess was made to say in one splendidly filthy cartoon, her hand located firmly under Lord Bute's kilt: 'A man of great parts is sure greatly to rise.'[38] And just how far were Scotsmen going to rise?

The question was canvassed in newspapers and novels but particularly in plays. Before the 1750s, Scottish characters had only featured in English drama in a very miscellaneous fashion. No stereotypical Scotsman had emerged, and few English dramatists had known how to mimic Scots language. In the second half of the century, all this changed. Two stock Scottish characters appeared. And, indicatively, they were challenging, not contemptible types – the intellectual and the careerist. Laughing at their antics and aspirations as exhibited on stage, English audiences tried to exorcise their apprehension at Scottish ambition. 'I ha' acquired a noble fortune, a princely fortune', boasts Sir Pertinax Macsycophant in Charles Macklin's *True-born Scotsman* (1764):

> . . . I raised it by boowing; by boowing, sir; I naver in my life could stond straight i' th' presence of a great mon; but awways boowed, and boowed, as it were by instinct . . . Sir, I boowed, and watched, and attended, and dangled upo' the then great mon, till I got intill the very bowels of his confidence.[39]

Macklin was an Irishman. But he knew full well that many Londoners were now sufficiently familiar with Scottish accents to enjoy hearing them caricatured on stage, and sufficiently envious of Scottish achievement to attribute it all to obsequiousness. (And how telling it was that sycophancy to those in power, not Jacobite treason, was now seen by Englishmen as the essential Scottish vice.) What Macklin failed to realise, perhaps, was that Scots were now just too powerfully entrenched for this kind of satire to be acceptable. Government censors kept his play out of the London theatres until 1781. Even then, they insisted on a change of title: *The True-born Scotsman* had to become the more neutral *Man of the World*.

Petty though this episode was, it supplied further proof that the shrill English complaints about the Scots taking over did have some basis in fact. As Christopher Smout puts it, the Scottish periphery was beginning to exert 'a pull on the core, the tail beginning ever so slightly to wag the dog'.[40] Part of the reason for this was Scotland's own greatly increased prosperity. Its economy expanded after the 1750s at a faster rate than ever before, in some respects at a faster rate than the English economy. Between 1750 and 1800, its overseas commerce grew by 300 per cent, England's by 200 per cent. In the same period, the proportion of Scots living in towns doubled, whereas England's more substantial urban population increased by only some 25 per cent.[41] And Scottish towns were now far more affluent places, secure in post-Jacobite stability, made fat on imperial trade and graced with new, broad streets, elegant private houses and imposing public buildings. The show-piece was Edinburgh New Town, its centre designed by James Craig in 1767 as a celebration of *British* patriotism, and as an assertion of Scotland's and the city's importance in the Union. Prince's Street, George Street and Queen Street intersected with Hanover and Frederick streets, thereby paying tribute to George III, his immediate family, his father and his dynasty. And while St Andrew's Square commemorated Scotland's own patron saint, it was balanced – in Craig's initial plan at least – by another square named after St George. The very heart of Scotland's capital was now a monument to its parity with England in loyal attachment to the House of Hanover.[42]

Yet, as both sides of the border came to recognise, there were senses in which Scotland was not England's peer but its superior. The fact that large numbers of people today have heard of the Scottish Enlightenment, whereas comparatively few know or care that an English Enlightenment even took place, shows both the stellar quality of the best Scottish intellects at this time – David Hume in philosophy, William Robertson in history, Joseph Black in science, John Millar in social theory and Adam Smith in economics – and their distinctive cliquishness. Coming from a small country, and under persistent pressure from English prejudice, Scots in the world of letters, and in other realms of activity, tended to stick together and advance each other. 'No Scot ever exerted himself but for a Scot', wrote Wilkes darkly, and this strong sense of collective identity enormously increased the impact they were able to make.[43] Ambitious Scots also benefited from having more and better universities as training grounds. In the century after 1750, for example, Oxford and Cambridge produced only 500 medical doctors. Scotland, by contrast, educated 10,000.[44] Many of these men naturally looked south of the border for employment. So did large numbers of Scottish engineers, like James Watt, who left Glasgow for Birmingham and collaboration with Matthew Boulton in 1774, and somewhat later the great road-builder Thomas Telford. And so did Scottish architects like Robert Adam and Sir William Chambers, both comfortably ensconced at the top of their profession as joint architects to George III and his queen.

Scots had been going south in search of greater opportunities for centuries, but not in such numbers, and rarely with the advantage – as now – of having fellow countrymen sufficiently highly placed in politics to act as influential patrons. To this extent, Wilkite laments that the Scots were getting above themselves were fundamentally correct. Because Jacobitism was dead, because London was desperately eager to secure Scottish collaboration in warfare and empire-building, and because Scotland itself was developing into a more prosperous country, equipped with impressive reserves of talent, men from the north were able to seize upon jobs and opportunities in the south to an unprecedented degree. And the results were considerable and complex. Whatever some Scottish

26. Thomas Rowlandson, *Walking up the High Street*, 1786. The greatest eighteenth-century friendship, between the English Samuel Johnson and James Boswell, a Scot.

WALKING UP THE HIGH STREET.
Mr. Johnson and I walked Arm in Arm up the High Street to my House in James Court; it was a dusky night; I could not prevent his being afsailed by the Evening effluvia of Edinburgh. ——
— As we marched along he grumbled in my Ear "I smell you in the dark."
Vide Journal p. 13.

nationalists choose to maintain today, it was not simply a case of Scottish ability being creamed off away from its proper home all for the benefit of an English empire. English resentment of this Scottish exodus is surely proof of that.

Scots who went south reacted – as people who uproot themselves from their homeland always do – in very different ways. Some returned home as soon as they could, deeply alienated and disillusioned. Others stayed on as foreign mercenaries, taking what advantage they could from their new surroundings while remaining fundamentally aloof. Still others, like James Boswell, were turned into perpetual exiles by the experience, feeling themselves too Scottish to settle comfortably in England, yet becoming too English ever to return to their native land. But some, particularly the most successful, were able to reconcile their Scottish past with their English present by the expedient of regarding themselves as British. James Watt, for example, remained throughout his career a Scottish patriot. Every invention he patented, every steam engine he pioneered, filled him with the glowing thought that in the future his own countrymen would be able to say: 'This was made by a Scot.' Yet when Catherine the Great tried to persuade him to come to Russia, Watt told her he could never leave his own nation which was Great Britain. Winning access to a wider stage of endeavour had also broadened his patriotism.[45]

Scots like Watt do not seem to have regarded themselves as stooges of English cultural hegemony. Far from succumbing helplessly to an alien identity imposed by others, in moving south they helped construct what being British was all about. In part, this was because many of the most successful of them were concentrated in certain well-defined areas of British life. A breakdown of the career patterns of Scotland's Members of Parliament illustrates this point very clearly:

Scottish MPs holding state office, 1747–1780[46]

	1747–53	1754–60	1761–67	1768–74	1780
Civilian posts in Scotland	5	8	9	10	2
Civilian posts in England	3	5	8	5	6
Army and Navy	0	5	11	8	15
Totals	8	18	28	23	23

As this table demonstrates, in the immediate aftermath of the Jacobite rebellion of 1745, hardly any of Scotland's forty-five MPs were in state employment of any kind. Yet in less than forty years, this situation was triumphantly reversed. By 1780, more than half of all Scotland's representatives were in receipt of state salaries, and this table actually *understates* the degree to which élite Scots were coming to profit from being British. It omits, for example, men like Sir James Cockburn, the MP for Linlithgow, who held no official post for most of his career, but who did pick up a state pension, as well as a valuable contract to supply 100,000 gallons of rum to the troops in America during the War of Independence.[47] The table also omits the growing number of Scotsmen who sat for English or Welsh rather than Scottish constituencies. Few Scots had been able to take this path to political life and its profits before the 1750s. But between 1754 and 1790, sixty did so, including Alexander Wedderburn. He came to London from the Scottish bar, invested some of his savings in elocution lessons so as to smooth down his natural brogue, and was duly returned to Parliament for a Yorkshire seat in 1768. Three years later, he had clawed his way to being Solicitor-General and was a Privy Councillor. By 1780, he was Attorney-General and Lord Loughborough. Still ahead for this son of a Dundee town clerk lay the Woolsack and, in the end, splendid incarceration in St Paul's cathedral.[48]

Yet, as the experience of Scotland's own MPs bears out, this kind of burrowing into the very heart of the *civilian* establishment in London was rarely possible for Scots before 1780. Some of those who tried succumbed to English discrimination, like James Oswald who made it to the Board of Trade, but missed being appointed Chancellor of the Exchequer in 1763 because he was a Scot.[49] Those few who did get to the very top were liable, like Lord Bute, to encounter vicious resentment. So it was easier and usually far more rewarding to explore rather different routes to advancement. Accepting an administrative post back in Scotland was one possibility. But far more attractive to Scots from a wide variety of social backgrounds were two arenas in which life was still sufficiently hard or uncertain to repel the more pampered and overbearing English patricians, and opportunities were consequently much more open – the less fashionable regiments of Britain's army, and the coal-face of its empire.

Ever since the Union, the British army had been one of the few departments of the state wide open to Scottish ambition. Perhaps one in four regimental officers in the mid-eighteenth century was a Scot.[50] Like their English, Welsh and Irish counterparts, these men needed money and contacts to get to the very top of their profession. But if they possessed these attributes, as well as proven loyalty, there were no barriers to what they might achieve. An extreme example of what was possible would be John Campbell, 4th Earl of Loudoun, a man of only mediocre ability who was none the less valued enormously by London because of his title, his territorial power in Ayrshire and his unflinching Whiggism. Loudoun advanced incompetently but inexorably in the army's hierarchy, ending up as Commander-in-Chief of the British forces in North America during the Seven Years War, a position from which he was soon fortunately recalled.[51] The majority of Scottish army officers were better but also poorer than this, more often than not the sons of impoverished gentry families. For them, the rapid succession of imperial wars in the second half of the century was a godsend. Of course, their chances of dying in battle soared, but so too did their prospects of rapid advancement through the ranks and their opportunities for booty. 'I was born a Scotsman and a bare one', Sir Walter Scott would write, 'Therefore I was born to fight my way in the world', and this gets the connexion between economics and aggression exactly right.[52] For Scottish younger sons, prevented by convention from going into trade like some of their English equivalents, the path to glory was also one of the few available pathways to fortune. Securing British victories could be the means of ensuring their own.

And for many, it was. Hector Munro came from a family in Cromartyshire which had mattered in the fifteenth century but had dwindled into poverty thereafter. A family friend bought him a commission in one of Loudoun's Highland regiments, but it was only when he sailed to India with his men in 1760 that his career took off. Munro literally fought his way to notice, in 1764 winning the Battle of Behar which effectively ensured that Britain would annex Bengal. He promptly went home and used his share of the loot to build up a Scottish estate and make himself a Member of Parliament. For some Scots, though, empire became a profession in itself, an opportunity for power, responsibilities and excitement on a scale they could never have enjoyed back home. James Murray had gone into the army in 1740 weighed down with two disadvantages. He was the fifth son of a poor Scottish peer and his brothers were Jacobites. It took him twenty years' active service to establish himself as a brigadier, and his big break came only when General James Wolfe chose him for his campaign against Quebec. Victory, together with Wolfe's death, gave him his chance. He stayed on in the province restoring order, and in 1760 was duly rewarded by being made Britain's first Governor of Canada.[53]

Such men were the stars of the imperial firmament, rich, resplendent and only rarely emulated. But there were a multitude of lesser lights as well, and in some parts of the empire a quite disproportionate number of these were Scottish. During the time he was Secretary of State, for example, Lord Bute seems to have ensured that his countrymen got the lion's share of crown appointments in East and West Florida, colonies only acquired in the Seven Years War and therefore singularly free of any prior English stranglehold.[54] It was India, though, that the Scots made their own, long before the reign of 'Harry the Ninth', Henry Dundas. More than a quarter of the East India Company's army officers were Scotsmen; so, by mid-century, were a good proportion of its civilian officers in Madras and Bengal – the Scottish bankers and stockholders who had a strong grip on the Company made sure of that. Yet, paradoxically, it seems to have been an Englishman, Warren Hastings, Governor of Bengal and subsequently Governor-General of India, who converted this stream of Caledonians into positions of influence in the East into a torrent.[55]

Hastings' career raises in an acute form questions that need to be posed more generally: What, if anything, was distinctive about the Scots' contribution to the British empire? And why did they invest in it in such large numbers and so enthusiastically? That Hastings advanced a disproportionate number of them is clear enough. In the decade after 1775, some 47 per cent of the 249 men appointed to serve as writers in Bengal were Scots; and so were 60 per cent of the 371 men allowed to reside in Bengal as free merchants. Most impressively of all, Hastings' inner circle of confidants, the men he personally selected to go on intricate diplomatic missions to courts in India and elsewhere, was dominated overwhelmingly by Scots. By men like George Bogle, sent by Hastings to negotiate trade relations with the Teshu Lama of Tibet in 1774, or Major Alexander Hannay, dispatched on an equally dangerous mission to the Mogul court the following year. These were the men whom Hastings called his 'Scotch guardians'.[56] But just what was it about them that made him value them so much?

One reason for their prominence may have been that the quality and the quantity of Scottish talent available in the colonies at this time, like the quality and quantity of Irish talent, were more abundant than that of the English variety. Well-born and/or well-educated Englishmen usually had the pick of jobs back home. With some conspicuous exceptions, like Hastings himself, those of them who abandoned these opportunities on their doorstep for the discomforts and dangers of colonial life tended to be outsiders in some way: the less affluent, the less fortunate, the less reputable and the less able. By contrast, even the rawest frontiers of the empire attracted men of first-rate ability from the Celtic fringe because they were usually poorer than their English counterparts with fewer prospects on the British mainland.

Having more to win and less to lose, Celtic adventurers were more willing to venture themselves in primitive conditions. Some of them were also more willing to spend time learning exotic new languages, as George Bogle did when he became the first European (apart from stray Jesuit priests) ever to make an intensive study of Tibetan culture, establishing a close friendship with the Teshu Lama and writing to him regularly after their meeting until his own savagely early death back in Calcutta.[57] There was an important sense in which this kind of venturesome behaviour was in keeping with Scottish tradition. Back in the seventeenth century, thousands of Scottish officers had served as mercenaries in Denmark, Sweden, the Netherlands and even Poland and Russia. So, for Scots, journeying to a foreign culture to work and fight was a familiar and unfrightening prospect. And the rewards could be considerable. As would be true until the twentieth century, Britain's empire, especially its Indian empire, gave the talented, the lucky and the high-ranking a chance to experience luxury as well as squalor, and the opportunity to build up a substantial personal fortune. Living expenses were few, house servants were abundant and, in this earlier period especially, the pickings in terms of presents, ransoms and booty could be enormous. Even the ultra-professional Bogle, who was only in his thirties when he died, was able to accumulate £2,500 from his time in India, and so pay off the debts on his family's estate at Daldowie near the River Clyde.[58] Once again, it was a case of comparative Scottish poverty spurring on aggressive Scottish interest in British imperial expansion.

And what was true for this tiny minority of active imperialists applied far more broadly. Investing in empire supplied Scots with a means of redressing some of the imbalance in wealth, power and enterprise between them and the English. For Scottish merchants and tradesmen, access to the newer colonial markets proved doubly advantageous because, unlike older settlements and the customary European markets, they were not dominated by English merchantmen. For Scots who had trained in medicine, the level of disease in the colonies ensured that there were always lucrative if dangerous openings available there. For skilled artisans, blacksmiths, wrights, coppersmiths, joiners and the like, leaving Scotland for the West Indies or other possessions could be a means of making enough money to buy their own slaves and set up a business. Other Scots found niches in the colonies as clerks, or as book-keepers, or as legal assistants. 'It is impossible to be precise about the numbers who left the country', one Scottish historian has written, 'but the surviving documentation suggests it was enormous.'[59] In many cases, those who emigrated must have found only failure, disillusionment and a speedy death waiting for them. But for all that, dynamic imperial growth still offered Scots chances that the Old World did not.

For some Scots, though, it was less the job and trading opportunities that empire provided, than the *idea* of empire that proved most compelling. If Britain's primary identity was to be an imperial one, then the English were put firmly and forever in their place, reduced to a component part of a much greater whole, exactly like the Scots, and no longer the people who ran virtually the whole show. A British imperium, in other words, enabled Scots to feel themselves peers of the English in a way still denied them in an island kingdom. The language bears this out very clearly. The English and the foreign are still all too inclined today to refer to the island of Great Britain as 'England'. But at no time have they ever customarily referred to an *English* empire. When it existed, as in retrospect, the empire has always been emphatically British. In terms of self-respect, then, as well as for the profits it could bestow, imperialism served as Scotland's opportunity.[60]

And this was exactly what some Britons who were not Scottish feared. In 1785, Edmund Burke would cite Warren Hastings' grants of 'contracts, allowances, and agencies' to Scots as proof of his attempt to create 'a prodigal and corrupt system of government in India'.[61] Those Scots who had been so active in Britain's Indian possessions were, he suggested, hard, unscrupulous men, with an eye turned unerringly to the main chance, all too prone to sacrifice native interests to ruthless centralisation and self-aggrandisement. Like those earlier Whigs in opposition, John Wilkes and his supporters, Burke took it for granted that Scotsmen were irremediably 'tinctured with notions of despotism'.[62] By employing them so enthusiastically, he argued, Hastings had revealed his own arbitrary politics and consequently merited impeachment. And impeached he duly was, in a long trial that dragged on from 1788 to his final, belated acquittal in 1795. In the eyes of his parliamentary critics he had committed two blatant wrongs. He had given preferential treatment to Scottish military and civilian officers in India, and he had governed in a high-handed and unscrupulous fashion, and the two offences were intimately connected.

Were these accusations against Hastings anything more than just another expression of English (or in Burke's case, Irish) envy and resentment at the increased scope for Scottish ambition? Was it really the case that Scots found empire congenial because it gave expression to an inherent taste for strong, even ruthless government? For some Scots, I suspect it was. Once again, the opposition critique contains an element of truth, something that simply cannot be explained away as prejudice and pique. Many of the Scotsmen who made successful military or civilian careers in the colonies at this time came from Jacobite families or had at one time been Jacobites themselves. James Murray, for example, the first Governor of Canada, had a Jacobite father and Jacobite brothers. John Murray, 4th Earl of Dunmore (no relation), served as Governor of New York in 1770 and was appointed Governor of Virginia one year later. Yet his father had fought for Charles Edward Stuart, the Young Pretender, in 1745, and he himself had acted as his page during his brief stay at Holyrood.[63]

Or take the case of Lord Adam Gordon, who fought for Britain in the West Indies and acquired 10,000 acres of land for himself in New York. His father had been a Roman Catholic and had taken up arms for the Pretender in 1715. He himself was entirely loyal but utterly hard-line, advising London in the 1760s that it should appoint centrally paid full-time royal governors in the American colonies, and that it should seize control of all religious property in Canada. And then there was Simon Fraser, a leading general in the Seven Years War and fervent opponent of American independence. His father, Lord Lovat, had been executed in 1747 for Jacobitism, while he himself had fought for that cause at the Battle of Falkirk. As for Warren Hastings' Scotsmen in India, almost all of them had Jacobite relations 'lurking in some cupboard'.[64]

The absorption of so many previously Jacobite families and individuals into imperial service represented an extreme example of that much wider and more important trend: namely, the increased integration of Scots into the British community in the aftermath of the 'Forty-Five and in response to war and its conquests. Yet Jacobite infiltration of the empire also stands as a powerful reminder of the ambiguities of integration. As I have argued, Scots were not just passively assimilated. They did not invariably become honorary or, according to one's point of view, dishonourable Englishmen. They brought their own ideas and prejudices to bear on the business of being British. And in the case of Scottish empire-builders who had once been closely linked with Jacobitism, this could mean applying certain attitudes to authority to virgin territory in North America, India and the West Indies.

Because of their political beliefs, these men were likely to adopt a sympathetic attitude towards royal authority, even if their king was now George III. Perhaps, too, they were more prone to take a strong line in suppressing colonial disorder, and more unapologetic in devising new and efficient forms of centralised control. Used back home in Scotland to an electorate that was tiny by English and Welsh standards, possessed of a strong military tradition and accustomed to exercising far more power over their tenants than most landowners in the south could expect to enjoy, it is possible that some Scottish imperialists, at least, found the business of presiding over thousands of unrepresented subjects in the colonies neither very uncongenial nor particularly unfamiliar. The same would be true of the later generation of Anglo-Irish proconsuls, classically Richard Colley Wellesley and his brother, Arthur Wellesley, the future Duke of Wellington.[65]

None of this lets the English off the hook, of course. As the careers of Wolfe, Hastings and Robert Clive demonstrate, many of them, too, relished the empire and the opportunities for unbounded power it brought with it. But if we are to understand the profound unease expressed by Edmund Burke, John Wilkes and so many other disgruntled Whigs, we must recognise that Scottish endeavour not only sought expression in a splendid and cosmopolitan Enlightenment, but had an aggressive and sometimes unscrupulous side as well. In the uncertain aftermath of the Seven Years War, Scots played a leading part in making British imperialism what it was, accelerating that drift towards greater authority in political style which became so marked after the American war.

Their disproportionate contribution to the Great Game persisted throughout the nineteenth century and on until the end of the empire. And in a strange, vestigial way, it still continues. Today, Scots are unusually well represented in Britain's foreign office, in its diplomatic service and, it would seem, in the upper echelons of its secret service. 'Why', John Le Carré's hero wonders in *Smiley's People* ('not for the first time in his career'), '. . . are Scots so attracted to the secret world? . . . Ships' engineers, colonial administrators, spies.'[66] Nor is this just a belated example of English suspicion of intriguing, domineering Scots operating in a cold-blooded, out-of-bounds manner, though it is certainly that. Can it be entirely accidental that the most famous fictional spy of them all, James Bond, Number 007, deadly marksman, intriguer, the ultimate man behind the curtain, sexual athlete and ruthless patriot, is also a Scot, as was the author, whose wish-fulfilment he was?[67]

AMERICA AND THE REVOLUTION IN BRITISH SENSIBILITIES

War and empire, then, were the means by which the union between Scotland and the rest of Great Britain was made real. But military and imperial strife would also define what Britishness was about

27. John Dixon, *The Oracle. Representing Britannia, Hibernia, Scotia and America*, mezzotint, 1774.

in another, far less congenial manner. In March 1774, a striking mezzotint was published in London. Entitled *The Oracle*, it showed Father Time giving a magic-lantern show to an audience consisting of Britannia (used in this case as a symbol for England alone), together with allegorical maidens representing Scotland, Ireland and America. Time's images are of the future, a brilliant future in which British freedom and British union triumph over the discord that is threatening to tear the empire apart. Wreathed in smiles, Britannia leans back from these happy prospects in relief, while a devoted Hibernia gestures to the globe, to the worldwide dominion that is now secure. Thus did John Dixon, a Dubliner by birth, imagine times to come. One year and one month later, shots rang out at Lexington, and Britain and the thirteen American colonies went to war.

It is easy to dismiss Dixon's vision of imperial concord as nothing more than ephemeral propaganda swiftly overtaken by events. Yet his recognition that the crisis over the Thirteen Colonies was also likely to involve the relationship between England, Scotland and Ireland was perceptive. So, too, was his allegory of America, which – looked at closely – is far more enigmatic than his superficial optimism might lead one to expect. Unlike her three companions who pose together amicably in the light, Dixon's America sits apart in the shadow, her face unclear. This isolation and ambiguity is only deepened by her appearance. She is brown-skinned, whereas the others are white. Her legs and arms are bare, and her rough costume and feathered headdress are in marked contrast with their flowing classical drapery and knotted hair. Portraying the American colonies in this way, as a somewhat romanticised Indian princess, was standard iconographic practice for both European and American artists, and would remain so until the 1780s.[68] But for the British, and particularly for the English, such representations had a special significance which Dixon played on very skilfully.

The main reason why an American Indian was used to symbolise the Thirteen Colonies was, of course, that their white inhabitants had yet to evolve a recognisable and autonomous identity of their own. The majority of American colonists at this time were of British descent and came for the most part from England. They dressed like Britons back home, purchased British manufactured goods, read books printed in the main in London, spoke English and – as David Fischer has triumphantly demonstrated – retained intact many of the folk ways, family ways, and sex ways of their place of origin.[69] In these respects, American colonists were the same people as their brethren on the British mainland. But they were also very different, set apart by their experiences as emigrants and pioneers in a completely different landscape, not to mention by 3,000 miles of water.

For mainland Britons, then, Americans were (and perhaps still are) mysterious and paradoxical people, physically distant but culturally close, engagingly similar yet irritatingly different. In this sense, the strangeness evoked by the Indian princess who figured so often in London cartoons as a symbol of the colonies was by no means inappropriate. The motif was a resonant one in other respects as well. On the one hand, it summoned up the idea of a noble savage and was therefore well suited to those Britons who wanted to idealise America as a second Eden, a haven untouched by the corruption and luxury of the Old World. On the other hand, the image of an American Indian carried with it also an element of menace, and this I suspect was often deliberate. Well-informed

Britons at this time were not unaware that imperial dominion might in the future shift from their own small island to the massive continent inhabited by their American colonists.[70] Dixon's Indian princess carries a bow and arrows. Far more than her sisters in empire, even Britannia, whose spear rests casually beside her, she is a warrior, a possible threat.

Americans as colonists subordinate to the mother country, Americans as Englishmen abroad and consequently the brethren of those at home, Americans as uncorrupted children of a promised land, Americans as potential competitors in empire: behind these conflicting images lay profound uncertainty about the workings of the imperial relationship itself. There have been many different explanations volunteered as to why the American Revolution broke out when it did and in the way that it did. But if one were rash enough to plump for only one underlying cause, it would have to be London's failure to establish the kind of strong institutions of imperial control in North America that the Spanish had been able to construct in their Latin American colonies.[71] This failure was due to domestic circumstances, more than to any lack of interest or lack of will. From the first substantial migrations of East Anglian puritans to Massachusetts in the 1630s, Englishmen had settled in America by order of the king alone. None of the colonies founded after this were authorised by an Act of Parliament, and none of them sent representatives to the House of Commons. Consequently, it was to successive English monarchs, not to the Legislature, that the colonists looked as the source of ultimate authority. But for much of the seventeenth century, the Stuart kings faced too many troubles at home to devote concentrated attention to their settlements overseas. And although Charles II and James II made serious attempts to clamp down on the American colonists' growing autonomy, the Revolution of 1688 quickly undid almost all of their efforts.[72]

Successive wars and the distractions of dynastic change prevented British administrations from again devoting sustained attention to American affairs until the 1740s. These belated attempts to reassert metropolitan control over the colonists were made more urgent, and at the same time far more difficult, by the impact of the Seven Years War. The conquest of Canada substantially removed the colonists' fears of a French invasion from that quarter. And this made for an obvious conflict of interests with the mother country. As far as the British were concerned, the massive increase in the geographical size and cultural diversity of their North American empire made a much larger and more permanent military presence there indispensable. Since the post-war National Debt was so corpulent that it sucked in almost five-eighths of the government's annual budget in interest payments, it was crystal clear to almost every member of both Houses of Parliament that the Thirteen Colonies must be made to contribute more to the cost of their own defence. But since the American colonists now felt much more secure than before, this line of argument fell on stony ground. Why, they asked, now that the French were no longer a threat, should they be taxed to pay for a standing army that was bound to increase centralised authority over them?

And what right had Parliament to tax them anyway? Their allegiance was owing to the King of England alone and, as far as taxation was concerned, only their own elected colonial assemblies had the right to demand it of them. 'Acts of Parliament have been passed to annex Wales . . . to the realm', the leading American patriot and future President, John Adams, reasoned in 1775, 'but none ever passed to annex America . . . The two realms of England and Scotland were, by the Act of Union, incorporated into one kingdom by the name of Great Britain; but there is not one word about America in that Act.'[73] Since the colonies owed neither their existence nor their connexion with Great Britain to acts passed by Parliament, but only to the king, the former could have no powers of taxation or legislation over them.

Perfectly logical in its own terms, this argument made no sense to the British governing classes and no sense in terms of recent British constitutional history. By the 1760s and '70s, British monarchs had long ceased to be able to function without the consent of Parliament. Consequently, the distinction Americans wanted to draw between royal authority on the one hand and parliamentary authority on the other seemed, on the British side of the Atlantic, grotesquely inapposite.[74]

This constitutional and fiscal quandary was not the only or, as far as the Americans were concerned, even the prime motor behind the outbreak of war. But for the British it was the central issue at stake. In the past, they had signally failed to do what the Spanish had done: namely, build an effective structure of royal authority and administration in their American colonies. As a result, no possibility existed of soothing and winning over influential and talented Americans, in the way that influential and talented Scotsmen were increasingly being won over, by giving them increased access to state employment. The existing state apparatus in North America was simply too small for that to be an option. Given these already glaring inadequacies in Britain's control over the Thirteen Colonies, on what basis could the imperial relationship be conceivably sustained in the future, if the Americans were to be allowed to reject Parliament's supremacy as well?

It was in these terms that the government put its case for going to war with the Americans in 1775. In George III's words, they were fighting 'the battle of the Legislature'.[75] As such, they could hope to appeal to those patriots who looked to Parliament as a crucial component of British identity and British superiority. But in other respects, as ministers acknowledged, the traditional rudiments of popular patriotism could not be drawn on with remotely as much confidence as in previous eighteenth-century wars. This time the enemy was not Roman Catholic. And while High Church clerics might find it easy to condemn the American colonists as latter-day puritans and vile republicans, large numbers of ordinary English, Welsh and Scottish Protestants, and not just dissenters, seem to have felt persistently uncomfortable about going to war with their co-religionists across the Atlantic. Then, of course, there was the matter of trade. By the early 1770s, the Thirteen Colonies took some 20 per cent by value of British exports and supplied 30 per cent of its imports. Only by bringing the Americans to heel, the government argued, could these jewels in Britain's commercial crown be kept intact. But while some merchants and traders agreed with this wholeheartedly, others bitterly resented the war's disruption of transatlantic trade in the meantime and feared that a defeated and ravaged America would make only a poor market for British goods in the future.[76]

But what chiefly compromised enthusiasm for the war at its start was quite simply that it was a *civil war*, not just in the sense that both sides had so much in common, but also in that each side was split within itself. One exasperated American estimated that one third of his countrymen were in favour of winning independence, another third were ardent loyalists, while the remainder had still to make up their mind – a wild guess that does at least have the virtue of conveying the confusion prevalent in the Thirteen Colonies in 1775. Opinion within Great Britain was just as seriously fractured. And this needs stressing, because so many historians have chosen to concentrate *either* on radical opposition to the war *or* on conservative support for it, whereas what mattered most at the time was that responses were neither overwhelmingly pro-war nor uncompromisingly anti-war, but instead profoundly mixed. 'Interested as we are in this contest', wrote the editor of the *Annual Register* carefully, '. . . It indeed little becomes us to be dogmatical and decided in our opinions in this matter, when the public, even on this side of the water, is so much divided.'[77]

Just how divided was suggested by the government's encouragement of what was in effect a rigged plebiscite on the war. Early in September 1775, the gentlemen, clergy, manufacturers and inhabitants of Manchester submitted an address to the king pledging support for the war. This was a spontaneous local initiative. But a delighted government promptly encouraged other bodies to follow suit. In all, some 150 corporations, town councils, militia regiments and groups of inhabitants sent in loyal addresses in favour of pursuing war with the Americans.[78] Together with the names of the signatories, these were duly reprinted in virtually every English and Scottish newspaper. No publicity campaign of this kind had been thought necessary in earlier wars, though indicatively one had been implemented after the Jacobite invasion in 1745. The intention, now as in that earlier emergency, was clearly to outface any domestic opposition. On this occasion, however, the tactic misfired. Twenty-five towns and counties retaliated against the loyal addresses by submitting rival peace petitions.[79] These documents were also signed, in some cases embarrassingly so. Hampshire's petition against the war with America, for example, collected 2,500 signatures, ten times more than the county's pro-war address. More than 1,200 Newcastle freemen, many of them small tradesmen and artisans, also petitioned for peace. Yet only 124 of their fellow citizens had signed up for war.

And looked at carefully, even the loyal addresses themselves bore testament to the extent of domestic division over the war, and particularly to the unevenness of response between different parts of the island. The counties of northern England – Cumberland, Northumberland, Westmorland, Durham, Cheshire, Yorkshire and Lancashire – had tended to be royalist enclaves during the Civil War, and many of them retained a strong Tory as well as a Roman Catholic presence in the eighteenth century. In accordance with this partisan tradition, many people here seem to have viewed what was happening across the Atlantic as yet another rebellion of seditious dissenters against a king, a second civil war in fact. Almost 6,500 men signed Lancashire's address in support of the war, while 1,200 signed Bolton's address – the largest number of pro-war signatories from a single town obtained in this campaign. Yet even this obviously conservative region was split assunder over America. Predominantly Anglican though it was, it also had a large population of Quakers who retained strong links with their brethren in Pennsylvania. Individual Friends seem to have played a conspicuous part in organising Lancashire's peace petition, which attracted some 4,000 signatories.

In fact, there were only three parts of Great Britain where public responses to the outbreak of the war were more or less monolithic: East Anglia, Wales and Scotland. The first of these, and particularly the counties of Suffolk, Essex and Norfolk, had supplied the bulk of those men, women and children who had journeyed across the Atlantic between 1620 and 1641 to become the first white settlers in New England. These early links with America, kept alive in local memory by way of folk histories, by records in family Bibles and by transatlantic correspondence, seem to have made many East Anglians deeply antipathetic to the war, not least because it was in the New England colonies that the first blood was spilt.[80] Only one small borough in Suffolk and one town in Essex dispatched loyal addresses to the king. Otherwise these two very well-populated counties remained silent. So did Norfolk, reserving its fire until 1778, when 5,400 of its inhabitants dispatched a petition to London demanding peace.[81] In this region, opposition to the war was never confined to just Protestant dissenters or radicals, but was a much wider phenomenon. Perhaps the most powerful evidence of this is the behaviour of Cambridge University's dons, all of whom at this time were required to be Anglicans. Whereas Oxford University (which had Lord North as its Chancellor) dispatched a loyal address supporting the war in October 1775, Cambridge remained stubbornly mute until the end of November. Even then, a motion to address the crown passed the University's senate by only eighty-four votes to forty-six.

The Welsh were even more taciturn, the whole country submitting only two pro-war addresses. This may simply have been because mobilising opinion in this way was still very much of a novelty in Wales. But its poor showing as far as the government was concerned may also have owed something to widespread unhappiness about the war. Protestant identity was very strong here, and the country had produced a good many emigrants to America, most of them concentrated in Virginia and Pennsylvania.[82] Richard Price, a leading opponent of the war, was Welsh, and surprisingly large numbers of his countrymen had supported John Wilkes in his campaign to get elected for Middlesex. 'The Welsh and the Scotch, who inhabit the remote ends of this kingdom', a Wilkite journalist had argued in 1769, 'are very opposite in their principles. The former are hot, generous, and great lovers of liberty. The latter violent and tyrannical.'[83] The first part of this typical piece of Wilkite ethnic stereotyping does seem to have had some basis in fact, in the sense that many pro-Wilkite Welshmen also went on to be pro-Americans. As for the second part, Wilkite suspicions of Scottish authoritarianism were only corroborated by the campaign of addresses in support of the war. Between

September 1775 and February 1776, over seventy addresses in support of armed coercion of the American colonists were submitted by Scottish counties and town councils, almost as many as issued from the whole of England, which had five times as large a population. Neither at this stage of the conflict nor later did a single Scottish petition for peace ever reach London.

As a guide to opinion in Scotland, this was actually less cut and dried than it appeared. All but three of the Scottish pro-war addresses had no signatures attached or only very few. Almost all of them were written and submitted solely by provosts, town councils and magistrates, and so reveal very little about reactions lower down the social scale. And, despite the lack of peace petitions, anti-war activism did exist in Scotland, among the Presbyterian clergy, among the legal fraternity, among Edinburgh's intellectual élite, and in Glasgow, where there was an abortive attempt to petition for conciliation. Support for the war, then, was no more unanimous here than in any other part of Great Britain. None the less, as far as *formal* expressions of opinion were concerned – addresses, propaganda, subscription lists, sermons and recruiting drives – the *Scots Magazine* was right to claim that 'in this part of the kingdom, the exertions in support of government have even exceeded the exertions in the southern part'[84] And Scottish support for the war was just as marked on the other side of the Atlantic. According to Bernard Bailyn, some 40,000 Scots emigrated to North America between 1760 and 1775, many of them desperately poor Highlanders in search of a better and more prosperous life. Yet, in marked contrast with the 50,000-odd Irishmen who emigrated to the Thirteen Colonies in the self-same period, these Scottish settlers seem to have opted overwhelmingly for the loyalist side in the War of American Independence.[85] Here, perhaps, is further evidence that Scots, even the very poor, had become much more reconciled to the British polity since the rising in '45, and deeply attached as well to a British empire that afforded them so many opportunities.

Many influential Scots, in fact, seized on the American war as a means to underline their political reliability to London, deliberately contrasting their own ostentatious loyalty with American disobedience, and with the anti-war activity of English radicals. The loyalty address submitted by the magistrates and council of Fortrose in Inverness-shire, for example, waxed scathing on that 'set of men . . . who, under the mask of patriotism, sow sedition', a clear reference to John Wilkes and his allies who were now spearheading opposition to the war in London.[86] The gentlemen of Nairnshire reminded the king how 'this county in the late war sent out many of its sons to defend your Majesty's ungrateful colonies', and assured him that they would fight just as hard now against 'the traitorous and the disaffected'.[87] 'Untainted by the vices that too often accompany affluence', declared the nobility of Caithness-shire, 'our people have been inured to industry, sobriety – And, when engaged in Your Majesty's service, have been distinguished for an exact obedience to discipline and a faithful discharge of duty.' The gentlemen and freeholders of Renfrewshire sent similar reassurances, but they at least were honest enough to spell out the mixed motives behind this epidemic of Scottish obsequiousness. In supporting the war effort, they admitted, they were acting out of 'loyalty, love of our country, [and] regard for our own interests'.[88]

As this candid admission suggests, it was not just concern for the maintenance of royal authority and a zest for empire that prompted so many politically active Scots to come out in favour of war with America, important though those motives were. The war also presented a splendid opportunity for impressing the authorities with their country's loyalty, thereby ensuring that its interests and inhabitants would receive even more positive attention from London in the future. Such a reminder of Scotland's value was judged all the more essential in the light of the recent Wilkite attempts to play on traditional Anglo-Scottish divisions. Wilkes's xenophobic Englishness and popular success had been viewed north of the border as seriously prejudicial to those attempts, in progress since 1746, to construct a more united Great Britain and a more imperial Great Britain, in which Scots might see themselves, and be seen by others, as peers of the English. But now, as Alexander Murdoch has written, 'the American War renewed their opportunity to prove their loyalty and enthusiasm for the concept of Britain'.[89]

In other ways, too, the American war compelled different groups of Britons to re-examine the nature and boundaries of their patriotism. As far as the radicals and other opponents of the war were concerned, the passage of time made their position increasingly difficult. Most of them had been anxious to keep their brethren on the other side of the Atlantic within the empire and had favoured conciliation as the best means of achieving this. The American Declaration of Independence in July 1776 cut the ground from under their feet, as well as leaving many Englishmen with the sense that part of their past history and collective identity had been brutally amputated. Openly supporting the Americans' right to establish themselves as a separate and independent nation, as distinct from advocating their appeasement, was very hard for those radicals who prided themselves on being patriots. It was harder still when the Americans allied themselves with the old

28. *The Parricide. A Sketch of Modern Patriotism.* Radicals (including a cross-eyed John Wilkes) as friends to America and therefore traitors to Britain: anonymous print, 1776.

Catholic enemy France in 1778. And it was lethal in the context of major battles involving large numbers of British casualties. 'I am sorry', John Wilkes told the House of Commons after Saratoga, 'that 800 valiant English and Germans were killed in a bad cause, in fighting against the best constitution on earth.'[90] This was brave, but it could hardly be popular. Indeed, individuals who were less prestigious and protected than Wilkes could have a very rough ride if they expressed their support for the Americans too openly. There are scattered references in the newspaper press to American sympathisers being beaten up, or on occasions tarred and feathered by their neighbours, a deliberate borrowing of the punishment riotous Americans had inflicted on royal officials before the Revolution.[91]

Critics of the government were thus put on the defensive, and their claims to patriotism contradicted in a very brutal way:

> How despicably must posterity consider those men, who amidst their boasted professions of loyalty and zealous attachment to the constitution, give their assistance to enemies who are openly aiming at dismemberment of the empire.[92]

In this sense, the American Revolution contributed to a revolution in the nature of radicalism in Britain. Before the war, critics of the constitution had experienced little difficulty in reconciling demands for change at home with the most blatant chauvinism, imperialism and bellicosity. The enemy then had always been France or Spain, Roman Catholic regimes that could easily be seen by prejudiced Protestant eyes as enemies to liberty. Wilkes, for example, had seen no contradiction between his advocacy of parliamentary reform and concessions to the American colonists on the one hand, and lambasting the administration for failing to go to war with Spain over the Falkland Islands in 1770 on the other. In both cases, in his view, he was fighting liberty's battles. But war with America destroyed this kind of complacency. The innovation, as far as British experience in the eighteenth century was concerned, of fighting Protestants on a large scale undermined this facile union of constitutional zeal and uninhibited jingoism. From now on, domestic critics of a British imperial state were more likely to face a hard choice between winning easy popularity by supporting successive war efforts, or risking unpopularity by concentrating on the need for political and social change at home.[93]

For those who governed the British state, too, the war proved in the short term peculiarly costly and brutal. It lasted much longer and was far more expensive than ministers had ever anticipated. It had to be pursued against a background of domestic division and debate and in dangerous isolation. France joined the Americans openly in 1778, followed by Spain one year later and Holland in 1780. Britain, by contrast, had no European allies at all, barring those few German states who lent it manpower. Encircled by enemies, it lacked the strength and the will to prevent one of its own peripheries, Ireland, from acquiring parliamentary independence in 1782. Worst of all, of course, and uniquely in this period, it lost. And the humiliation of defeat at the hands of a former colony was profound for a ruling élite possessed of strict notions of hierarchy and massive pride: 'Your armies are captured', London's Livery told George III after his forces' definitive defeat at the Battle of Yorktown, 'the wonted superiority of your navies is annihilated; your dominions are lost'.[94]

Yet, paradoxically, this defeat proved more constructive in the long term than the glossy victories achieved in the Seven Years War. At the level of ordinary opinion, the experience of an unsuccessful and unhappy war, fought in isolation from or opposition to the rest of Europe, seems actually to have resolved some of the uncertainties and divisions of the 1760s and early 1770s. Alienation from the administration that had gone to war there certainly was. But once the Prime Minister, Lord North, accepted the position of scapegoat and resigned in 1782, a sense of embattled identity, of Britain against Europe and, now, of Britain against America became more prominent than anything else. An entirely obscure Staffordshire clergyman summed up the mood well when he scribbled in his parish register that,

> To future ages it will appear to be an incredible thing . . . that these kingdoms should maintain (as they have done) a glorious, but unequal conflict for several years with the most formidable and unprovoked confederacy that should be formed against them.[95]

Instead of being sated with conquests, alarmed at their own presumptuous grandeur as they been after 1763, the British could now unite in feeling hard done by. Their backs were once more well and truly to the wall, filling many of them with grim relish and renewed strength.

The war refurbished their unity in another important respect. True, one important periphery, the American colonies, had been lost. But another, Scotland, had become linked to the centre to a greater degree than ever before, fastened tight by cords of mutual self-interest. This did not mean that antipathy towards the English in Scotland, or antipathy towards the Scots in England promptly evaporated in the warmth of a new tolerance and understanding. Obviously not. But never again was there an outcry against Scottish influence in the state on the scale initiated by John Wilkes and his supporters.[96] And this was not because that influence declined, but rather because southerners became accustomed to its increasing. The English had been able to regard the heartland of their first empire, the American colonies, as peculiarly their own, pioneered by their own ancestors long before the Act of Union with Scotland. By contrast, in terms of those who won it, those who governed it and those who settled it, the Second British Empire would indeed be emphatically British. And a major share in the work (and the profits) of constructing Greater Britain would for a long time be sufficient for Scottish ambition.

I have suggested that Scottish penetration of the new British empire was one element in the shift towards a much firmer governing style at the end of the eighteenth century. But there were many other elements, and defeat in America was one of the most important. It has sometimes been argued that the War of American Independence was for Great Britain what Vietnam would be for the United States some two hundred years later, a David and Goliath conflict which divided and demoralised the great power in question even before it went down to unexpected defeat. If this seems a valid analogy, then we can push it further. In the case of both of these world powers, loss of face was followed by a sharp move to the Right, a new impatience with opposition and a hard determination to shore up the fabric of the state. The lesson drawn by London from the American war, wrote Frederick Madden and David Fieldhouse, was 'not that the first British empire had been too strictly governed or that policy had been too selfish or inflexible, but rather that it had been too permissive, conciliatory and ineffective'.[97] In the wake of the Seven Years War, some leading Britons had been embarrassed by the weight of empire, even going so far as to question its morality. By 1783, however, many of these scruples and uncertainties had gone. The result was a series of imperial reforms designed to clarify and strengthen London's control: the India Act of 1784, the Canada Act of 1791 and the Act of Union with Ireland in 1800 being only the more important.

But the governing élite would also work to strengthen its position at home, reconstructing its authority, image and ideas, and – as we shall see – devoting far more attention than before to questions of Britishness. In the half-century after the American war, there would emerge in Great Britain a far more consciously and officially constructed patriotism which stressed attachment to the monarchy, the importance of empire, the value of military and naval achievement, and the desirability of strong, stable government by a virtuous, able and authentically British élite. Everyone knows that the War of American Independence created a new nation in the United States of America and undermined an old nation, *ancien régime* France. But it did even more than this. It helped to forge a very different Great Britain in which both men and women would have to work out their ideas of patriotism as never before.

29. Sir Joshua Reynolds, *Charles Stanhope, 3rd Earl of Harrington*, 1782.

4 *Dominance*

In May 1778, a medieval tournament took place on the banks of the Delaware River. Seven self-proclaimed knights of the blended rose, caparisoned like their horses in red and white silk, challenged the seven black and orange knights of the burning mountain. On a field 150 yards square, ringed with troops and set out 'according to the customs and ordinances of ancient chivalry', they broke lances, fought each other with swords, and finally – for this was the eighteenth century after all – fired pistol shots above each others' sweat-sodden, powdered wigs. Only when urged to desist by the ladies they were championing, fourteen Philadelphian maidens got up in Turkish costume and bright, silken turbans, did the knights retire from the field and rejoin their fellow British officers. The ball that followed lasted until midnight; the feasting until the early hours of the morning. Sated and entranced, served by black slaves in silver collars, guests from among the élite of Philadelphia and the army that occupied it, saw themselves reflected in hundreds of specially imported mirrors, and were dazzled finally by fireworks. They ended with an illuminated triumphal arch and a pyrotechnic figure of fame blowing from its trumpet (in French) the words: 'Thy laurels shall never fade'.[1]

This was the *mischianza* or triumph held, ostensibly, to honour the departure of the Commander-in-Chief of the British land forces in America, the Honourable William Howe. Superficially, the event was just one more manifestation of that taste for gothic romance and orientalism that was so prevalent in European polite culture at this time. Yet more was at stake here than just a stylish entertainment. Chivalry's essential function, Maurice Keen has written, is always to hold up an idealised image of armed conflict in defiance of the harsh realities of actual warfare.[2] By definition, chivalry also reaffirms the paramount importance of custom, hierarchy and inherited rank. General Howe's tournament occurred just seven months after the crushing British defeat at Saratoga and was organised, we know, by a set of idealistic young army officers from comfortably landed backgrounds. As such, it can be seen as a window on the minds and manners of an élite under stress. After three years of indecisive war in raw, uncongenial territory, and in the face of doubt, disappointment and vague premonitions of defeat, the cream of the British officer corps sought a brief escape in an ordered and glamorous past. Sword-in-hand and on horseback, they reconstructed the war with the American colonists as they would ideally have liked it to be: a splendid crusade fought according to the rules by men of birth, and fought successfully.

The reality was very different. Just one month after Howe's chivalric triumph, the British were driven out of Philadelphia. Two years later, Major John André, one of the gallant knights of the blended rose and author of an elaborate account of the tournament, would be hanged as a common spy on the orders of George Washington himself. And in 1783, all the king's horses and all the king's men would be forced to give up the battle, leaving behind them an independent United States of America:

> The boast of heraldry, the pomp of power,
> And all that beauty, all that wealth e'er gave.
> Awaits alike th'inevitable hour.
> The paths of glory lead but to the grave.[3]

All military defeats are shattering to those caught up in them, but this defeat proved particularly so. Great Britain, which in the wake of the Seven Years War had assumed for itself the rank of the world's foremost imperial power, had been decisively vanquished by the French and by its own relatively puny colonists. The colonists in question had been overwhelmingly Protestant and predominantly British in origin. Yet this common ethnicity and religion had conspicuously failed to keep them attached to the mother country. Instead, they had been willing to kill and be killed by fellow Britons, and in the end to declare that they were not British at all but something very different. In practice, Americans would find it difficult to hammer out a new and completely autonomous identity. But the British whom they had rejected would also find the process of adjustment hard. They had been deprived of a part of themselves, and now had to re-examine their own identities and boundaries. Their leaders also had to think seriously about their public image. For the most immediate way in which defeat in America proved devastating was that it called into question the competence of the British governing élite.

Virtually every war fought since the Act of Union had gone badly at some stage, but before 1783 none had ended in defeat. Nor would any major war in which Britain was involved after this date end in defeat. (Those who are curious about this country's peculiar social and political stability probably need look no further than this for the essential cause.) The American war, then, was the great exception. A British army led by a succession of patrician generals, Burgoyne, Howe and Cornwallis, and an administration under the leadership of the eldest son of a peer, Frederick, Lord North, had suffered a humiliating defeat, as had the monarch who had persistently supported the war, George III. Those who feared, like Horace Walpole, that Great Britain would now moulder piecemeal into insignificant islandhood were absurdly premature, but the blow to the ruling order's pride and reputation was immediate and immense.

Yet in a quite remarkable way the British élite recovered. The half-century that followed the outbreak of the American war would be one of the most formative and violent periods in the making of modern Britain and in the making of the modern world – a time of accelerating industrialisation and urbanisation, of growing class consciousness and demands for reform, of revolution in France, and of war in Europe so massive that it swept into every other continent. Virtually every European state in this period would undergo political change, military reorganisation, and social and ideological upheaval. And all but one of the world's great empires would experience a substantial reduction in the territory they ruled, or a decline in the vigour with which they ruled it. Great Britain, however, would be a conspicuous exception to this general crisis. Not an exception in the sense that it escaped crisis. Quite obviously it did not. But an exception in the extent of its resilience. By the 1820s, its rulers would claim dominion over some 200 million men and women, more than a quarter of the world's population. Unlike its European and extra-European rivals, it would keep its mainland free from civil war and serious invasion from abroad. Most remarkable of all, perhaps, far from giving ground to any substantial degree, Britain's ruling class would actually increase in size, in homogeneity, in wealth and in range of power. The first of the European élites in the eighteenth century to experience revolutionary and imperial crisis would also be the first to evolve a strategy for endurance and recovery. From the 1780s onwards, its members would set about re-ordering their authority, their image, their ideas and their composition. In the process, they not only reshaped the exercise of power in Great Britain, they also contributed to a substantial change in the content of British patriotism.

CRISIS OF AN ORDER

To understand the dimensions of this patrician renaissance, we need to appreciate just how extensive the crisis was. As for every other

European élite at this time, the foremost challenge was war on an unprecedented scale. Britain had barely recovered financially from the American war before it was caught up in a conflict with Revolutionary and Napoleonic France. This lasted from 1793 to 1815, with only a brief and phoney truce in the middle, and cost £1,657,854,518 – close to three times the total cost of all the other major wars Britain had fought since the Glorious Revolution, and approximately six times its pre-war national income.[4] To most men of power, however, the cost of losing seemed far more terrifying than the cost of winning. In part, and as William Pitt the Younger openly admitted, war with France represented a desperate struggle to defend rank, and above all, property against the 'example of successful pillage' set by the revolutionaries of 1789. Imagine, Edmund Burke asked his fellow MPs one year later, what it would be like,

> to have their mansions pulled down and pillaged, their persons abused, insulted, and destroyed, their title-deeds brought out and burned before their faces, and themselves and their families driven to seek refuge in every nation throughout Europe, for no other reason than this, that, without any fault of theirs, they were born gentlemen and men of property, and were suspected of a desire to preserve their consideration and their estates.[5]

Even after Napoleon Bonaparte had muffled the egalitarianism of the early French Republic, the prospect of Britain's traditional rulers losing face (if not their heads) persisted. Most of the officers in Napoleon's *grande armée*, like the bulk of his imperial nobility, possessed no claim to land or ancient lineage, but had risen to prominence since the Revolution through their own exertions. In this sense, Napoleonic France could still be seen – and was seen by its British opponents – as a meritocracy. Consequently, the prolonged success of French arms in Continental Europe did more than threaten British territorial autonomy. It was also politically subversive, casting doubt on the belief that men of land and birth were inherently more suited to the exercise of authority than any other social group. 'The diadem of Bonaparte', declared the *Edinburgh Review* in 1809, 'has dimmed the lustre of all the ancient crowns of Europe; and her nobles have been outshone and out-generalled, and out-negotiated, by men raised by their own exertions from the common level of the populace.'[6]

Inordinately expensive war fought out on a global scale also meant that those in authority after 1775 had to sustain a far greater volume of public business than ever before. This was obviously true in the case of men holding places in central government, in the

Treasury for example, where the fiscal demands of war doubled the work-load between 1792 and 1805, or in Parliament, where the amount of legislation passed, committees formed and late-night sittings endured quintupled between 1761 and 1813.[7] But it was no less true of those landowners and plutocrats who exerted influence in their own localities, not least because civil defence duties expanded, to a brief and patchy degree during the invasion threats of 1779–82, relentlessly and for much longer after 1793. Most dramatic of all, perhaps, was the increased weight of responsibility and danger sustained by those holding high military or naval rank, and by those holding key posts in an empire which was now so much larger, so much more geographically diverse, and so different in ethnic composition from that which had existed prior to 1776.

Defeat in America, revolution in France, and war with both, together with the expanding volume and diversity of domestic and imperial government, imposed a massive strain on the lives, nerves and confidence of the British élite. One result was a spate of high-level casualties, and not just on the battlefield. William Pitt the Younger, Prime Minister from 1783 to 1801 and again from 1804 to 1806, died at the age of forty-seven, a victim of incessant work and compensatory drinking. His political disciple, George Canning, was barely able to get a stab at the premiership in 1827, before succumbing completely under the burden, just like 'any poor horse that drops down dead in the road', as one contemporary put it.[8] Some less gritty spirits killed themselves before work could do it for them. The suicides of a leading Whig politician, Samuel Whitbread II, in 1815, of the prime spokesman in Parliament for penal reform, Samuel Romilly, three years later, and of the Foreign Secretary, Lord Castlereagh, in 1822, were all attributed at the time to the relentless demands of public life. All three of them exited by slashing their throats.

There was, indeed, a distinctively *sturm-und-drang* quality about British patrician life in the late eighteenth and early nineteenth centuries that has never been properly investigated since, a special kind of emotionalism and violence. Think of the Earl of Chatham collapsing in the House of Lords as he made his last manic and incoherent speech against war with America in 1778, or of Edmund Burke flinging a dagger onto the floor of the House of Commons in December 1792 as a symbol of his departure from the Foxite Whigs, and of Charles James Fox bursting into tears in response. Stiff upper-class lips in this period gave way very easily to sobs, histrionics and highly charged rhetoric; and sometimes gave way entirely. In all, nineteen Members of Parliament are known to have committed suicide between 1790 and 1820; more than twenty lapsed into what seemed like insanity, as did their monarch George III.[9] Beyond the walls of Westminster, rich commoners and peers alike played Russian and real roulette, duelling and gambling to an unprecedented degree, as if choosing to put their lives and fortunes at risk in these ways was somehow preferable to facing those strains and dangers that threatened to engulf them against their will.

Yet the most corrosive challenge to patrician confidence and authority at this time may not have been the wars with Revolutionary America and France, or the exotic demands and seductions of a new, predominantly eastern empire, or even the pace of administrative and industrial change at home, but rather a calling into question of the very legitimacy of the power élite. Denunciation of the landed classes as a discrete group, as distinct from assaults on an individual monarch, minister or party group, had appeared occasionally in polemics issued on behalf of John Wilkes and parliamentary reform in the 1760s and '70s. But only from the 1780s did this kind of criticism enter the mainstream of political discourse in Britain, where it was popularised through the journalism of Thomas Paine, Joel Barlow, Thomas Spence and above all, William Cobbett, and made still more abrasive by those radicals who buttressed their arguments with names, numbers and lists. Compilations such as T.H.B. Oldfield's *Representative History of Great Britain and Ireland* (1816) revealed the extent to which landowners, and particularly members of the peerage, interfered in the electoral process; while the *Extraordinary Red Book* (1816) and John Wade's *Black Book: or corruption unmasked* (1819) spelt out in relentless detail exactly why they bothered to do so. Fifty thousand copies of Wade's anatomy of graft were sold; and even reading it today, it is easy to see why. Quite simply, Wade documented the folk cynicism of politics. He proved, or seemed to prove, that everyone in the British Establishment had his hand in the till, advanced his own male and female relations and was closely related by blood or marriage to everyone else in high office:

> The aristocracy, usurping the power of the state, have the means under various pretexts of extorting for the junior branches of their families, a forced subsistence. They patronise a ponderous and sinecure church establishment; they wage long and unnecessary wars to create employments in the army and navy; they conquer and retain useless colonies; they set on foot expensive missions of diplomacy and keep an ambassador or consul, and often both, at almost every petty state and petty port in the world; they create offices without duties, grant unmerited pensions, keep up unnecessary places in the royal household, in

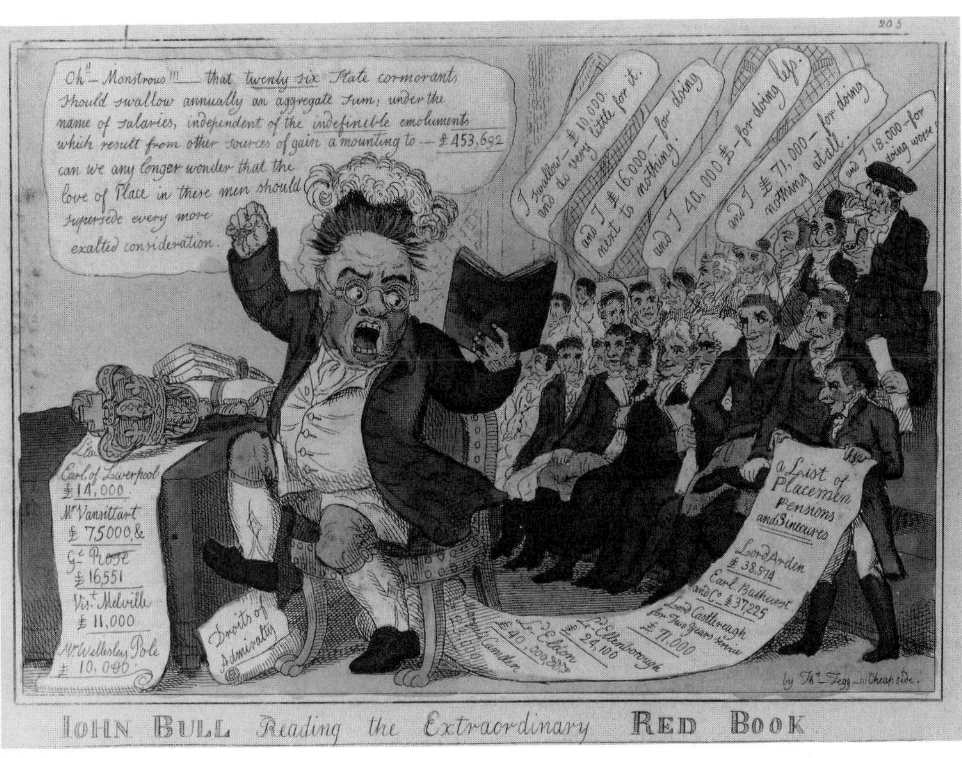

30. *John Bull Reading the Extraordinary Red Book*. A satire on patrician greed, 1816.

> the admiralty, the treasury, the customs, excise, courts of law, and every department of the public administration.[10]

Wars were fought, taxes were inflated, policy was distorted and jobbery multiplied, all so that this oligarchy might grow fat.

Such analyses were damaging not because they were correct in detail (they were not), but because they treated the landed interest as a separate class parasitic on the nation, rather than as part of the nation and as its natural leaders. Instead of taking authority for granted, they quantified it cold-bloodedly and condemned. Crudely but raucously, the radical critique stripped public men in Britain of their pretensions to patriotism. It announced to these rulers of an empire that they had no clothes, and no real civic virtue either. The honour of the aristocratic male, Charles Pigott argued, meant no more than 'debauching your neighbour's wife or daughter, killing your man, and being a member of the Jockey club, and Brooks's gaming house'. Titles, declared Paine, were like rickets, a disease one needed to grow out of.[11] Had this line of attack been confined to the political radicals, it might not have mattered so much. But the argument that patrician degeneracy was subverting Britain also ran through a great deal of otherwise conservative middle-class comment. 'Our nobility', declared one anonymous writer,

> placed on an eminence among the people, instead of supporting the dignity of their station, are become a shame and disgrace to it. Our young noblemen are jockies, whoremasters, and spendthrifts, while those advanced in years are repairing the waste of their youth, by a shameful plunder of the public.

'To attempt to reform the poor while the opulent are corrupt', the impeccably Tory Hannah More would write in the 1780s, was 'to throw odours into the stream while the springs are poisoned'.[12]

This kind of alienation from those in authority would be fostered throughout Europe by the French Revolution, but in some respects, Great Britain's élite was particularly vulnerable to it. It was, as we have seen, a working, capitalist élite, actively supportive of commerce and in love with every form of economic modernisation that might enrich it. And its members did not claim the seigneurial dues and fiscal immunities that made the old French and German nobilities such easy targets for attack. Moreover, at its lower levels, the landed class was always open to new recruits from industry, trade and the professions, and seems to have become rather more so in precisely this period.[13] None the less, in terms of size and sociology, the higher echelons of the British governing élite were peculiarly narrow by contemporary standards. If Jean Meyer is right, nobles on the eve of the French Revolution made up on average between one and two per cent of the population in Continental European states. A decade later, all of the peers, baronets and knights added together made up only an infinitesimal 0.0000857 per cent of the British population.[14] Naturally there were many rich and influential men without titles as well. But once again, *at the higher levels* of the British élite, there were not as many of these more self-made commoners as some historians have suggested. John Burke (he of *Burke's Peerage*) calculated that there were no more than four hundred families in the 1830s 'uninvested with heritable honours' who owned really substantial estates or possessed high official rank, and this was in the United Kingdom as a whole.[15]

And as John Burke knew better than anyone else, there were close links of blood and marriage between these four hundred families, and between them and the peerage. The composition of the House of Commons alone demonstrated that. In the early nineteenth century, one in four MPs was married to a daughter of another MP. Many others married the daughters of peers, or were themselves related to the peerage.[16] Such connexions with noble families were a common path to being elected to Parliament in the first place. For as Cobbett and others repeatedly complained, their lordships not only filled their own upper house, but influenced the election and subsequently the conduct of members of the lower house as well. In 1807, at least 234 of the MPs representing constituencies in England, Wales and Scotland owed their seats in some way to aristocratic intervention. This was the high–or (according to one's point of view) the low–point of aristocratic influence over the House of Commons. Even so, in 1831, one year before the passage of the first Reform Act, 90 members of the peerage still controlled the election of more than one third of Great Britain's MPs.[17]

So the position of the British governing élite in the half-century after the American war was a deeply paradoxical one. It was relatively homogeneous. At its higher levels, it was extraordinarily compact. Its wealth and power were very great and, as Wade and Cobbett correctly diagnosed at the time, actually becoming greater still in some respects. All of these qualities helped it to sustain the challenge of war, empire, revolution, social change and political dissent. But these self-same qualities–homogeneity, compactness, wealth and power–naturally invited attack as well. If it was to restore its reputation and confidence after defeat in America and win support for a prolonged war against an avowedly egalitarian and meritocratic France, the British élite required far more than coercive power. It needed to be able to repel suggestions that it was an exclusive and over-lavish oligarchy and legitimise its authority anew. Most of all, perhaps, its members needed to demonstrate to themselves as well as to others that they were authentically and enthusiastically British: to prove, as Edmund Burke put it, that 'a true natural aristocracy is *not* a separate interest in the state, or separable from it'.[18] Maintaining their close social identity, they had at the same time to assert their rightful place as patriots. And to a much greater degree than is sometimes acknowledged, they succeeded in doing precisely this.

Let us see how.

THE MAKING OF THE BRITISH RULING CLASS

> The leading members of the provincial aristocracies . . . migrate to the capital in permanence; they purchase mansions at Rome, villas and estates in the fashionable vicinity; they invade the high

> strata of society; they contract marriage alliances with Italian families, and even with the old Roman aristocracy.

This was how the great New Zealand historian Sir Ronald Syme once described the reconstruction of the Roman empire under Augustus. Ambitious and influential men from the outer provinces of the empire, he argued, had moved to its centre, bringing with them an abundance of fresh ideas, fresh talent and fresh energy, and gaining in return greater opportunities and wealth for themselves. 'The strength and vitality of an empire', Syme concluded, 'is frequently due to the new aristocracy from the periphery.'[19] Much the same might be said of the British empire from the last third of the eighteenth century onwards. Members of the Welsh, Scottish and Anglo-Irish landed élites, who had often in the past been excluded, as well as temperamentally aloof and geographically distant, from the centre of political power, now moved or were drawn into it. In the wake of the loss of the American colonies, these Celtic élites amalgamated with their English counterparts far more extensively than before, reinvigorating the power structure of the British empire and forging a unified and genuinely British ruling class that endured until the twentieth century.

Such an important development could not occur all at once, nor in its origins was it the result of conscious deliberation. As is the case with all hereditary élites, the earliest and most crucial determinants were the vagaries of sex and biology. From the later seventeenth century to the 1770s, the landed establishments of England, Wales, Ireland and Scotland had been caught up in a major demographic crisis. For reasons that are still unclear, many landowners did not marry, and many who did marry failed to produce male heirs. For nearly a century, landed families were thus not reproducing themselves, in the sense that, on average, two parents failed to produce two children. And the consequences of this were widespread and considerable. In Scotland, some famous families like the Queensberrys became extinct in the male line. Others, like the Breadalbanes, ony survived because the titles and estates passed to very distant cousins.[20]

Very similar developments were apparent in Ireland and in Wales. The demise of ancient gentry familes in Cardigan, Merioneth, Pembroke and Carmarthen is well attested. In Monmouthshire, between 1700 and 1780, there were thirty-one failures in the male line affecting ten estates; and in Glamorgan, only ten of the thirty-one great estates were occupied in 1750 by heirs in the male line of the head of the family of fifty years before.[21] In England, too, many ancient landowning families faded away. Between 1700 and

1750, the old dynasties of Catholic gentry all but disappeared in the north-east. In Essex, only a handful of the great county families in possession in the 1770s had been established there before 1700. In Cambridgeshire, half of the county's élite disappeared between the mid-seventeenth and mid-eighteenth centuries; and in Yorkshire, of the ninety-three baronetcies created between 1611 and 1800, fifty-one were already extinct by the latter date.[22]

So however much they may have been primarily conscious of themselves as Englishmen, or Irishmen, or Welshmen, or Scotsmen, the members of these separate landed élites were affected by the same, broad demographic trend. And, in all four cases, the results were identical. As families died out, because of their inability to produce male heirs, their estates passed to other landowners: through indirect inheritance to distant male cousins, or through the female line, or through sale. Altogether, about one third of all landed estates seem to have changed hands this way in this period, many of them coming into the possession of owners who were completely new to the area in which the land lay. In Essex, for instance, the Mildmays had been a famous and illustrious county family established there since the sixteenth century. But in 1796, the male line died out completely, and the estates passed, via a Mildmay niece, to Sir Henry Paulet St. John, an out-county landowner whose own lands were in Hertfordshire. And such mergers were common across an even wider gap, out-country instead of out-county, as in 1779, when the Goggerdan estate in Cardiganshire passed to an Edward Lovedon who already owned land in Berkshire, thereby transforming him from a small-scale *English* squire into a *British* landowner.[23]

In counties where the local élite suffered with a special severity during the demographic crisis, this could result in the creation of an almost entirely new and British landed establishment in place of the old and local gentry. In Glamorgan, as Philip Jenkins has shown, there was an almost complete remaking of the county élite during George III's reign, as estates passed by marriage to major out-county owners like the Butes, the Dunravens, the Dynevors and the Windsors, all of whom already held land in England, and some of whom were also major owners in other parts of the Celtic fringe.[24] The Dunravens, for example, eventually went on to accumulate 40,000 acres of land in estates scattered throughout Wales, Ireland and England. The Butes did even better, ensnaring four heiresses in three generations, and in the process acquiring 116,000 acres in England, Wales and Scotland.[25] Whether these families wanted to be British or not thus became immaterial. The shift of landed property virtually compelled them, as it did many others, to think in terms of Great Britain, and often in terms of the United Kingdom as a whole.

The social, political and cultural repercussions of this consolidation of estates across county boundaries and across country boundaries were made more profound by yet another demographic development, or to be more precise by the demographic crisis turned inside out. In the last third of the eighteenth century, population growth throughout Britain and Ireland accelerated, demand for food crops soared and the price of wheat skyrocketed. By 1789, wheat sold for 45 shillings a quarter. It reached 84 shillings a quarter in 1800 and went on to average 102 shillings between 1810 and 1814, prices that had never been attained before. As a result, large landowners grew fatter than ever. Rentals on most English estates increased by between 70 and 90 per cent. In Wales, they rose by at least 60 per cent, as on the Wynn estates in Merioneth between 1790 and 1815, and in some cases by as much as 200 per cent. In Ireland, the increase averaged 90 per cent and in much of Scotland, it was probably eightfold between 1750 and 1815.[26] The economic experience of landowners throughout the United Kingdom thus became increasingly similar, as the previously poorer Celtic fringe caught up with England in terms of profits and rentals, and the whole of the landed interest was in a state of unrivalled prosperity. Even though there was a slump after Waterloo, rentals settled down in the late 1820s at about double the pre-1790 figure.

This increase in the profitability of land, and the standardisation of those profits throughout Great Britain and Ireland, hastened still further the merging of the English, Welsh, Scottish and Anglo-Irish élites. It became more common now for Englishmen in search of an estate to be willing to purchase one in the Celtic fringe. By the 1820s, even land in the Scottish Highlands, so long despised in the south as an unprofitable and backward region, was attracting a stream of greedy Sassenach purchasers. More broadly, their new shared prosperity allowed members of the landed class to purchase into an increasingly homogenised lifestyle and culture.

Consider the case of Francis Humberston Mackenzie, Lord Seaforth (1754–1815).[27] An Anglo-Scot with lands in Lincolnshire as well as the massive Seaforth estate in the Highlands, he was a direct beneficiary of the demographic crisis, being only a distant cousin of the original Seaforth dynasty which had died out in 1781. And since his rentals rose sharply after the 1780s, he was able to live in a far grander and more cosmopolitan style than his predecessors in the title. He purchased not just one but two town houses in London, as well as another in Edinburgh's most fashionable square. He also restored the family's ancestral seat, Brahan Castle, which had been devastated by an English army back in 1725 as punishment for the 5th Earl of Seaforth's uninhibited Jacobitism. Away went many of the grimmer aspects of architecture which might have revealed that Brahan had once been a chieftain's fortress, built to repel invading forces from the south. In its place, the new Lord Seaforth constructed a house that would have been perfectly acceptable in design on both sides of the border. Inside it went new carpets, fine porcelain and paintings by two of George III's favourite artists, Benjamin West and Thomas Lawrence. Outside, there was a landscaped garden, abounding in 'exquisite walks, wooded dells and hollows'. It is tempting to accuse Seaforth of swallowing English aesthetics whole, but this would be unfair. Just as it would be unfair to indict those of his English patrician contemporaries who commissioned new houses from the Scottish architect, Robert Adam, with abandoning their Englishness. It was rather a case of all British men of substantial property now taking certain common patterns of consumerism for granted. And those who spend together, live together.

In some cases, quite literally so; for the fusing of the English and Celtic élites was increasingly cemented in marriage. Between 1750 and 1800, there were more than twice as many marriages between daughters of the Scottish peerage and Englishmen than there had been in the first half of the century. And by the nineteenth century, women of this type were more likely to opt for English husbands than marry fellow Scots.[28] It was greater Celtic affluence that lay at the root of this romantic revolution. Because more Scottish, Welsh and Anglo-Irish peers could now afford to live in London, because their families were now far more equipped to shine in its social season, and because the dowries they gave their daughters were now so much more commodious, they could play to win in the fashionable marriage market as never before. Though few women from any part of the island were as well provided for as Scotland's most celebrated heiress in this period, Elizabeth, Countess of Sutherland. When she settled on an English husband in 1785, George Granville Leveson-Gower, the future Marquess of Stafford, she brought with her 800,000 acres of her titular county. Here was another example, and a most spectacular one, of a family's landholdings coming to cross the boundaries of country.[29]

Why English patricians now sought Celtic spouses more enthusiastically than before is therefore clear enough. But what was the attraction on the other side? The answer very often was improved access to influence and power. As we have already seen, Scottish penetration of military and imperial posts had been steadily increasing since 1745. But the top jobs in the civilian establishment had tended to remain very much an English preserve. It was marriage alliances with members of the English élite that did most to ease the entry of men who were not English by birth into these higher echelons of state employment at home, something which greater Celtic affluence could not by itself necessarily accomplish. The power of family attachments, so strong in all hereditary élites, helped to dissolve greedy English parochialism as nothing else could have done. It was, for instance, two marriages with well-connected Englishwomen that transformed Robert Stewart (1739–1821) from a clever Anglo-Irish landowner and member of the Dublin Parliament into a United Kingdom grandee with a place at Westminster and a bevy of sons emphatically in place as well. His first wife had been the daughter of the Marquess of Hertford; when she died, he married the Hon. Frances Pratt, daughter of the 1st Earl Camden, ex-Lord Chancellor of England. Frances's dowry was poor, but as Stewart must have known, her family's influence was magnificent. It brought Stewart an Irish peerage and subsequently a seat in the Upper House as Earl (later Marquess) of Londonderry; and when Camden's heir was appointed Lord Lieutenant of Ireland in 1798, he made Stewart's eldest son, Robert, his secretary, and his second son, Charles William, his aide-de-camp. For both of them, this proved the vital foot in the door. Charles William went on to be a general in the British army and ambassador to Austria. His brother, the future Viscount Castlereagh, went even further and faster, to a place in the cabinet, to the Foreign Secretaryship, and ultimately, of course, to that dark night of the soul and cut-throat razor which alone prevented him from going on still further to the premiership.[30]

The impact of these cross-border marriages on attitudes and behaviour became more powerful as generations succeeded each other. Take the case, for instance, of the Williams Wynns, still sonorously described by *Burke's Peerage* today as 'second to none among the Cambrian families in territorial possessions and political influence'. In the early eighteenth century, the men who held this title had been very Welsh and very Jacobite. Sir Watkin Williams Wynn, 3rd Bt., publicly burnt a picture of King George II in Denbigh in 1727, kept a private army to cow his political opponents and, like all of his predecessors, chose a Welsh woman for his wife. Offered a peerage as an enticement to political orthodoxy, he rejected it with scorn, spending most of his time in his North Wales fastness until, bloody-minded and bucolic to the end, he broke his neck while out hunting rabbits.[31]

His son, who did not reach maturity until the 1770s, might have come from a different planet. A member of London's Dilettanti Society and a passionate devotee of amateur theatricals, he married not just one Englishwoman, but two. And the transition from quasi-feudal local overlord to responsible and blandly cultivated British patrician became still more marked in the next generation. The Sir Watkin Williams Wynn who became fifth baronet in 1789 was an exquisite young man, educated at Westminster and Christchurch and equipped, of course, with an English wife:

> Wynnstay in his time ceased to be a [Welsh] cultural centre and became a focus of military exercises, country sports, agricultural meetings, and an appanage of Sir Watkin's mother's family, the Grenvilles, under whose aegis, inevitably, he entered public life.[32]

Inevitably. So, no less inevitably, did his two brothers. When Lord Grenville was appointed Prime Minister in 1806, Charles Watkin William Wynn duly became Under Secretary of State for Home Affairs; Henry Watkin Williams Wynn, not a man of overwhelming ability, had already been comfortably placed in the diplomatic service under the same beneficent auspices.

All of these developments – a massive transfer of land by way of inheritance and purchase, an unprecedented rise in the profitability of land and increasing intermarriage between Celtic and English dynasties – helped to consolidate a new unitary ruling class in place of those separate and specific landed establishments that had characterised England, Scotland, Wales and Ireland in the Tudor and Stuart eras. And this change was recognised at the time and in the most explicit of ways. Before 1770, most reference books on the peerage printed in Britain had either been about England and Wales, or Scotland, or Ireland: separate books for nobilities that were still substantially separate in fact. But from 1770 to 1830, fifty-five of the seventy-five guides to the nobility that were published – and it is revealing that there were so many – treated the peerage of the United Kingdom as a single unit.[33] This was what *Collins's Peerage*, did for instance, which came out augmented in 1812 in nine volumes, edited by Sir Samuel Egerton Bridges. So did John Stockdale's *Peerage of the United Kingdom* in 1808. More lastingly, John Debrett produced the first edition of his *Peerage of England, Scotland and Ireland* in 1802, as yet another explicitly unitary reference book, in which peers were arranged in alphabetical order, irrespective of which country's nobility they belonged to. And when John Burke decided to catalogue the leading commoners in the 1830s, he, too, took it for granted that the arena in question was Great Britain and Ireland, not England alone.

How far was this more integrated ruling class authentically and innovatively British as distinct from merely Anglicised? Some have suggested that the Celtic aristocracies became strangers in their own lands, so much did they succumb to English politics, English manners, English culture and English spouses.[34] To many Scottish, Welsh and above all, Irish tenants and agricultural labourers, this may well have seemed the case. But in the eyes of the patricians themselves, what was happening was far more complex and variegated. Some of them did become so caught up in metropolitan life and values as to regard themselves as honorary Englishmen. But by 'England', they usually meant much more than just one part of the island they inhabited. The term became for them (as it did for Horatio Nelson at Trafalgar) a synonym for Great Britain as a whole and very often for its empire as well. High political language reflects this very clearly:

> We commonly when speaking of British subjects call them English, be they English, Scotch, or Irish; he, therefore, I hope, will never be offended with the word English being applied in future to express any of His Majesty's subjects, or suppose it can be meant as an allusion to any particular part of the United Kingdom.[35]

These words, addressed to the House of Commons in 1805, were not those of some pompous English representative. They were spoken by David Scott, a Forfar man who sat for a Perthshire constituency. In the same way, Lord Palmerston, an Anglo-Irishman who became Prime Minister in 1855, always called himself English, and could never understand why – when he paid political visits to Scotland – the people there were not willing to be called English also.[36] 'England', for men like these, was an all-inclusive term and not an expression of a narrow attachment at all.

For the majority of Welsh, Scottish and Anglo-Irish patricians, however, greater integration with their English equivalents meant only that dual nationality became a highly profitable reality. They could partake of London's bounty to an unprecedented extent, while still retaining considerable autonomy in their own countries. Take the case of George Gordon, 4th earl of Aberdeen, for example, who would be educated at Harrow and at Cambridge University, would go on to be launched into Westminster politics as the ward of William Pitt the Younger and would see his brothers and sisters comfortably ensconced in high-ranking positions in the army, diplomatic service and royal court, before going on himself to be Prime Minister in 1852. Yet, Muriel Chamberlain remarks, 'nothing brought Aberdeen to his feet quicker than what he saw as an attack upon the Scottish legal system, marriage laws or banking system'. He knew what was still distinctive about his own homeland, and despised any 'English interference in Scottish affairs'.[37] For him, there was no conflict at all between working as a British politican in London, and being assertively Scottish. Many others took a similar view. The same Lord Seaforth who gentrified Brahan Castle and relished the London season also made a scholarly study of the Gaelic language and was a fervent patron of Sir Walter Scott.[38] Even the exquisite Sir Watkin Williams Wynn, 5th Bt., devoted protégé of the Grenvilles though he was, persistently refused London's offer of a peerage and took pleasure instead in being called 'Prince *in* Wales'.[39] Human beings are many-layered creatures, and do not succumb to the hegemony of others as easily as historians and politicians sometimes imply. Those Welsh, Scottish and Anglo-Irish individuals who became part of the British Establishment in this period did not in the main sell out in the sense of becoming Anglicised look-alikes. Instead, they became British in a new and intensely profitable fashion, while remaining in their own minds and behaviour Welsh, or Scottish, or Irish as well.

Far more striking than Celtic subservience, in fact, was the degree to which English patricians in this period were prepared to concede a substantial quota of employments and patronage to their Welsh, or Scottish, or Anglo-Irish counterparts. Prejudice persisted on all sides, of course. Sydney Smith, fashionable clergyman and wit, gibed how an English-dominated House of Commons still disliked the invasion of 'young men of conseederable taalents from the North', with their unsettling brogues and still more unsettling ambition.[40] But from now on, in Parliament and the cabinet, as in the legal profession, in the diplomatic service, in the foreign office, in the military and especially in the colonial service, bright, privileged and greedy Englishmen took it for granted that they would have to co-operate and compete with their equivalents in the Celtic fringe, so far had the assumptions of public life altered since the Earl of Bute's premiership. The point was hammered home provocatively by John Hay Beith in an essay published during the First World War called *The Oppressed English*:

> Today a Scot is leading the British army in France [Field Marshall Douglas Haig], another is commanding the British grand fleet at sea [Admiral David Beatty], while a third directs the Imperial General Staff at home [Sir William Robertson]. The Lord Chancellor is a Scot [Viscount Finlay]; so are the Chancellor of the Exchequer and the Foreign Secretary [Bonar Law and Arthur Balfour]. The Prime Minister is a Welshman [David Lloyd

> George], and the First Lord of the Admiralty is an Irishman [Lord Carson]. Yet no one has ever brought in a bill to give home rule to England![41]

Tellingly, this was not a belated outburst of frustrated English xenophobia. It was a spoof. Beith was a professional humourist and, as his name suggests, a man of Scottish descent. Yet beneath his schoolboy satire lay the explanation of why, finally, the rivalries and prejudices between the different élites of the British Isles had to some degree been adjusted and resolved in the last third of the eighteenth century. The massive wars and empire-building of that period not only compelled the landed classes to act together for reasons of self-interest, but also brought them into unprecedented contact with men and women who were unquestionably alien. Fighting Americans in the Thirteen Colonies, or the French in Europe and Asia, or subduing the luckless inhabitants of India, Africa, Australia and the West Indies made it very much easier for men who were English, or Welsh, or Scottish, or Anglo-Irish to perceive what they had in common. If the inhabitants of the United Kingdom are now more conscious of their internal divisions, this conversely is part of the price they pay for peace and the end of world-power status. They are no longer under the same obligation to unite against a hostile Other, against the outside.

THE CULTURAL RECONSTRUCTION OF AN ÉLITE

The last quarter of the eighteenth century and the first quarter of the nineteenth century witnessed, then, the emergence of a genuinely British ruling group. Nobles and notables closed ranks and became more homogeneous in terms of wealth, marriage patterns, lifestyles and ambition, thereby rendering themselves more secure in the face of extreme pressure from without. But by itself, this process was not enough to repel accusations that those who dominated Britain were a separate and malign interest in the nation. Greater integration into metropolitan society and politics could actually make the Celtic aristocracies appear even more divorced from the majority of the Welsh, Irish and Scots than before, just as its increasing opulence widened still further the gulf that separated the English landed class from lesser mortals. Here, then, was an obvious dilemma. How was consolidation as a caste to be combined with demonstration of broad patriotic utility? How, crudely, could the distinctive wealth, status and power of the new British ruling class be packaged and presented so as to seem beneficent rather than burdensome, a national asset rather than an alien growth?

This dilemma was made more acute by the fact that the cultural practices of the patrician and fashionable classes were in some respects ostentatiously unBritish. True, they differed from many other European élites in not favouring French as their first language. But it was still a prerequisite for entry into high society or high office. When the American ambassador, Richard Rush, went to his first official dinner party at Lord Castlereagh's London town house in 1818, for example, he was astonished to find that 'the conversation was nearly all in French':

> This was not only the case when the English addressed the foreigners, but in speaking to each other . . . Here, at the house of an English minister of state, French literature, the French language, French topics were all about me; I add, French entrées, French wines![42]

And had he been in London high society fifty years before, Rush might well have had to add French fashions as well. Up to the American Revolution and even beyond, élite male costume for attendance at court was the *habit à la française*, an 'elaborate and colourful silk, satin, or velvet coat and waistcoat, with lace collar and cuffs', as Philip Mansel describes it.[43] The equivalent female costume was the *robe à la française*, a lavish petticoat stretched out on each side by paniers – side hoops – with a matching open dress worn on top, ruthlessly boned and corseted above the waist so that the breasts were pressed upwards and half-exposed. Variations on these costumes could be seen in every European capital, and in Philadelphia, Boston, New York, and Madras and Calcutta as well. But in all cases the original was the same: the court dress of Louis XIV's Versailles.

France was not the only foreign state that British magnificos bought or borrowed from. Presbyterian landowners from Scotland often sent their heirs to the universities of Utrecht or Leiden. A progress through some of the German states was sometimes included in the itinerary of the Grand Tour out of an interest in things military or musical, or simply out of the pragmatic consideration that the ruling dynasty came from the electorate of Hanover.[44] But it was southern Europe that exerted the most powerful attraction. In the 1700s, even more than after, rich, hedonistic and/or cultivated Britons cherished Italy, and particularly Italian art. Fifty per cent of the paintings sold in London auctions rooms for more than £40 between 1711 and 1760 – that is, at a price that only the rich and the titled were likely to afford –

were by Italian masters.[45] And one of the attractions of including Venice, or Florence, or Rome in the Grand Tour was to see the art in those cities and preferably to buy some of it.

In the eyes of the patricians themselves, none of this behaviour necessarily detracted from conventional patriotism. They rarely travelled in or purchased from foreign states out of any strong sense of identification with *their* culture or politics, so much as out of a desire to assert and confirm the prejudices and position that they themselves already held. Of course, there were always a few aesthetes like Lord Chesterfield who genuinely prided themselves on being citizens of the world, but in the main an appearance of cosmopolitanism was valued, as it still is today, because of what it signified: leisure, education and wealth. French fashions appealed, for instance, primarily because their elegance, cost and complete impracticality advertised the gentle status of the wearer. Dressed in this manner, women declared themselves to be artificial and mannered creatures of the flesh who scarcely needed even to move; while men became peacocks who manifestly did not need to work. This was why Laurence Shirley, 4th Earl Ferrers, was so careful to wear an *habit à la française*, made of white silk and ornamented with silver embroidery, when he was hanged for the murder of his steward in 1760.[46] At the very time that the strange democracy of the English law was compelling him to die like a common felon, his 'foreign' clothes reaffirmed his quite uncommon rank. By the same token, Dutch and Italian old masters, like Gobelin and Beauvais tapestries, or illuminated manuscripts, or Greek vases, were sought after because they were blue-chip art, rare commodities that could be displayed as evidence of one's educated taste and of the depth of one's pocket.

A selective aping and acquiring of what was foreign, then, was one of the ways in which Britain's élite proclaimed its social, cultural and economic superiority at home. But by the last quarter of the eighteenth century, this strategy was coming to be seen as decidedly imprudent. As we have already seen, newspapers, magazines, novels and cartoons had long been indicting patrician cosmopolitanism as an expensive, degenerate and suspect failure of home-grown Protestant plainness.[47] Now that a more profound alienation from the élite had emerged, these stock accusations of cultural treason appeared much more ominous than before. At the same time, the opportunities for admiring contact with the rest of Europe were being brutally curtailed. The free movement of men and manufactures between Great Britain and the Continent was disrupted by the Franco-American agreement in 1778 and suspended for more than two decades by the wars with Revolutionary and Napoleonic France. By the time of Waterloo, a generation of patrician Britons had grown up for whom Continental Europe was more a cockpit for battle, and a landscape of revolutionary subversion, than a fashionable playground and cultural shrine. Out of necessity, therefore, as well as for reasons of prudence and patriotic choice, members of the ruling order were encouraged to seek out new forms of cultural expression that were unquestionably British. They remained as concerned as ever to stress what distinguished them from their lesser countrymen, but in ways now that were indigenous to themselves, not borrowed from abroad.

'My education resembled that of most young men of my rank . . . I went through Eton and Oxford': Lord Holland's casual remark at the start of his memoirs points us to one of the most important sources of this new cultural identity.[48] In the early 1700s, it had been common for young patrician males to be educated at home by private tutors, and common, too, for them to bypass the universities. In 1701, less than 35 per cent of English peers attended Oxford or Cambridge; the proportion of Scottish, Welsh or Irish peers who did so was smaller still.[49] But as the century progressed, all this changed. By the time Holland came to write – around 1800 – over 70 per cent of all English peers received their education at just four public schools, Eton, Westminster, Winchester and Harrow. And in the first half of the nineteenth century, sons of the peerage and the landed gentry together made up 50 per cent of the pupils of all the major public schools.[50] For boys from this social background, education now almost invariably meant absorption into institutions catering to Great Britain as a whole, not attendance at purely local academies. Removed from the private, introspective worlds of home and rural estate, they were brought into protracted contact with their social peers, were exposed to a uniform set of ideas and learnt how to speak the English language in a distinctive and characteristic way. This was increasingly the case after school as well. By 1799, over 60 per cent of English peers spent some years at a university; by 1815, a similar proportion of English, Welsh, Scottish and Irish MPs did so too.[51]

How did the emergence of a more uniform patrician education shape attitudes to the British nation? As yet, little work has been done on the ideology as distinct from the sociology of public schools and universities in this period, but what we do know is suggestive. Patriotic duty was stressed in practical ways, as when public-school masters encouraged boys to participate in national subscriptions and to celebrate British military and naval victories. And patriotism of a kind was embedded in the classical curriculum. The emphasis on Greek and Roman authors and ancient history meant a constant diet of stories of war, empire, bravery and sacrifice for the state. School and university prize poems and essays from this period creak under the weight of such themes, as well as exuding a lush appreciation of masculine heroism: the

> . . . true proportions of resistless might;
> Heroic mien, and lineaments, and height:
> The brow that looks security – the soul
> That speaks from limbs of adamant control.
> (Oxford University prize poem, 1817)[52]

In the early nineteenth century, the Chancellor's English prize at Oxford went to essays on 'A Sense of Honour' (1805), 'Posthumous Fame' (1806), 'The Love of our Country' (1809) and 'Funeral and Sepulchral Honours' (1811).[53]

Classical literature was doubly congenial because the kind of patriotic achievement it celebrated was a highly specific one. The heroes of Homer, Cicero and Plutarch were emphatically men of rank and title. As such, they reminded Britain's élite of its duty to serve and fight, but in addition, affirmed its superior qualifications to do both.[54] And the classics had a further practical advantage. The societies they celebrated were emphatically dead. Consequently, they could inspire without being in any way threatening. Indeed, familiarity with the recorded glories of ancient empires could throw into even greater relief the superior virtue and power of imperial Britain. Rome, a Christ Church undergraduate versified in 1810, had spent its heroism on 'pomps of death, and theatres of blood'; but British power was quite different. It was constructive. It was Christian. It was free. Most of all – it was contemporary. William Cowper, whose verse translations of the *Iliad* and the *Odyssey* (1791) were swiftly absorbed into the curriculum of both Oxbridge and the Scottish universities, was entirely typical in being swept by his love for the classics into unabashed celebration of his native land. 'Empire is on us bestow'd', crows Boadicea to the Romans in one of his poems, 'Shame and ruin wait for you'.[55]

It was patrician patriotism *in the British present* that the public schools and universities sought to inculcate, not just an academic interest in the antique past. Dr Barnard, headmaster and subsequently Provost of Eton from 1754 to 1781, invented the tradition of having the most distinguished sixth formers – which in practice meant young men of rank intent on political careers – donate portraits to the school. This supplied a fillip to their own ambition, as well as an incentive to younger Etonians who spent their schooldays under the painted gaze of arrogantly superior alumni like Charles James Fox, Samuel Whitbread, the future Earl

31. Eton leaving portrait of Charles Grey by George Romney, *c.*1788.

Grey and the Hon. Richard Wellesley, future Governor General of India.[56] Barnard also reorganised that peculiar Etonian ritual, the Montem, converting it into a triennial ceremony in which the senior scholars were allotted military titles (captain, marshal, ensign and serjeant-major) and wore junior versions of British military uniforms. Utterly transformed from its origins as a violent teenage revel, a charivari for nobs, the Montem became a patriotic pageant delighting proud parents and important visitors like George III or the Duke of Wellington.[57] And when Etonians, and Harrovians, and Wykehamists went up to Oxbridge, or Edinburgh, or Glasgow, or even Trinity College, Dublin, they soon found themselves, particularly if they were bright, competing to produce Greek and Latin verses or English essays on British and imperial themes. In 1804, for example, the Vice-President of Fort William College in Bengal founded an annual prize at Cambridge University for the best essay on British India. Undergraduates were invited to discuss 'the best means of civilising the subjects of the British empire in those parts of India' controlled by the East India Company, or 'The

Probable Design of the Divine Providence in subjecting so large a portion of Asia to the British dominion'.[58]

Yet for many young men, the ideas that the public schools and universities increasingly strove to inculcate must have been less important than the male bonding and physical toughness they necessarily engendered. As Lord William Russell argued, a public school would ideally fit 'a boy to be a man . . . to be able to contend with the difficulties of life – to attach friends to him – to take part in public affairs'.[59] Separated for long periods of time from their families, plunged into an almost exclusively masculine world, boys could become acutely conscious of their membership of a caste and prepared for future absences from home on military or colonial service. This cult of juvenile fortitude was important for political as well as patriotic reasons. Paine's *Rights of Man* (1791–2) had attacked Britain's ruling class in many ways, but one of his cruellest, cleverest insults was to dismiss its members as 'drones', as a 'seraglio of males'. To an élite wanting to claim that its status was founded on service to the nation, this was the most offensive slur possible. Some of the emphasis in public-school and university language at this time on physical toughness, on vigour and virility should almost certainly be understood as a conscious attempt to counteract such a negative image. During the invasion crisis of 1803, the London *Times* specifically cited the calibre of élite education as a proof that Paine was wrong:

> Our young nobility and gentry are not brought up in the solitary confinement of a seraglio, but in the hardy discipline of a public school; and in manly sports and exercises from their earliest years.[60]

Cambridge University's Regius Professor of Modern History employed very similar language and reasoning when he delivered a public ode at the installation of a new Chancellor in 1811. Britain's greatness and survival, he versified, came from its law, its piety, its valour, its freedom and, of course, from God. But before anything else, it came 'From hardy sports, from manly schools'.[61] Great Britain was not just another and a greater Rome, it was also a latter-day Sparta. Its patrician youths were warriors not wimps.

A very similar message was being relayed at the same time on the hunting field. For much of the eighteenth century, fox-hunting had been the casual and disorganised pursuit of backwoods squires and farmers, emphatically less prestigious than stag-hunting and initially not much more common at patrician level than hare-coursing. But from the 1750s, when a Leicestershire country gentleman called Hugo Meynell began to develop a new and faster breed of foxhound, the range and reputation of the sport began to rise. As F.M.L. Thompson writes:

> It was in the later eighteenth century, and above all in the first third of the nineteenth century, that the hunting countryside was quartered out between regular hunts, their 'countries' or territories receiving defined and well understood boundaries, and their meets becoming sufficiently ordered and controlled to provide for thorough hunting of the whole of their country.[62]

By the 1830s, there were over ninety different hunts scattered throughout Great Britain, with still more based in Ireland. The very scenery of Great Britain was now reorganised and re-envisioned in keeping with the leisure priorities of men of land and substance. Hedges were torn down, ditches filled, gates and bridges built, tenants' privacy invaded, all in pursuit of the unfortunate, uneatable fox.

And the inedibility of the quarry was, of course, the great give-away. Here was one of those rare sports where *taking part* really was far more important than winning. Fox-hunting attracted a broad spectrum of rural society, but the main expense of breeding and feeding hounds and hunters fell to the great landowners, who thereby reaffirmed their prominence in the local community. They reaffirmed much more as well. Fox-hunting, in contrast with stag-

32. Benjamin Marshall, *George, 5th Duke of Gordon on 'Tiny'*, *c.*1806–7. Complete with fox-hounds.

hunting or hare-coursing, was a peculiarly British sport. It was fast, physically dangerous, splendid to watch, carried out in a dashing, close-to-the-body costume that quite obviously mimicked military uniform, and at this stage was confined almost exclusively to men. In short, the invention of fox-hunting can be seen, as it was seen at the time, as another expression of the new patriotic, patrician machismo: 'The same men who will ride straight across a county at a gallop, taking their fences generally as they come', reasoned Lord Seaton, a veteran of Waterloo, '. . . will be likely to do anything or everything which may be required of them in action, be it the leading a charge of cavalry, the mounting a rampart or breach, or . . . storming a battery.'[63] The only difference was that the Frenchman stood in for the fox.

Hunting enabled a gentleman to flaunt his leisure without seeming in the process to be idle or effete. It distinguished him from the poor and the labouring, the urban and the mercantile, the sedentary and the professional, without in any way compromising his pretensions to patriotism. Foxes were vermin. By hunting them to the death – and thereby safeguarding the smallholder's chickens or lambs – élite males proclaimed their social utility, while at the same time enjoying themselves enormously. And because of its healthy, outdoor quality, fox-hunting could be presented as an aid to manly readiness and pluck. 'I need not enlarge', wrote one peer's son in 1802, 'upon the political advantages of encouraging a sport which propagates a fine breed of horses, and prevents our young men from growing quite effeminate in Bond Street.' Fox-hunting, wrote the sport's most celebrated journalist, 'Nimrod', was 'one of the lion supporters of the Crown', Britishness, virility and rank in action.[64]

Here, then, was an example of a far more conscious and aggressive effort on the part of the landed élite to assert its status as arbiter and guardian of the national culture. I am not suggesting, of course, that such developments resulted in any simple or direct way from the élite's perception of the challenges confronting it. Often, it was a case of pre-existing trends and practices being seized upon and interpreted in a new way. Thus the tendency for male and female members of the élite to practise internal tourism rather than foreign travel began to be noticeable as early as the 1760s, and was a consequence initially of major war shutting off access to the Continent. One of the pioneers of the trend was Sir Watkin Williams Wynn, 4th Bt. In 1771, he embarked on a two-week tour of North Wales, together with nine servants and the fledgling artist Paul Sandby, whom he hired to record the more picturesque views.[65] As internal tourism developed, others ventured much further than this. Sir George Beaumont, for instance, an Essex baronet and art collector, turned to regular sketching tours in the Lake District and Wales when war cut him off from his beloved Italy. Still other patricians travelled to collect rare minerals, to botanise, to view or to kill. By the early 1800s, roads and sporting guns were sufficiently advanced to make shooting trips in the bleakest and dampest regions of the Scottish Highlands practical and attractive. Like several other Highland landlords, the Duke of Gordon took to advertising the hunting and fishing opportunities on his estates in *The Times*, catering to more well-heeled and bloodthirsty tourists by renting out special hunting lodges at £70 a time.[66]

Exploring the more isolated regions of Great Britain at this time had something of the same cachet as Continental travel, and was far more reassuring. In contrast with the more well-established watering places and spas which had long been taken up by the bourgeoisie, North Wales, the Lake District and the Highlands were still relatively expensive to get to and consequently, much more select. Far less industrialised and urbanised than South Wales, Lowland Scotland or England, their people were less likely to be infected with radical ideas, and far more willing, perhaps, to know their place and keep to it. Visiting these regions, patrician tourists enjoyed the comforting illusion that they had travelled back in time, to when their world was still safe. Moreover, to appreciate 'the remotest parts of Britain', as the guidebooks called them, in the proper manner, as to appreciate Rome, or Florence, or Paris, one needed to have acquired a fashionable, aesthetic education: a knowledge of Edmund Burke's theory of the sublime, a properly developed understanding of the picturesque and the ability to read key texts like William Gilpin's *Observations on the River Wye* (1782) which was littered with untranslated Latin quotations and allusions to Old Masters such as Claude Lorraine and Salvator Rosa.[67]

Just like the Grand Tour, therefore, informed internal tourism came to be a way of proclaiming who one was, a point made with characteristic precision by Jane Austen in *Northanger Abbey* (1798–1803). At one point, its *ingénue* heroine, Catherine Morland, is ridiculed for her naïvely lyrical appreciation of the Bath landscape by her admirer Henry Tilney and his sister, Eleanor:

> In the present instance, she confessed and lamented her want of knowledge, declared that she would give any thing in the world to be able to draw; and a lecture on the picturesque immediately followed, in which his instructions were so clear that she soon began to see beauty in every thing admired by him, and her

> attention was so earnest, that he became perfectly satisfied of her having a great deal of natural taste. He talked of fore-grounds, distances, and second distances – side-screens and perspectives – lights and shades; and Catherine was so hopeful a scholar, that when they gained the top of Beechen cliff, she voluntarily rejected the whole city of Bath, as unworthy to make part of a landscape.[68]

As always in her novels, Austen lets us know exactly how much each of these characters is worth in the social and money stakes. Henry is the Oxford-educated son of an army general with a fortune and a country estate; his sister is the future wife of a viscount. Superior social status and education have allowed them to appropriate the scenery of their own land: to see and describe it ('fore-grounds', 'distances', 'second distances', 'side-screens' etc.) in ways that Catherine, who is only the daughter of a modest country clergyman, simply cannot hope to do.

This insistence on the primacy of the polite vision was increasingly extended to the fine arts as well. Of course, the aristocracy and the very rich had long dominated the upper echelons of the art market, but now they exercised and rationalised this supremacy in a rather different way. For much of the eighteenth century, titled British patrons, and particularly English patrons, had laid themselves open to the accusation that they nourished foreign artists and virtually ignored their own. They might turn to a William Aikman, or a William Hogarth, or a Thomas Hudson, and later to a Reynolds or a Gainsborough, to record themselves, their posterity, their dogs, their horses and their wives. But when they wanted to spend big money on fine art, it was to the Continent they looked, and most especially to Old Masters who were dead, uncontroversial and a sound investment. Demands that British art should be taken seriously, and actively fostered as a matter of national interest, had been left to the artists themselves and to a succession of bourgeois activists, men like John Wilkes, for example, who pleaded in Parliament for a national gallery, or John Boydell, the London alderman who ruined himself commissioning British artists to paint scenes from Shakespeare's plays.[69]

The men who governed the British state were conspicuously slow in lending their support to these cultural initiatives. The French established a national gallery in 1793; the Swedish followed suit a year later. The Rijksmuseum was founded in 1808 and the Museo del Prado in 1819. But Parliament made provision for the National Gallery in London only in 1824, and even then, no adequate building was made available for it until the late 1830s.

'That nation', a French art theorist had jeered during the Revolutionary wars, 'has no centralised, dominant collection, despite all the acquisitions made by its private citizens who have *naturally* retained them for their private enjoyment.'[70] And although this was republican venom, he had a point. As long as they were at war with the armies and ideas of the French Revolution, the majority of British patricians were disinclined to violate the sanctity and splendour of private property, and loan or donate art from their own country-house collections to set up a national gallery. To do so would be expensive, and might even appear subversive.

Yet if art in Britain was not to be made a state concern, it was still desirable that it should be seen now to flourish under patrician auspices. And increasingly it was. Gentleman collectors such as Sir George Beaumont, Sir John Fleming Leicester, Samuel Whitbread II (Lord Grey's brother-in-law) and the novelist Sir Walter Scott acquired and commissioned native art with a fervour, and at a price, that would have seemed incomprehensible to earlier generations.[71] So, on a much grander scale, did George O'Brien Wyndham, 3rd Earl of Egremont. His father, the 2nd Earl, had also been a compulsive collector, but he had confined his purchases almost entirely to Italian masters and antique marbles. The new Egremont, by contrast, bought British. Not just Old Masters like Gainsborough and Reynolds, but paintings by new boys like John Constable, William Blake, David Wilkie and Benjamin Haydon, as well as neo-classical sculptures from John Flaxman and Charles Felix Rossi. Then there was Turner. Egremont purchased no fewer than twenty of his paintings, and from 1827 to his death ten years later, regularly invited the artist to his country house, Petworth, letting him immortalise its lakes, gardens and sun-drenched rooms.[72]

Interior at Petworth, which glows today from the walls of the Tate Gallery in London, is one of the most stunning celebrations of patrician generosity ever painted, but it was still an exception to the general rule of art patronage in early nineteenth-century Britain. Most aristocrats continued to concentrate on Continental art and were even more successful than before in acquiring it now that the French Revolution had brought so many royalist collections onto the market. Far more than before, however, care was taken to give these old collecting habits a new and more acceptable twist of meaning. Increasingly, the art purchases of the patrician order were presented as a public benefit, as an asset to the nation. One way in which this was accomplished was by opening up art collections in country houses to acceptable members of the public on a far more generous scale than before.[73] More affluent patricians sometimes founded their own private galleries in London as well, which were then opened selectively to visitors. In 1803, for example, the Duke of Bridgwater, leader of the syndicate of English peers that purchased the fabulous Orléans collection of Old Masters from France for £43,000, died and left his share to the Marquess of Stafford. He promptly opened up a gallery at Cleveland House in London to exhibit the paintings, grandly staffed by twelve servants whose liveries had cost forty guineas apiece. Other peers commissioned guidebooks to their art collections and then allowed them to be published. This was what the 2nd Earl Grosvenor did after he had spent £10,000 on four canvases by Rubens, and aquired Reynolds's *Mrs Siddons as the Tragic Muse* and Gainsborough's *Blue Boy* for patriotic good measure.[74]

But perhaps the most effective means by which patrician art collectors were able to make their private possessions appear a public good was through the British Institution for Promoting the Fine Arts in the United Kingdom, established in Pall Mall, London, in May 1805.[75] This was both a highly exclusive and a quasi-official venture. George III was asked to approve its foundation. The Prince of Wales acted as its Honorary President. Particularly rich subscribers were allowed to purchase hereditary governorships; and its most active supporters included the Earl of Dartmouth, Viscount Lowther, the Marquess of Stafford and Sir Charles Long, all staunch government supporters. Its avowed aim and much of its work was entirely benevolent. It provided a permanent gallery where British artists could exhibit their work, and it also displayed Old Masters borrowed from country-house collections for the edification of the general public and home-grown, fledgling artists alike. Yet as critics argued at the time, there was undoubtedly a hidden agenda as well. The British Institution allowed patricians to influence the development of British art without conceding a national gallery, which might seem to challenge the principle of private ownership. By lending some of his Old Masters to the Institution, a gentleman collector could flaunt his wealth and culture, and seem a patriot into the bargain, without needing himself to purchase any British art at all.

In all of these ways, the British Institution helped to forge a set of cultural assumptions that remain enormously influential today: namely, the quite extraordinary idea that even if an art object comes from abroad, and even if it remains securely in private ownership, as long as it resides in a country house it must somehow belong to the nation and enhance it. As early as 1812, Sir Egerton Brydges was able to make this argument in his edition of *Collins's Peerage*:

> The Stafford, Carlisle, and Grosvenor collections of pictures; the Spencer, Marlborough, Devonshire, Bridgwater, and Pembroke libraries are *national* treasures, becoming a people who are contending for the empire of the world.[76]

In virtually every Continental state at this time, aristocracies had to live with the risk that their property might be pillaged or confiscated. Only in Great Britain did it prove possible to float the idea that aristocratic property was in some magical and strictly intangible way *the people's property also*. The fact that hundreds of thousands of men and women today are willing to accept that privately owned country houses and their contents are part of Britain's *national* heritage is one more proof of how successfully the British élite reconstructed its cultural image in an age of revolutions.

HEROES OF THEIR OWN EPIC

In 1818, an impressionable foreign observer attending his first royal levee at the court of St James saw the upper echelons of the British élite as they themselves liked to be seen:

> Men of genius and science were there. The nobility were numerous; so were the military. There were from forty to fifty generals; perhaps as many admirals . . . 'That's General Walker', I was told, 'pierced with bayonets, leading on the assault at Badajos'. And he, close by, tall but limping? 'Colonel Ponsonby, he was left for dead at Waterloo . . .' Then came one of like port, but deprived of a leg, slowly moving, and the whisper went, 'That's Lord Anglesea'. A fourth had been wounded at Seringapatam; a fifth at Talavera; some had suffered in Egypt; some in America. There were those who had received scars on the deck with Nelson; others who carried them from the days of Howe. One, yes one, had fought at Saratoga . . . It was so that my inquiries were answered. All had 'done their duty', this was the favourite praise bestowed.[77]

All élites buttress their rule with theatre, and the men who had dominated Great Britain in the eighteenth century had been as resourceful as any in this respect, employing the robes and rituals of the law to underline their powers to punish and pardon, and their massive country houses to advertise their individual wealth and local clout. But what the American ambassador witnessed on this occasion was theatre on a much grander scale, in which men of rank mingled with men of action, and blue-blooded peers acquired lustre from association with red-blooded heroism: a splendid tableau of immaculately cut uniforms, glorious wounds, heroic mutilations, with even a sprinkling of intellectual achievement and meritocracy thrown in for good measure. As he was explicitly told, the moral such displays were intended to convey was that the British élite was a service élite. Under enormous political, military and social pressures, its members needed more than ever to convince themselves as well as others that they had indeed done their duty to Great Britain, and done it well.

Recognising that an ostentatious cult of heroism and state service served an important propaganda function for the British élite does not mean, of course, that we should dismiss it as artificial or insincere. All aristocracies have a strong military tradition, and for many British patricians the protracted warfare of this period was a godsend. It gave them a job and, more important, a purpose, an opportunity to carry out what they had been trained to do since childhood: ride horses, fire guns, exercise their undoubted physical courage and tell other people what to do. Even more parvenu members of the élite were likely, as we have seen, to have been exposed to an aggressively patriotic curriculum at public school or in the universities. And almost all of them were influenced by an exhilarating sense of expanding British power in the world, a particular kind of arrogance of place which was badly dented but not long depressed by defeat in America. One sees this arrogance, a pride in nation as well as a pride in blood, reflected very clearly in the portraits of the time. Sir Joshua Reynolds made his fortune by capturing and even accentuating it, borrowing the pose inspired by the classical statue *Apollo Belvedere* and using it for a succession of portraits of high-ranking British males. But, even more than Reynolds, it was the American artist, Benjamin West, who encouraged prominent Britons to see themselves as heroes of a national and imperial epic.

His painting *The Death of General Wolfe*, first exhibited to the public at the Royal Academy in 1771, was in content a splendid fraud.[78] Wolfe had been a young, neurotic, highly controversial and by no means well-born commander-in-chief of the British forces in Canada. He had died taking Quebec in 1759 in the usual degree of squalor and agony. None of the officers West painted around his deathbed had actually been there at the time. Nor had the pensive Indian warrior, shown watching how the great white man died, been there, since men like him had fought on the other side. And in reality, there had been no furled Union Jack raised above the dying hero like a cross denuded of its victim. Only in one crucial and innovative respect was the painting authentic.

33. Benjamin West, *The Death of General Wolfe*, 1770.

Instead of clothing his subjects in timeless togas or chivalric armour, West showed them wearing contemporary British military uniform. He took classical and Biblical poses of sacrifice and heroism and brought them into the British here and now. And this was why the painting caused a sensation, why it was made into a best-selling print, why George III ordered a copy, and why Lord Robert Grosvenor paid £400 – a remarkably large sum then – for the original.[79]

The Death of Wolfe started a vogue for paintings of members of the British officer class defying the world, or directing it, or dying in battle at the moment of victory. West's countryman John Singleton Copley would repeat almost all of the master's tricks in his version of the death of Major Peirson, killed as he recaptured the town of St Helier, Jersey, from an invading French army in 1781. Once again, a single moment and incident of warfare was frozen in time. Once again, a notably young officer was shown expiring dramatically under the Union flag, duty triumphantly done. And, once again, the artist provided marginal figures to draw out the meaning of the central event and lend it epic stature: the fleeing women and children whom Peirson's exploits are about to rescue; the private soldier, a drummer on this occasion, distracted from his own mortal wound by grief for his lost leader; and, most vivid of all, Peirson's black servant – the only black in British military service, as far as I know, to be commemorated in heroic fashion in eighteenth-century art – killing the Frenchman who had fired the fatal bullet. Johann Zoffany would produce paintings broadly similar in composition to celebrate the exploits of British army officers in India; so would David Wilkie, particularly to glorify his fellow Scots. But the genre reached the zenith of its effectiveness in Britain with Arthur William Devis's canvas of the death of Admiral Horatio Nelson at Trafalgar in 1805.

In this, as in so many of the other paintings, it was death at the moment of victory and victory in death that was caught and commemorated. But this time there was no Union Jack suspended over the dying hero, only the great wooden beams of the Victory's blood-stained lower decks, rising like a crucifix above him. And Nelson was shown quite literally divested of his British uniform. Instead, Devis very deliberately painted him draped in white, haloed by the ship's lantern, surrounded by his disciples of the sea, already canonised as the redeemer of his country, the navy's patron saint.

Because these paintings are at once too narrative and too unabashedly chauvinistic for modern taste, we tend to forget the sheer scale of their contemporary impact. Tens, often hundreds of thousands of prints and crude woodcuts based on them were sold over the years. Designs on mass-produced fabrics and ceramics were drawn from them, as were cheap black and white or coloured cut-outs for children and a multiplicity of inn signs.[80] But though the market for patriotic iconography was a broad and deep one by the early 1800s, the polite classes – and most of all, élite males – were probably affected by it to a peculiar degree. It was they, after all, who had the money and freedom to see the original paintings when they were exhibited, and the means to buy them. It was they who had been indoctrinated already with Greek and Roman classics in which heroes sternly sacrificed their lives for the sake of honour and country: *dulce et decorum est pro patria mori*. And it was they who identified most powerfully with images in which high-ranking officers were singled out from the pain, anonymity and predictable slaughter of war by dint of sheer personal distinction. A highly selective cult of heroism, never focussing on ordinary soldiers or seamen but only on those commanding them, was deeply congenial to men intensely proud of their personal status and honour. One

34. John Singleton Copley, *The Death of Major Peirson, 6 January 1781*, 1783.

35. Arthur William Devis, *Death of Nelson*, *c.*1805.

very public aspect of it was Parliament's decision in the early 1790s to employ state revenue to place statues of military and naval officer heroes in St Paul's cathedral in London – something which had never been done before.[81]

But the new cult of élite heroism also shaped individual conduct. Some men became so caught up and entranced by it that the reality of their lives, and even more of their deaths, became inextricably mixed with the highly coloured images of heroism available in Plutarch and Homer, or in the art of West, or Copley, or Devis. It is, I suppose, just possible that the waiter who brought along William Pitt the Younger's last meal was correct, and that he really did expire on 23 January 1806 with the line: 'I could just do with one of Bellamy's meat pies.' But it seems far more probable that the pious version of his deathbed is the true one, and that this strange, intensely priggish man who read the classics every moment he could spare from public business and alcohol, died with the words: 'Oh, my country! How I love my country!'[82] Just as General Sir John Moore, mortally wounded at the Battle of Coruna in 1809, gasped out at the end: 'I hope the people of England will be satisfied. I hope my country will do me justice.'[83] (Moore, incidentally, was a Scot.) The sentiments were clearly heartfelt, the programming perfect. These men, and many others like them, died as their culture told them to do, and became thereby a vital part of the ideal of patrician valour and self-sacrifice.

Those most susceptible to the ideal were often not so much the great landowners, or peers of the realm equipped with gilt-edged genealogies, but relative newcomers to the élite who had less to lose and more to prove. Horatio Nelson was the son of a Norfolk parson. He had influential relations in high office (had he not done so, he would scarcely have risen so far in the Royal Navy so fast), but he and his immediate family had negligible land and little disposable cash. So pursuing glory was his only sure path to eminence, a realisation that came to him with all the force of a religious conversion. Convalescing from malaria in 1776, he thought he saw a radiant orb before him:

> A sudden glow of patriotism was kindled within me and presented my King and Country as my patron. Well then, I exclaimed, 'I will be a hero, and confiding in Providence I will brave every danger'.[84]

On this blend of euphoric bravery and beguiling egotism, he based his career. 'Before this time tomorrow', he wrote on the day before the Battle of the Nile in 1798, 'I shall have gained a peerage or Westminster Abbey.'[85] He would be famous and a lord, or famous and dead. And in the end, of course, he was all of these things. Making his will in the long hours before Trafalgar, it seemed to him entirely appropriate to bequeath Emma Hamilton to the nation. Serving Great Britain had made him what he was. Was it not logical that after his death, the nation should keep his mistress as well?

Because Nelson was a larger-than-life figure, it is easy to dismiss his profoundly romantic but also self-interested patriotism as something quite exceptional. In its intensity and candour perhaps it was. But Nelson only practised to a remarkable degree what the cult of heroic individualism fostered very broadly among the class he aspired to. His showmanship and sense of audience, too, were entirely typical. Like other members of the British élite at this time, indeed like the members of virtually all of the European élites in the Napoleonic era, Nelson was acutely sensitive to the importance of medals and uniforms, all the outward pomp of state service. Being the man that he was, though, he exploited them more flamboyantly than most. Only five feet two inches tall, prematurely white-haired, with a badly damaged eye, only one arm, and with hardly any of his upper teeth left by the end of his life, he devoted enormous thought to his public and naval image not just because he was vain, but because it was necessary. After the Battle of St Vincent (1797), he made it clear to the authorities that he wanted the Order of the Bath as a reward rather than a baronetcy, since the former carried with it a splendid red ribbon. He got it, of course, and invariably wore it, just as he wore every other gong he received from Britain and its allies, including a jewelled clockwork star from the Sultan of Turkey which rotated when it was wound up.[86]

It was this side of Nelson, the little man in a big uniform, that Gillray satirised so brilliantly in 1798. Nelson: the indisputable, incandescent hero who would be picked off by a French marksman at Trafalgar because he refused to cover up the medals, epaulettes and gold braid which made him so conspicuous. And it was this calculated exhibitionism, this theatre, that embarrassed and appalled many of his more genuinely patrician contemporaries. For it seemed to caricature to a vulgar degree the very style and strategy that they themselves were increasingly adopting. Splendidly, unabashedly and utterly successfully, Nelson did what the majority of the men who dominated Great Britain sought to do more elegantly and discreetly: use patriotic display to impress the public and cement their own authority.

They were helped in this aim by the sheer scale of contemporary warfare which put an unprecedented proportion of them into military uniform. The number of officers in the Royal Navy rose

36. James Gillray's satire on the newly ennobled Nelson, 1798.

from 2,000 in 1792 to 10,000 in 1806, by which time some 40 per cent of them were men from landed backgrounds, a higher proportion than ever before.[87] Men of landed birth were more prominent still in the officer ranks of the British army, particularly right at the top and in the crack regiments. Between 1750 and 1800, 124 peers and sons of peers had served in the Life Guards, the Blues, the First Foot Guards and the Scots Guards. During the next half-century, 228 did so.[88] But it was the explosion of volunteer and militia regiments after 1793, even more than the expansion of the regular forces, that allowed almost every young and middle-aged Briton who exerted influence in the state or in the localities to adopt uniform if he so wished. Of the more than two thousand men who sat as Members of Parliament between 1790 and 1820, almost half served as militia or volunteer officers. A further fifth of all MPs, twice as many as in any pre-1790 Parliament, were officers

37. The importance of uniform: *The Protean Figure and Metamorphic Costumes*. A cut-out doll published in London in 1811 to aid artists called on to paint uniformed clients.

with the regular army; one hundred more were naval officers.[89] The supreme legislative body of Great Britain had not just become a military headquarters conducting a world war for territorial integrity, empire and property. It now looked like a military headquarters as well.

The significance of this change in patrician appearance was a profound one. As far as individuals were concerned, military uniform did what it always does when sufficiently splendid and well cut: enhance the physical impressiveness of the wearer however inadequate he might be in fact. Contemporary guides to

38. The importance of uniform according to a radical card game: *The Habit Makes the Man*, London, early nineteenth century.

39a and b. Robert Dighton, cavalry-officer uniforms, *c.*1805.

'correct' male dress were engagingly candid on this point. In a cavalry officer's uniform, one of them commented,

> an insignificant head is hidden under a martial plumed helmet. The coat, padded well in every direction . . . is rendered small at the back by the use of stays . . . Then, as for bandy-legs, or knock-knees, they are totally unseen in long, stiff, leather boots, that extend up on the thigh, to which two inch heels may be very safely appended, so that with the cuirass and different accoutrement straps, it offers an effectual screen.[90]

Prints and portraits from the Napoleonic era bear this out. Never before or since have British military uniforms been so impractically gorgeous, so brilliant in colour, so richly ornamented or so closely and cunningly tailored. And the more exclusive a regiment an officer belonged to, and the higher his rank, the more dazzling his uniform was likely to be. In every sense he was dressed to kill.

Worn on private as well as on public occasions, in the street or in the ballroom quite as much as on the parade ground or the field of battle, these elaborate and extremely expensive uniforms did far more than cater to an individual's vanity or charisma, however. They served to distinguish members of the British élite from the rest of the population, while at the same time underlining their wearers' patriotic function. Uniforms were the embodiment of authority, but they also denoted service to the nation. This was why so much time and creativity were devoted to the business of designing and multiplying uniform in the wake of the American war. George III prescribed a new form of state dress for general officers in 1786 and a special uniform for field marshals in 1793; while the first regulations for the dress of junior staff officers appear to date from 1799. Naval uniforms received similar attention, the Board of Admiralty issuing new and exhaustive dress regulations whereby 'the distinctions of rank in the service are rendered more clear and becoming'.[91] After peace broke out in 1815 and the volunteer regiments had to be disbanded, the Prince Regent took care to establish new, civil uniforms for all senior court and government officials and for the Lords Lieutenant of counties in England, Scotland, Wales and Ireland.[92]

The revolution in the appearance of the British male élite was not confined to men holding military or official positions. Every European élite had taken note of the sartorial and political disaster represented by the first procession of the Estates General in Paris in 1789, the prelude to the French Revolution. On that occasion, the representatives of the Third Estate, dressed in sombre black, had been cheered; but the traditionally lavish costumes of the nobility and clergy had met with jeers or silent disgust. 'The magic of ostentation', as Jean Starobinski puts it, had 'stopped having an effect on spectators who had learned to add up the cost.'[93] From now on, the *habit à la française*, the wigs, powdered hair, brocades, silks, lace and parrot colours, which had been fashionable from Boston to Berlin, and Moscow to Manchester, was increasingly abandoned in favour of far more subdued and functional male dress. The significant point, however, is that Great Britain seems to have been one of the first European nations in which this shift in style from peacock male to sombre man of action became apparent. As early as the 1780s, even peers of the realm were regularly to be seen attending the House of Lords in a costume that evoked a plain, quasi-military masculinity: a dull-coloured riding-coat, white or cream breeches or pantaloons, and boots.[94] And by the early 1800s, superbly cut but essentially subdued and understated London tailoring had not only become fashionable throughout the western world, but had spawned its own powerful etiquette at home. The apparently unwritten rules that senior civil servants in Britain still abide by today – that only black, grey or navy suits are suitable for London wear, that brown or green are permissable only in the countryside, and that any other colour is simply not acceptable for a gentleman at all – were, in fact, promulgated in a spate of dress-guides issued in the early nineteenth century.[95] However formal the occasion, patrician males now dressed in British fashions – and like men with work to do.

But it was not enough just to look the part. If British patricians were to convince as patriots, cultural change and sartorial change had to be accompanied by a change in élite conduct. In practice, this did not mean ceasing to expect inflated monetary rewards for serving the state, or an end to nepotism or sinecures. In 1809, the House of Commons would establish that well over one million pounds of public money was still being distributed in pensions every year, of which only 8 per cent went to reward conspicuous public service. A year later, it revealed that, despite administrative reform, 250 men and women were still in receipt of sinecures. To this extent, accusations that the British aristocracy and their relations were, in William Cobbett's words, 'a prodigious band of spongers', had some truth to them.[96] More candid patricians admitted as much in their private correspondence. 'Everyone here past five and twenty', wrote Lord Lansdowne, a former Whig Chancellor of the Exchequer, 'knows that public virtue is all a farce and that private ends, not patriotic principles, activate the puppets that dance before our eyes.'[97] Lord William Bentinck, second son of the Duke of Portland, supplied a more subtle and more accurate appraisal of élite motivation and expectations. The true reward of public service, he wrote in 1813, was 'the public respect which you will enjoy if you deserve it . . . this depends wholly . . . upon my own conduct. But the Government can give me what the public cannot, which is income and comfort. Respect is very good for the mind, but not for the body.' In other words, an acute awareness of the importance of being seen to serve the public well was often accompanied by an eagerness to serve oneself as lavishly as possible. Bentinck would prove a highly active, even inspired Governor of Madras (1803–7) and later Governor of Bengal (1828–35). He also took care to accumulate £90,000 in the process.[98]

Office-holders and aristocrats found different ways to compromise between the lures of private enrichment and the heightened demand for public probity, to have their cake and eat it too. Many of them became workaholics to a degree that older generations found positively strange: 'It is the fashion among the young ones', Lord Holland wrote wonderingly in the 1820s, 'to attend to parliamentary business'.[99] For others, religion became the essential spur and rationale of their lives. Lord Kenyon, a Tory High Churchman who used his position as Master of the Rolls to secure two expensive sinecures for his sons, preached high morality in the courtroom and practised active Christian charity outside it. He took a hard line with any patrician duellists and adulterers who came before him, and subscribed in all to a dozen different charitable societies. Behaving in this manner was a form of insurance made doubly necessary by the pressure of events, as he himself told a courtroom the year that the French Revolution broke out:

> Mankind will never forget that governors are not made for the sake of themselves, but are placed in their respective stations to discharge the functions of their office *for the benefit of the public.*[100]

Even less aggressively religious public men acknowledged the vital importance of practising regular church-going and conventional sexual morality. In the early and mid-eighteenth century, it had been possible for high-ranking politicians like Viscount Bolingbroke or Robert Walpole or the Earl of Sandwich to flaunt the fact that they were keeping mistresses and to be blithely unconcerned about newspapers and cartoons publicising it. But by 1800, the fashion among politicians in office at home (out-of-office Whigs and colonial officials were always a different matter) was for ostentatious uxoriousness. Spencer Perceval, Lord Liverpool, George Canning, Lord Sidmouth, Lord Castlereagh and Robert Peel all wallowed in domesticity. As a life-long bachelor, William Pitt the Younger was the great exception to this trend. But he was careful to die a virgin.[101]

This greater emphasis on an impeccable private life – or at least, the appearance of it – was part of a wider idealisation of the statesman. Far from being confined to the military sphere, the cult of heroism was used to embellish the higher echelons of civilian service to the state as well. Pitt, in particular, son of an earl, ostensibly scrupulous, an unabashed professional 'for whom the business of government was a passion and not a refuge', became the talisman for a whole generation of British politicians and an influence on official attitudes and behaviour throughout the nineteenth century.[102] After his death, Pitt clubs sprang up in major towns throughout England, Scotland and Wales, hundreds of their highly prosperous members assembling every year in London to commemorate his birth and legend:

> And shall not his memory to Britons be dear,
> Whose example all nations with envy behold,
> A statesman unbiased by interest or fear,
> By power uncorrupted, untainted by gold.
>
> Who when terror and doubt through the universe reigned,
> While rapine and treason their standard unfurled,
> The heart and the hope of his country sustained.
> And this kingdom preserved midst the wreck of a world.[103]

40. Joseph Nollekens, *William Pitt*, 1807.

'The Pilot who Weathered the Storm', as the title of this hymn to statesmanship significantly described him, Pitt was the prototype on which subsequent British politicians such as Liverpool, Canning, Peel, William Gladstone and hundreds of lesser men would consciously base their careers. And in their own terms, this adulation was justified. Not only had Pitt's own industry, efficiency, financial expertise and morality given patrician dominance a more acceptable face at a time of acute stress, but he had also been one of the first to recognise that this dominance must be finely adjusted in the direction of meritocracy. As Michael McCahill has shown, the rapid expansion of the peerage by more than two hundred between the American war and 1830 saw an unprecedented number of men being raised to the Upper House for state service. Thirty-five politicians, judges, diplomats and above all, military heroes received titles between 1780 and 1801 that allowed them to sit in the House of Lords; forty-five more did so between 1802 and 1830.[104]

The classic beneficiary of this trend was Arthur Wellesley, the younger son of a relatively impecunious Irish peer, whose military endeavours in India and Europe made him first a baron, then a viscount, then an earl, then a marquess and finally, Duke of Wellington. Among naval men, St. Vincent, Camperdown and Collingwood were all ennobled in recognition of their service at sea, as were all of Wellington's lieutenants in the Peninsular campaigns, Beresford, Hope and Hill. Gestures towards a kind of meritocracy occurred in the civilian professions as well. The penal reformer, Samuel Romilly, made the shrewd observation in 1806 that during the past twenty-five years, George III had taken great care to bestow knighthoods on all attorneys-general, solicitors-general and judges as soon as they were appointed, whereas before 1780, 'he had never seen the necessity or propriety of it'.[105] Here again, in the field of the law, we can see a heightened awareness on the part of Britain's rulers of the importance of being seen to reward exceptional talent *and* to incorporate that talent within the ranks of those who had merely inherited their titles.

For the official intention was not so much to make the upper ranks of the British polity easily accessible to talent, as to admit in a controlled fashion a number of truly exceptional men for the sake of efficiency, and for the sake, too, of preserving the existing order. Outstanding talent and remarkable achievement were used like yeast. Absorbing a limited amount helped the dough of hereditary peers and younger sons to rise in the public estimation. The bulk of the peerage continued to owe their titles primarily to who they were, and not to what they did for the state. More than 70 per cent of the most active Members of Parliament between 1790 and 1820 were, according to a recent estimate, not self-made men at all but individuals who owed their prominence in the state at least originally to their landed estates.[106] The bulk of admirals were of landed birth, as were almost all of the generals and diplomats. Social and political dominance in Great Britain was still in the main in the hands of its traditional rulers.[107] But because many of these traditionalists were also men of high competence and courage, because they admitted a limited quota of landless talent to their ranks, because they catered to commercial and industrial interests, and because after the disasters of the American war, they showed themselves willing to modify their style, ethos and even their appearance, they endured.

All of this would have been much less effective if the British had lost the war against Napoleon. But they won. Waterloo made the world safe for gentlemen again. A British army led by a duke, and officered overwhelmingly by men of landed background who had purchased their commissions, helped destroy a self-made emperor and his legions. Won on the playing fields of Eton, it was not, but Waterloo indubitably preserved the social and political prominence of old Etonians and their kind. It could be cited as ultimate confirmation that those who dominated Great Britain owed their position to genuine distinction and devotion to duty, not just to birth or property – final proof that they were heroes indeed.

There were many who remained unimpressed, of course. Yet even though attacks on their exclusivity, rapacity and overweening power continued in some quarters after Waterloo, the men who dominated Great Britain still had substantial cause to congratulate themselves. They had bounced back from the humiliation of defeat in America. They had resisted French republicanism and quashed any attempts to imitate it at home. They had destroyed Napoleon Bonaparte's military machine in Continental Europe. And, in the process, they had dramatically increased the size of Britain's empire. They had done something else as well: assumed many of the characteristics of a service élite, and gained much of the credit for being a service élite, without, in fact, conceding all that much in the way of meritocratic change. Without opening the upper echelons of power and rank to more than a limited number of self-made men, a far more self-conscious rhetoric and appearance of service to the public and to the nation had been broadly adopted which proved remarkably effective.

The new British élite dressed itself in a workmanlike and quasi-military fashion. A much greater proportion of its members than ever before attended public schools and universities. Many of them now took more than usual care to appear scrupulously religious and morally impeccable, and to identify themselves with military achievement on the battlefield and with a cult of civilian heroism at home. Relentless hard work, complete professionalism, an uncompromising private virtue and an ostentatious patriotism: this had been the governing style preached by Pitt the Younger and his disciples, quite as much as by Robespierre and his allies in Revolutionary France. In this respect, as in many others, the British ruling classes borrowed from the enemy across the Channel in order to defeat him. But the change in patrician style was also prompted by domestic considerations, by the need to appease middle-class opinion at home and to repel (if possible) extra-parliamentary demands for extensive social and political change. Of course, there was far more to the survival of the British élite than the changes I have described. Its efficient suppression of dissidence at home and its sheer economic and territorial power also played an important part. Yet in the end, just how dominant and durable a ruling order can be depends on how far it convinces others – and itself – of its right to rule and its ability to rule. In this sense, the British élite's ability in the aftermath of the American war to associate itself with patriotism and with the nation in a new and self-conscious fashion proved invaluable to its continuing authority and confidence.

The landed establishment's willingness and ability to change at this time has been too much neglected or denied recently. Because the middle classes in this country did not succeed in storming the citadels of high political and economic power until the second half of the nineteenth century, some historians have been content to concentrate only on the 'ongoing power' of Britain's traditional élite, as if a change in its social composition was the only one that could conceivably have mattered.[108] Yet, as we have seen, change the élite did in many other directions, and especially in the direction of greater Britishness. Particularly in the last quarter of the eighteenth and in the first quarter of the nineteenth centuries, there was, throughout the British Isles, a consolidation of the top personnel into a new and far more integrated upper class. The formerly separate landed establishments of England, Wales, Scotland and Ireland gradually fused, their members intermarrying, acquiring estates scattered throughout the kingdom, competing for office at home and in the empire, adopting similar lifestyles and forms of expenditure, and laying claim to be the guardians of a 'national' – in the sense of British – culture. As a journalist writing in 1819 commented, 'The manners of the nobility and gentry assimilate over the whole Kingdom.'[109]

By becoming a more unitary élite in this way, top Britons not only buttressed and consolidated their own social and political primacy, they also helped influence what Britishness was all about. Public schools, fox-hunting, a cult of military heroism and of a particular brand of 'manliness', the belief that stately homes are part of the nation's heritage, a love of uniforms: all of these characteristic components of British life, which still remain powerful today, first became prominent under patrician auspices in the half-century after the American war. And there was another and connected sense in which these years witnessed both the remodelling of authority within Great Britain, and a recasting of what it meant to be British. The same period that saw the making of the British ruling class would also see the British monarchy assuming many of the characteristics and much of the patriotic importance that it retains today.

41. Francis Bartolozzi, *King George III*, stipple engraving, 1800.

5 *Majesty*

In November 1788, George III appeared to go mad. Foaming at the mouth, growing steadily redder in the face, refusing to sleep, he chattered deliriously and incessantly of building new palaces, founding new orders of chivalry and bedding Lady Pembroke – in short, of all the indulgences he had so conscientiously denied himself since coming to the throne in 1760. When purges and opiates, the two stand-bys of eighteenth-century medicine, proved ineffective, his frantic family and ministers agreed to call in one Dr Francis Willis, a clergyman turned keeper of the insane. And it was Willis and his band of heavyweight assistants who terrified the king back to normalcy. Whenever he refused to eat, or lie down, or swallow his medicine, or stop talking, or tried to tear off the leeches clamped greedily on his forehead, or the mustard and spanish fly plasters blistering his legs, his keepers would force him into a straitjacket, and fasten him down on his bed with an iron band and rope. On one such occasion, prone, humiliated and in reality probably not mad at all, the poor man cried out that no ruler except a British king could be so utterly confined.[1]

In retrospect, the king's despair seems profoundly ironic. For although the first half of his reign had proved deeply controversial and sometimes unhappy, the second half would witness a royal apotheosis. Just as Britain's governing class in general revived and reconstructed itself in the half-century after the lost war with America, so at the same time and for some of the same reasons, the British monarchy succeeded in becoming more celebrated, more broadly popular and more unalloyedly patriotic than it had been for a century at least. Yet none of this portentous transformation can have meant much to the demented creature writhing in the hands of his keepers. And in a sense, George III's bitter outburst at the extraordinary restraints on his power and his dignity was a profoundly revealing one.

Revealing, first of all, because it was literally true. A mad sovereign, or a sovereign who appeared to be mad, was one of the risks of hereditary monarchy that almost every European state experienced at some time. But hardly ever was a royal sufferer exposed to such unceremonious treatment as George III; still less were the details of such treatment made known to the general public. When Christian VII of Denmark (1749–1808) became genuinely insane in the 1760s, he was allowed, none the less, to continue in some of his royal duties, while a discreet silence was maintained about his condition both inside and outside the Danish court.[2] But George III's symptoms, as his medical biographers remark, were 'freely discussed in private, in public, in Parliament, in the press, by doctors, laymen, and indeed by the King himself', a lack of restraint that bore witness both to the broad dissemination of political information in Great Britain and to the peculiarities of the royal image within it.[3] It was surely his recognition of these peculiarities, and his resentment of them, that lay behind the king's words. Confronted by the absolute power of the egregious Dr Willis, his freedom to command and his ruthless ability to enforce, how could he not be reminded of the cruel limitations of British royalty?

A ROYAL CULTURE CONFINED

In terms of legal and constitutional theory, of course, such limitations were few. Neither the Bill of Rights of 1689 nor the Act of Settlement of 1701 prevented a British king from declaring war or making peace, from calling or dissolving Parliament, from appointing any qualified Protestant Britons he wanted as cabinet ministers, courtiers, army and naval officers, from nominating peers, bishops, judges and ambassadors exactly as he pleased, or from pardoning completely any criminal he chose to favour.[4] Great Britain remained, or so it seemed on paper, a strong monarchy in a Europe where strong monarchies were the norm, and where those few states that deviated from that norm – Venice, or the Dutch Republic, or Poland – were in evident decline. Yet in practice, British kings had long experienced greater constraints than most of their Continental equivalents, constraints imposed not just by constitutional convention but also by their particular circumstances and temperaments.

The most brutally explicit constraint, and the most longstanding, was money. Even after the dissolution of the monasteries in the early sixteenth century, no Tudor monarch had ever enjoyed finances equal to his or her needs or ambitions. Nor in the seventeenth century was any of the Stuart kings able to balance his budget or achieve the level of grandeur he desired. Inigo Jones designed for Charles I a palace that would have outshone the Buen Retiro that his contemporary Philip IV was building in Spain; but avid for royal spectacle and the visual arts though he unquestionably was, Charles could never afford it.[5] The Civil Wars depleted the crown's material splendour as well as challenging its mystique. Many of the great medieval and Tudor palaces, Greenwich, Nonsuch, Theobalds, Woodstock and Winchester among them, were destroyed in the fighting, or demolished by victorious parliamentarians, or fell irretrievably into disrepair. So whereas Henry VIII had been able to hunt game, or women, or heretics out of more than twenty great houses scattered throughout England, Charles II returned in 1660 to only seven: Whitehall, St James's, Somerset House, Hampton Court, Greenwich, Windsor Castle and the Tower of London.[6]

Over the next hundred years, every British monarch made some addition to this reduced inheritance. None was able or willing to concentrate on one architectural project that might embody royal grandeur in stone, marble and statuary to remotely the same degree as Versailles in France, or the Winter Palace in St Petersburg, or the Belvedere in Potsdam, or Herrenhausen in Hanover, or the royal palaces of Madrid, Naples and Turin. Lack of resources accounted for part – but only part – of this failure. True, even after Parliament guaranteed that the king would receive the full value of the Civil List, £700,000 per annum under George I, and £800,000 per annum under George II and at the start of George III's reign, the possibilities for adventurous building were never very great. Once the king had paid the salaries, as he had to, of his courtiers, ministers, judges, diplomatic and secret services out of this sum, and maintained his family in an appropriate style, any pocket-money remaining was likely to be sparse.[7] Just how sparse is suggested by an incident in the early 1760s. A speculative builder snapped up some vacant land opposite the gardens of Buckingham House (the future Buckingham Palace) and promptly erected a new row of houses whose prime selling point was the good view they afforded of the Royal Family whenever it ventured out of doors. The king had pleaded with the Treasury to grant him an extra £20,000 to buy up the offending property and so safeguard his privacy. But the First Lord of the Treasury, the penny-pinching George Grenville, refused, and royalty's private perambulations became public property.[8]

But lack of cash was not the only and not the most important restraint on royal building in Britain. All of the great royal builders of Continental Europe, not least Louis XIV, spent far more money on their creations than they could afford, but believed that their magnificence was worth the investment. The apparent inability of British monarchs to behave with the same calculating abandon, at least before the war with America, derived more than anything else from a failure of nerve and from a lack of dynastic confidence and continuity. Short and contentious reigns always compromise the evolution of a developed royal image; and in the century or so separating Charles I's accession in 1625 from George I's death in 1727, Britain had in all seven monarchs, five of whom reigned for less than thirteen years. Had this rate of royal turnover been due only to the accidents of mortality, it would still have been damaging; the traumatic shifts in rule enforced first by the Civil War, then by the Glorious Revolution and lastly, by the Hanoverian Succession in 1714 made it inevitably much more so. It was these successive disruptions, together with the differences in style and taste between the monarchs in question and their frequent dislike for each other's memory, that precluded the building in Britain of a palace fit for a king.

As soon as he returned from exile in 1660, Charles II embarked on new palaces at Greenwich and Winchester, as well as major improvements at Windsor and Holyroodhouse in Edinburgh. But his successor, James II, reigned too briefly to consolidate these projects; and after the Revolution, William III abandoned all of them – turning Greenwich, for example, into a hospital for retired seamen – and concentrating instead on refurbishing Hampton Court. Christopher Wren's plans to turn it into a massive baroque palace proved, however, as abortive as Inigo Jones's earlier dreams of a transformed Whitehall.[9] When Queen Anne succeeded in 1702, she left Hampton Court largely alone and spent most of her time at Windsor. George I, by contrast, disliked Windsor and confined his own very limited architectural commissions to Kensington Palace. His son, George II, never went near this building if he could avoid it, reverting instead to Hampton Court and to St James's. And this pattern of disgruntled royal mobility continued into George III's early reign. Scorning to live where his immediate predecessor had done, he purchased Buckingham House for his personal retreat.[10] It was all like a very grand and slightly mad game of musical chairs. And, like many games, it did little for the dignity of the players. Under sustained royal pressure, the Treasury and Parliament might well in the end have consented to the building of a British Versailles, if only as another expression of national rivalry with the French. It was the uncertainties and the vicissitudes of the royal self-image in Britain that ultimately obstructed royal architectural splendour.

The British monarchy's failure to associate itself with one particular set of splendid buildings had practical as well as symbolic repercussions. Most obviously, the physical space available for the court was inadequate. The Hanoverian dynasty's recurrent bouts of Oedipal combat – George I's quarrel with his elder son, the future George II, George II's difficulties first with his son, Frederick, Prince of Wales, and then with his grandson, the future George III, and so on – probably tell us as much about the pressures and politics of space as about the family's neuroses. Very simply, there was no palace big enough to accommodate all the different royal generations together with their servants and courtiers. This had not been a problem under the Tudors or the Stuarts, because highly sexed though these princes were, they did not – with the exception of James I and Charles I – produce large families of healthy children. But the Hanoverians were prolific, and most of their offspring survived to adulthood. This was one very basic reason why the dynasty endured, but also why it fought among itself. Lacking enough space to keep the heir apparent and his family close to him and under his surveillance, a Hanoverian king was likely to find them purchasing their own London establishments, Leicester House and later Carlton House, so creating rival centres to the court and potential bases for political opposition.

Spatial politics also restricted the court's role as a social and cultural centre. The beehive court that Versailles made fashionable, with its ranks of drones and worker-bees all coming together to service the ruler in a single, self-sufficient environment, demanded a massive amount of space as well as massive resources. Space to accommodate an abundance of artists, actors, singers, scientists, huntsmen, fencers, mistresses, cooks, courtiers and servants – there were 10,000 of them living in Versailles by the 1740s – within the confines of the royal palace, thereby compelling fashionable society to revolve around the inclinations and pursuits of the monarch and enabling him to live free from dependence on his capital city.[11] British court society was quite different. It was on a much smaller scale. The Royal Household under George I and his immediate successors never contained more than 1,500 individuals, not all of them in attendance at the same time. It included bands of musicians as well as a tame poet laureate, but it lacked the human or spatial resources to forge a discrete court culture or generate all of its own large-scale entertainments. Whenever George II or George III wanted to see an opera or a play, for example, they had to leave St James's or Buckingham House and visit the London theatres, just like the rest of the public did. In this sense, Britain's royal court was always parasitic on the capital city and never independent of it.[12] And because it was situated amidst London's theatres, opera houses, pleasure gardens, clubs and the magnificent town houses of the aristocracy, the court was never the *only* focus for fashionable society, though it was always an important one.

These points are highlighted by an anecdote in Lord Hervey's waspish journal of the court of George II. In 1728, he tells us, the Duchess of Queensberry – 'proverbially beautiful, and at the top of the polite and fashionable world' – was caught by the king raising subscriptions in the royal drawing-room for John Gay's *Beggar's Opera*. Since this highly successful musical satirised the king's minister, Sir Robert Walpole, the duchess was promptly forbidden the court. But neither she nor her husband was at all cowed by this royal veto; nor were they cold-shouldered by other members of the nobility. The duke resigned his offices in protest at the insult to his wife; and she wrote to George II thus:

> The Duchess of Queensberry is surprised and well pleased that the King hath given her so agreeable a command as to stay from Court, where she never came for diversion, but to bestow a great civility on the King and Queen; she hopes that by such an unprecedented order as this is, the King will see as few as he wishes at his Court, particularly such as dare to think or speak truth.[13]

It is hard to imagine such deliberate *lèse-majesté* going unpunished in many European courts or, indeed, in many non-European centres of power. Yet it seems to have done neither of the Queensberrys any permanent harm with either polite society or the ruling dynasty. The duke was promptly appointed a Lord of the Bedchamber by the Prince of Wales, then at odds with his father, and subsequently became a privy councillor; his duchess continued to give balls, masquerades and suppers that high society in London fought to attend. Royal displeasure did John Gay no harm either. *The Beggar's Opera* became, as it remains, a classic; and though its sequel, *Polly*, was banned from the stage by royal order, it, too, promptly became a bestseller. One did not need to please the Royal Family to be a cultural success in London; indeed, entertaining the City was likely to prove far more profitable to an artist than flattering the court.

The British monarchy, then, up to and after George III's accession, was still powerful but only sporadically splendid and assured. Its setting was inadequate, and the tastes and standards of its court no longer determined the content or directions of polite culture, or even the behaviour of polite society. Of course, these very disadvantages might have been turned into a political asset. The large, expensive, inward-looking courts that flourished in some European states, crammed with members of the nobility and claiming to set the cultural tone, were impressive institutions, but rarely popular with the masses who paid for them but never witnessed their magnificence. The British monarchy's comparative restraint could easily have been presented as proof of its rare patriotic virtue; just as its residence in the island's most populous city could have been used to cement its ceremonial appeal and underline the kings' essential oneness with their people. But from the Revolution of 1688 until the end of the eighteenth century, royal propagandists and courtiers made little consistent endeavour to foster a popular cult of the monarchy along these or any other lines. Insufficiently grand in its private circumstances and in its relations with the patrician classes, the monarchy was also too aloof, too unconcerned and too controversial to be invariably or broadly popular.

This was particularly apparent under the first two Hanoverian sovereigns, and not just because they were uncharismatic foreigners. When James VI of Scotland travelled south to become James I of England in 1603, he can scarcely have struck his new Sassenach subjects as being anything other than alien and physically unprepossessing. Yet both he and his dynasty appear to have become speedily assimilated. If the Hanoverians did not, this was partly their own and their advisers' fault. James I only returned to his original kingdom once after 1603 (as the Scots legitimately complained). But George I visited Hanover five times after 1714, died and was buried there; while George II took extended summer vacations in his homeland on a dozen different occasions. By contrast, neither of them took the trouble to visit Wales, or Scotland, or the Midlands, or the north of England. The peripatetic style of the Tudor kings, their great cross-country progresses and royal entries that dazzled plebeian spectators and ruined their hapless patrician hosts, was not to the early Hanoverians' taste. Neither was cheap, mass-produced secular propaganda issued on a regular basis. 'Tis pity', someone wrote to an English newspaper in 1723, 'but some way could be devised, whereby his Majesty's speeches and all other loyal papers might be dispersed more publicly through the nation . . . The news coming only to some particular houses in market towns, the vulgar commonly take things by hear-say, and live all their time in ignorance.'[14] It was a pity; but for a long time little was done outside of the churches to remedy this state of affairs. Royal reportage in the newspapers and periodicals remained patchy and impersonal, and Jacobite ballads were often easier for the poor to come by than tributes to the ruling dynasty, and far more entertaining.

This is not to say that the early Hanoverians lost the propaganda war with their Stuart rivals. On the contrary, when it mattered most, they won hands down. After the exposure of the Atterbury Plot in the summer of 1723, George I's ministers promptly issued an order that 'all and every person whatsoever' over the age of eighteen in England, Scotland and Wales, whether male or female, propertied or not, should take the oaths of allegiance, an astonishing demand for nationwide ratification of the ruling monarch that has never yet been properly investigated.[15] And when the Young Pretender invaded in 1745, clergymen of all denominations and journalists of both parties buried him under a weight of sermons and written polemics on behalf of the Hanoverian dynasty. They argued that George II, like George I, owed his throne to Divine Providence *and* to the people's choice: that both his kingship and the celestial protection he enjoyed were earned by his maintenance of British civil liberties, laws, property and domestic peace. Whereas apologists for the Stuarts celebrated them primarily in terms of who they were, the Hanoverians were vindicated in terms of what they did and what they abstained from doing. Jacobites dealt essentially in personalities and romance; their opponents were far more likely to invoke the Protestant faith and constitutional utility of the ruling dynasty and to appeal to reason and caution. And, in every dynastic crisis experienced by the first two Hanoverians, appeals to Protestantism, constitutionality, reason and caution triumphed.

But on its own, this was not enough to keep the Hanoverian monarchy and its public appeal warm. The war for dynastic survival was emphatically won, but the everyday battles for a wider and richer popularity were a rather different matter. It is tempting to speculate just how much of the Jacobitism some historians have detected in British culture during the first half of the eighteenth century was at base a far more neutral hunger for a sentimental, highly coloured royalism that the early Hanoverians left unsatisfied. From the night of 20 September 1714, when George I entered his new capital for the first time, driving along in pitch darkness as if deliberately to outrage the crowds of Londoners who had waited long hours to see him, through to the Royal Fireworks display in Green Park in 1749, when the patriotic slogans on show were rendered only in Latin, and on to George III's coronation on 22 September 1761, when he and his queen were taken to Westminster Abbey in separate sedan chairs just like ordinary mortals going about their everyday business, royal ceremonial and celebration in this period regularly plumbed the art of sinking to its very depths. All too often, as Samuel Johnson complained, the crown was 'worn out of sight of the people', or seen by them only in a less than impressive guise.[16]

Why was this? Why did the early Hanoverians not devote more attention and imagination to the challenge of appearing as splendid rulers and as *British* rulers? It would be wrong to couch an explanation only or even primarily in terms of the personalities of the kings or the ineptitude of their advisers. The real obstacles to a popular monarchy, a monarchy that could be broadly and continuously celebrated as a patriotic symbol, were far more structural and fundamental. One problem, which would not be entirely resolved until the end of Queen Victoria's reign, was that British monarchs were also active politicians, though to a diminishing degree. For as long as they were seen as actively making and unmaking administrations, they were likely to alienate one partisan group or another among their subjects. Particularly if – like the first two Hanoverian kings – they associated themselves consistently with just one political party. Rightly or wrongly, George I and George II were regarded by many Britons as Whig kings, partisan figures not agents of national unity. As the kings themselves fully realised, this perceived bias curbed their freedom of political action and dented their public appeal. But for most, though not all of the time, they allowed themselves to believe that they had no alternative. That only a succession of Whig administrations could keep them safe from conspiracies and invasion attempts on behalf of the exiled Stuarts.

However unreal it proved in the event, the spectre of the Stuarts made the first two Hanoverian kings defensive. Instead of responding as they might have done, by increasing the momentum of royal ceremonial, public display and propaganda, George I and his successor all too often sought refuge in the seclusion of the court, or in the poisoned embrace of unalloyed Whiggery, or in periodic escapes to Hanover. Irritated, or austere, or self-conscious, or simply absent, only rarely did either man seem entirely assured and happy in his new inheritance.[17] And this lack of confidence showed, not least in the images they left behind.

Typically, these images were few in number and mainly private. The only outdoor statue erected to George I in London during his lifetime was placed on top of a church tower, out of view except at a distance. The two metropolitan statues of George II were both commissioned by private donors, not placed there by royal command with public money.[18] Neither king was interested in using the arts to foster a personality cult around himself; and neither liked posing for portrait busts and court paintings. The few that survive suggest more than anything else the inability of both men to relax into their status. Like other European monarchs by this time, they had no desire to be painted or sculpted in the trappings of classical or Christian divinity: no wish to appear, as Rubens had once apotheosised James I, in the guise of Solomon, or as David, or as any other actor immediately under the direction of the Deity. Even Sir James Thornhill's celebration of George I and his family at Greenwich, crammed full with allegory though it is, makes it absolutely clear that the king himself is human not divine.[19]

But having shed the buttress of divinity, either the kings or their artists shrank from going all the way and adopting the easy conversation-piece style that was becoming so fashionable in royal portraiture on the Continent. Hogarth did get as far as making a preparatory sketch for a royal conversation piece in 1733, showing the younger princes and princesses playing in front of their parents, George II and Queen Caroline; but royal approval was notably unforthcoming.[20] Instead, the first two Hanoverian monarchs were almost invariably represented wearing formal court dress, or clad in full armour, or warlike on horseback, or as Roman emperors; and almost without exception, they were portrayed alone. It was as if, in these earlier royal images, the sword could never be seen to be sheathed nor the royal stance softened. Even the last, strangely moving portrait of George II, painted by Robin Edge Pine in 1759, when Britannia was conquering the world, shows the elderly king, blind, toothless and evidently frail, corseted still in his court dress, standing aloof in his dark palace, with only his armed guards waiting in the wings – waiting in case they are needed.

WHY GEORGE III WAS DIFFERENT

The stolid and priggish young man who succeeded as king on 25 October 1760 has, for more than fifty years now, more often than not been described as politically orthodox and personally conventional. Anxious to dispel the cruder myths that he was bad as well as mad, historians have fallen over themselves to redress the balance and portray George III as being in essence not very much different from his grandfather, George II, or his great-grandfather, George I.[21] Yet the mere act of reciting these relationships, and the passage of time and generations they evoke, should warn us that this interpretation is flawed. How many young men in any society are like or want to be like their grandfathers? Both George I and George II had been born before the Glorious Revolution. Both had grown up in war-torn Germany, led armies into battle and become kings only in their middle age. And for both of them, as we have seen, the British throne was a new and nervous acquisition, never

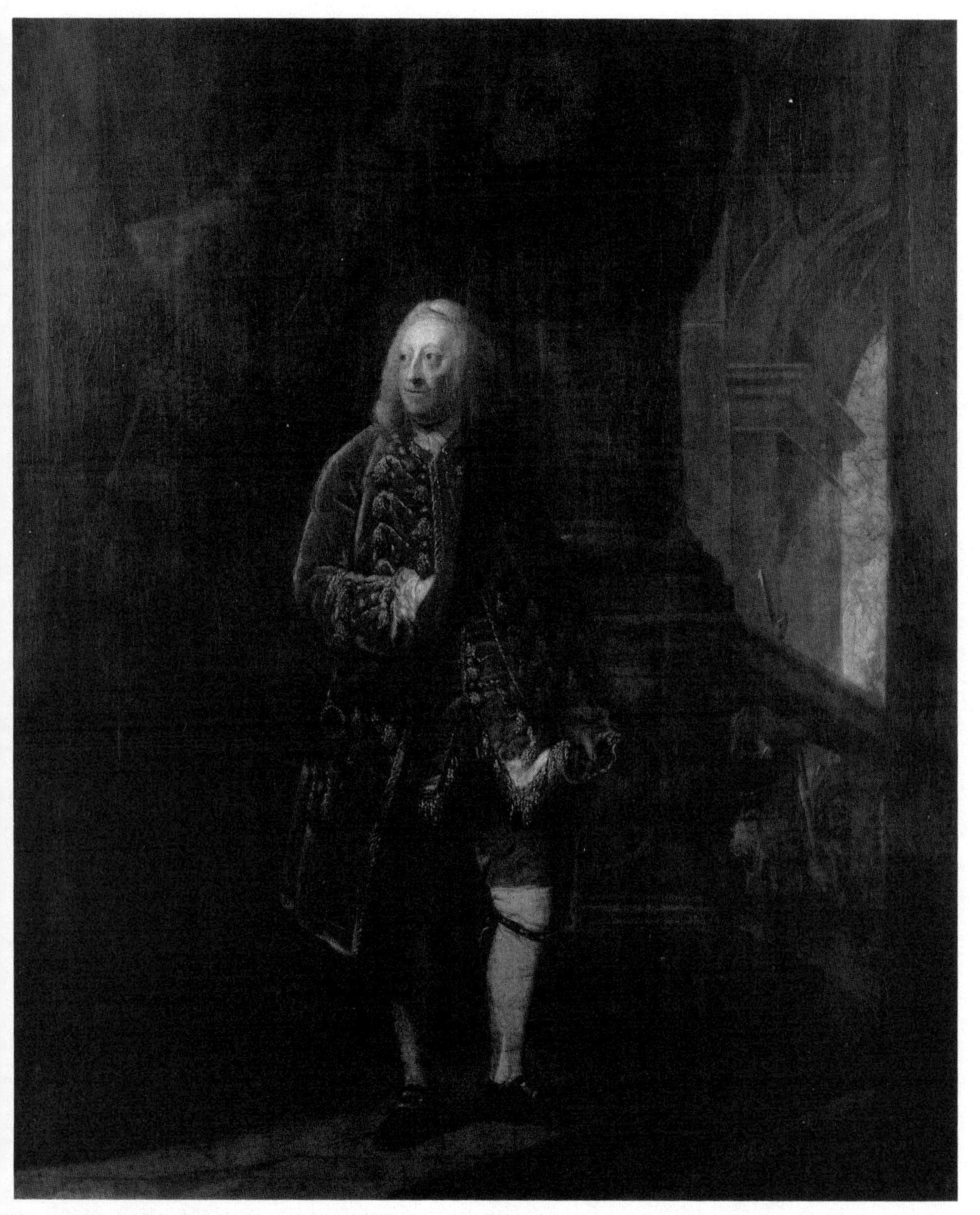

42. Robin Edge Pine, *George II* (copy).

to be taken comfortably for granted. But George III was different. Different not just because he was only twenty-two in 1760, born and bred – as he boasted to Parliament – in Britain. But different, too, because he had grown up in a much safer and a much grander political world than his forbears, exposed to new circumstances and new ideas.

The ideas in question were not his own. Nor did they originate with his elegant, ineffectual mentor Lord Bute. They came to him through his father, Frederick Lewis, one of the great might-have-beens of British history. From the 1730s, Frederick – so often dismissed as just another puny princeling – had recognised what was wrong with the Hanoverian dynasty's practice of monarchy and tried, in so far as his limited resources allowed, to improve matters. He had refused to be a creature of the Whigs, choosing his friends and allies from all political groupings.[22] He had spent money and time associating himself with the making of a patriotic culture, planning the creation of a national academy of art, and commissioning Thomas Arne and James Thomson to write 'Rule Britannia'. And he had forged an image for himself that was a cunning and influential blend of ritual splendour and winning domesticity. His gold and graceful state barge, now in the National Maritime Museum at Greenwich, shows how very much he wanted to make a visual impact, how much he relished letting the Thames carry him through his capital city in style. But his private life also served a public function. From being a conventionally promiscuous bachelor prince, he had become after marriage a devoted husband and a fond father of nine children. All of these domestic assets Frederick had celebrated in art. Just as he had himself painted playing the cello with his sisters, and helping to put out a fire in London.[23] With Frederick, the image of the Hanoverian dynasty changed, becoming softer and markedly more sympathetic. George I and George II had sought primarily to survive; Frederick, like his successor, wanted to appeal and to impress.

Much of George III's reign would be a reprise in more favourable circumstances of what Frederick attempted to do before his early death in 1751. Frederick had wanted to extirpate traditional party divisions; George presided over their dissolution. Frederick had wanted British art institutionalised in the service of crown and state; George had copies of the highly successful portrait of himself by Allan Ramsay circulated to every British embassy and major government office, and helped found the Royal Academy of Art in 1768. Frederick sowed his wild oats and then reaped the private and public advantages of playing bourgeois paterfamilias; George wallowed in paternity earlier, more abundantly and without the detours on the way. And both men knew that the warmth of the domestic hearth must, for best public effect, be balanced by the chill of regal splendour. 'The prince . . . will be feared and respected abroad, [and] adored at home', George had written in one of his schoolboy essays, 'by mixing private economy with public magnificence'.[24]

The careful weighing of how a king might best *appear* to his subjects was prophetic. The revival of the monarchy in George III's reign would be very much a matter of a renovated and far more assertively nationalistic royal image, not a resurgence of royal power in political terms. Initially, George himself probably hoped for something rather different. Like his father, he looked back to the Stuart monarchs of the seventeenth century, particularly Charles I, with fervent admiration, modelling much of his art patronage on theirs, for example. When Zoffany painted the king's two elder sons at Buckingham House in 1764, he showed them – and this can only have been on royal instructions – standing under Van Dyck's portrait of Charles I's children.[25] Discreet signals of this kind may have been all that the king could do to express his private ambition: his hope that with Jacobitism extinguished, and the tactical mistakes of the earlier Hanoverians rectified, monarchy in Britain might return to what it once had been. Those radicals on both sides of the Atlantic who claimed to detect in the new reign a return to Stuart principles may have seen more clearly into the royal mind than they knew.

But all of the new king's wider ambitions were doomed to disappointment. Hence, perhaps, his bitter complaint of confinement in 1788 as he lay struggling, shackled in his straitjacket. The invisible but potent straitjackets imposed on previous British monarchs by custom, by political change, by the increasing complexity and scale of government business and by their own variable ability and application, were not removed in George III's reign. There was no marked upsurge of royal influence over the cabinet after 1760, rather the reverse. And there was no dramatic rise in royal interest and initiative in foreign and imperial policy or in the administration of the state. Formidably powerful still in terms of blocking measures and men he disapproved of, at no stage in his reign could George III ever have been described, as Frederick the Great of Prussia was, as 'normally almost the sole driving power in all departments of state'; nor did he ever attempt personally to shake up the organisation of his state in the manner, say, of Joseph II in Austria.[26] In Britain, as in many other European states, there was a process of royal resurgence in the second half of the eighteenth century. But whereas in Prussia, or Austria, Russia, Sweden or

Napoleonic France this process took the form of an increase in royal or quasi-royal power, in Great Britain what changed was the image and popularity of the monarch. And even this change did not occur immediately.

Samuel Romilly, deist, reformer, follower of Rousseau, and so with nothing in common with George III other than the fact that he, too, in the end appeared to go mad, analysed better than any other contemporary the reasons for and the timing of the king's belated apotheosis:

> From the beginning of his reign to the close of the American War, he was one of the most unpopular princes that ever sat upon the throne: he is now [1809] one of the most popular; and yet in nothing is the character or spirit of his government altered. *But the truth is that it is to the conduct of others, and to events over which His Majesty had no control, that all his popularity is to be ascribed.* When the coalition between Lord North and Mr. Fox took place [that is, in 1783] the tide turned in his favour . . . The King's joining the people on so important an occasion, against his Ministers and against the Parliament, laid the foundation of his popularity. Then followed an attempt upon his life by a maniac; then the irregularities and dissipation of the Prince destined to be his successor; next his own unfortunate derangement of mind . . . and last of all, but which added tenfold strength to every motive of endearment to the King, the horrors of the French Revolution.[27]

Romilly's analysis was not entirely correct. *Some* of the improvement in the royal image was due, as we have seen, to George III's own determination to be a different kind of monarch than his predecessors. But it was the case that only after the American war did this determination really pay off in terms of public response. In the 1760s and '70s, there is certainly evidence that many Britons approved of their new king. But there is also ample evidence that the king was widely and actively disliked, not just in radical London, where Wilkite rioters once drove a hearse into the grounds of St James's Palace to remind its royal occupant of the fate of tyrants, but throughout the provinces as well. 'The bulk of the people in every city, town, and village', warned John Wesley in 1775, having just returned from one of his cross-country missions, '. . . do not so much aim at the ministry . . . but at the King himself . . . They heartily despise his Majesty, and hate him with a perfect hatred.'[28] It was only in that mood of defensive introspection which followed on Britain's declining fortunes and

The State Watchman discover'd by the Genius of Britain. studying plans for the Reduction of America.

43. Satire on George III by Thomas Rowlandson, 1781.

eventual defeat in America, that a marked and sustained change in mass attitudes to the monarchy began to be apparent.

The change manifested itself in simple as well as in complex ways. Between George III's accession in 1760 and 1781, the records of the London theatres show that 'God Save the King' received only four formal performances. Over the next twenty years, however, it was to receive more than ninety performances. And by the early nineteenth century, Britons were regularly calling this rather dismal piece of music – as they had not done before – the *national* anthem.[29] An analogous shift in the royal image, occurring at the same time, can be seen in cartoons. Before and during the American war, graphic images of George III were far more likely to be derisory than not; and sometimes worse than derisory. Although usually portrayed as a blind simpleton, kept in leading strings by his mother and her reputed lover, Lord Bute, he figured sometimes as a villain in his own right: as an oriental tyrant who just happened to rule in the West, as an auxiliary of corruption, or – than which there could be few worse accusations as far as most Britons were concerned – as a closet Catholic.[30] But from the end of the war, the bulk of cartoonists grew markedly kinder to the king. From the 1780s onwards, he was repeatedly caricatured as a genial, homespun farmer, or as John Bull, or as St George, or even – in one of James Gillray's earthiest productions – as Britain personified.[31] At first glance, *The French Invasion: or John Bull, bombarding the Bum-Boats* seems little more than a blatant piece of scatological disrespect, George III's patriotic pretensions reduced to a capacity for directing shit at the enemy. Yet the dirt misleads. Rarely since the 'Ditchley' portrait of Queen Elizabeth I had the fusion of monarch and kingdom been so explicitly expressed in art. George III is shown as being in the most intimate sense possible entirely at one with England and Wales (interestingly, not yet with Scotland). They give him shape, but he gives them identity. Looked at again – and Gillray's work is full of such ambiguities – this can be read as a deeply conservative print.

It is also very funny; and this, too, was significant. With the exception of a few savage prints issued by the radical underground in London, graphic criticism of the monarchy from the 1780s onwards usually sought to provoke ridicule not hatred. Even those artists who refused to join unequivocally in the new patriotic cult of the monarchy were more likely now to present the king as a figure of fun than as a corrupt or over-powerful monarch. Gillray's images of George III, like the Cruikshank family's caricatures of George IV a generation later, doubtless led to snorts of irreverent amusement among the multitudes who bought them for a few pence or gazed at them in the windows of print shops. But laughter takes the sting out of criticism. And laughing at royal individuals led in practice very easily to amused tolerance for royalty itself. Those who satirise the British Royal Family today, lampooning their corgis, their reputed philistinism, their funny clothes and their even funnier accents, may imagine they are being subversive, but, of course, they are not. The shift in criticism of the monarchy which first became apparent in the 1780s, a shift away from anger at the institution to mockery of individual royals and their foibles, helped – as it still helps – to preserve it.

But why did such a shift take place at all? Why did Britain's monarchy become so much more celebrated, and so much more successful as a focus for patriotic celebration, in the second half of George III's reign? As Samuel Romilly suggested, the immediate

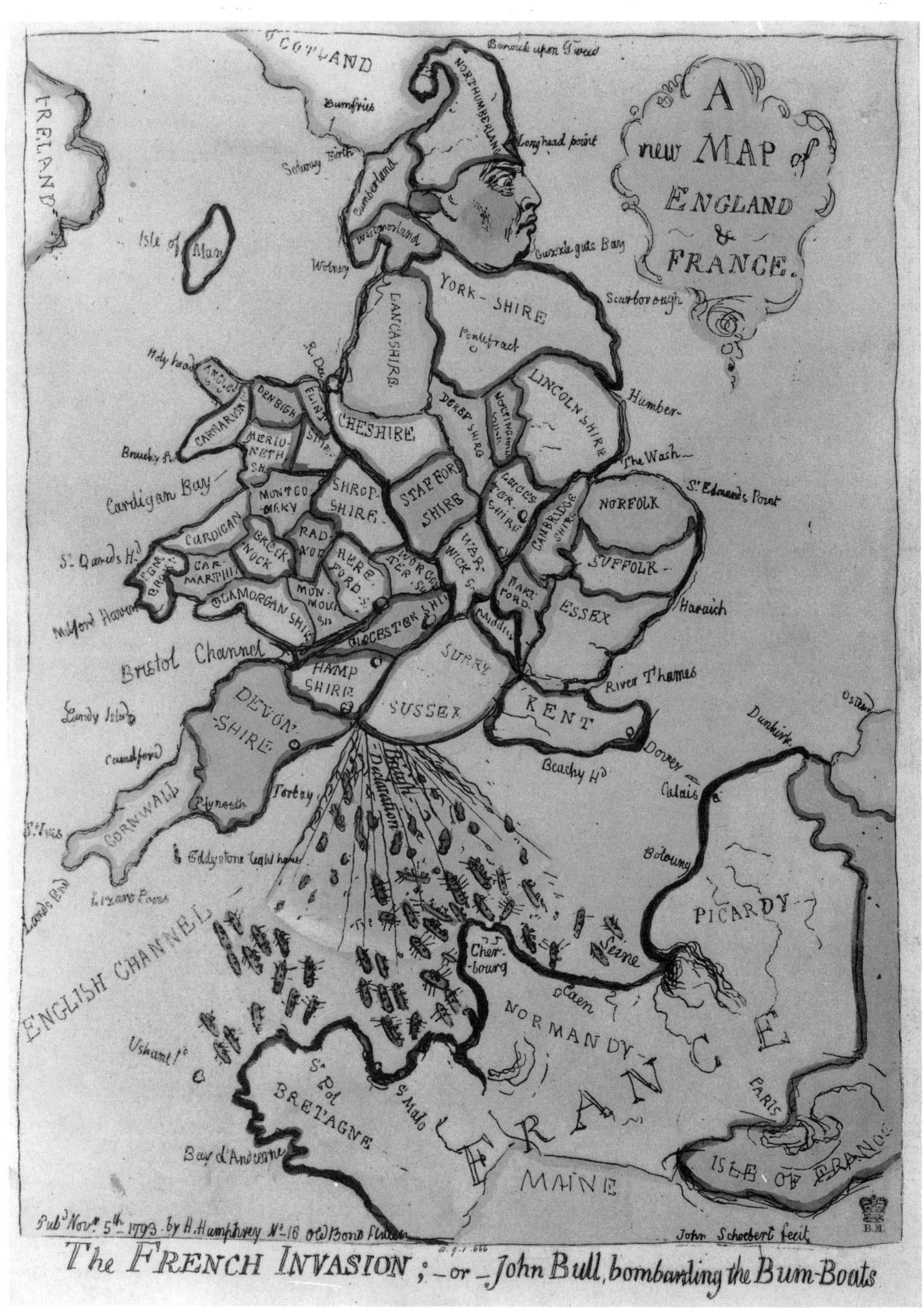

44. James Gillray, *The French Invasion; or John Bull, bombarding the Bum-Boats*, 1793.

cause lay in the politics of the 1780s. As a limited monarch, George was able to evade most of the blame for British defeat in America. The former Prime Minister, Lord North, was made the scapegoat for national humiliation; while the king himself, because of his undoubted domestic probity, his obstinate patriotism and his adroit alliance with the boy wonder, William Pitt the Younger, came to represent for many Britons reassuring stability and honest, uncomplicated worth in the midst of disaster and disillusionment.[32] This might have counted for little, however, without two more protracted developments. The horrifying illness he suffered in the winter of 1788 made the king appear deeply vulnerable, and the surge of public pity that ensued cancelled out many of the earlier fears of his arbitrary and corrupt intentions. From now on, ill-health, reduced activity and ultimately old age would serve to protect George III (just as they later protected Queen Victoria) from the kind of scathing criticism and controversy that had previously dogged him. In these new circumstances, it was far easier for propagandists to argue that the monarchy was *the* uncontentious point of national union, an argument that the French Revolution made ubiquitous and indispensable. After 1789, royal celebration throughout Great Britain would increase dramatically in scale and tempo. It would take many forms, and satisfy a surprisingly wide variety of private needs. But for the agents of authority, its primary significance would be as a means to enlist wider public support for war abroad and good order at home.

Before 1789, Parliament and ministers had kept a wary and envious eye on the Civil List, and on any royal expenditure that seemed likely to exceed it. After 1789, however, and until the military successes of the 1810s, all but extreme Whigs tended to accept, however grudgingly, that national security necessitated greater monetary investment in royal splendour. The most obvious result of this loosening of purse strings was a transformation in royal living space. In the first half of his reign, the king's building exploits had been modest. But in the two decades before 1811, he spent an estimated £168,000 renovating Windsor Castle, a further £50,000 on alterations to Buckingham House, and a mammoth £500,000 on the construction of a completely new castle at Kew.[33] At the same time, the heir to the throne – the future George IV – was pouring money into the oriental splendours of the Brighton Pavilion, and paying scores of artists, architects, craftsmen, decorators, cabinet-makers, metal-workers and wood-carvers to turn Carlton House from an already substantial town house into 'one of the finest royal residences anywhere in contemporary Europe'.[34]

In terms of what had gone before, these royal building projects

45. Buckingham House before 1800, anonymous engraving.

46. William Gauci, *Buckingham Palace*, lithograph, *c.*1830.

47. The King's Audience Chamber at Windsor Castle after it had been redesigned for George III and with Benjamin West's wall paintings in place. William Henry Pyne, *The History of the Royal Residences*, London, 1819.

represented something more than a massive increase in cost and scale. In style and symbolism, too, they marked an abrupt change that was at least in part politically driven. Before the 1780s, George III's taste had been cosmopolitan. Insofar as he built or bought pictures, he favoured neo-classical design and French and Italian masters. When refurbishing Buckingham House, for instance, both he and his court painter, the American Benjamin West, 'had gone out of their way to be international in their perspective'.[35] But defeat in America, and the move from residence in London to Windsor Castle – a move finalised only in 1789 – seem to have prompted a shift in royal aesthetics. From Benjamin West, George now demanded a series of massive wall paintings for Windsor glorifying Britain's real and mythic history; while his castle at Kew, like the new state apartments at Windsor, was an exercise in runaway gothic revival: turrets, moats, arrow windows and serried ranks of castellated walls. By building this way, the king was following current fashions. But a great deal of gothic's fashionable appeal lay in its evocation of chivalry, hierarchy and times past when the institution of monarchy went unquestioned.[36] For George, I am sure, Kew was a counterblast to revolution, whether in America, or France, or Great Britain, just as West's history paintings were an assertion of Britain's heroic (and monarchical) past against the doubts, dangers and defeats of its present.

His successor's opposition to the French Revolution, though just as heartfelt, took a different aesthetic form. Instead of finding inspiration in his own kingdom's medieval past, George IV looked to pre-Revolutionary France. Carlton House was filled to overflowing with artifacts that had once belonged to Louis XIV, with medals, pictures and figurines of the Sun King and his royal descendants, with souvenirs of the French *ancien régime* of every kind: Van der Meulen's study of the building of Versailles, for instance, or Louis XV's coronation book which George's agents snapped up for him in readiness for his own coronation in 1821. Whether as Prince of Wales, or Prince Regent, or king, the last of the four Hanoverian Georges was always – as Talleyrand recognised – *un roi grand seigneur*, a man bent on championing the old France against the principles and ruling personnel of the new.[37] If, in the dregs of his life, drugged, corpulent and foolishly amorous, George IV came to believe that he had fought in person on the blood-soaked fields of Waterloo, this was not perhaps as utterly ridiculous as it appeared. In his own mind, and, more importantly, in his artistic and architectural patronage, George had been fighting Napoleon and his republican predecessors virtually all of his adult life. How else can we understand his instructions to his architect John Nash that he must rebuild Regency London so that it could outshine Napoleonic Paris?[38]

Defeat in America and, above all, revolution in France fostered in Britain a more splendid monarchy and influenced the nature and direction of that splendour. This was as true of public royal ritual as it was of private royal space. We know that George III, like a great many other Britons, was aware of and fascinated by the didactic state festivals that Jacques-Louis David and others stage-managed for the new French leaders, the Fête de la Fédération of 1790, the Fête de l'Unité of 1793, and the Festival of the Supreme Being held a year later.[39] And it seems likely that the extent of popular participation in these French patriotic festivals, the way in which they were co-ordinated so as to occur both in Paris and the major provincial towns on the same day and, above all, their sheer propaganda impact, determined the king and his ministers to make some attempts at emulation. In December 1797, George III would process in state through the London streets past a crowd of well over 200,000 people to give thanks at St Paul's cathedral for British naval victories over the Dutch, French and Spanish fleets. Royal Thanksgivings for military victories had occurred in Britain before (though not since Queen Anne's reign), but the press rightly detected that more was involved here than just a return to old, indigenous traditions. The Naval Thanksgiving, the *Morning Chronicle* judged, was a 'Frenchified farce', not least because it broke with normal British practice and copied Revolutionary French precedent (and advertised the Royal Navy's return to loyal obedience after the recent mutinies at Spithead and Nore) by including in its ranks 250 ordinary sailors and marines. The king himself had been responsible for this innovation and for the initial decision to hold a thanksgiving.[40]

This cross-Channel competition in ritual and aesthetics posed an obvious problem for the British authorities. How could they organise public display so as to distinguish it from that spawned by an illegitimate and enemy regime? Their solution was twofold. First, British patriotic and public display was rendered distinctive by focussing it on the monarch. Whereas Revolutionary and Napoleonic France retained many of the ceremonial forms used by Louis XVI and his predecessors, while giving them a far more nationalist and militarist emphasis, in wartime Britain, almost all official celebrations subsumed national achievement in glorification of the monarch. Thus the press took care to note that Jubilee Day on 25 October 1809, the beginning of the fiftieth year of George III's reign, was also, but only incidentally, the anniversary of the Battle of Agincourt.[41] So, too, in 1814, the Prince Regent arranged that London's prime peace festival should occur on 1 August. This ensured that it coincided with and was indeed overshadowed by the centenary celebrations for the Hanoverian Succession.[42] Officially sponsored patriotic celebrations were thus made, as far as possible, identical with celebration of the king.

The second way in which ceremonial in Britain was made to seem distinctive in this period was through the claim that it was hallowed by tradition, as distinct from the upstart and synthetic contrivances of the French. Such an analysis may seem over-intellectualised, but an examination of the peculiarly splendid Installation of Garter Knights held at Windsor Castle on St George's Day 1805 suggests that it is not. The money lavished on this ceremony – over £50,000 according to one estimate – was quite unprecedented, as were the invitations to attend sent out to all foreign ambassadors and ministers of the crown. Yet the official emphasis was on the *antiquity* of the ceremony: 'It was His

Majesty's particular wish, that as many of the old customs should be kept up as possible.'[43] The reaction to the Installation of one well-informed spectator, William Windham, the future Secretary of State for War, suggests just why it was that George III and his advisers indulged in such expense and ceremonial, while at the same time claiming that their endeavours were fully in line with tradition: 'It is better than the formal shows at Versailles.'[44] Less than a year earlier, in July 1804, Napoleon had held a special assembly at the Invalides to award the first stars of the Légion d'honneur, an Order he had created in 1802. Five months later, he had crowned himself emperor in a brilliantly invented ceremony at Nôtre Dame which was well reported in the British press. The peculiarly lavish Garter ceremony of 1805 must be understood as a calculated royal, aristocratic and British riposte, intended to parry the pretensions of a mushroom emperor: a slap in the face, as the London *Times* put it, to an 'unprincipled and sanguinary usurper', who had dared 'to imitate, by a splendid mockery, the long recognised, the consecrated and venerable institutions of the unpolluted honour of ancient states'.[45]

THE MECHANICS OF ROYAL CELEBRATION

The resurgence of the British monarchy's national reputation and celebration in the last quarter of the eighteenth century can, then, partly be explained by the determination of George III and his ministers to reassert rank and to rally public opinion in the wake of defeat in America and in the face of the French Revolution and the threat of Napoleon and his armies. But royal apotheosis in Britain was not just engineered from above. To understand why it happened as it did, and when it did, we need to explore as well why so many ordinary Britons were apparently willing to celebrate their monarchy in a new way. We can start by considering the tale of two, very different women.

On 14 October 1809, an obscure, middle-class widow from the Welsh borders, one Mrs Biggs, wrote a letter to the Earl of Dartmouth, the Lord Chamberlain, boasting about a singular piece of patriotic initiative. The year had been a deeply embarrassing one for the Royal Family. Not only were the Prince and Princess of Wales still living outrageously apart, as they had done virtually ever since their disastrous marriage in 1795; but the king's second son, Frederick Augustus, Duke of York, Commander-in-Chief of the British Army, had also become caught up in sexual scandal. His mistress, a shrewd *demi-mondaine* called Mary Anne Clarke, had used her bedtime influence with the duke to attract bribes from men seeking more than usually rapid military promotion, an arrangement finally revealed to the House of Commons by one of Clarke's former lovers, Colonel Wardle, MP for Salisbury. After a long and messy inquiry, the duke had been found guilty of extreme *naïveté*, though not of corruption, and had resigned his post amidst self-righteous meetings of reformers nationwide and a bevy of prurient pamphlets and apologias from all of the major protagonists.[46]

What redeemed this affair from some of its tedium and squalor was the unabashed ingenuity of Mrs Clarke and Mrs Biggs. Clarke was a printer's daughter, and reacted to imminent social disgrace with a characteristic blend of chutzpah and professionalism. She wrote and published a splendidly uninhibited pamphlet trouncing Wardle; and then secured her future by privately printing all of the Duke of York's love letters. It cost the crown £7,000 down and a pension of £400 per annum to buy her off and the copies up. Thus provided, Clarke settled down to a life of smiling respectability, always taking care to keep one secret copy of the letters in Drummond's Bank as her insurance. For the Royal Family, the situation proved less immediately retrievable. With George III himself now blind, increasingly senile and virtually a recluse at Windsor, and with growing war-weariness and economic discontent, the monarchy was in danger, or so at least it seemed to a leading opposition peer, Lord Grey, of 'losing all hold on the affections of the people'. It was Mrs Biggs who thought of a remedy. As she wrote to Dartmouth:

> In the early part of the summer when Colonel Wardle's popularity and the meetings for reform appeared likely to become inimical to the peace and happiness of the country, it occurred to me that the ensuing October would be his majesty's fiftieth anniversary and that if the idea of a jubilee or general festival could be successfully suggested it might excite a spirit of loyal enthusiasm well calculated to counteract the pernicious efforts of Mr Wardle.[47]

Accordingly, throughout late July and early August, this bizarre conspirator had written 'nearly three hundred [anonymous] letters, to most of the principal places and to many people of popular habits & influence, recommending a Jubilee which should include both festivity and beneficence'.[48]

The idea took off. The Jubilee of 25 October 1809, the first royal event of this kind ever held, was celebrated in outposts of the British empire, thoughout Scotland and Wales and in well over 650 different locations in England:

48. Jubilee celebrations in front of London's Mansion House in 1809, anonymous print.

A People, happy, great, and free;
That People with one common voice,
From Thames' to Ganges' common shores rejoice,
In universal Jubilee.[49]

These very different acts of female initiative and self-aggrandisement had a wider significance, however. Clarke and Biggs personified, almost caricatured, the two faces of the relationship between the Royal Family and their sex. On the one hand, women were (and would continue to be) a persistent source of scandal, particularly when unmarried princes were available. On the other, sentimental female attachment to the British monarchy, an attachment that first became prominent in George III's reign, would from now on supply an increasingly important part of its popular base.[50] In Clarke and Biggs, too, was acted out the paradoxical relationship between monarchy and publicity. Too much of the wrong kind of publicity, and monarchy was (and is) in peril; yet calculated acts of publicity are indispensable to its appeal. Lastly, and crucially, Mrs Biggs's resourcefulness is a potent reminder that royal resurgence after 1780 was not just a product of ministerial sponsorship, nor even of the local exertions of conservative landowners, clergymen and Church-and-King vigilantes, important though all of those forces undoubtedly were. The increase in the scale and co-ordination of royal celebration was also made possible by the active enthusiasm of men and women well outside the formal political élite; and it was aided beyond measure by an increasingly sophisticated infrastructure of communications. In the grandiloquent words of the *Scotsman*: 'The post, the press, and the stage-coach, have made it easier to unite twenty millions of men in a common cause in our own days, than it was to unite the fiftieth part of the number in the days of Philip of Macedon.'[51]

By now, the newspaper press had conquered even the more peripheral areas of Great Britain. South Wales acquired its first successful English-language newspaper in 1804, and three years later, the *North Wales Chronicle* was founded in Bangor. In Scotland, too, the press was expanding at a much faster rate than before. Back in 1750, its five newspapers had been concentrated in Aberdeen, Glasgow and Edinburgh. Fifty years on, there were at least thirteen Scottish papers; and, by the time of George III's death, there were more than twice as many again, circulating, thanks to better roads and an expanding mail-coach service, even to the most northerly counties, Sutherland and Caithness. In all, Great Britain had over three hundred different newspapers by 1820.[52]

But it was not just a case of a greater volume of newsprint becoming available: different print techniques were also being used more adventurously to spread information. When the Prince Regent's daughter and heir presumptive to the throne, Princess Charlotte, died in childbirth in November 1817, several provincial newspapers experimented with outlining their front pages in black for the occasion. This became the standard practice for subsequent royal casualties, adding drama to reportage and instantly communicating the fact of national loss to those who could only look at print, not read it. It was at this time, too, that newspaper editors seem to have learnt the technique of printing the more sensational pieces of headline news in large typeface on placards. These were then put up outside the newspaper office and affixed as well to mail-coaches, which duly carried the news (and advertised the paper in question) along all of the post roads. When the news of William IV's sudden death in 1837 was placarded in this fashion by the printers of the *Reading Mercury*, they calculated that 'in less than an hour . . . there was scarcely a person within the borough, who was not aware of the severe loss the country had sustained'.[53]

Since a quota of the London newspapers were always subsidised by the administration, and provincial newspapers invariably

49. Richard Gilson Reeve, *The Royal Mails at the Angel Inn, Islington, on the Night of His Majesty's Birthday*, aquatint, *c.*1825.

borrowed from the London press, the intensity and direction of royal reportage could sometimes be regulated from above. It seems likely, for example, that when the *Courier* predicted nationwide mourning for Princess Charlotte in 1817 – 'There is no doubt that on Wednesday next, the day of the funeral, all business will be suspended; and that the empire will afford the awful and appropriate spectacle of a whole people spontaneously engaged in religious exercise and devotion' – it was acting on the instructions of its Treasury paymasters.[54] The Pentridge Rising in Yorkshire had just been suppressed. The highly unpopular and repressive Gagging Acts were still in force. And with the death of the princess, the future of the British monarchy had suddenly come to seem acutely vulnerable. The Prince Regent now had no direct, legitimate heir. Nor, separated from his wife, the unfortunate Caroline of Brunswick, was he likely to supply one. So until one of his elderly brothers could be persuaded to put aside his mistress, marry and procreate, a posthumous cult of Charlotte, built around her sex, youth, virtue, imminent maternity and tragic demise, seemed one of the few reliable barriers behind which an embattled dynasty, apparently on the verge of extinction, could shelter.[55]

But although successive British governments certainly tried to prod the newspaper press in the right royal direction, blanket control of its coverage of the monarchy was never remotely possible or necessary. Far more than had been the case in the early and mid-eighteenth century, papers competed with each other to publicise royal events. Just how valuable this could be was shown in the run-up to George III's Jubilee in 1809. Since its genesis was eccentric, and neither royal nor ministerial supervision was available, the sheer scale of this event was a remarkable tribute to the activism of the press and, it would seem, to public opinion which compelled many local authorities into action.[56] From August 1809 onwards, almost every newspaper in Britain served to heighten anticipation of the event by printing readers' suggestions and emotive editorials, as well as mayoral notices about Jubilee meetings, advertisements for Jubilee souvenirs and details of subscriptions, procession routes and projected bean-feasts.[57] Newspapers were even more important in those few cities where the local government was dilatory or equivocal in its Jubilee arrangements. In Bristol, the mayor did not summon a Jubilee meeting until four days before the celebration was due to occur. But since the *Bristol Journal* had for several weeks been regaling its readers with details of what other towns were preparing, blatantly appealing to touchy civic pride ('Every provincial paper, that we have perused, proclaims the universal attention which this day has excited. Why is this ancient and loyal, this opulent City, the last to announce its intention to join in the universal joy?'), the city's parish authorities were sufficiently informed to be able to arrange a Jubilee programme by themselves.[58]

Only rarely did urban authorities need such prodding to participate in royal celebration. Increasingly, indeed, they seized upon it as a means to advertise their town's particular affluence, identity and culture, as an outlet for civic pride as well as British patriotism. Instead of the traditional, muted rites for royal occasions, a special church service, a private dinner for the corporation and perhaps a bonfire for the plebs, affluent or ambitious towns now had the will and the facilities to indulge in far more lavish ceremonies designed to exhibit pride of place. Wider and more graciously planned high streets made full-scale processions possible and irresistible; and new assembly rooms were called into service for balls or public dinners for the local élite. It also became fashionable to use days set aside for royal celebration to inaugurate some solid work of local improvement. Edinburgh commemorated George III's Jubilee by extending the docks at Leith; Birmingham, by unveiling its first ever public statue, Richard Westmacott's bronze

50. A typical cheap, mass-produced memento of George III, *c.*1810.

monument to Horatio Nelson; Oswestry marked the day by christening its new gas lights; and Bangor in Wales opened a public dispensary.[59]

Strategies of this kind helped to ensure good crowd attendance at royal celebration. The busy and the poor, in particular, were more likely to turn out to see a concrete change in their own environment, than just to stand around passively and cheer – or perhaps not cheer. But there was also a more subliminal message involved in this synchronisation of loyalist display and real local benefits. One of the most powerful arguments employed by royal apologists at this time was that, whereas republican experiments in Continental Europe had led inexorably to anarchy, military despotism, mass conscription and the despoliation of property, in Great Britain – because the existing order had been preserved – things were blessedly different: 'We have heard the storm indeed', one Anglican clergyman conceded on Jubilee day in 1809, 'but it has been as he, who, under the warm domestic roof, hears without the whistling of the wintry wind; we have heard it, but to endear to us still more our native comforts.'[60] With the toppling of so many European monarchies, George III's unusual longevity both as a king and as a man could be seen as a symbol of his nation's relative stability, confirmation of its status as the Protestant Israel, 'this favoured land'. Very easily, the king became a lucky charm, a totem by which evil spirits might be repelled. In the words of one Dundee song:

For under him we sit and crack,
In peace and unity compact,
Whist every nation's on the rack
That does nae like our Geordie.[61]

And what better way could there be to hammer this piece of superstition home (quite literally) than by demonstrating that with every royal event, civic welfare was materially advanced?

The more successful a town felt itself to be, the more likely it was to invest in royal celebration. In Norwich, once the second city in the kingdom but now barely scraping into its top ten in terms of wealth and population size, civic dignitaries proved noticeably reluctant to organise mass celebrations for either the Jubilee in 1809 or George IV's coronation in 1821, a failure that stemmed from diminished confidence and not just out of nervousness of local radicalism.[62] The contrast with Liverpool, newly established as the second city of the empire, was absolute. As its Jubilee address reveals, its leaders relished celebrating George III as a means of celebrating what Liverpool itself had become: 'You found us, Sire, unknown to fame. Under the protecting influence of Your Majesty's government, we have now arrived at so high a degree of commercial . . . importance, as to be left almost without a rival throughout your Majesty's extensive empire.'[63] The city went on to commemorate the event by founding a society for the prevention of cruelty to animals and by commissioning an equestrian statue of the king to be paid for out of a public subscription. As a local handbill explained, it was modelled on the statue of Marcus Aurelius in Rome. But it was better. While the original was cramped in front of the Capitol, Liverpool's royal statue would dominate its entrance by the London road, dazzling those travellers who came from the metropolis to the new Rome of the north.[64]

Pride of place and pride in affluence went hand-in-hand with pride in numbers. It is often argued that French Revolutionary violence, coming on top of the haunting memories of the Gordon Riots, made the British propertied classes apprehensive of their poorer neighbours in the mass. Yet printed accounts of mass-attended royal events in this period more commonly convey delight at the size of the crowd than anxiety about its volatility. Liverpool's newspapers boasted that the 50,000 men and women who reputedly participated in the Jubilee formed but half of its population.[65] A much smaller city, Plymouth, also felt able to rejoice in a Jubilee crowd of roughly the same size, because it demonstrated its status as a regional capital. Country bumpkins and country gentry alike had flocked in from Cornwall and rural Devonshire, giving a splendid boost to the city's shops and victuallers and gawking appreciatively at the elaborate procession: 'the grandest and best conducted ever seen in the West of England'.[66] In the absence of a professional police force, it was the proliferation of different kinds of voluntary societies that made this kind of complacency possible: private organisations that supplied civic and royal ritual with numbers, but numbers that were self-regulated and kept within bounds.

The volunteer and militia regiments brought into being by the war with France were an obvious case in point, and were particularly important in making the capital city a more reliable arena for royal display than it had been before. In the late seventeenth and earlier eighteenth centuries, widespread dislike of standing armies had meant that the military component of state processions was often unpopular. Nor, in wartime, were there always sufficient regular troops available to undertake widespread ceremonial duties. Yet, without an adequate military presence, public royal ritual could be unsafe. Fears of inadequate crowd control reputedly deterred many people from watching the thanksgiving procession in London for George III's recovery in April 1789. The availability of large numbers of citizen volunteers changed all this. Although they could still encounter popular hostility in some regions, their local provenance and (crucially) their importance in the event of French invasion, meant that metropolitan and local processions could now be lent the policing and glamour of an armed soldiery without too much loss of popularity. One of the best-attended royal events of this period was the king's review of 27,000 volunteers at Hyde Park on 26 and 28 October 1803, the height of the invasion crisis. An estimated 500,000 people turned up on each of the two days, and to John Carrington, Chief Constable of Bramfield, who journeyed all the way from Hertfordshire to see it, the display was entrancing: 'I never saw such a sight all my days.'[67] By the end of the nineteenth century, Queen Victoria incurred her subjects' displeasure if she was *not* accompanied on official occasions by military magnificence, a revolution in civilian response that had its origin in the Napoleonic period.[68]

Aided by an amateur soldiery, embellished with their brightly coloured uniforms, glistening firearms and martial music, civic processions in Britain came to be much bigger and more intricate affairs than ever before, often choreographed by specially appointed committees. Instead of being confined to members of the local corporation only, or to a select number of trade groups (the usual participants on high days and holidays before 1789), provincial processions on royal occasions were increasingly organised around both sexes, all age-groups and all classes–and for good reason. The more ambitiously inclusive such celebrations could be made, the more they could be seen as advertising broad local agreement in national and royal celebration.

Involvement started early. We are still very ignorant about the politicisation of children in Britain at this time, yet they were increasingly prominent in both radical and royal demonstrations. As far as the latter was concerned (and, who knows, perhaps the former also) the rapid growth of various kinds of charity and Sunday schools was an enormous boon. By 1800, there were some 200,000 children attending Sunday schools in England and Wales; thirty years later, there were almost 6,000 such schools, instructing 1,400,000 children. In addition, there was a massive rise in the number of schools providing cheap or, in some cases, free day education for the children of the poor. Just how amenable these children were to the ideas put to them by their social betters has been much disputed.[69] In all ages and in all countries, children are rarely as naïve and impressionable as adults would like to believe. But the temptation to involve what seemed a captive and comparatively docile audience in loyalist propaganda was certainly not one that Britain's ruling orders chose to resist at this time. On George III's birthday in 1813, for example, a group of fashionable ladies and gentlemen descended on a school for poor children in London. They paid for the boys and girls to be given a special celebratory dinner which they served themselves so that:

> they [the children] might be taught from ocular demonstration that goodness levels all ranks and conditions . . . Their susceptible little hearts had received, as it were, an electric stroke which had stamped them for ever as good men and true–the defenders till death of their King and Country.[70]

The burgeoning literacy rate in many parts of Britain meant that the children of the poor could now be supplied with patriotic tracts (as they were in Shrewsbury on George IV's coronation), or with copies of the national anthem (given to the Sunday School children of York on the same occasion). Since they were already pre-assembled and disciplined at fixed school buildings, it was very easy to incorporate such children in loyalist processions; and if their parents flocked to join the appreciative spectators, so much the better. Lancaster marched its Catholic, Methodist, non-conformist, and free-grammar-school children in four large blocs at its procession to mark George IV's coronation in 1821. And children were cheaply bribed. Manchester was one of many cities that started distributing free medals to children on a massive scale at royal events in this period; other places offered toys, Bibles, three-penny cakes or flags.[71]

The mobilisation of children, the most vulnerable sector of the population, shows the desire to use royal celebration to control and indoctrinate at its most naked and unashamed. But by no means all, or even the majority of men and women caught up in these jamborees can be regarded as passive and pliant victims of manipulation from above. Many must have attached themselves to a procession because it was something different and entertaining, or because they were given the day off and the promise of a free meal, or because participation was a way of signalling one's importance in the local community. The women who marched through towns singing the national anthem dressed as Britannia, or as Mrs John Bull, or even as classically draped virgins might well – as we shall see later – have their own agenda to serve.[72] So might freemasons. By 1800, almost all of the male members of the Royal Family were masons, and the Prince of Wales was Grand Master from 1790 to 1813. So the prominent masonic participation in royal celebration in this period was part a tribute to brothers who happened to be royal, part advertisement of the lodges' local clout and part a means for men who were prosperous but by no means necessarily top drawer to demonstrate their clubbery and cohesion.[73]

Lower down the social scale, friendly societies and trade groups were drawn into royal events not so much because of pressure from employers, but rather because marching through a town's streets, carrying trade banners as well as Union Jacks, was one of the few legal means available to demonstrate worker solidarity. Moreover, the trend towards *mass* royal celebration bestowed on workers a brief moment of power: the power to say no. And the evidence suggests that working men and women sometimes did say no. In 1821, only ten trade groups in Bristol consented to join the city's procession in honour of George IV's coronation. Ten years later, when William IV was crowned, no fewer than twenty-eight different trade groups marched through the city to celebrate Britain's new monarch and the commitment to parliamentary reform he supposedly represented.[74]

As Mark Harrison has argued, it is in practice wrong to study the dissident popular demonstrations that took place throughout Great Britain in the late eighteenth and early nineteenth centuries in isolation from large-scale loyalist events, as though only the former were radical in impact and the latter always and invariably conservative.[75] In both kinds of mass action, what was most striking was the dramatic rise in the number of Britons and also the kinds of Britons who were getting involved in public politics. A constricted polity was having to become very much wider. In this sense, there was surprisingly little difference between monarchical Britain and Revolutionary France, where, as Lynn Hunt has described, post-1789 regimes deliberately involved more and more people in politics as a means of strengthening themselves:

> The power of the revolutionary state . . . expanded at every level as people of various stations invented and learned new political 'microtechniques'. Taking minutes, sitting in a club meeting, reading a republican poem, wearing a cockade, sewing a banner, singing a song, filling out a form, making a patriotic donation, electing an official – all these actions converged to produce a republican citizenry and a legitimate government.[76]

Such 'microtechniques', such acts of individual initiative, commitment and participation, were not uniquely French. Nor were they the monopoly of republicans and radicals. In Great Britain, similar political devices had become more common and more widespread from the mid-eighteenth century onwards. But now they were being channelled into royal celebration to a quite unprecedented extent. As a result, more men and women learnt loyalty and found it absorbing in a new way. But some of them at least must have learnt other things as well: how to march in a procession, how to fabricate and display banners, how to attend organisational meetings – in short, how to plan and stage a political event out of doors. The massive workers' procession that preceded Peterloo in August 1819 – 'the discipline and pageantry with which the contingents moved towards Manchester – a leader to every hundred men (distinguished by a sprig of laurel in his hat), the bands and the great embroidered banners . . . the contingent of "our handsomest girls" at the front' – clearly owed a great deal to recently acquired popular familiarity with large-scale royal ritual.[77] As was so often the case, mass patriotism challenged the existing order even as it helped to support it.

MEANINGS AND MAGIC

Manifestly, then, George III's kingship meant very different things to different groups of Britons at different stages of his long reign. At one time denounced as tyrannical or mad; at another, cherished as the Father of his People and as a national totem; applauded by some of his subjects as the guarantor of British prosperity and stability; celebrated by others for their own private and sectional reasons; and consistently dismissed by a republican minority as an expensive irrelevance: more than most rulers, this ultimately mediocre man evoked a bewildering variety of vivid responses. Reaching through the detail and divergence to the broad significance of his reign for the evolution of the monarchy's public and patriotic image is therefore difficult, and one can arrive at two rather different conclusions.

Viewed against the background of his Hanoverian predecessors, the transformation that George III effected by his own actions and experienced through the actions of others was dramatic. George I and George II had been handicapped by their perceived partisanship, by their German upbringing, by the spectre of Jacobitism and by having too much power to avoid controversy and not enough to finance sustained grandeur or dominate government. George III, by contrast, was dynastically secure, ostentatiously British and a-party; and sufficiently uncontroversial by the 1780s to be celebrated nationwide to an unprecedented degree, and to be supported in this belated apotheosis by most of the governing class.

Death marked the change with massive clarity. When George I expired while visiting Hanover in 1727, no one in Britain seems to have clamoured for the return of the body, and no monument to him was ever erected. George II fared little better in 1760. Outside the court, the newspapers did not scruple to report that he had died in the lavatory, anymore than the *Gentleman's Magazine* was abashed at printing a coloured diagram of his dissected heart.[78]

51. Diagram of George II's dissected heart published in the *Gentleman's Magazine* in November 1762.

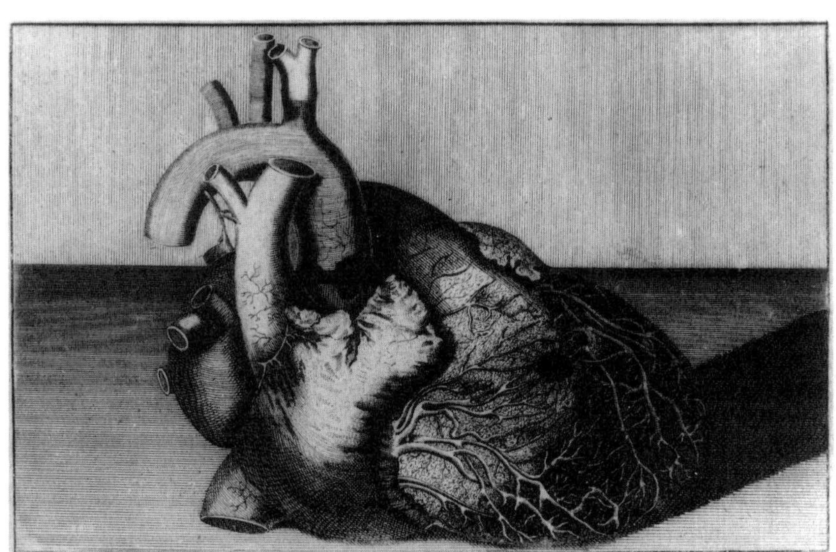

Polite society was not much more reverential. The funeral of the man who had ruled Great Britain for more than thirty years noted one politician was 'not well attended by the peers nor even the king's old servants'.[79] Yet when George III died sixty years later, shops shut throughout the kingdom; even the London poor were reported as wearing some signs of mourning; both government and opposition politicians paid their respects; and over 30,000 people descended on the town of Windsor for the funeral, even though it was a strictly private occasion.[80]

This was impressive. Yet in terms of what happened to his successors, George III's apotheosis can easily seem much less decisive. From the day of George IV's coronation in 1821, when his estranged wife Caroline stumped around Westminster Abbey in a vain attempt to gain admission, through to his unlamented death in 1830, this British king was both widely denounced and mercilessly ridiculed.[81] Later in the nineteenth century, many of the criticisms levelled against the early Hanoverian kings seemed to undergo a revival. Married to Albert, Queen Victoria would be attacked for being partisan and pro-German; newly widowed, she would be censured for presiding over a dull court and for living like a recluse shut off from her subjects.[82] Not until the end of the nineteenth and the beginning of the twentieth century would there be another, and far more sustained rise in the British monarchy's popularity and ceremonial appeal, a rise connected with many of the same forces that had underpinned celebration of George III a century before: imperial grandeur and anxiety, the need to control a growing and disorderly population infected by more democratic ideas, and the accident of successful war.[83]

Starkly contradictory though these two views of the significance of George III's reign may seem to be, in reality they are far from being mutually exclusive. It should come as no surprise that monarchy's reputation in Great Britain – as in other nations – fluctuated wildly over time, or that its current popularity is a product of cyclical, not of steady growth. The unevenness of the British monarchy's public appeal and ritual splendour after 1820, in other words, should not be seen as detracting from the importance of what went before. Like other members of the patrician class, George III had succeeded in reconstructing his authority in the face of defeat in America and revolution in France by coming to terms with the nation in a new and far more self-conscious way. And in three respects, at least, his legacy proved a durable one. By the end of his reign, the monarchy was more genuinely and assertively British than it had been before; it was indisputably more splendid;

and it was more securely at one with the politics of unreason and emotionalism.

It was now axiomatic that royal celebration should ideally involve all political affiliations, all religious groupings and all parts of Great Britain: in other words, that it should at least *seem* to be authentically national and not sectional celebration. This had by no means always been the case. When George II had been crowned in 1727, Whig and Tory activists in many provincial centres organised separate and competing festivities for the occasion. By contrast, most of the local committees organising celebrations in 1821 (George IV's coronation), 1831 (William IV's coronation) and 1837 (Queen Victoria's coronation) were ostentatiously bi-partisan, and controversial emblems, mottos or colours were banned from their arrangements.[84] This did not automatically make them consensual affairs, of course. But that they should ideally be consensual was now explicitly the official intention.

By the same token, it had become common for special religious services for royal occasions to occur in all places of worship, not just in Protestant churches: 'The cathedral, the abbey, the parochial church, the meeting house of the dissenter, the chapel of the Methodist and the Catholic and the synagogue of the Israelite', catalogued *The Times* on Jubilee Day in 1809, 'were alike opened on this interesting occasion.' 'The whole nation', agreed the *Day*, was 'like one great family . . . in solemn prayer and thanksgiving, for . . . the Father of his People.'[85] Even though royal assent had still to be given to Catholic emancipation and Jewish emancipation, religious pluralism was now firmly built into patriotic display and directly encouraged by the Royal Family itself. Several of George III's sons, for example, made a point of paying formal visits to the more fashionable London synagogues, if only because of the importance of Jewish finance in funding the National Debt during the Napoleonic wars.[86]

The centre of this web of royal celebration was far more splendid and far more stable than it had been when George III succeeded to the throne. Later monarchs would continue to stage small aesthetic rebellions – George IV blew up Kew Castle and Brighton Pavilion was sold off by Victoria and Albert – but none of them disputed that what really mattered was Windsor Castle and Buckingham Palace, both now sumptuously decorated establishments comparable with anything Continental Europe had to offer. As regent and king, George IV spent £1,650,000 from the Civil List, and more from his own funds, extending these two palaces even further and refurbishing the dynasty's base in Scotland, Holyroodhouse. He also coaxed £787,000 from Parliament towards the creation of Regent Street, Marble Arch, Trafalgar Square, an enlarged British Museum, a new Mint and a new building, designed by Robert Smirke, 'worthy of the first Post Office in the World'.[87] His own and John Nash's plans to marmorealise the metropolis were never fully completed. But London was now equipped as a stage for ceremonial to a degree that would have been unthinkable fifty years before. It was also led by plutocrats fattened on the French wars, who relished their city's status as the seat of worldwide empire. Back in the 1760s and '70s, London's Common Council had bombarded the king with petitions in favour of John Wilkes and against the American war. Now the city's rulers lavished money on royal banquets, bestowed their Freedom on as many members of the Royal Family as would accept it and invested in special banners to be used on all occasions of royal celebration, emblazoned with the letters S.P.Q.L. Leading citizens of the new Rome, they wanted Caesar in their midst and were prepared to fête him.[88]

But for the bulk of Britain's population, it was not so much these material developments that made a difference as the evolution of a new kind of royal magic and mystique. The essence of Edmund Burke's *Reflections on the Revolution in France* (1790) had been an assault on the notion that kings were to be valued only for their civic usefulness. Monarchy, as he rightly diagnosed, could never survive on constitutional abstractions alone. If it was to flourish, it required romance, glamour, irrationality and uncritical devotion. It also needed a human face, to 'be embodied . . . in persons'.[89] For these purposes, it was no longer enough for royal apologists to emphasise that George III ruled with divine approval because he was a Protestant and a constitutional monarch. A more personal foundation for monarchy was wanted. And it was duly found, found by giving the very old notion of the king's two bodies a new and more secular twist. Yes, the line now went, George III was on a different level from all of his subjects, the inhabitant of splendid palaces and the fulcrum of unprecedented ceremony; but he was also a husband, a father, a mortal man subject to illness, age and every kind of mundane vulnerability, and, therefore, essentially the same as his subjects. 'It is an important truth', *The Times* would declare on the day of his funeral in 1820, 'that most of the qualities which George III possessed . . . were imitable and attainable by *all classes* of mankind.'[90] Herein lay the essence of a newly invented royal magic. At one and the same time, Britons were being invited to see their monarch as unique and as typical, as ritually splendid and remorselessly prosaic, as glorious and *gemütlich* both.

This brand of magic helped to transmute George III's weaknesses into strengths. By way of its alchemy, his severe bouts of illness, his encroaching age and his bevy of dissolute sons seem not so much to have detracted from the reputation of the monarchy, as to have increased public protectiveness towards the king himself. By being manifestly vulnerable, he became more not less appealing. But the magic also made the most of those qualities he undoubtedly possessed: his morality, his domesticity, his taste outside of ceremonial occasions for the simple life generously defined. It was qualities of this kind that made possible his absorption into a very traditional piece of folklore: namely, the recurrent myth of a king going about his people incognito and hearing their unstudied comments. Stories of George III doing precisely this became increasingly common in newspapers and broadsheets from the 1780s onwards:

> The farmer grown familiar asked the gentleman, as he thought, if he had seen the King; and being answered in the affirmative, the farmer said 'Our neighbours say, he's a good sort of man, but dresses very plain'. 'Aye', said his Majesty, 'as plain as you see me now', and rode on.[91]

All of those aspects of the king's life which might have seemed merely dull – and certainly did seem so to patrician sophisticates at court – were conjured by royal propagandists, and even by some of their opponents, into evidence for the king's winning humanity. When the royal couple could be pictured by Gillray, parsimoniously eating boiled eggs in front of the fire, or when a mock epitaph could be issued for Queen Charlotte, characterising her as an over-frugal housewife killed by falling into a washing tub, it was clear that even the satirists had become hopelessly entangled in the myth of royal ordinariness.

The deeply appealing myth that members of the Royal Family were just like everyone else, yet at the same time somehow different was spread by the marked increase in royalty's physical mobility. George III himself was too frail to travel after 1800, but his numerous sons – too often dismissed by historians as either entertaining or deplorable wastrels – visited almost every region of Great Britain, wooing local opinion as they went along by accepting the Freedom of major cities. Prince William of Gloucester, for example, visited Edinburgh on his way to accepting the Freedom of Glasgow in 1795, and subsequently journeyed to receive the Freedom of Cambridge (1799), of Liverpool (1804), of Birmingham (1805), of Bristol (1809) and of London (1816). The reputedly liberal Duke of Sussex was even more enterprising, not just accepting Freedoms from old cathedral cities like Bath, Bristol and

52. James Gillray, *Temperance enjoying a Frugal Meal*, engraving, 1792.

Chester, but also visiting Wales, the industrial north, Sunderland, Doncaster and Newcastle.[92]

Few of these visits were as impeccably organised as royal excursions would be in the later nineteenth and twentieth centuries.[93] But they did enable far more Britons than ever before to see members of the Royal Family, to see – though at a carefully regulated distance – what they looked like, how they dressed, and how they behaved. Something of the impact that exposure to royalty could have on unsophisticated spectators is suggested by this eye-witness account of George IV's visit to Edinburgh in 1822, the first visit to Scotland by a ruling monarch since the 1630s:

> A continued line of pale faces, with expectation wound up to actual pain, and a sort of bewildered smile on their first glimpse of that being called a king – Britain's king – Scotland's king – their own king! The moment come, the first in their lives, when they could compare the actual thing called Majesty, with all they had from childhood dreamed and fancied of it![94]

Yet again the magic was working. Being seen in person seems often to have made members of the Royal Family, not, to say the least, a physically beguiling group of individuals at this time, more remarkable to the public not less.

Growing up around the British monarchy, not fully recognised by the kings themselves, perhaps, but certainly perceived by more astute courtiers and politicians, was a formula for unprecedented public success, a new kind of patriotic significance and a peculiar brand of subjugation. The Marquess of Anglesey, Waterloo veteran, cabinet minister and courtier, would set out the formula with damning and admirable clarity in a conversation with the future William IV in 1830:

> Your Royal Highness must bear this in mind – You must keep a brilliant Court . . . without making yourself too common, you must nevertheless frequently show yourself amongst your subjects.

In other words, the monarchy must be seen to be splendid, but above all, it must be *seen*.

> The advantages of a female Court after so long an absence of any thing of that sort, were incalculable.

That is, royalty must go hand in hand with an appearance of domestic bliss; without, however, remaining too long behind the shelter of palace walls:

> I observed upon the propriety of a King visiting periodically the various parts of his dominions.[95]

Ritual splendour, an appearance of domesticity, and ubiquity: this was the formula that George III taught and bequeathed to his royal successors. That it made them captives after a fashion, at the same time as it captivated large numbers of Britons, was the price of its success.

6 *Womanpower*

On 22 June 1814, the men and women of Taunton in Somerset took the day off and celebrated the outbreak of peace. Happily unaware that it would require yet another massive battle finally to destroy Napoleon and his armies, they gave themselves over to what the journalists called a 'lavish display of public exaltation'. The local poor were buried in free beef, beer and plum pudding. A triumphal arch was manufactured over the western approach to the town, topped with a banner proclaiming that John Bull had done his duty. And through this unsteady construction of canvas and plyboard marched a procession: the army and navy veterans, the volunteer corps, the civic dignitaries and clergymen, the schoolchildren, and the trade groups, tailors, stonemasons, coal carriers, carpenters, printers and the like, each with the emblems and banners of their particular craft. To the unobservant, it must have seemed a typical civic celebration, well meant, a little under-rehearsed, perhaps, and certainly over-long. Yet here, in Taunton's peace festival, and in many similar events taking place throughout Great Britain, something new and significant was happening.

Marching alongside Taunton's trade groups were members of six female friendly societies. The bourgeois gentleman allotted the satisfying task of playing the part of the Duke of Wellington for the occasion was joined in his carriage by a woman of the same social rank dressed as Britannia. Following decently behind, came not only 'a respectable yeoman' got up as John Bull, but also a woman from a similar background posing as Mrs Bull.[1] Deliberately, and across the social spectrum, patriotic celebration had been given a female component. And, as far as Britain was concerned, this was a recent innovation. In the past, women had occasionally served as anonymous props in civic processions, posing as Liberty or – as here – Britannia.[2] But rarely had they marched, as the female societies of Taunton did, in their own right. Nor had the character of Mrs Bull been a familiar one in British civic and patriotic ritual before the American Revolution. Her presence, now, side by side with her 'husband', John Bull, suggested that the claims of women were coming to be recognised in this society in a new way. By participating as actors and not just as spectators in this victory procession, and in many others that took place throughout Great Britain in 1814 and 1815, women proclaimed that they, too, were patriots who could make an active contribution to the nation's welfare and progress. Yet just what kind of patriots could female Britons hope to be?

BEATING AGAINST THE BONDS OF WOMANHOOD

The debate over woman's proper place in society had become increasingly intense as the eighteenth century progressed, not just in Great Britain but throughout western Europe and North America. In all of these areas, women were formally excluded from exercising political rights, and in England and Wales the restrictions on them were harsher in some respects than elsewhere. The author of *The Laws Respecting Women* summed up the position conventionally enough in 1777: 'By marriage the very being or legal existence of a woman is suspended'. Every wife except a queen regnant was under the legal authority of her husband, and so was her movable property: 'She can't let, set, sell, give away, or alienate any thing without her husband's consent. Her very necessary apparel, by the law, is not her's in property.'[3] The law of Scotland was kinder to women in matters to do with divorce, but here, too, it was the rule that 'on marriage, the husband acquired power over the person of his wife, who was considered to have no legal *persona*'.[4] Throughout Great Britain, the end result of all this was the same. Stripped by marriage of a separate identity and autonomous property, a woman could not by definition be a citizen and could never look to possess political rights. 'In Britain', a Scotsman explained in 1779,

> we allow a woman to sway our sceptre, but by law and custom we debar her from every other government but that of her own family, as if there were not a public employment between that of superintending the kingdom, and the affairs of her own kitchen, which could be managed by the genius and capacity of women. We neither allow women to officiate at our altars, to debate in our councils, nor to fight for us in the field.[5]

Only in the bleakest way possible was a woman's freedom of political action in Great Britain formally acknowledged. If she committed high treason, she could be put on trial and burnt (not eviscerated like male traitors might be). A female Briton could be punished for plotting against the state, but – in law – she could never play the part of an active patriot within it.

The law though, if not an ass, is rarely an adequate reflector of social realities. The true position of British women was more diverse than the statute books suggested, and increasingly in flux. Many adult women, possibly the majority of those who were poor, worked for money wages, in agriculture, in cottage industries, in domestic service, in shops, in the mines, in anything they could get. If they were single or widowed, their wages and any other property they might possess, was their own by right. And if their parents were affluent and careful, even women who married could have property settled on them in advance which their husbands could not subsequently touch. To this extent, female Britons were in much the same position as the majority of their male countrymen. They might well possess some property to their name. But under the existing representative system, they had no vote. This was one reason why male anxieties about female pretensions became markedly sharper in the second half of the eighteenth century. If men without land but possessed of movable property were to start campaigning for admission to the political process, as they were by the 1760s, and if some radicals were to advance further and demand universal manhood suffrage, as they had by the 1780s, what was there to stop single or widowed, and possibly in the end, even married women seeking access to similar rights? How were upwardly mobile and politically ambitious British men to legitimise their claims to active citizenship, without taking women along with them?

One answer was by placing renewed emphasis on the physical, intellectual, emotional and functional differences between men and women. Jean-Jacques Rousseau's *Emile* (1762), which appeared in at least five different English-language editions before 1770, was only the most dazzlingly successful statement of this kind of highly polarised treatment of the sexes. Woman, Rousseau claimed, was born to obey. Less clever and physically weaker, she was an essentially relative creature, more dependent on her menfolk than they were on her. Yet her contribution to the well-being of the state was vital, as vital, indeed, as that of men, but essentially and necessarily different from it. The confines of the home were the boundaries of her kingdom. This was where she exercised a gentle and improving sway over her husband and forged the next generation, breast-feeding and brainwashing her children into patriotic virtue. Women who neglected their families for the outside world, who put their infants out to nurse, or worst of all, practised birth control, endangered the polity and violated their own natures. So did women who sought public recognition of any kind. 'Even if she possesses genuine talents', Rousseau argued, 'any pretension on her part would degrade them. Her dignity depends on remaining unknown; her glory lies in her husband's esteem, her greatest pleasure in the happiness of her family.'[6] Her contribution to the welfare of the nation was essentially private and always indirect.

Rousseau's sexual politics proved immensely influential in Britain, both among conservative moralists like James Fordyce, Hannah More and Jane Austen, and – almost against her will – on the feminist Mary Wollstonecraft who found it impossible and undesirable to escape entirely from the notion of separate male and female spheres: 'Man must necessarily fulfil the duties of a citizen, or be despised', she would write in her *Vindication of the Rights of Woman* (1792), and '. . . while he was employed in any of the departments of civil life, his wife, also an active citizen, should be equally intent to manage her family, educate her children, and assist her neighbours'.[7] To many, though not to her, the doctrine of separate spheres offered a reassurance that, although changes in the rights of man might be necessary and imminent, these need not and should not be accompanied by an alteration in the position of women either in the home or outside it.

For some, indeed, the welfare of Great Britain made it absolutely vital that women should continue to behave in a traditional manner. A cult of prolific maternity was immensely attractive to those who believed (as many did before the introduction of a census in 1800) that Britain's population was in decline, and to those who simply wanted more live births so that the nation might better compete in terms of cannon-fodder with France. This particular concern increased along with the scale of European warfare, as witnessed by the spate of maternity hospitals established for the benefit of the poor in London and elsewhere from mid-century onwards. Encouraging women to breed, urging the benefits of maternal breast-feeding over wet-nursing, rescuing foundlings and orphans, all of these causes became increasingly attractive to British legislators, pundits and charitable bodies in the second half of the eighteenth century, for practical as well as humanitarian reasons.[8] The motto of the Lying-in Charity for Married Women at their own Habitations, a smart London charity patronised by the Prince of Wales in the 1780s, was frank and typical: 'Increase of Children a Nation's Strength'.

And anxiety about keeping British women fertile, busy and contented within the domestic sphere only deepened as more and more of them appeared to be active outside it. The chief omens and agents of change were as always the towns. Women formed the majority of urban populations, as servants, as workers in shops and taverns, as vagrants and as prostitutes at one end of the social sprectrum; and, at the other, as residents and visitors drawn to amenities that the countryside could not offer: theatres, assembly rooms, lending libraries, concert halls, elegant squares and enticing bow-windowed shops.[9] As the rate of urbanisation accelerated, moralists became more anxious about its impact on female manners and behaviour. They worried about the increasing number of young women abandoning the safety and supervision of the countryside to take up employment as domestic servants in the towns. They worried even more about what this rise in the number of servants signified, the fact that female leisure was no longer just the prerogative of the well-born or the very rich. Relieved of the heavier domestic duties, middle-class wives and daughters, and even the wives and daughters of petty tradesmen, were more likely to wallow in consumerism and vanity. They might come into contact with new and disreputable ideas. They might, like Sheridan's Lydia Languish, read unwholesome novels, or still worse, write them. (Increasingly, of course, women did both.) They might, free from the supervision of husbands and fathers, encounter men. They might cease to be virtuous.

The close connexion between the progress of urbanisation and apprehension about the roles of the sexes emerges very clearly in the case of Scotland, where the growth of Edinburgh, Aberdeen, Glasgow and many lesser towns can be measured by the rate of gloomy pronouncements on the deterioration of female manners. Who in the future would bear the children, worried Lord Kames, now that so many women were intent on enjoying themselves outside the home?[10] Public places, argued John Gregory, Professor of Medicine at Edinburgh University, were not 'suited to make people acquainted together'. Wives and particularly daughters should ideally conduct their social encounters under the shelter of the patriarchal roof. Women were the 'principal springs' of society, flattered the Aberdeen divine James Fordyce in 1776, but all the more reason why they should be confined to an acceptable role and to a separate sphere: 'the sons of reason should converse only with the daughters of virtue'.[11] Once, recollected the historian James Ramsay, Scottish women had 'made their most brilliant appearance at funerals'. Now there had been a 'wonderful change upon female manners, in consequence of playhouses, assemblies and concerts'.[12]

By the time Ramsay was writing, a much closer monitoring of female socialising was occurring in the towns themselves. In the 1750s, Edinburgh's one assembly room had been presided over by a woman, the sister of Lord Mansfield, and its account books had been 'open to the ladies at all times'. By the 1780s, the city had three assembly rooms. But the most fashionable, in New Town, was run by a male steward, and its rules specifically banned 'young ladies out of women's dress'.[13] Anxiety about women wearing pseudo-masculine dress was particularly prominent at this time, and seems in retrospect absurdly overdone. All that was happening in reality was that a minority of fashionable women had taken to wearing a version of a man's riding-coat, on top of a more severely tailored skirt for outdoor pursuits such as walking, horseback-riding and tourism. Yet, as the dozens of satirical prints devoted to this topic make clear, the changing silhouette of some women was interpreted as a further demonstration that the world was shifting dangerously. As so often happens, the debate over the position of women at this time became the meeting point of much broader anxieties. Under enormous pressure from war and revolution without, and more rapid social and economic transformations at home, Britons seized upon the comparatively minor changes in women's state as a symbol of all that seemed disturbing and subversive.

Just how fierce reactions could be was shown in the protracted campaign to elect Members of Parliament for the city of Westminster in 1784. This was the first general election to be held after the war with America, and the first ever in British history in which the position of women became a contentious political issue argued over in speeches, ballads, prints and the press. At one level the debate settled, interestingly enough, on maid-servants. The Prime Minister, William Pitt the Younger, had acknowledged their new pervasiveness by proposing to levy a tax on their employers. This was seen by the servants themselves as a possible threat to their jobs, and the opposition candidate at Westminster, Charles James Fox, duly canvassed against it. But it was women from a very different social background, and one woman in particular, who attracted far more attention.

It is a mark of the residual sexism of British historiography that we still know so little about Georgiana, Duchess of Devonshire, and that even now she can be referred to as an 'aristocratic supertramp'.[14] Contemporaries knew better. When she died in 1806, one of her obituaries described her as 'well read in the history and polity of all countries', and making due allowance for flattery, she does seem to have read avidly and to have been fascinated by the ideas as well as the personnel of politics. We know that she was an enthusiastic disciple of Rousseau, reading him, of course, in the original French; and that she was sufficiently interested in the new ideas about women's education to employ the daughter of the

53. *An Officer in the Light Infantry driven by his Lady to Cox-Heath.* A satire on female cross-dressing, *c.*1780.

redoubtable Sarah Trimmer, friend of Johnson and influential author, as governess to her children. But if she was clever enough to write at least one successful novel herself, she was also fundamentally bored. Married at sixteen, very much on her parents' instructions, to William Cavendish, 5th Duke of Devonshire, who was grand, dull, sexually unfaithful and completely unambitious, she lived 'in a continual bustle without having literally anything to do'. Partly because of this, she became an ardent Whig, acting as a political hostess in London, passing letters and rumours between great men and serving as the platonic confidante of both Fox and the Prince of Wales. (It was only later that she had an adulterous affair with the future Lord Grey of the Reform Act.)[15] To this extent, Georgiana was doing no more than many other patrician women who were always allowed a certain degree of political influence behind the scenes. But at the Westminster election, she crossed the divide separating private female influence on male politicians (which was acceptable) from autonomous and political public action (which was not).

It was not unusual for rich and aristocratic women to take part in canvassing at elections on behalf of male relations.[16] Georgiana's own mother, the sedate and highly religious Countess Spencer, had canvassed the borough of Northampton on behalf of her son, seeing this as a perfectly acceptable extension of her family duties, not a deviation from them. But by involving herself in the Westminster election in 1784, Georgiana broke with precedent in two crucial respects. Self-evidently, Westminster was not a family borough. Nor was it rural, or secluded, or safely distant from the public gaze. It was the constituency in which the Houses of Parliament were situated, the largest and most democratic borough in Great Britain in terms of its electorate, and the most likely to attract the attention of the newspaper press. Moreover, the candidate she was assisting, Charles James Fox, was not a blood relation. He was the highly controversial leader of the Whig opposition contingent in the Commons, a gambler and a rake, a fierce critic of monarchy, an advocate by this stage of a broad household suffrage, a man who was even prepared to suggest in 1797 that well-educated women should, conceivably, have the vote.[17] By supporting him out of doors and not just in the smug seclusion of the great Whig town houses, Georgiana laid herself open to the accusation that he was her lover, or that she was interfering in the political process out of conviction rather than from a suitably feminine attachment to individuals. The latter charge was true, and the language she used to vindicate herself reveals how conscious she was of the barriers confronting her, and how much she had to steel herself in

54. *The Devonshire Amusement*, anonymous print, 1784.

order to cross them: 'I am as calm about politics *as is decent*', she reassured her mother during the campaign, '. . . for really, *without pretending to wisdom*, the state of things is alarming for the constitution'. And again, 'This is an odious subject, and *yet considering all things, do what one will*, it is a subject one must think and feel about.'[18]

The scores of satirical prints issued about her electioneering activities in 1784, most of them hostile, have usually attracted attention only for their facile obscenity. But claims that the duchess had traded sexual favours in return for votes for Fox were not in fact the heart of the matter. It was the unnaturalness of female participation in the public sphere that the cartoonists returned to again and again, and the image of a wife of a peer breaking class ranks to embrace plebeian voters was summoned up only as part of this much greater breach of the accepted order. A print called *Political Affection* showed the duchess pressing a fox to her breasts while her hungry child clamoured for milk. The obvious implication, that she was neglecting her own realm of private affection in order to interfere in the public, was hammered home in another caricature showing the hapless Duke of Devonshire being forced to change his child's nappy in the absence of its mother. This print is divided into two halves, mimicking the two separate spheres in which men and women supposedly operate. But there has been a dramatic transfer of roles. For while the duke surveys his offspring's raw behind in the narrow confinement of the home, a portrait of himself with cuckold's horns behind him, the duchess – as in almost all the cartoons of her in 1784 – is out in the open air, her hair wild, her dress windswept, her garter undone and a staff of liberty surmounted by Fox's head and two phallic fox tails clutched in her hand.

But perhaps the most powerful comment on the abnormality of the duchess's endeavours was an anonymous drawing of one half of her plucked and powdered face joined, but only partially joined, to half of Charles James Fox's blue, unshaven visage. As the accompanying verse made clear, the point was not just that their alliance was irregular, even monstrous, but that the split between rough and virulent political man on the one side, and simpering, fashionable femininity on the other, was simply too great for fusion between them to be possible. And if the coming together of political man and would-be political woman was not to be represented visually, neither could it easily be expressed in words. To his supporters in the Westminster election, Fox was pre-eminently 'The Man of the People', a reformer and a democrat. For the duchess to assume an analogous title and become the woman of the people would have meant, as her critics pointed out, proclaiming herself to be a prostitute. The same English language that dignified a public man, demeaned a public woman.

Try as they might, Georgiana's champions were unable to construct a satisfying way of legitimising and explaining her endeavours. One writer made a stab of mocking the idea 'that ladies of quality have no business with the affairs of the nation [and] . . . ought never to come out of the nursery except to make a pudding'.[19] But many others contented themselves with celebrating the duchess's beauty, delicacy and innocent friendship with Fox, thereby converting her support for political ideas into a more acceptable and sentimental attachment to an individual. Even more turned her into a muse. Cartoons issued in her defence show her being escorted by Liberty and Fame to receive a wreath of laurel from Britannia, or raised above the prone body of Scandal by the loosely draped figures of Truth and Virtue. Such conceits were just another and very useful way of sanitising her actions. Taken in hand by the Virtues (who are often shown holding her arms as though physically to restrain her), she became just another female allegory that could be admired as a symbol, without in any way

Cheek by Joul or the MASK
Two faces here in one you see deſign'd,
Each ſtrongly mark'd declares the inward mind,
One ſeems ambitious of a daring ſoul,
The other ſoft the paſsions to controul.
One rough & virulent, th' other fair & free,
With looks that promiſe ſenſibility.
When ſuch as theſe in harmony unite,
The contraſt ſurely muſt amaze the ſight.
Publish'd by E Hedges No 92 Cornhill May 3d 1784

55. *Cheek by Joul or the Mask*, anonymous print, 1784.

56. *The Apotheosis of the Dutchess*, anonymous print, 1784.

challenging or even speaking to current ideas of woman's place in the nation. When Fox was finally declared elected as MP for Westminster in May 1784, his supporters staged a celebratory procession which wound past Devonshire House in Piccadilly. Taking part in it was the Duchess of Devonshire's carriage, topped with a banner inscribed 'Sacred to Female Patriotism'. Even her co-workers in the Foxite camp had been unable to admit Georgiana to the ranks of a single and communal patriotism embracing women as well as men. As for the carriage itself, it was empty.[20] At the next general election in 1790, Georgiana remained out of town, cowed into silence and private life.

The Westminster election was a minor event, but it encapsulates an important paradox in the position of women in Britain and elsewhere during the half-century or so after the American Revolution. On the one hand, as this episode abundantly confirms, anxiety over women's freedom of action increased during this period, as did the determination to regulate it more closely. In particular, there was far more emphasis than ever before in print, in art and in the spoken word on the need to exclude women from public life. In 1778, six years before the pillorying of the Duchess of Devonshire, the House of Commons barred women from listening to its debates from the gallery or floor of the House, as they had tended to do from the early eighteenth century onwards. And close to the end of the period covered by this book, in 1832, womens' exclusion from the franchise – hitherto taken tacitly for granted – would be formalised by the Reform Act specifically limiting the vote to suitably qualified 'adult males'.[21] In the intervening period, female Britons would be deluged with prescriptive literature of all kinds warning them that theirs was the private sphere and that this was where they must remain. 'As well as particular employments', thundered a male writer in the *Lady's Magazine* a month before the Westminster election ended,

> there are also particular subjects of conversation adapted to the different sexes; and as a very great judge of mankind hath said before me, that politics belong to the men, and to hear a woman talk with virulence of one party or the other, is as unbecoming as to hear one of us declaim against the particular cut of a pair of ruffles.[22]

We have already seen how challenges to the existing order in the late eighteenth and early nineteenth centuries were met in Great Britain by a reassertion of royal splendour and patrician power. It was not particularly surprising that these same massive disruptions – defeat in America, revolution in France and an unprece-

57. Thomas Rowlandson, *Procession to the Hustings after a Successful Canvass*, 1784.

dented rate of economic and social change in Britain itself – should also have provoked a restatement of the differences between the sexes and of the need for female subordination.

Yet those who argue that this period witnessed an actual contraction in women's public role in Britain as elsewhere and an unprecedented confinement of women to the private sphere confuse, it seems to me, angry polemic and symbolic gestures with what was happening in fact.[23] Yes: the House of Commons excluded women from listening to its debates after 1778. But only a very few patrician women had listened to them before that date; and those who wanted to eavesdrop on Parliament thereafter seem to have found ways of doing so. Yes: the Reform Act specifically prohibited women from voting in 1832. But even before this formal veto women had been unable to vote. And yes: the Duchess of Devonshire was savagely treated in 1784. Yet what is surely striking is that she was active in the Westminster election in the first place, as, incidentally, were many other fashionable women who attracted far less fire than she did. The very stridency of the opposition that greeted the duchess was itself a give-away. It demonstrated – more eloquently than anything else could do – that in Britain the boundaries supposedly separating men and women were, in fact, unstable *and becoming more so*.

At one and the same time, separate sexual spheres were being increasingly prescribed in theory, yet increasingly broken through in practice. The half-century after the American war would witness a marked expansion in the range of British women's public and patriotic activities, as well as changes in how those activities were viewed and legitimised. Women from different social backgrounds would take part in pro-war activism. Women would make a major contribution to the growing tempo of royal celebration. And even the most conventional British women would come to accept that formal exclusion from active citizenship did not exclude them from playing a patriotic role – and a political role of a kind.

WAR AND THE SEXES

All conventional wars in which men go away to fight and women stay behind at home focus attention on the divisions between the sexes. But the wars against Revolutionary and Napoleonic France did so to a peculiar degree and for particular reasons. Eighteenth-century Britons, as we have seen, regularly defined themselves in opposition to what they saw as being French characteristics and manners. And, even before 1789, it had been common for writers on proper female conduct, whatever their politics, to invoke the supposed behaviour of Frenchwomen as exemplifying what must at all costs be avoided in Britain. Frenchwomen, John Andrews observed in 1783, had whiter teeth than their sisters across the Channel, but this small merit was cancelled out by their heavy use of cosmetics. Frenchwomen, Mary Wollstonecraft agreed, were too vain, too frivolous, too self-indulgent, too prone to sensuality to be the model for rational and modest womankind.[24] The charge most frequently made, however, usually by men, was more serious: it was that Frenchwomen had too much of the wrong kind of power.

By way of the Parisian salons, in which both sexes gathered to exchange cultural and scientific ideas, a minority of Frenchwomen had acquired pretensions to intellectual autonomy. Such women, wrote the conservative evangelical Thomas Gisborne, proved 'the least eligible of wives', but were fortunately '. . . phenomena rarely seen in the meridian of Great Britain'.[25] He felt less complacent about another supposed characteristic of Frenchwomen. Since France had been an absolutist monarchy, lacking responsible representative institutions, women there had been able to use their prominence at the royal court to engage in political intrigues with kings and ministers alike. And although the superiority of Britain's constitution, with its limited monarchy and all-male Houses of Parliament, had thus far prevented comparable female intrusions into high politics, in the actions of women like the Duchess of Devonshire, Gisborne saw signs of impending rot:

> The pattern . . . exhibited at Paris, has long been imitated in London as nearly as circumstances would allow. In proportion as the example of ladies in the highest circles affords encouragement to vanity or to hope; it is studied and followed by numbers of their female acquaintance whose situation gives them an opportunity of treading, though at an humble distance, in the same steps. Even women who have no connection with the political hemisphere are seen to be inspired by the passion communicated from their superiors; imbibe the quintessence of political attachment and antipathy; and by the ardour with which they copy the only part of their model which they have the means of emulating show that it is not through want of ambition that they are left behind in the race.[26]

Just like the French Jacobins would do after 1789, British moralists condemned *ancien régime* France for allowing women an unnatural prominence.[27] 'In France', asserted James Fordyce in 1776, 'the women are supreme: they govern all from the court down to the cottage.' 'The lust of power and dominion', agreed his fellow Scot John Andrews seven years later, 'has now taken possession of their ideas, and supplanted those sentimental attachments that used to characterise them.'[28] Describing 'inappropriate' female behaviour as French in this way was partly a polemical tactic: a means by which British moralists could stress how alien and unwelcome they found such behaviour to be. A woman who tried to act like a man was manifestly unnatural. And what better way could there be of making this clear to a British audience than by characterising such improper conduct as being peculiarly French?

But this coming together of Francophobia and preconceptions about sexual roles also operated at a deeper, less calculating level. There was a sense at this time – as perhaps there still is – in which the British conceived of themselves as an essentially 'masculine' culture – bluff, forthright, rational, down-to-earth to the extent of being philistine – caught up in an eternal rivalry with an essentially 'effeminate' France – subtle, intellectually devious, preoccupied with high fashion, fine cuisine and etiquette, and so obsessed with sex that boudoir politics were bound to direct it. All of these complex prejudices, which drew their substance from a modicum of fact, enabled conservatives in Britain in particular to see in the outbreak of the French Revolution a grim demonstration of the dangers that ensued when women were allowed to stray outside their proper sphere.

The actual events of the Revolution made this kind of analysis even more attractive. In October 1789, the market women of Paris, driven mad with famine, marched on Versailles, storming the apartments of the French Royal Family and forcing them to leave the palace and return under guard to their capital. These were the 'furies of hell, in the abused shape of the vilest of women' whom Edmund Burke stigmatised in his *Reflections on the Revolution in France* (1790). But the more influential part of this marvellously written, marvellously tendentious polemic was his description of the market women's victim, Marie-Antoinette, who had escaped from their clutches to seek refuge, as a proper woman should, 'at the feet of a king and husband':

> It is now sixteen or seventeen years since I saw the queen of France . . . and surely never lighted on this orb, which she hardly seemed to touch a more delightful vision . . . glittering like the morning star, full of life, and splendour, and joy . . . Little did I dream that I should live to see such disasters fallen upon her in a nation of gallant men, in a nation of men of honour and of cavaliers. I thought 10,000 swords must have leaped from their scabbards to avenge even a look that threatened her with

> insult. – But the age of chivalry is gone. – That of sophisters, economists, and calculators, has succeeded; and the glory of Europe is extinguished for ever . . . On this scheme of things, a king is but a man; a queen is but a woman; a woman is but an animal; and an animal not of the highest order. All homage paid to the sex in general as such, and without distinct views, is to be regarded as romance and folly.[29]

Although the impact of Burke's *Reflections* on the evolution of conservative ideology in general is now taken for granted, this particular paragraph – which made an enormous impression on contemporaries – has often been dismissed as over-the-top romanticism signifying very little. Yet if one seeks proof of Joan Scott's contention that 'gender is one of the recurrent references by which political power has been conceived, legitimated, and criticized', here it emphatically is.[30] Like most thinkers touched by the Enlightenment, Burke was accustomed to gauging the quality of a civilisation by the way that women were treated within it. For him, the twin phenomena of working women daring to seize the initiative in public events, and of a queen who was also a wife and mother being driven by force from her home, were alike proof that events in France threatened to undermine society as he knew and valued it. Deference to monarchy, deference to rank and religion, deference to the proper ordering of the sexes: all these, for Burke, were interconnected and put at risk by the Revolution.

For these reasons then – because of the outbreak of an increasingly radical revolution in a nation viewed as peculiarly 'feminine' and susceptible to female influence, and because of the active participation of women in the early stages of that revolution and the well-publicised fate of Marie-Antoinette – it was scarcely surprising that pre-existing anxieties about the position of women should have become still more intense in Britain after war with France broke out in 1793. Even more than before, both sexes, but particularly women, were deluged by conduct books, sermons, homilies, novels and magazine articles insisting that good order and political stability necessitated the maintenance of separate sexual spheres.[31] Women should remember, argued the High Tory clergyman Richard Polwhele, that 'the crimsoning blush of modesty, will be always more attractive than the sparkle of confident intelligence'.[32] 'Natural timidity and amiable softness', wrote a gentleman from Edinburgh, perturbed by a report that women there were engaging in target practice in readiness for a French invasion, were women's essential characteristics: '. . . Let them leave military duties and the defence of our national dignity to their fathers, their brothers, and their countrymen'. Women must never forget, urged Thomas Gisborne in his best-selling *Enquiry into the Duties of the Female Sex* (1796), Pericles' words to the matrons of Athens: 'Cherish your instinctive modesty; and look upon it as your highest commendation not to be the subject of public discourse.'[33]

Yet, at the same time as they were being urged to look, feel and behave in ways that were unambiguously womanly, many female Britons were in practice becoming more involved in the public sphere than ever before, not least in terms of patriotic activism. This does not mean that the majority of women, any more than the majority of men, invariably supported the wars against Revolutionary and Napoleonic France. They did not. Abundant evidence exists of women at all social levels who believed either that war was always sinful, or that these wars in particular were wrong and oppressive. Some more plebeian women simply resented the state's appropriation of their menfolk, hiding deserters, mutilating their husbands to save them from being conscripted, and – in Scotland at least – participating in violent anti-recruitment riots.[34] Yet none of this should obscure the fact that women were more prominently represented among the ranks of conventional patriots in this conflict than in any of Britain's previous wars. And this was recognised at the time by the politicians at Westminster. In 1804, for example, William Windham reminded the House of Commons that military victory would depend on civilian exertions, not just on the armed forces:

> We need go no further for a proof of this, than to enquire what the influence is, in promoting the military spirit, of that half of the community, which certainly takes no part in [armed] service, namely women.[35]

Those women who supported the war did so, in many cases, from the same motives as their menfolk: out of conventional chauvinism, out of ideological conviction, out of fear of a French invasion or of revolution at home, out of conformity with their neighbours even. But female patriotism also had more specialised sources. Many women, and not just the prosperous, seem to have believed that their own security and the security of the family unit were at stake in this French war as they had not been in earlier conflicts. In part, this was because the risk of a French invasion of Britain was so much greater in this war than ever before. But crucial, too, as an ingredient in female anxiety was the destruction of Marie-Antoinette and the rest of the French Royal Family.

Accustomed as we are now to assassination attempts against prominent women, and to women in general being slaughtered alongside of men in wars and revolutions, it is easy to forget just how much of an impression was made in the 1790s by tales of the guillotine's appetite for female and not just male victims, and by the guillotining of the French queen in particular.[36] Not since the execution of Henry VIII's wives in the early sixteenth century had such a high-ranking woman been *publicly* tried and *publicly* executed (Mary, Queen of Scots, remember, was done to death in decent obscurity). The greatly improved levels of literacy and communications ensured that Marie-Antoinette's grisly end was known and felt far more widely than these earlier female exits: *and it was shocking*. Shocking because – as Edmund Burke pointed out – it raised the issues of what, if anything, was due to female vulnerability, of just how safe women were, in fact.

If a woman could be violently done to death after a rigged trial in which she was accused among other crimes of child abuse, what else might happen to members of her sex? It is no accident that the language used in Britain to describe Marie-Antoinette's end frequently drew on images of violation. Here, for example, is Mary Wollstonecraft – not remotely a royalist sympathiser – describing the mob invasion of the queen's rooms in the Tuilleries:

> The sanctuary of repose, the asylum of care and fatigue, the chaste temple of a woman, *I consider the Queen only as one*, the apartment where she consigns her senses to the bosom of sleep, folded in it's arms forgetful of the world, was violated with murderous fury.[37]

Here was the destruction of Marie-Antoinette re-imagined as a prolonged and public rape.

Not everyone saw things so starkly. But among the propertied – and, I suspect, more widely – Marie-Antoinette's fall, imprisonment, trial and execution, were felt to be profoundly unnerving in a way that the demise of her husband, Louis XVI, was not. 'The impression of the Queen's death is constantly before my eyes', wrote the Duchess of Devonshire; 'The Queen of France is never for three minutes out of my head', claimed Horace Walpole: '. . . they have made her immortal'; and these kinds of highly emotional reactions were very common.[38] The stories circulating in France about Marie-Antoinette's reputed corruption, infidelities, lesbianism and incest with her son were far less current in Britain and insofar as they were known, seem only to have deepened the sense of horror at her fate. As Hannah More, no admirer of the queen, wrote on hearing the incest charge: 'It is so diabolical, that if they had studied an invention on purpose to whitewash her from every charge, they could not have done it more effectively.'[39]

Massively and gruesomely publicised in British conservative propaganda, the fate of Marie-Antoinette and her family seems genuinely to have appalled many women, encouraging them to see this war with France as a cause in which their own welfare and status were peculiarly involved.[40] Their responses might have been more mixed if Republican France had extended to its female population the kind of civil and educational advances advocated by radicals like Condorcet on one side of the Channel and Wollstonecraft on the other. But, of course, this did not happen. Just two weeks after Marie-Antoinette's execution in October 1793, the French government banned all women's political associations. In November, leading female republicans like Madame Roland and Olympe de Gouges were guillotined. And in 1804, the Napoleonic Code explicitly reinforced the authority of husbands and fathers over wives and daughters. The French Revolution, it seemed, had exposed women to political violence as never before, but in return, had given them few if any concrete advantages. Indeed, it could even be said to have deprived them of something. As Joan Landes and others have shown, much of the language and imagery of the French Revolution, particularly in its early stages, elevated obedience to an impersonal state over the importance of more homely, human ties.[41] Duty to the stern commands of the new French republic was now to come before attachment to the family, the only sphere of influence that most women possessed. Confronted with this state of affairs, more well-informed female Britons may well have decided that supporting the war against France was not just prudent but essential to their safety. 'The whole world might be at war', Laetitia Hawkins would argue in 1793,

> and yet not the rumour of it reached the ears of an Englishwoman – empires might be lost, and states overthrown, and still she might pursue the peaceful occupations of her home; and her natural lord might change his governor at pleasure, and she feel neither change nor hardship.[42]

In Great Britain, woman was subordinate and confined. But at least she was also safe.

The twin themes of the peculiar safety of British women and of their danger from the French were played on assiduously by loyalist propaganda during the wars. Pamphleteers, cartoonists and above all, clergymen summoned up the threat of pillage, massacre and rape at the hands of an invading French soldiery, apparently with considerable success. After the small French expeditionary force that landed in Fishguard, Pembrokeshire, in 1797 was rounded up, the captives had to be guarded from the fury of local villagers, and particularly from the anger of the women. 'The women were more clamorous than the men', reported Lord Cawdor, whose responsibility it was to escort the French prisoners to London, 'making signs to cut their throats, and desiring I would not take the trouble of carrying them further'.[43] A similar angry insecurity seems to have been felt by women in Leicester in September 1798, a time when a French invasion of Britain seemed more than usually likely. Leicestershire's militia had been urged by the government (which could not compel it) to volunteer for active service against the current Irish rising. Only half of the militiamen were willing to go, and the rest returned to their cosy local duties, marching through the county town on the way. They encountered 'the most marked disrespect', especially from the women.[44] This was not just because they had failed to fight, but because they had failed to fight in Ireland which was a logical jumping-off spot for any French invasion force aimed at the British mainland. When they jeered at the passing militiamen, Leicester's women were condemning the men of their own county for failing in their masculine as well as in their patriotic duty to protect them, for raising once again the spectre of the possibility that the age of chivalry was dead.

But female interest in the wars with Revolutionary and Napoleonic France also had far more positive, less passive sources, of which sex was undoubtedly one. An unprecedented number of uniformed males, marching, parading and engaging in mock battles in every region of Great Britain brought a pleasant *frisson* of excitement into many normally quiet and deeply repetitive female lives. One has only to remember how Mrs Bennet and her sillier daughters react in Jane Austen's *Pride and Prejudice* (1813) when a militia regiment is stationed within walking distance of their home. The fifteen-year-old Lydia Bennet's dreams of 'all the glories of the camp; its tents stretched forth in beauteous uniformity of lines, crowded with the young and the gay, and dazzling with scarlet', like Mrs Bennet's calculating fantasies about 'a smart young colonel with five or six thousand a year' suddenly materialising to take one of her girls off her hands, found many echoes during the war years outside the realm of fiction, and among plebeian Britons as well as the gentrified classes. William Rowbottom, an observant and literate weaver who lived and worked in Oldham near Manchester, was forever noting in his ungrammatical and miraculously surviving diary how the local working girls hung on the arms of soldiers, and how avidly they watched every recruiting parade they could get to see.[45]

The cult of heroism that flourished, as far as Great Britain was concerned, far more in these wars than in preceding conflicts, owed a great deal to this kind of female enthusiasm. Charlotte Brontë for one was a fervent admirer of the Duke of Wellington from when she was five years old. She collected pictures of him, scanned the Yorkshire newspapers for news of him and made him a prime actor in the fables of Glass Town and Angria that she devised with her sisters, Emily and Anne, and with her brother, Branwell. The obsession persisted into her mature writings. Arthur Wellesley, 1st Duke of Wellington, victor of Waterloo, was the germ from which the dark and masterful Mr Rochester of *Jane Eyre* would ultimately be created.[46] The power this character still exerts over women readers of all ages today should give us some insight into the intensely romantic, and often blatantly sexual fantasies that gathered around warriors such as Nelson and Wellington. Anyone wanting more substantial evidence for this need only go as far as Hyde Park in London, to the statue of Achilles, commissioned by the women of Britain in honour of the Duke of Wellington.

The idea for such a monument had originated with Lavinia, Countess Spencer, the staunchly evangelical wife of the 2nd Earl Spencer. In 1814, she launched a public subscription – confined, however, to women – and in due course collected more than £10,000. The commission was awarded to the eminently respectable Richard Westmacott, who promptly designed London's first nude statue, a bronze replica of one of the famous Quirinale horse-tamers, divested of his horse and transformed into the hero of the *Iliad* by the addition of a shield and a sword. What fascinated the majority of people at the time, however, was less the statue's impeccably classical pedigree, than the fact that a strictly female subscription had been expended on representing so much resplendent male nudity. Originally entitled 'The Ladies' Trophy', the statue when it was completed in 1822 very swiftly came to be known as the ladies' fancy. 'A difficulty has arisen', wrote Lady Holland, tongue in cheek:

> and the artist had submitted to the female subscribers whether this colossal figure should preserve its antique nudity or should be garnished with a fig leaf. It was carried for the leaf by a majority . . . The names of the *minority* have not transpired.[47]

The truth, however, was still more piquant, and more suggestive, too, of masculine anxieties in the face of unabashed female enterprise. It was apparently the gentlemen whom the very proper Lady Spencer had arranged to head the statue committee, not the lady subscribers, who insisted on the fig leaf.

For all of the prurient anecdotage surrounding it, Lady Spencer's initiative was in fact symptomatic of a wide-ranging and important

To ARTHUR DUKE of WELLINGTON
And his Brave companions in arms
This Statue of Achilles
cast in French Brass
Is inscribed by their Countrywomen!!
June 18th 1822
Making Decent——!!
Pubd by G Humphrey 27 St James's St London — August 8th 1822
This Print Commemorative of Anglo French BRASS & true British Chastity, is inscribed with veneration to that worthy man
Mr Willbyforce who with saintlike regard for the Morals of his Country, has undertaken to make the above fig Decent, from 10 in the Mg till Dusk

58. George Cruikshank, *Making Decent!!*, 1822.

CHARLES XII
FLANNEL-ARMOUR; _FEMALE-PATRIOTISM, _or _ Modern Heroes accoutred for the Wars
To the benevolent Ladies of Great Britain, who have so liberally supported the new system of Military Cloathing, this Print is dedicated

59. James Gillray, *Flannel-Armour – Female-Patriotism*, 1793.

development. Far more than in any previous war, British women discovered in patriotic activism in this conflict an outlet for their energies and organisational capacities, and a *public* role of a kind. As soon as the war broke out in 1793, groups of prosperous women banded together in all parts of the country to provide warm clothing for British troops about to set sail for Flanders. They organised collections of money and flannel garments and a depot in London in which to store the clothes until they were needed.[48] Other women from similar social backgrounds busied themselves making flags and banners for the volunteer and militia units that were sprouting up all over the island. These were then presented to the soldiers at open-air ceremonies in front of large audiences. Between 1798 and 1800 alone, over ninety different women are known to have presented colours to volunteer regiments in this way, sometimes making speeches to the assembled troops and spectators in the process.[49] But it was more common for women to advertise their loyalty by instigating subscriptions or joining in existing ones alongside the men. In 1798, so many women subscribed to the state-sponsored Voluntary Contribution to the war that the London *Times* wondered nervously whether separate subscription lists should not be set up for them.[50] Women were just as prominent in local and private subscriptions. In 1803, 20 per cent of those who subscribed towards the volunteer corps in the Welsh county of Monmouthshire were women. The following year, 120 women contributed to the London-based Patriotic Fund which distributed prizes and relief to wounded soldiers and seamen. The donors ranged from the dowager Lady Amherst, who gave 100 guineas, to seventeen farm girls who clubbed together (whether voluntarily or not is unknown) to the tune of eight shillings.[51]

Such contributions to the war effort were socially acceptable because they could be seen as an extension into the military sphere of the traditional female virtues of charity, nurture and needlework. For women to be supplying the soldiery with banners, flannel shirts and other material comforts was, superficially, all of a piece with their ministrations to their menfolk at home. Yet, in reality, what the women were doing represented the thin end of a far more radical wedge. By extending their solicitude to the nation's armed forces, men who were not in the main related to them by blood or marriage, women demonstrated that their domestic virtues possessed a public as well as a private relevance. Consciously or not, these female patriots were staking out a civic role for themselves.[52] And many of them relished it. Like the religious and local charity work in which middle- and upper-class women were becoming increasingly active at this time, war work took women out of the house and taught them how to lobby, run committees and organise: 'This has been a hurrying week for me', Hannah More wrote happily enough in 1794: '. . . trying to raise money for the militia's shoes; so much writing and talking'.[53]

Participating in wartime subscriptions could also involve women in organisational work, as well as allowing them to demonstrate that they enjoyed a measure of economic power. Those who gave usually acted on their own initiative, donating money in their own name and not waiting for their husbands or fathers to contribute. Women who subscribed alongside their husbands did sometimes make an appropriate genuflexion to patriarchy. A Mrs Roberts, for example, a civil servant's wife who subscribed to the Patriotic Fund in 1804, donated markedly less money than her husband did. Her son gave less than she did; and her daughter gave even less again, thereby underlining her place on the bottom rung of the family ladder. But not all families behaved as hierarchically as this. Mrs

Morris, the wife of a gardener at Brentford in Middlesex, gave the Patriotic Fund a guinea, exactly the same amount as her husband. Their children – both boys and girls – gave half a guinea each.[54]

Women's historians have largely ignored the wealth of evidence about female property and family politics contained in these patriotic subscription lists (and hundreds of them survive), perhaps because of the lingering belief that women are or should be more pacifist than men. Yet in the wars against Revolutionary and Napoleonic France, as in so many later conflicts, British women seem, in fact, to have been no more markedly pacifist than men. Instead, and exactly like many of their male countrymen, some women found ways of combining support for the national interest with a measure of self-promotion. By assisting the war effort, women demonstrated – in a highly acceptable fashion – that their concerns were by no means confined to the domestic sphere. Under cover of a patriotism that was often genuine and profound, they carved out for themselves a real if precarious place in the public sphere.

MAKING SEPARATE SPHERES WORK FOR WOMEN

Large-scale and protracted warfare, then, had something of the paradoxical impact on the British home front in these years that it would have to a much greater degree in the twentieth century. It accentuated the functional differences between the sexes, while at the same time widening the scope of female activity and endeavour. Those female Britons who invested heavily in patriotic activism remained, of course, very much the minority. Most women continued to acquiesce in the rightness of separate sexual spheres in the sense that they accepted that home and children, together with a measure of subordination to fathers and even more to husbands, were their primary duties, though not their only duties. For many working-class women with small, dependent children there was little choice in the matter. Home, with perhaps some poorly paid piece-work carried out inside it, was not a choice and certainly not a vocation. It was what there was.

Acknowledging that this was so, however, I would still want to differ from those historians who have presented this period as one of unambiguous retreat and restriction for women, and from those who would go on to argue that 'in the nineteenth century women were restricted to the private sphere more than ever before'.[55] There was a renovated cult of female propriety and domesticity evident in Great Britain from at least the 1770s: yes. It could and did restrict women: agreed. Women were prevented from participating in those political advances that the French Revolution seemed to promise and that British reformers increasingly demanded for adult males: of course. But the more calculated deployment of separate spheres rhetoric in this period also had a more unexpected set of consequences. It could supply a way for women to assert their important role in British society and to protect their rights such as they were.

One reason for this was that the doctrine of separate spheres – like many other political concepts – was ideally profoundly contractual. Women refrained, at least in theory, from invading the public sphere, the realm of action, on the understanding that their moral influence would be respected and recognised. They accepted a vulnerable position in life, on condition that men would maintain and respect them. Consider, for example, this speech made by a Miss Patterson, daughter of Lieutenant-Colonel Patterson, as she presented the colours to a London volunteer regiment in 1799:

> Though the duties imposed on our sex are confined to private life, and civil and military functions are your exclusive prerogative, it must not be supposed that because we cannot participate in your labours, we are indifferent to their object . . . The subversion of those principles which hold society together, is the aim of our implacable foe [that is, the French]. In the preservation of those principles we are as much interested as yourselves. For should you once acquire the character of modern revolutionists, should you cease to fear God and honour the King, female influence must be extinguished for ever. You would no longer respect us for that propriety of conduct, which we feel to be our highest ornament.[56]

How are we to read this pronouncement? Clearly it is utterly conservative in its absolute condemnation of everything the French Revolution stood for. Patterson even echoes Edmund Burke's prediction that the glory of Europe would be 'extinguished for ever', which she, very significantly, paraphrases as 'female influence must' – in the event of revolutionary contagion – 'be extinguished for ever'. The speech is conservative, too, in the sense that Patterson explicitly accepts, indeed celebrates, the way that her society confines her sphere of action. On the other hand, there she was on a London parade ground *publicly* lecturing squads of men standing silent before her, an action that very few non-royal females can have carried out in Britain before 1789. And in effect, what she was insisting upon was a mutually binding contract: I, as a woman, will do my duty. But you, as men, must do yours.

This was a very limited kind of female politics. And Patterson's words would have seemed a bitter mockery to many poorer

60. *Massacre at St. Peter's or "Britons Strike Home"!!!*. A satire on Peterloo published in August 1819.

women, struggling to keep themselves and their children alive, with very little to hope for from male chivalry, or from anything else. Yet the point that separate spheres was an essentially contractual doctrine was hammered home by various incidents in early nineteenth-century Britain, affecting all classes of women and men. Think, for example, of the furious public reaction to the Peterloo massacre in August 1819, when a troop of yeoman cavalry charged a mixed crowd which had assembled in St Peter's Field, Manchester, to hear the parliamentary reformer Henry Hunt. Of the 400 or so wounded in this débâcle, more than 100 were women; and two women as well as nine men were killed.[57] On this occasion, femaleness had conspicuously failed to ward off masculine aggression. The unwritten contract between the sexes had been broken in the most public manner possible: and the price the authorities paid for this was considerable. Without exception, every political cartoon published attacking this episode gave prominence to armed men pursuing, or riding over, or cutting down women, even though four times as many men as women had suffered. And it was very largely the power of this representation of Peterloo – of helpless British women being hurt rather than protected by men in uniform – that made it such a propaganda defeat for the British state. An even more telling propaganda defeat was the mirror image of Marie-Antoinette's execution in France, the trial of Queen Caroline in Britain.

Caroline's marriage to George, Prince of Wales, eldest son of George III, had been arranged in 1795 without either of them having seen each other. When they did see each other, it was mutual distaste at first sight. Legend has it, and it probably is nothing more than legend, that they spent only their wedding night together. Certainly, once their only child Charlotte was born in 1796, they went their separate ways. The prince reverted to gluttony, architecture and mistresses. His wife was caught up in a succession of rumoured and possibly real sexual scandals. In 1813, she was finally persuaded by the grant of a generous pension to go abroad, where she probably had an affair with her Italian major-domo, Bartolomeo Bergami. When her husband became King George IV in 1820, Caroline decided to return to Britain to claim her position as queen. To stop her, the king insisted that she be put on trial for adultery in the House of Lords. This was serious. Under a fourteenth-century law which had never been repealed, adultery on the part of a queen consort was accounted treason; and some arch royalists suggested that Caroline might pay for her transgressions with her life.[58]

But it did not happen, and we now know that one aspect of its not happening was a nationwide campaign on Caroline's behalf in which middle-class and working women were remarkably prominent: 14,000 Bristol women, more than 9,000 women from Edinburgh, 11,000 women from Sheffield, 17,600 married women from London, 3,700 'ladies' from Halifax, 7,800 from Nottingham, 9,000 from Exeter and tens of thousands more signed addresses in support of the queen. In Newcastle-upon-Tyne, where the pro-Caroline address was confined to men, one woman brought along her five sons and made them all sign, complaining to the organisers at the same time about her own exclusion: 'for it was a woman's cause'.[59] Those women who were able to sign lent their names to documents that reiterated the queen's virtue, attacked George IV for seeking to legitimate the double standard and expressed fears that a royal divorce would compromise the marital security of all British women. 'If an adultery can be established by remote inference', the Bristol women were made to argue, 'pleas for divorce will be indefinitely multiplied'. Or, as a contemporary ballad put it:

Attend ye virtuous British wives
Support your injured Queen,
Assert her rights; *they are your own*,
As plainly may be seen.[60]

As in the war years, British women showed themselves willing to leave the confines of their homes to defend their right to security within them.

At the same time, Whig and radical politicians, together with the newspaper press which was largely pro-Caroline, harped insistently on the sacred right to safety and security of all British women: 'The beauty – the goodness – the very helplessness of the sex', declared one MP, 'are so many claims on our support, are so many sacred calls on the assistance of every manly and courageous arm'.[61] At one level, such language demonstrated very starkly the severe limitations that the ideology of separate spheres imposed on women. Caroline – and by implication her female supporters – were not represented as citizens possessed of rights that had to be respected; but rather, as women who – because of their sex – merited masculine protection from all wrongs. A radical pamphlet called *The Queen and Magna Charta; or, the Thing that John Signed* summed up the contrast between the civic rights of British men on the one hand, and the strictly private prerogatives of their womenfolk on the other, by means of verse and the brilliant pen-and-ink drawings of William Hone. Under a picture of an Englishman, an Irishman and a Scotsman, was written:

These are
THE BRITONS,
By upstarts put down,
Who contend
For the honour of
CAROLINE'S CROWN.

This was followed by a drawing of an undifferentiated group of women and the lines:

These are
THE LADIES
Whose husbands and sons,
Can wield for their safety,
Both sabres and guns
Our solace, our happiness,
Charm of our lives
Our
MOTHERS,

THE QUEEN
AND
Magna Charta;
OR, THE
THING
THAT
JOHN SIGNED.
Dedicated to the Ladies of Great Britain.

" The Muses still with Freedom found,
" Shall to thy happy coast repair;
" Blest Isle! with matchless Beauty crown'd,
" And manly Hearts to guard the Fair!"
RULE BRITANNIA.

LONDON:
PRINTED FOR AND PUBLISHED BY T. DOLBY, 299, STRAND, AND
34, WARDOUR STREET, SOHO.
1820.

61. Title-page of William Hone's defence of Queen Caroline in 1820.

Our
SISTERS,
Our
DAUGHTERS,
Our
WIVES.

Men could be Britons, or Scotsmen, or Irishmen, or Englishmen. But women, according to this view of things, were not to be described in terms of such public allegiances.[62] They were ladies, who were to be characterised only according to their private relationships with men. And they were vulnerable.

Yet stressing female helplessness *and what was due to it* in this way could – up to a point – serve women's interests. The agitation surrounding Queen Caroline was so widespread and the rhetoric employed by her supporters was so emotive that the authorities were forced to retreat. The connexion Edmund Burke had drawn so many years before between the maltreatment of Marie-Antoinette and the rottenness of French politics was now disinterred and levelled with savage effect against Britain's Tory government and George IV. 'Marie-Antoinette had a faithful, virtuous, tender, affectionate husband', declared the London *Times*, 'so that if *she* were guilty of any licentiousness, her conduct was the more inexcusable'.[63] But Caroline – so the argument went – was a blameless woman married to a notoriously immoral monarch. And not just a blameless woman, but a blameless *British* woman. By prosecuting her, the state and its ruler stood condemned. In the face of this kind of language, the king, his ministers and the House of Lords were reduced to impotence. The queen was in effect acquitted, and the ghost of Marie-Antoinette was finally laid.

It has been suggested that 'the sentimental sensationalism and domestic melodrama' surrounding the Queen Caroline affair distracted many of its supporters from the real political business in hand, namely, an assault on the unreformed British state and its monarchy.[64] But, of course, it all depends what you think politics should be about. For many female Britons, the sentimental and the domestic were not peripheral to the pro-Caroline campaign: they *were* the campaign. To understand why, we need to put the Caroline affair in a much broader context.

Caroline was only one of a gallery of royal females who helped to transform public attitudes to the British monarchy from the last quarter of the eighteenth century onwards, and who influenced at the same time women's attitudes towards themselves. In sharp contrast with George I, who had locked his wife in a German prison for committing adultery, or George II, whose queen had pre-deceased him by almost a quarter of a century, George III was married, and faithfully married, to Queen Charlotte from his coronation in 1761 to the end of his effective reign in 1810. She was plain, docile, conventional and remarkably prolific, producing fifteen children of whom thirteen survived. Usually dismissed as colourless, she was, in reality, a hard woman and just as important as a totem of morality as her husband was.

From the start, she delighted in having her smiling and abundant maternity commemorated in art, often posing with books on child care in her hands or on her dressing table. During the American war, Benjamin West painted twin portraits of her and the king. He

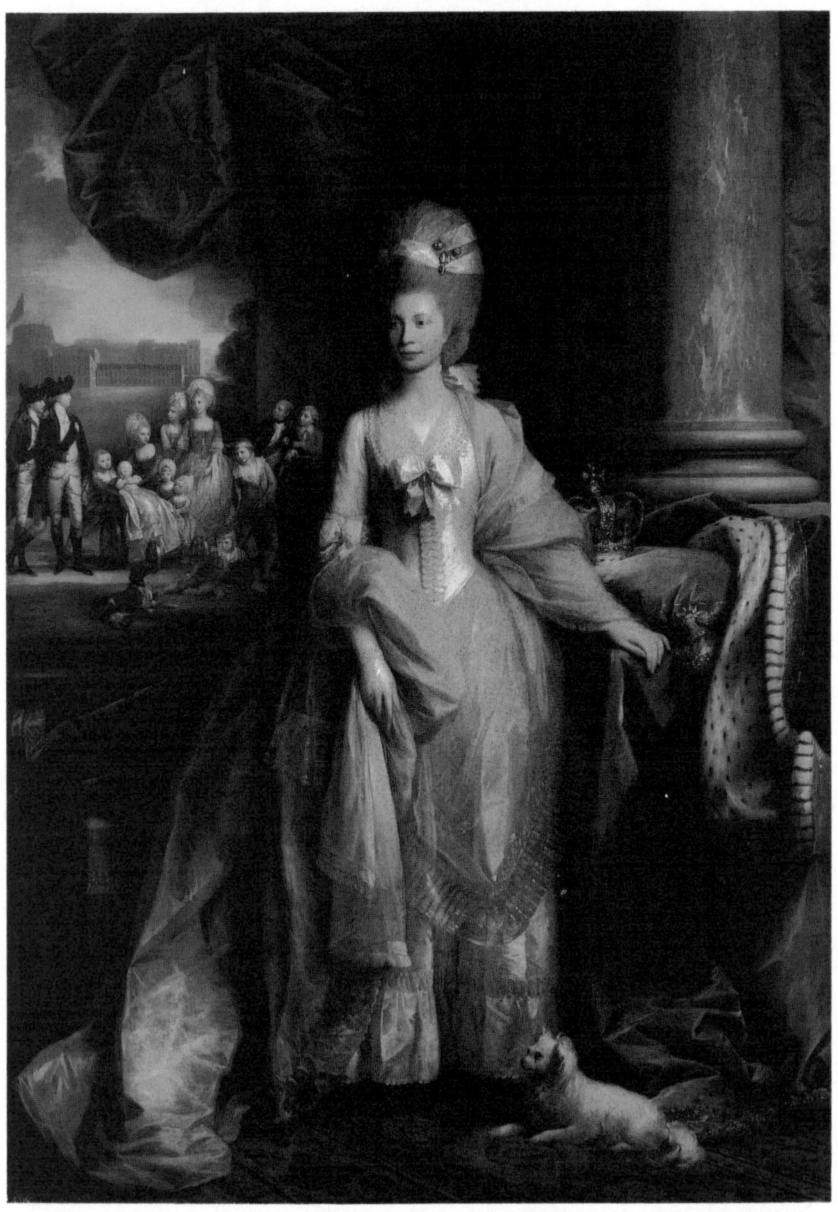

62. Benjamin West, *Queen Charlotte.*

was shown against a background of soldiers, horses, cannon and war. She was painted, no less grandly, standing before her contribution to the nation, her massive family of pretty princesses and arrogant princelings. Separate spheres has sometimes been claimed

63. Francis Bartolozzi after Richard Cosway, *Princess Charlotte Augusta*, stipple engraving 1797.

as a peculiarly middle-class notion.[65] Yet in reality, important cultural attitudes of this kind are never socially segregated in this way, but instead influence behaviour and perceptions at all levels of society. Benjamin West could never have adopted this format for his twin portraits without royal approval. And it was a format that, as Charlotte must have understood, exalted her position in the Royal Family even as it confined it. But her real apotheosis occurred in 1789, in the celebrations that greeted the king's recovery from what had seemed like insanity. Almost a quarter of the more than 700 loyal addresses dispatched from different parts of the island were sent specifically to her. 'No female ever more justly deserved it', remarked one newspaper, 'she is a pattern of domestic virtue which cannot be too much admired'.[66]

None of her daughters made a similar impact on the public, mewed up as they were in Windsor Castle like nuns. But her granddaughter and namesake, the Princess Charlotte, was another matter. From her birth in 1796, she seems to have become a focus for sentimental attachment, particularly among women. As a plump and wayward adolescent, she quarrelled with her father, the Prince Regent, supported her mother, the future Queen Caroline,

64. Matthew Wyatt's monument to Princess Charlotte in St George's Chapel, Windsor.

insisted on marrying Leopold of Saxe Gotha for love, having earlier rejected the suitor her father had chosen for her, and finally completed her role as a romantic heroine by dying in childbirth in November 1817, just twenty-one years old. 'It really was', one opposition politician recalled, 'as if every household throughout Great Britain had lost a favourite child.'[67] A subscription to build a monument to the dead princess was inaugurated, initially confined to women. All donations were accepted, and no one was allowed to donate more than a guinea; yet the final sum collected was well over £12,000. It went to fund a tremendous marble by Matthew Wyatt which can still be seen in St George's Chapel at Windsor. Mourned by the four quarters of the globe, the dead princess is shown utterly collapsed under a shroud, just one limp hand protruding. But safe above this sad wreck of mortal humanity, an immortal Charlotte, together with her baby folded in the arms of an angel, soars triumphantly towards heaven.[68] In death, the princess has become a female hero, and something more than a hero. And it was because of her death, and George IV's inability to tolerate Caroline or to sire legitimate heirs without her, that a teenage girl called Victoria succeeded to the British throne in 1837, yet another woman attaining prominence in what some now referred to as the Queendom, and this time ruling in her own right.

The feminisation of the British monarchy, occurring as it did at a time when the press and the souvenir industries allowed royal events and personalities to reach a very wide public, was immensely important for all classes of women. It provided them, to paraphrase Walter Bagehot, with a splendid edition of the universal facts of life that they themselves were likely to experience. Women who had been worn out by repeated childbirths, who knew the peculiar burden of coping with a large and discordant family could see in Queen Charlotte's life their own idealised. Young girls who had quarrelled with their parents or striven to marry the man of their choice could and did identify with Princess Charlotte. Her death in childbirth horrified, fascinated, but may also have comforted young wives who feared, quite legitimately, the same fate; just as Queen Caroline's trial touched a nerve and aroused compassion among women who feared desertion or their menfolk's ill-treatment.

In a Roman Catholic country, the cult of the Virgin Mary can satisfy some of this need for an idealisation of conventional female experience. But, for the Welsh, the Scots and the English, this consolation had been officially removed by the Reformation. The remarkable prominence of the female component of the British Royal Family from the end of the eighteenth century right down to the present day, a prominence that has coincided with a gradual decline in church attendance, can be seen in part as a kind of substitute religion, a strictly Protestant version of the cult of the Virgin. At some level, Matthew Wyatt must have known this very well. His monument to Princess Charlotte, like many of the cheap prints issued in her memory, borrows its pose from much older images of the Assumption of the Virgin. A sad and dumpy Hanoverian princess who would have become, had she lived, Queen of Great Britain and its empire, had merged in death with the Queen of Heaven.

The wider significance of this cult of royal women was twofold. On the one hand, Princess Charlotte, like Queen Charlotte, like Queen Caroline, and like the future Queen Victoria, supplied British women with a focus for their patriotism that was peculiarly their own. But, in addition, monarchy as soap opera made (and arguably still makes) the wrongs and rites of passage of ordinary women's lives seem important and valuable in a way that no other aspect of British political life could or can do, run exclusively by men as it was then, and as it still largely is today. The dead Princess Charlotte might be a weak Protestant stand-in for the Virgin Mary, but she also dignified by example the mundane, private life of many ordinary female Britons. As one, anonymous woman wrote in a poem she submitted to the *Gentleman's Magazine*:

> T'was hers with calm and condescending grace,
> To rule in woman's chiefest empire, Home;–
> T'was hers to keep the sabbath in its place,
> Mid the meek worship of the village dome.[69]

Female royals, as the public liked to conceive of them, lent yet more moral weight and heroic stature to the idea of a separate women's sphere. And the consequences of this were both limiting and liberating.

A WOMAN'S PLACE IS IN THE NATION

I have argued that the spread of separate-spheres ideology, which had been increasingly evident in prescriptive literature in Great Britain, as in so much of Europe and in North America, from the 1770s onwards, could be drawn on in practice to defend the position of women. I have suggested, too, that the existence of prominent royal females who had to act out the roles of wife, daughter, sister or mother, helped other British women to assert the dignity and importance of these private relationships. But belief in a distinctive female sphere could also, paradoxically, legitimise women's intervention in affairs hitherto regarded as the preserve of men.

To understand why, we need to return to Rousseau. Subordinate and artificial though his ideal woman was, she was also indispensable to the well-being of the state through her private influence on her citizen husband and education of her children. Without the wholesome domesticity that she presided over, male citizenship would have no foundation, 'the legislative hallways would grow silent and empty, or become noisily corrupt'.[70] From these initial premises, two very different conclusions were drawn. As far as the Jacobins in France and the evangelical conservatives in Great Britain were concerned, since woman's place at home was so valuable, it was important that she stay there. But Rousseau's arguments could also be understood very differently, and this was why feminists like Georgiana, Duchess of Devonshire, and Mary Wollstonecraft found his writings so valuable. In previously prevailing political theory, citizenship had been linked with the possession of land and/or the ability to bear arms–in other words, as an inescapably masculine prerogative. By breaking away from this model and stressing instead the connexion between civic virtue and the family, Rousseau, whether he recognised it or not, supplied women with a rationale for intervening in political affairs. Confining women to the private sphere, he none the less helped to dissolve the distinction between it and the public. For if politics was indistinguishable from morality, as he always claimed, then surely women as guardians of morality must have some right of access to the political?

Wollstonecraft saw the potential in Rousseau's arguments very clearly and was careful to construct her claims for women's rights in the *Vindication* out of their contribution to the family. 'If children are to be educated to understand the principle of patriotism', she pointed out, then 'their mother must be a patriot' as well. Only if women were able to 'acquire a rational affection for their country', could they become truly useful in the home.[71] Wollstonecraft died from the effects of childbirth in 1797, and the subsequent revelations about her private life savagely limited her influence. Instead, the subversive potential of Rousseau's analysis of politics was popularised in Britain by a very different woman, Hannah More.

Feminists have never quite known what to do with More, sometimes applauding her as one of themselves, sometimes dismissing her as a reactionary and an apostate. More herself experienced no such contradiction. It was precisely because she appeared (and was) conservative in general, that she was able to get away with her own unconventional life and with her writings on women, which are rather less orthodox than they appear at first glance. She was born in 1745, the daughter of a downwardly mobile gentleman schoolteacher. To keep herself, she set up a girls' boarding school in Bristol with her sisters. But she soon went on to higher things, first to writing bad but successful plays in London, and then to a full-time literary career as a Tory evangelical. More's bias and personal faults are clear enough. She was pushy, humourless and complacent, and could be unctuously sycophantic where influential men were concerned, whether they were politicians, peers, ecclesiastics or cultural lions like Samuel Johnson and David Garrick. But like many women who know how to flatter influential men, she was also a tremendous success. When the Bishop of London was in search of a writer of loyalist tracts for the masses in 1793, he bypassed the university-trained male clerisy and went straight to Hannah. The result was the so-called Cheap Repository Tracts, several million copies of which were sold during the wars, mainly to anxious landowners, clergymen and employers in search of something lucid to distribute among the poor. Many of More's didactic tracts and novels for the middle and upper classes also became best-sellers; and at her death in 1833, she was worth £30,000.[72] Self-made and a life-long spinster, More had become the first British woman ever to make a fortune with her pen, and this fact alone should warn us against seeing her simply as a conservative figure.

For More, as for Rousseau, women were born to be wives and mothers, and their spirit must be curbed to this end. 'There is perhaps no animal so much indebted to its subordination for its good behaviour as women', she wrote, paraphrasing Rousseau's dictum that 'Girls must be thwarted early in life'.[73] Female politicians, like female warriors, were, she insisted, wrong because unnatural, but still more so because they were improper: 'Propriety is to a woman what the great Roman critic says action is to the orator; it is the first, and second, the third requisite.' Decorum, modesty and forbearance, she argued repeatedly, were essential tactics for women in a man's world, and so was pragmatism: 'They should learn not to murmur at expostulation, but should be accustomed to expect and to endure opposition. It is a lesson with which the world will not fail to furnish them.'[74]

This was obviously very different from Mary Wollstonecraft's insistence that British society as a whole must be changed so that women could possess rights *as citizens* rather than just *as women*. But by writing what were in effect survivors' handbooks urging women to adapt themselves to the status quo, More was no less concerned than Wollstonecraft to call them into action. Women, she argued repeatedly, must abandon frivolity and gossip for serious study which 'serves to harden the mind' and 'lifts the reader from sensation to intellect'. In the home, where they were naturally prominent, they must 'not content themselves with polishing, when they are able to reform; with entertaining, when they may awaken'. And though they could not and should not exercise power directly, through their influence on men they might determine how power was used:

> On the use which women of the superior class may be disposed to make of that power delegated to them by the courtesy of custom, by the honest gallantry of the heart, by the imperious control of virtuous affections, by the habits of civilized states, by the usages of polished society; on the use, I say, which they shall hereafter make of this influence, will depend, in no low degree, the well-being of those states . . . and the virtue and happiness, nay perhaps the very existence of that society.[75]

This (to us) contradictory set of arguments, an insistence that women must stay within the private sphere, while at the same time exerting moral influence outside it, dominated though it did not exhaust discussion of female rights in Great Britain in the first half of the nineteenth century. The anonymous, but clearly Anglican and conservative author of *Females of the Present Day, Considered as to their Influence on Society* (1831), for example, echoed More in her belief that '*our* influence in the country at this period is extensive', insisted that such influence was founded on woman's place in the home, yet warned, too, that domestic duties were incompatible with passivity: 'We were sent into this busy world to be useful.'[76] 'How intimate is the connexion', Sarah Stickney Ellis would assure her literally millions of readers after 1840, 'which exists between the *women* of England, and the moral character maintained by this country in the scale of nations.'[77]

Such assertions may strike us as unacceptable invitations to complacency and quietism at a time when all British women, like most British men, were still without the vote, still excluded from most public buildings and political clubs, still denied a free choice of career if they were educated and still likely to be grossly underpaid if they were in employment. Yet it seems inherently unlikely that authors like More and Ellis, and the hundreds of others who imitated them, would have proved as popular as they did among women themselves, had they been understood only as preaching resignation and retreat. Instead, their interpretation of woman's sphere seems to have made possible for some a greater sense of purpose, an opportunity for escape into action and commitment. The assurance that they were Great Britain's moral arbiters gave women what Georgiana, Duchess of Devonshire, had so conspicuously lacked in her foray into Westminster politics in 1784: authority and legitimation for initiatives outside the home.

This was true even of those working-class women in the north of England and in Scotland who formed their own reform societies in the second decade of the nineteenth century. When they attended public meetings with their male peers, such women tended to dress in white as a token both of their virtue and their disinterestedness. They did not, they claimed, want the vote for themselves. Their actions stemmed from their role within the home and in the family, and they were fired by the suffering they witnessed there and by duty to their menfolk. As one working woman wrote to the radical newspaper the *Black Dwarf* in 1819:

> We do not wish to be fitted for orators, nor do we wish to claim a right to vote for representatives in the great council of the nation . . . We wish to be instructed in what way the ascendency we possess, and wish to retain over your sex, may be most beneficially exerted . . . There are many mothers, who, like myself, wish to rear patriot sons.[78]

Rousseau himself could scarcely have expressed proper female aspirations better. And the female reformers were following still older models of desirable female behaviour in their practice of sewing caps of liberty to award to their male comrades. Some of these liberty caps were extremely ornate affairs, like the one that Blackburn's Female Reform Society presented to a radical orator at a public meeting in the town in July 1819: 'made of scarlet, silk or satin, lined with green, with a serpentined gold lace, terminating with a rich gold tassel'.[79] The precedent here – recognised or not – was clearly those exquisitely embroidered favours that high-born ladies supposedly awarded their chosen knights before they went into battle or entered the lists on their behalf in a tournament. The Blackburn woman who presented the cap made this clear when she told the radical spokesman not to give it up 'but with the forfeiture of your existence'.[80]

Borrowing from chivalric myths in this fashion provided another opportunity for female reformers to present themselves as embodiments of virtue and high morality, whose function it was to inspire their menfolk to proper political actions. Only thus could they hope to reconcile what was undeniably a departure from orthodox female behaviour – their involvement in independent political associations – with what was expected of their sex. And only by achieving such a reconciliation, would they stand any chance of defusing masculine prejudice. But there was almost certainly another reason why most of the female Britons who attached themselves to different pressure groups at this time felt obliged to explain their actions in terms of disinterestedness and duty to their families. They needed to convince themselves, as well as men, of the rightness of their commitment. As newcomers to public life, they were often nervous, insecure and inexperienced. Invoking woman's superior morality and virtue proved enormously helpful because it converted the *desire* to act into an overwhelming *duty* to do so. Women could think to themselves, and say to others, that they had no choice but to do what they did. And this was true of those women who became involved in movements like Chartism, the Anti-Corn Law League and anti-slavery, as well as individual reformers like Elizabeth Fry and, later, Florence Nightingale.

Women were also helped by the fact that a wide variety of pressure groups already existed among British men. It was obviously much easier for women to infiltrate public matters now that politics were less confined to the exclusively male world of Parliament and Whitehall, and now that so many moral campaigns were initiated independently of the exclusively male Anglican and Presbyterian hierarchies. Informality and improvisation bred new opportunities. The first serious inroads by British women into the campaign against the slave trade, for instance, occurred in 1791, when the male organisers launched a nationwide boycott of slave-grown sugar. Whether intentionally or not, this brought the campaign against slavery into the centre of woman's traditional sphere of influence–the home. By refusing to serve West Indian sugar at home, by giving preference on shopping trips to dealers in 'free' sugar, a woman could feel that she was making a difference. And though this particular sugar strike achieved very little, the same tactic proved far more successful when it was revived in the mid-1820s.[81]

By then, large numbers of women throughout Great Britain had integrated themselves into the anti-slavery movement, managing to convince others as well as themselves that their particular skills and contacts could be put to a wider use. The same kind of tireless neighbourhood visiting and assiduous fund-collecting that middle-class women so often engaged in for philanthropic causes, the same kind of ladies' committees that had flourished during the wars to knit socks for soldiers, organise subscriptions or celebrate royal Jubilees, the same kind of detailed knowledge of how communities worked, who had money, and who talked to whom that women made use of among themselves: all of these female skills were drawn on first to raise support for ending British participation in the slave trade, and then in the struggle to abolish slavery as an institution in British colonies.[82] By 1830, there were ladies' anti-slavery societies in almost every British town, the biggest in Birmingham distributing some 35,000 items of propaganda every year and regularly forwarding sums of £50 to the parent anti-slavery society in London. Very much to the horror of William Wilberforce, the ladies also collected signatures for petitions against slavery, cheerfully exploiting the fact that male householders found it hard to override conventional etiquette and insult a woman canvasser to her face or turn her from the door. And though it remained rare for women to sign these men's petitions, by 1830 they were regularly submitting their own. The largest, delivered to the House of Commons in 1838 contained the signatures of half a million women.[83]

Women also increasingly affixed their signatures to petitions on other political issues. A great many of them, mainly from the labouring classes, seem to have petitioned against Roman Catholic emancipation in 1829; and in some towns, women also contributed to the massive petitioning campaign in support of parliamentary reform that took place between 1830 and 1832. Male reactions, both at grass-roots level and in Parliament, were often hostile. The organisers of Bristol's anti-Catholic petition in 1829, for example, simply struck out the name of every woman who had signed it before sending it up to Westminster.[84] Once there, mixed or women's petitions had to run the gauntlet of gentlemanly condescension. 'He was as ready as any man to admit that women were very well in their place', Robert Waithman told the Commons in March 1829 – *Hansard* recorded a laugh at this point – 'but he did not think they were in their proper place when they came forward to petition Parliament.'[85] Neither did the newly elected MP for Oldham, William Cobbett. In 1832, he condemned female interference in the reform struggle: 'because he thought that when ladies once got out of the domestic circle, and got into the political, they lost much of the influence they would otherwise properly possess'.[86]

More was involved here than conventional prejudice. Both Waithman and Cobbett were radical MPs, committed to the inclusion of all men of property as well as the educated working class within the electorate. Anxious that the state should concede more political recognition to the nation out-of-doors, they disliked female participation in extra-parliamentary politics because they feared it would bring those politics into disrepute. Stray female forays into the political sphere must not be allowed to disrupt the onward march to a wider, but still exclusively masculine citizenship. Condemnation of female involvement in public affairs was not, of course, confined to radicals. When the High Tory Lord Eldon wonderingly produced an anti-Catholic petition in the House of Lords signed 'by a great many ladies', a fellow peer convulsed the House by enquiring 'whether the petition expressed the sentiments of young or old ladies'.[87]

This kind of unthinking male resistance to female forays into public affairs should be borne in mind in any judgement of separate-spheres arguments, which did at least have the virtue of legitimising women's occasional intervention in politics on the grounds of their superior morality. Such arguments might be limiting, but, in the absence of any other effective form of justification, they had their place. 'Some persons had been found to attempt to cast ridicule upon the petitions to which he had been alluding, on the score of their having been signed chiefly by females', declared Daniel O'Connell of a glut of anti-slavery petitions to the House of Commons in 1833:

> He would say – and he cared not who the person was of whom he said it – he would say, that that person had had the audacity to taunt the maids and matrons of England with the offence of

> demanding that their fellow-subjects in another clime should be emancipated. He would say nothing of the bad taste and the bad feeling which such a taunt betrayed – he would merely confine himself to the expression of an opinion, in which he was sure that every Member of that House would concur with him, namely, that if ever the females had a right to interfere, it was upon that occasion. Assuredly, the crying grievance of slavery must have sunk deep into the hearts, and strongly excited the feelings of the British nation, before the females of this country could have laid aside the retiredness of their character to come forward and interfere in political matters . . . and, he hesitated not to say, that the man, whoever he might be, who had taunted the females of Great Britain with having petitioned Parliament – the man who could do that, was almost as great a ruffian as the wielder of the cart-whip.[88]

Indicatively, no Member of Parliament was prepared to risk replying to this kind of language with levity or disapproval. When British women posed as the nation's conscience, as selfless activists who had left their customary domesticity only in order to further the greater good, they put on powerful armour against the lances of misogyny and condescension. In this guise, female voices *could* reach Westminster and be listened to there.

Self-evidently, this was a limited kind of female politics. Limited, in that only a minority of women participated in extra-parliamentary campaigns of this sort. But limited, too, in the sense that – in order to be effective – the women who did take part found themselves having to act as the angels of the state, rather than as British citizens on a par with their menfolk. Female opponents of slavery, like female supporters of parliamentary reform, like the female Chartists and Anti-Corn Law League campaigners of the 1830s and '40s, were obliged to operate on the peripheries of movements designed and driven by men. In none of them were they able to advance demands that would specifically have benefited themselves. They had almost always to present themselves as working for others in a self-denying and morally superior fashion, confined in the words of Harriet and John Stuart Mill to being 'a sort of sentimental priesthood'.[89]

Yet priests can be important people. And being thought of as moral exemplars is a lot better than being dismissed as merely inferior and irrelevant. There seems no doubt that, insofar as the position of women changed in Britain in the half-century after the American war, the effect was to increase – rather than diminish – their opportunities for participating in public life. The wars with

Revolutionary and Napoleonic France tempted much greater numbers of female Britons out of the home and into pro-war activism (and into pacifist agitation, too) than any previous conflict. A new idealisation of the female members of the Royal Family provided women from many different social backgrounds with their own distinctive brand of patriotism, as well as a way of celebrating by example their domestic roles as mothers, daughters, sisters and wives. And, throughout this period, women were exposed as never before to the bustle and seductions of urban life, to newspapers, magazines, books and broadsheets, available in greater numbers and more cheaply than ever before, to new kinds of charitable, patriotic and political associations, and – of course – to new types of paid work. For many of them, as for many of their male contemporaries, the cumulative result of all these developments must have been wider access to people, information and ideas.

It is in this context that the renewed emphasis in a great deal of prescriptive literature on the importance of separate spheres must be understood. If British women were being urged to remain at home more stridently in this period than ever before, it was largely because so many of them were finding an increasing amount to do outside the home. The literature of separate spheres was more didactic than descriptive. Yet, as some women discovered, it could still serve a useful purpose. Proclaiming their reputed vulnerability and moral superiority – and men's duty to respect both – provided them with a means to legitimise their intervention in public affairs and a means, as well, of protecting themselves. Posing as the pure-minded Women of Britain was, in practice, a way of insisting on the right to public spirit.

Of course, the vast majority of women continued to find most of their satisfaction, such as it was, in the domestic sphere. But so, too, did large numbers of men. And, of course, women remained unenfranchised – as did the majority of British men until 1884. The significant point, however, is that for both sexes, the last quarter of the eighteenth century and the first quarter of the nineteenth century saw a sharper rate of change at home, massive and demanding wars abroad and the challenge of new forms of patriotism. This was the period in which women first had to come to terms with the demands and meanings of Britishness. The demands that the nation made of their menfolk in these years were, as we shall see next, still more pressing and unprecedented.

65. James Gillray, *Buonaparte 48 hours after Landing!*, 1803.

7 *Manpower*

On 26 July 1803, when panic about an imminent French invasion was at its height, James Gillray published one of his most striking yet most ambiguous prints. An English volunteer soldier, oak leaves flourishing from out of his lumpy three-cornered hat like holly out of a Christmas pudding, waves aloft a pitchfork. On top of it, is the head of Napoleon Bonaparte. It is just forty-eight hours since the French have landed, and the man who has conquered most of Continental Europe has been defeated and destroyed by a corps of plebeian volunteers, the Union Jack raised high in their midst. So far, so inspiring. A typically professional piece of patriotic propaganda – we might think – from a master artist. Yet the closer we look at this imaginary scene, the more likely we are to feel troubled. The face of the volunteer hero is bloated and coarse, his lips are glutinous, his eyes dull. Bumptious and trite, he celebrates his victory as if the French consul were deaf not dead: 'Plunder Old England, hay? Make French slaves of us all, hay? Ravish all our wives & daughters, hay? O Lord help that silly head!' Despite all this bluster, it is, in fact, the victim's severed head, not the oafs who have decapitated him, that captures our attention. Gaunt, drained of blood, ruthlessly exposed, Napoleon Bonaparte still retains his high cheekbones, his finely chiselled Roman nose, his hair fashionably cut *à la Titus*, his altogether classical profile. Britain's arch-enemy, he is still in death an officer and a gentleman, and Gillray clearly cannot resist drawing him as such. Equally clearly, the artist has found it impossible to celebrate the ordinary volunteer soldier who is his fellow countryman without simultaneously demeaning him.[1]

Gillray's inability to come to terms with plebeian patriotism was by no means exceptional at this time. All over Europe, the scale and danger of the French Revolutionary and Napoleonic wars dictated mass arming on an unprecedented scale. War, as Clausewitz put it, became 'the business of the people'.[2] And all over Europe, there was considerable anxiety and bewilderment among the propertied classes about the social and political repercussions of such extraordinary levels of mobilisation. Societies that had been accustomed to regarding their common soldiery as uncouth, mercenary and dangerous, the scum of the earth as the Duke of Wellington described them, now found themselves dependent as never before on mass military endeavour. As a result, some effort had to be made to re-imagine plebeian soldiers as potential heroes and as patriots: and as Gillray's print bears witness, this process of adjustment often proved difficult. As far as Great Britain is concerned, however, the uncertainty about how to *see* the ordinary fighting man of this period has been remarkably persistent. We now know a great deal about the mechanics and meanings of mass arming in Revolutionary and Napoleonic France, and about the dynamics of popular resistance to the French army in Spain, Russia and the various German states.[3] But the hundreds of thousands of Britons who committed themselves, for whatever reason, to fight the French, remain in the shadows. Just like Gillray, we still fail to see these men as they really were.

In part, this is because Great Britain, unlike so many other European and extra-European states between 1789 and 1815, never experienced a French invasion. Consequently, the impression has persisted that for the British, these were essentially wars fought abroad for the sake of property, dominion and the maintenance of the established order, with very little voluntary popular input at home. But popular patriotism in Britain in this, as in so many other periods, has also been relatively little explored because the evidence for popular protest at this time is so distractingly abundant. The last quarter of the eighteenth century and the first quarter of the nineteenth witnessed rapid and disruptive population growth in Britain's industrial regions, a dramatic spread of radical ideas and political organisation among the artisanal classes, and sharp and often violent expressions of discontent over food, labour conditions and taxation. In these circumstances, Roger Wells has suggested, 'it would be idiotic to assume the loyalty of the British masses' during these final and most dangerous wars with France.[4] True enough. But there are two important reasons why it is just as inappropriate to leave the real extent and quality of mass loyalty unexplored.

First of all, Britain's rulers themselves had no choice but to investigate the quality of popular patriotism – and to rely on it. The danger of a massive French invasion was so great after 1793, and so protracted, that they were compelled to establish how many Britons would take up arms in defence of their nation. In order to do so, London was obliged to accumulate an unprecedented amount of information about ordinary Britons and their capacity and willingness to fight. And this is the second reason why investigating popular patriotism in this period is vital and desirable:

66. *After the Invasion – the Levee en Masse*, 1803. Another version of the patriotic pleb.

simply and unusually, enough evidence exists to let us do so. Normally, the labouring poor and the illiterate feature in the historical record only when they make trouble in some way, when they break the law or attract the disapproval of the powerful. By contrast, the conforming working man usually left few traces of his ideas and actions behind him. But this was not the case at the end of the eighteenth century and at the beginning of the nineteenth century. We have already seen how external dangers and internal tensions together combined to make royal, patrician and female investment in patriotism conspicuous at this time. But, still more dramatically perhaps, this was an era which saw the mobilisation of British working men on a scale that would not be attempted again until the First World War. This was when the authorities first found out just how many Britons were willing to fight – and this is the first occasion in British history when we can find out too.

A NATION IN ARMS

How were large numbers of men living on the edge of poverty to be brought to risk life and limb for a nation in which active citizenship was denied them? What kind of appeals could make them take up arms? And what meaning was to be given to their service and possible sacrifice?

Since the Union in 1707, these questions had become more urgent without having to be addressed head on. True, recurrent war with France puffed up Britain's armed forces to some 135,000 men during the War of Spanish Succession, to 170,000 men in the Seven Years War, and to a record 190,000 men in the lost American war.[5] But although this expansion demanded fiscal and administrative innovations, it did not lead to any radical changes in ideas about the common fighting man, or effect a fundamental transformation in recruiting practices. Like the other European powers, in time of war Great Britain continued to rely on large numbers of foreign mercenaries (mainly Germans), and to supplement the artisans and labourers who enlisted in its armed forces voluntarily with men seized by press gangs against their will. Moreover, in marked contrast with many other states, Great Britain was for the most part free from invading armies and internal warfare. With the significant exceptions of the brief Jacobite rising in 1715 and Charles Edward Stuart's more serious invasion in 1745, Great Britain was able to remain a warlike state with no compelling need to convert itself into a nation in arms.

But all this, like so much else in Great Britain, changed after the American war with the coming of a very different kind of armed conflict. More than twice as long as the First and Second World Wars added together, the wars against Revolutionary and Napoleonic France were almost as geographically extensive as far as British involvement was concerned, sweeping through Europe, into Asia, Africa, North America, Latin America, and even precipitating sea battles off the coast of Australia. As it turned out, war did not cross the Channel into Great Britain itself, but those living between 1793 and 1815 could not know that. Napoleon's Army of England was by far the most formidable invasion force assembled against Great Britain up to that time, the threat it represented was a protracted one, and it came very close to succeeding. There was a major but abortive invasion attempt against Ireland in 1796, and a more successful French landing there two years later. In 1797, a small expeditionary force landed in Wales. From 1798 to 1805, the conquest of Britain was Napoleon's primary strategic objective. And even after the Franco-Spanish fleet had been smashed at Trafalgar, and Britain had said it in stone by entombing Nelson's pickled corpse in St Paul's cathedral, there was still the prolonged challenge posed by the French blockade.[6]

In the face of these dangers, Britain's armed forces had to grow at a faster rate than those of any other European power. When the Bastille shattered in 1789, the British army was 40,000 strong. By 1814, it had expanded more than sixfold to some quarter of a million men. The Royal Navy, bedrock of defence, aggression, empire and trade, grew faster still. Before 1789, it had employed 16,000 men. By 1812, it employed over 140,000.[7] Supplementing these regular land and sea forces was an expanding penumbra of part-time and volunteer units defending the home front itself, almost half a million men by 1804. Mobilising these civilians presented an enormous challenge to the nerve and ingenuity of those in power.[8] It was simply not enough anymore to maintain civil order and obedience by way of professional soldiers, barracks, surveillance and sermons. Nor was it even enough to foster loyalty by means of an intensive campaign of propaganda and patriotic ceremonial. In the face of economic distress, social upheaval and the lures of French Revolutionary doctrines, a major effort had to be made for almost a quarter of a century to encourage large numbers of men from a wide range of social backgrounds to take up arms in support of the British state. In these circumstances, the question became imperative. How many Britons could be got to fight?

The only civil defence force in existence at the onset of the wars with France was the militia. This had been remodelled in 1757, when Parliament ordered that every English and Welsh county was to supply a given quota of men between the ages of eighteen and forty-five and pay for them out of the rates. Thirty-two thousand men, all of them good Protestants, were to be chosen by ballot, subjected to martial law in time of active service, and dispatched during peacetime for a month's military training every year under the enthusiastic and voluntary leadership of the local gentry.[9] This, at least, was the law. In practice, the system proved only patchily effective and was profoundly unpopular. As in France, the burden of militia service fell overwhelmingly on the illiterate poor.[10] And for this task, there were simply not enough of them available. County quotas were rarely met; and no attempt was made to adjust them to the changing balance of Britain's population. In 1796, the proportion of eligible men serving in the militia in heavily agricultural counties such as Dorset, Bedfordshire and Montgomeryshire was more than one in ten. By contrast, more industrialised counties where population growth had accelerated since the 1750s got off lightly. Only one in thirty eligible men was serving in the militia in the West Riding of Yorkshire, only one in forty-five in Lancashire.[11]

For five years after the outbreak of war with Revolutionary France in 1793, the British government's response to these inadequacies was careful and limited. By the Supplementary Militia

Act of 1796, it demanded a further 60,000 militiamen from England and another 4,400 from Wales, taking care this time to ensure that quotas fell far more equally on every county. The following year, it extended the militia for the first time to Scotland, hoping thereby to raise another 6,000 men for home defence duties. This brought the total strength of the militia throughout Great Britain to some 100,000 men.[12] In addition, the authorities encouraged 'gentlemen' to found their own private volunteer corps of infantry or cavalry. No state subsidies were given to these early volunteers. And London had no say over what they wore or who officered them, and no control over what their precise duties should be. Instead, the fact that these corps were self-funding was seen as a further guarantee of their members' social respectability and political soundness. What the government wanted at this stage of the war were landowners or substantial manufacturers to enrol as volunteer officers, with farmers, professionals, shopkeepers and men with established trades to their name serving as their rank and file. This was very largely what they got. Some 40 per cent of Edinburgh's volunteers in 1797, for example, were lawyers. And of the seventy-five heroes who volunteered to defend Ely in Cambridgeshire, sixty-nine were farmers, or attorneys, or snug tradesmen, butchers, blacksmiths, victuallers and the like; only six were labourers.[13]

As artists and cartoonists delighted in pointing out, it was their uniforms that gave many of these initial volunteer corps away. Very often, they were gorgeous, impractical and extremely expensive. Even a private's uniform in a fashionable London volunteer corps could set a man back £50, with a further £10 a year needed to maintain its smartness, and to provide ammunition. Cheaper at some £10 a head, but still very grand, was the costume the Earl of Egremont designed for his corps of yeoman cavalry at Petworth in Sussex in 1795. A finely tailored green jacket lined with white was draped tastefully over a white waistcoat and breeches and topped with a daringly contrasting dark-blue cloak edged in scarlet. On their heads, these sons of Mars wore bearskin helmets, with cockades, gilt ornaments and a scarlet feather. The earl made sure his own uniform was finer still, and that the feather on his helmet was extra large. Then, like scores of other volunteer commanders throughout the land, he rushed off to have his portrait painted.[14]

We have already seen how – as far as the British élite was concerned – the wearing of uniform in this period was boosted by a heightened concern with heroism and virility. But the splendour of these early volunteer uniforms had a broader significance. More graphically than anything else could do, it indicated that volunteering at this stage of the war was primarily, though not exclusively, a prosperous man's game. In some counties, generous subscriptions were raised to clothe and equip poorer men. But many volunteers took pride in equipping themselves. And many attached themselves to volunteer corps not so much to fight for survival against the French, as to defend their shops, homes, businesses or land against the more seditious and riotous of their own countrymen.

The evidence suggests, then, that in the early years of the war the British government was – rightly or wrongly – as afraid of its own people as it was of the enemy.[15] Labouring men might be the bedrock of the regular forces and fill the ranks of the militia, but they were neither welcome nor very much trusted in the less structured world of the volunteers. Not an armed people, but a propertied and respectable home guard to restrain domestic disorder was what the authorities were most anxious to create at this stage of the conflict. The change came in the winter of 1797, when Napoleon's Army of England encamped along the French coastline. Desperate, and by now without European allies, the government had no choice but to make the shift from seeking quality support at home to seeking it in quantity.

The most well-known outcome of this frantic search for numbers was Great Britain's first census, ordered by Parliament in 1800, on the grounds that 'in every war, especially in a defensive war, it must be of the highest importance to enrol and discipline the greatest possible number of men'.[16] Much less well-known are the detailed returns that the Defence of the Realm Act of April 1798 demanded from each county: details of the number of able-bodied men in each parish, details of what service, if any, each man was prepared to offer to the state, details of what weapons he possessed, details of the amount of live-stock, carts, mills, boats, barges and grain available, details of how many elderly people there were, how many alien and infirm. Compiled by harassed constables or schoolmasters, checked by clergymen, parochial vestries, and deputy lieutenants, these returns, which were repeated in 1803, supplied the British state with the most ambitious and precise taxonomy of its people compiled since the Domesday Book. These same documents, singularly neglected by historians and demographers, allow us to get behind the administrative details of civil defence, to reach the men themselves, the 'living beings in action', as Richard Cobb called their French counterparts.[17]

Of course, these questionnaires cannot provide an infallible index of popular patriotism. Some have simply not survived; and almost certainly many more – particularly those relating to Wales and Scotland – still lie undiscovered in dusty private archives. Those returns that do exist are not always complete or reliable. Not all of the participating constables and schoolmasters did an efficient job.

Not all of them told the truth. In some areas, they did not even try. The most outlying parts of the kingdom, Orkney, off the coast of Scotland, and the Isle of Man (only brought under crown control in the 1760s), seem never to have completed the government's various questionnaires. More integrated but still isolated and sparsely populated regions responded slowly, unevenly and at times, not at all. In mid-1804, Sutherland, Caithness and Nairn in Scotland, and Montgomeryshire and Radnorshire in Wales seem still not to have supplied London with all the detailed breakdowns of civilian volunteers that it had asked for the previous August.[18]

None the less, the statistics of civilian response that survive are impressive. Impressive in the thoroughness and care with which they were generally garnered. But impressive, too, in terms of what they reveal. In 1798, the state demanded that local officials interrogate every eligible male between the ages of fifteen and sixty about his willingness to take up arms in the event of an invasion. In 1803, it wanted further examinations, this time of all eligible men between seventeen and fifty-five years of age. It would have been easy, and it must have been tempting for the men who had to scurry round implementing these directives, simply to claim that their respective localities were united in a patriotic consensus. Some did just that. John Kinsey, for example, acting constable of Crickadarn parish in Brecknockshire, assured the authorities in 1803 that all of its eligible men were 'ready and willing to serve for the defence of the Kingdom'.[19] We shall never know how close to the truth this statement was.

Yet the crucial point is that such blanket assurances were not what the government sought or asked for. The detailed returns demanded in 1798 and 1803 were never printed in full and were never intended as propaganda to impress a doubting people. Most of the information they provided was only for the eyes of the local Lords Lieutenant and members of the central government, and what these men badly wanted was accuracy not reassurance. The majority of the constables and schoolmasters seem to have done their level best to provide exactly that, reporting – often verbatim – the candid and widely varying replies they received as they trudged round asking men if they were willing to fight. That is why these returns were and are so valuable. They undermine almost every facile generalisation made at the time and since about civilian responses in Britain during the Revolutionary and Napoleonic wars. They confront those who argue on the one hand for widespread loyalty and deference throughout Great Britain at this time, and those who want to claim on the other that the mass of Britons were alienated from their rulers, with grittily assembled, unaccommodating facts. What were they?

WHO WAS WILLING TO FIGHT?

The Defence of the Realm returns that survive demonstrate conclusively that even at the height of patriotic excitement about a possible French invasion, in 1803, some Britons were averse to fighting for their country and felt able to tell the authorities so point-blank. In East Grinstead in Sussex, the local constable estimated that there were 556 men between the ages of seventeen and fifty-five eligible to volunteer. Thirty-four of these had already enrolled in private volunteer corps, and a further 169 declared that they were willing to serve in the event of invasion. But that still left some 350 men who were not willing to serve.[20] Most of these, as the return makes clear, were older, married men with children, naturally disinclined to leave their families. But in other towns and villages, there were younger men who said no as well. Jacob Phillips, a seventeen-year-old unmarried articled clerk in Exeter refused to join a volunteer corps that year; so did his fellow townsman Francis Ellis, a young weaver who stoutly refused the local constable's suggestions that he should take up arms for his country not just once but twice.[21] We do not know why these two men refused. They may have disliked the prospect of military discipline. They may have been too engrossed in their personal affairs to care. Or, like one London coachmaker who actually scribbled his reasons on the local constable's return, their refusal may have been politically based:

> No law or power under the canopy of Heaven shall force me to take up arms . . . I pray to God, that I may never live to see my country become a province of France, but if this war is suffered to go on I know it will be conquered, for I am positively sure that the King, Lords and Commons . . . have long since lost the hearts, goodwill and affection of a very great majority of the people of this nation.[22]

To judge by his own words, this man was neither actively seditious nor irreligious. Nor was he poor. He owned a substantial house in Oxford Street and had a good trade. Those who refused to cooperate at this time, like those who conformed, cannot easily be slotted into any of the more predictable categories.

They did not, for instance, come from any particular occupational groups. And this is true even of those men whose leanings towards radicalism have become legendary, the shoemakers. True, in the parish of Sharnbrook in Bedfordshire, six men belonging to this trade – possibly all that there were in this community of under 600 people – refused to volunteer in 1803. But in the slightly smaller parish of Litcham, Norfolk, five shoemakers were among the founder members of the local armed association, dedicated 'to our King, Country and Constitution'.[23] Nor do areas in England and Wales where Protestant non-conformity was strong seem to have responded differently from securely Anglican regions. Though the old Puritan heartland of East Anglia *may* have been an exception. Cambridgeshire had been one of the last counties to obey the Militia Act of 1757, refusing to ballot its men until 1778. Twenty years later, this county, together with Huntingdonshire, had the smallest proportion of men enrolled in volunteer corps of any of the English counties. In 1803–4, Cambridgeshire, like Bedfordshire, failed to supply the state with adequate details of its defence arrangements; while only 13 per cent of eligible men volunteered in Huntingdonshire, and only 20 per cent did so in Essex.[24]

Yet even here, religious dissent may not have been the crucial factor behind this unevenness in war patriotism. Anyone familiar with the East Anglian countryside today knows its peculiar separateness, its distinct scenery, its bare and dismal fens, huge skies and omnipresent water, felt in the damp air and regulated by strange networks of sluices and dykes. Not until 1914, would nationwide mobilisation penetrate this waterland to any significant degree, and even then – as one local historian has written – 'the queues of recruits seen in other parts of the country did not materialise'.[25] The rural hinterland of East Anglia was simply too sparsely populated, too insulated, too complacent within itself to care much about the nation beyond its borders.

Very different, was the experience of that broad swathe of counties on the western and southern coasts of England – Gloucestershire, Somerset, Devon, Wiltshire, Hampshire, Sussex and Kent – which had stronger military traditions and was geographically far more vulnerable to French attack. On average, 50 per cent of all men aged between seventeen and fifty-five in these counties volunteered to take up arms in 1803. In Great Britain, as in other European states at this time, it was these kinds of peculiarities of place more than anything else that seem to have influenced men's willingness to fight. The kind of region and community in which they lived, rather than how they worshipped God, or what social class or occupational group they belonged to, was the factor that mattered most.

How, then, should we see the map of war patriotism in Great Britain in this period? Granted that there were individual and regional discrepancies in response to the call for volunteers, what sort of broad generalisations can be made about the declared willingness to fight? There are three conclusions that can be drawn. First, Wales and Scotland responded to the demands of mobilisation differently from England, and differently, too, from each other. Second, the more industrialised and urbanised a region was, the more likely it was to produce a high level of volunteers. Third, the nation's call for large numbers of men to defend it after 1798 was answered, not indeed unanimously but certainly abundantly.

In May 1804, the House of Commons was informed that some 176,000 Britons were already serving *within* Great Britain in the militia, in the regular army and in various private volunteer corps. A further 482,000 men had indicated their willingness to arm in the event of an invasion, and many of these were now training in state-subsidised volunteer corps (see Appendix 2). Some of these men had agreed to serve throughout the military district in which their town or village was situated (there were fourteen military districts throughout Great Britain); but the majority had been told that in an emergency they must serve anywhere in Great Britain, and had volunteered on these terms.[26] Over 200,000 of the volunteers had also been equipped with firearms, which were usually stacked between training sessions inside the nearest church.[27] All of this was highly impressive, but if Members of Parliament studied the figures before them carefully, they would have noticed not only the regional differences in response that I have already discussed, but also differences between the three component parts of Great Britain. Whereas all but three of the English counties had sent in their returns, five of the Welsh counties had failed to supply the central government with adequate information, as had eleven of the Scottish counties.

Why was this? As far as both Wales and Scotland are concerned, we can put aside any simple assumption that their people remained aloof from the war effort. They did not. Before the British state committed itself to popularising civil defence in 1798, the statistics it compiled revealed that a *higher* proportion of Welshmen and Scots had attached themselves to volunteer corps than had Englishmen. Just under 4 per cent of the total male population in Wales and Scotland had volunteered to join home defence units in the first five years of the war as against just over 2 per cent in England. And in this early stage of the war, Scots and men from *South* Wales were far more extrovert in their military commitment than their English neighbours. Almost half of the 84,000 volunteers known to have enrolled in England by the start of 1798 stipulated that in the event of a French invasion they were prepared to defend only their own town or village. By contrast, 88 per cent of volunteers in Pembrokeshire and Glamorgan claimed to be willing to defend their military district as a whole. And over 90 per cent of the Scottish volunteer corps were willing to serve throughout all of Scotland. Only in Selkirk and Lanark, prosperous Lowland counties, did substantial numbers of Scots reveal an inclination to defend just their own back yard (see Appendix 3).

At this early stage of the war – before 1798 – the fact that England was a richer and more highly populated country than either Wales or Scotland probably worked against efficient home defence in this particular part of Great Britain. Many comfortable Englishmen saw no reason to join volunteer corps at this stage. Those who did so were often more interested in defending their own homes and businesses against domestic unrest than in protecting the nation at large from a foreign enemy. Comparative prosperity in these circumstances fostered the most outrageous localism. By contrast, the poorer and more rural economies of Scotland and Wales seem initially to have aided militarisation. Landowners in these two countries, and particularly in Scotland, were often able to exercise a much greater control over their tenants than was possible in England.[28] It was largely because of this that a higher proportion of Welshmen and Scots were drawn into the early volunteer corps, and on much more generous terms than their English counterparts. Many must have undertaken to serve over long distances because their landlords gave them no choice in the matter. The peculiarities of place may have helped in this direction too. The Scottish Highlands had a strong martial tradition, and many of its inhabitants were used to travelling long distances into the Lowlands or northern England to find work. These factors – as well as the region's massively powerful territorial élite – may have helped to make its volunteer corps in the earlier 1790s more responsive, more extrovert and more numerous.

But precisely because defence measures in parts of Wales and Scotland were more heavily dependent on widespread deference to local landlords than in England, the response of Welshmen and Scots to the call to arms was sometimes less impressive after 1798. The Defence of the Realm Act passed that year, and the mass of civil defence legislation that followed it, showed that the initiative in home defence had now passed from local magnates to Parliament. As a result, some Scottish and Welsh landlords, who had been happy enough to organise their own private volunteer corps, seem to have given these new measures less than their full backing.

And without such backing, the state's directives could have only a muffled impact in areas so distant from London.

These difficulties need to be kept in perspective, however. By the end of 1803, more than 52,000 Scots were serving as rank-and-file members of volunteer regiments, some 15 per cent of the total number in arms throughout Great Britain.[29] It was only some of the more isolated regions – Inverness-shire and Bute for example – that proved noticeably resistant to London's demands. And, as always, Scotland as a whole proved far more responsive to the call to arms than Wales. The eight returns sent in by Welsh counties in 1804 (five Welsh counties failed to send in complete returns altogether) suggested that on average only 28 per cent of their eligible menfolk were willing to volunteer.[30] Predominantly rural and agricultural, with the bulk of its men and women still monolingual Welsh speakers, and lacking the strong military tradition that the Scots valued so much, North and central Wales especially remained at the start of the nineteenth century the part of Great Britain most resistant to control from the centre.

Economic factors, as well as cultural characteristics, go to explain the divergences in response in the three component parts of Great Britain. Englishmen were more widely prosperous than were the Welsh or the Scottish. Their patriotism was therefore more likely to be reinforced by self-interest, *if they could be convinced that a French invasion was genuinely imminent*. By 1803, most of them do seem to have been convinced of this, with predictable results: 'England never can be overrun', purred Arthur Young, '. . . her infantry is as numerous as her property is diffused'.[31] England was also a more urbanised country than Wales or Scotland, with much better communications; and this, too, made a difference. As has been argued repeatedly in this book, active commitment to Great Britain was not, could not be a given. It had to be learnt; and men and women needed to see some advantage in learning it. Those who lived far from centres of wealth, population, information and activity learned it very slowly, and *some* Scots and Welshmen, like some of the inhabitants of the more isolated and peripheral regions of England, chose not to learn it at all. The Lord Advocate of Scotland tried to explain this point to his English colleagues in 1804:

> Sandy and Donald are thinking, calculating animals, who don't plunge enthusiastically into measures, without much reflection, as John Bull does. Besides we are here remote from the centre of public affairs, and from all those scenes which serve so powerfully to rouse the spirit of the people in England.[32]

Only good and consistent communications, and economic and

cultural change, would override some of these longstanding differences. The Welsh record in civil defence after 1798 bears this out. Counties such as Brecknockshire, Carmarthenshire and Radnorshire which were isolated, mountainous, sparsely populated, and heavily dependent on agriculture, responded poorly to the government's defence measures. Flintshire, by contrast, enriched by urban centres like Wrexham and by its close trading links with Chester, over the English border, responded well: over half of its eligible males were enrolled as volunteers by 1804. And over 4,400 men joined the volunteers in Glamorgan, the most Anglicised, urbanised and accessible of the Welsh counties. War patriotism, it seems clear, was more likely to flourish where towns and trade did.

And this was not what Britain's rulers had anticipated. As soon as war with Revolutionary France broke out, Pitt the Younger's government had acted on the straightforward assumption that loyalty was likely to be commensurate with property. Those without some stake in society were regarded as potentially unreliable. But not all were suspect to the same degree. Rural labourers in England and Wales, Highlanders in Scotland and domestic servants everywhere, it was believed, were likely to be personally bound to their landlords and employers and therefore more tractable.[33] Simple, traditional and picturesque folk living in the depths of the countryside, pursuing their lives in time-hallowed fashion, undisturbed by any hint of modernity, were assumed to be more deferential *and therefore more loyal.* Just like many social historians today, however, ministers anticipated protest and sedition from those 'accustomed to associate together'–from workers in manufacturing industries, or urban artisans, or miners, or colliers, or dockers. Men massed together in towns and large workplaces were widely believed to be potentially volatile. Rural Britons, on the other hand, were expected to be useful and willing like the beasts of the field.[34] Yet if the Defence of the Realm returns showed anything at all, it was that these assumptions about the split between urban and rural responses were by no means invariably justified in fact.

Some of the most detailed information we have about civilian responses in 1798 concerns the predominantly agricultural parishes of north Hampshire.[35] This was an area running close to the boundaries with Berkshire and Surrey, stocked with small parishes like Steventon, where Jane Austen's father served as vicar and she herself wrote the early novels. A quiet and conservative area, then, virtually untouched by modernity or mobility of any kind. The first census revealed that all but six of Steventon's 150-odd inhabitants worked on the land. In nearby Cliddesden, only ten men and women earned their living in occupations other than agriculture. In Mapledurwell, only three did so; in Stratfield Turgis, only two, and in Tunworth none at all. In this unquestionably rural backwater, there was sometimes deference to local authorities; to the siren calls of the nation state however, most people remained stubbornly deaf. As a conscientious clergyman, Revd Austen was able to undertake that thirty-five Steventon men would volunteer if need be. But no such promises came from Cliddesden or Mapledurwell, where the responsible constables left the relevant part of the government forms blank. Nor was active loyalty to be found in Stratfield Turgis, where the constable wrote honestly: 'No one would say he was *willing* to serve'. As for Tunworth, its scrappy and incoherent return suggests that the local constable was either incapable of understanding his instructions or simply unable to write.

What was true of rural north Hampshire seems to have been true also of many other profoundly rural areas in England. Take the case of the parish of Tilbrook in Bedfordshire which had 219 inhabitants in 1800, only five of whom did not work on the land. In 1803, the local constable calculated that only forty of its menfolk were eligible to volunteer, and only eleven of them were willing to do so. Every farmer on his list declined to serve, and one brave man explained to the authorities why:

> This is to inform you gentlemen that we are in great want of men at this time to get our harvest, so I cannot spare time for our wheat is mildewing very fast at this time. But when we have got our harvest, I and my men are at your service.[36]

This was not disloyalty or defeatism. But it was August, after all, and as a farmer with a crop to get in, William Baker knew his own priorities. Much the same kind of responses, from much the same kind of men, have been found in the North Riding of Yorkshire. There, large numbers of men are known to have volunteered in those parishes situated near the boundary with Lancashire, a populous and increasingly industrialised region. But 'on the eastern borders of Craven, in the isolated and sparsely populated Upper Wharfedale there was scarcely any enthusiasm for volunteering: in Kettlewell parish there were no volunteers, in Arncliffe there were 3 and in Linton 3'.[37] Rural villages of this kind were essentially isolated and inward-looking. Their inhabitants responded to national mobilisation in much the same way as the villagers of Provence reacted to the ambitious centralisation attempted by the new French Republic after 1789: with stolid unconcern, marked suspicion, dumb resentment and sometimes downright resistance.[38]

In England and in Wales, though not in Scotland, it was the more urbanised and industrialised regions that supplied the largest proportion of volunteer soldiers (just as these same regions supplied the bulk of men for the regular army and the militia).[39] The Defence of the Realm returns demonstrate this very clearly. The census of 1800 revealed that in seven English counties only, the number of agricultural workers was more than double the number of men and women engaged in other occupations: Oxfordshire, Cambridgeshire, Berkshire, Essex, Herefordshire, Huntingdonshire and Lincolnshire. Of these seven predominantly rural counties, two – Cambridgeshire and Oxfordshire – failed to supply the government with adequate volunteering statistics in 1803–4. In the other five, the proportion of men who enrolled as volunteers at that time was on average only 22 per cent. A very different pattern emerges if we look at those provincial English counties where the workforce was predominantly engaged in trade or industry. According to the census, there were eleven such. Ten of these – Cheshire, Derbyshire, Durham, Lancashire, Leicestershire, Northamptonshire, Nottinghamshire, Staffordshire, Surrey and Warwickshire – supplied the authorities with detailed returns of their volunteers in 1803–4. These show that on average 35 per cent of the eligible male population in these counties volunteered to defend the nation.[40] Only one English county deviates conspicuously from this general rule that population density and industrialisation were actually more congenial to mobilisation during the invasion crisis than a predominantly agricultural economy. That county is Yorkshire, where only 20 per cent of the male population was willing to volunteer. And it is Yorkshire, of course, that supplies much of the evidence for mass alienation during the Napoleonic Wars in Edward Thompson's marvellous classic *The Making of the English Working Class*.

We should recognise that in terms of war patriotism, popular responses in Yorkshire *may* have been more the exception than the rule. And we need to recognise something of far more wide-ranging importance. Historians of France have explored grass-roots responses to war in this period far more extensively than have their counterparts in Britain. As a result, they have been quicker to recognise that new economic forces, in particular the massing of men that occurs with urbanisation and industrialisation, usually aided the militarisation of society.[41] British historians, by contrast, have often written as though economic change was invariably disruptive: as if the countryside naturally fostered obedience, while the towns spawned only protest. The reality, as we have seen, was rather different. In 1804, a writer in the *Edinburgh Review* com-

7. William Henry Bunbury, *Recruits*, *c.*1780. Derision and unconcern in a small country village.

plained that rural labourers had been so idealised by conservatives that the civic potential of the urban artisan had been badly ignored. Yet, he argued:

> if the bodily strength of artisans is less than that of ploughmen, they possess, in a much greater degree, that manual dexterity and skill, so necessary in the evolutions, especially of modern war . . . Modern warfare consists in reducing men to a state of

> mechanical activity, and combining them as parts of a great machine. For this use, which of the two is most fitted by his previous habits – he who has been all his life acting the part of a mechanical implement in a combination of movements – or he who has been constantly employed as a thinking, independent, separate, and insulated agent?[42]

The urban artisan, because he had been acculturated, because he was more easily reached by propaganda and recruiting parties, and because, crucially, he was not tied to the land, could be a more useful citizen in time of war than the solitary ploughman. In this respect, far from automatically making Great Britain more susceptible to revolution, precocious industrialisation and urbanisation may well have helped to keep the forces of the French Revolution at bay.

THE PRIVATE REASONS WHY

Establishing how many Britons attached themselves to volunteer corps during the Revolutionary and Napoleonic wars, who they were and where they came from is relatively straightforward. But what was it exactly that led so many men to volunteer? It should come as no surprise that patriotism was not the only motive, or that in some cases it was not a motive at all. Economic pressures drove some men to take up arms, so did coercion of different kinds, and so, too, did self-interest.

Like every other army that there has ever been, Britain's volunteer corps benefited from large-scale unemployment. This was one reason why so many more men joined the volunteers from the towns than from the countryside. In the latter, there was usually enough agricultural work available to go round, at least in summertime. By contrast, the economic disruptions of the war increased the pool of surplus labour in many urban areas. Some town dwellers must have put themselves down as volunteers because they had no other occupation, and because the pocket money they received while training was better than nothing.[43] Moreover, the authorities had been careful to build an element of compulsion into their defence legislation. In 1803, they made it known that unless a sufficient number of men came forward as volunteers, they would implement full-scale conscription on the French model to which all male adults up to the age of fifty-five would be liable. It seems likely, therefore, that in some communities at least, young single men came under pressure to volunteer from those of their neighbours and fellow workers who had wives and children or other dependents to look after, and who were desperately afraid of being called up against their will.

In addition, there is ample evidence of employers, landowners and clergymen using their influence to persuade workers and tenants into joining volunteer corps. (Though there is also evidence of employers forbidding their workers to volunteer because the training in arms involved meant that they had to be given time off from work.[44]) In the Scottish county of Midlothian as a whole, for instance, one in every seven eligible men was serving in a volunteer corps in 1798. But in the parish of Dalkeith, some six miles south-east of Edinburgh, where virtually all of the land was owned by the Duke of Buccleuch, the proportion of male inhabitants signing up as volunteers was markedly higher, almost one in two.[45] Such willingness to please the local territorial magnate was most pronounced in Scotland, but it was by no means confined there. English landowners exerted similar pressures on their tenants, just as English clergymen made use of their traditional influence over parishioners in order to summon them to arms. 'The Reverend Mr. Morton has the pleasure of acquainting Mr Trevor', wrote one Bedfordshire cleric rather unctuously to his deputy lieutenant, 'that on Sunday, after an address to his parishioners, the whole number of men from the age of 17 to 55, amounting to 103, volunteered their service, with a shout of God Save the King and three cheers.'[46]

Yet it would be wrong to see the bulk of volunteers as being driven to take up arms against their will, or because they succumbed to the blandishments of their superiors. To begin with, this would be to neglect the element of individual calculation that was often involved. Volunteers were exempted by law from the militia ballot. So, for some men, volunteering must have seemed if not a soft option, at least the best option available, a welcome opportunity to serve in a part-time corps in company with their friends instead of being compelled to join the militia with its much tougher discipline and close links with the regular army. And for tradesmen and shopkeepers, especially, the risk of possible death or mutilation at the hands of the French was balanced by the virtual certainty of making money. Volunteer corps were not just paramilitary organisations. Viewed cold-bloodedly, they were also ready-made groups of healthy male customers who needed constant supplies of clothes, shoes, food, drink and equipment. This was certainly how Peter Laurie, the son of a small East Lothian farmer, viewed them. Laurie started work as a printer's apprentice in Edinburgh in the early 1790s. But he showed too much interest in local radical politics for his family's comfort and was summarily dispatched to London to make his fortune. He did just that. After setting himself up as a saddler, he joined one of the metropolitan volunteer corps: 'I much disliked soldiering', he subsequently confided in his memoirs, 'but I never failed to avail myself of any thing that should increase my business and reputation.'[47] He sold saddles and uniform belts to his comrades at special discount prices, and went on to use his military contacts to acquire profitable orders from the East India Company's regiments in India. A model self-made man, Laurie ended his days as a director of the East India Company and Lord Mayor of London.

Thousands of other men shared Laurie's opportunism if not his candour and outrageous success. A break-down of Bristol's volunteer infantry corps in the 1790s illustrates this point very nicely.[48] The corps attracted few of the city's many booksellers, school-teachers and luxury traders; nor did it contain many men employed in the maritime industries. But one-sixth of the 845 men who joined it as privates earned their everyday living in the food and drinks trade, as wine merchants, grocers, butchers, innkeepers, bakers and the like. A further eighty Bristol volunteers were shoe-makers, linen-drapers, haberdashers, tailors, woollen-drapers, hatters and hosiers. There were also no fewer than thirteen hair-dressers serving in its ranks. Some of these tradesmen undoubtedly volunteered out of an attachment to their city and nation. But even these men will have been aware that their comrades-in-arms were also potential clients and customers. Even they will have been sensitive to the fact that fellow volunteers needed to eat and drink, to lavish money on smart new uniforms and to have their hair cut to appease their officers and impress their womenfolk. Patriotism, for this social class as for so many other Britons, paid.

Yet, in recognising that some men volunteered to suit themselves, and that others did so because they had no job, or out of deference, or because they felt coerced in some way, we must be careful not to duplicate the condescension of some more well-to-do contemporaries. The failure of imagination and sympathy that led James Gillray to dismiss the volunteers as no more than gullible bumpkins or self-serving plebs should not be our failure as well. The role of ordinary human courage, of aggression and excitement, of a natural desire to protect one's own hearth should not be downplayed just because those who experienced these emotions happened in the main to be poor. All the evidence suggests that volunteers who were working men, like volunteers who were not, could be swayed by a variety of different motives, not just by direct incentives or because of pressure from above, but also by instinct, by idealism, by a desperate concern for their homeland and by their youth.

It mattered a great deal that by the early nineteenth century, going on for 55 per cent of the British population were under twenty-five years old.[49] In absolute terms, more young, unmarried men were available than ever before, brash, eager, hungry for a chance to fight (particularly perhaps on home ground) and desperately concerned not to seem a coward in the eyes of friends and lovers. The cult of heroic endeavour and aggressive maleness that was so pronounced in patrician art and literature at this time, was just as prominent in popular ballads and songs. As in this Newcastle song, where hope for a speedy peace mingles uneasily with relish at the prospect of clobbering the French:

> Then to parade the pitmen went,
> Wi' hearts both stout and strong man,
> God smash the French we are so strang;
> We'll shoot them every one, man:
> God smash me sark if I would stick,
> To tumble them a down the pit,
> As fast as I cou'd thra a coal . . .[50]

It seems probable that some Britons at least volunteered not so much because they were anxious to fight for anything in particular, but simply because they wanted to fight – period.

And the prospect of fighting as a volunteer could be immensely attractive, not least because the system *was* supposedly a voluntary one. All the accounts we have of popular rioting against recruitment for the regular forces and the militia during these and earlier British wars suggest that it was the element of arbitrary compulsion that grated the most. When press gangs invaded communities and seized men by force, or when men were selected for the militia by way of a ballot against which the poor had no means of redress, there was always bitter resentment and often violent resistance. But crowds regularly protested, as the anti-militia rioters did in Lanarkshire in 1797, that their actions were not prompted by disaffection as such or by a disinclination to fight:

> That there are not wanting a sufficient number of men in this part of the United Kingdom, who will voluntarily and cheerfully come forward in defence of Your Majesty's person and government against all invasions and rebellions, whenever Your Majesty shall be pleased to put arms in their hands and upon whom it cannot be so great a hardship to serve as upon persons in the situation of your petititoners, *levied indiscriminately or by ballot*.[51]

Anti-militia rioters in Lincolnshire the previous year had taken a similar line, shouting repeatedly 'We will fight the French whenever they come. Why do not the gentlemen come out? We will fight with them.'[52] Allowing for the men's natural desire to vindicate their actions in the most acceptable terms possible, there does seem to have been some substance in these claims. Poor men would not be compelled to join up if they could help it. Nor would they willingly be sent to die for rich men curled up safe at home. But neither would most of them sit back and let the French invade without a fight. In 1798, and again in 1803, the nation's rulers *asked* men to serve rather than *forced* them to serve. Those who volunteered usually found themselves in the company of neighbours from many different social backgrounds, so that the poor did not feel that they alone had to bear the brunt of military mobilisation. The hundred-man-strong volunteer corps formed in the parish of Machen in Monmouthshire in 1803 was a typical case in point, its members ranging from a gentleman, to a lawyer's clerk, to a bevy of farmers and agricultural labourers, and on through the usual spectrum of rural trades, to ten men working in the local ironworks.[53]

This kind of enthusiastic collaboration between different social and occupational groups was rarely maintained once the immediate excitement of the invasion crisis had subsided. By the end of 1805, it is clear, many Britons had dropped out of the volunteer corps, or had refused to turn up for military training every week, or had quarrelled with each other or with their essentially amateur officers. Since the volunteer corps were not liable to martial law unless an invasion actually took place, this kind of disarray proved very difficult to check.[54] But while the fear and the adrenalin lasted, the voluntary nature of these corps, like their broad social recruitment, proved a tremendous attraction to those who joined them. And so did the strong local attachments on which they were founded.

Like the men of 1914, the men of 1798 and 1803 were encouraged to volunteer by promises that they would be able to serve alongside of friends and relations from their own village and county. Every clergyman and school-teacher doing the rounds of potential volunteers was instructed by the Lords Lieutenant to lay great stress on the fact that the men would 'have the special privilege of not being drafted into any regiment, battalion, or corps of regulars, militia, or fencibles, but will serve only in company with their relations, friends and neighbours'.[55] As so often happens, intense local loyalties turned out not to be obstacles to effective nationwide mobilisation in practice. Instead, and as in subsequent wars, they became the building blocks out of which a wider patriotic response was constructed. Men invited to take up arms alongside of brothers, or cousins, or drinking companions, or fellow workers were not only cheered on by the prospect of such company, they also came under intense peer pressure if they did not join in like the others. Thus the supervisor of an ironworks in Monmouthshire wrote that he believed 'full two thirds of our men are really volunteers – the rest have signed through influence or *for fear of being rallied by the rest*'.[56]

But, between 1798 and 1805 at least, the prime incentive to volunteer was not camaraderie, or aggression, or greed, or the fear of seeming less than a man, or coercion from above, but quite simply fear of invasion. Of course, we know now that Great Britain, unlike Russia, Switzerland, the Netherlands, Spain, Poland, or various Italian and German states, was never overrun by French armies. No patriotic war of liberation was required here of the sort that took place in Prussia after 1807, or still more in Spain after the *Dos de Mayo* in 1808. In those countries, men and women were swept into the fighting to defend their homes, families and culture, because the stark alternatives to resistance were annihilation or conquest. As it happened, Britain escaped these brutal imperatives. But it is vital to remember that those living at the time could feel no assurance that this would be the case. Indeed, the sheer extent of

68. Anti-invasion propaganda, 1795.

the civil-defence effort, together with the weight of propaganda, and the knowledge of what had happened in other parts of Europe made anxiety or feverish anticipation almost inescapable.

We know from diaries of the time just how common nightmares of a violent French invasion of Britain were at the end of the eighteenth and the beginning of the nineteenth centuries, and how easily rumours that the enemy had in fact landed gained ground among the credulous and frightened. The poet John Clare, son of a poor labourer from Northamptonshire and just ten years old in 1803, recalled later how the people in his village had been 'chin-deep' in invasion fears. How they gathered:

> at their doors in the evening to talk over the rebellion of '45 when the rebels reached Derby and even listened at intervals to fancy they heard the French 'rebels' at Northampton knocking it down with their cannon.[57]

Nerves were kept at fever pitch by preparations for evacuation, by long lines of wagons in village streets waiting to transport women, children and the infirm away from the scene of battle, and by instructions distributed by local clergymen and constables, urging people to prepare 'a change of linen, and one blanket for each person, wrapped up in the coverlid of your bed, and bring with you all the food in your possession' in readiness for when the order came to flee or fight.[58]

In these circumstances, many Britons must have volunteered without calculating too much about the precise benefits that might accrue to them. Indeed, we know that they did. The male inhabitants of the Cinque Ports, Dover, Hastings, Hythe, New Romney, Rye, Sandwich, Seaford and Winchelsea, were all exempt by law from being balloted for the militia. So, in their case, there was no question of volunteering being used as a soft option to dodge the sterner obligations involved in militia service. None the less, over 50 per cent of the eligible male population in these ports – more than 5,000 men – had volunteered to serve by 1804.[59] The reason why seems clear enough. Strung along the south-east coast of England, the Cinque Ports were acutely vulnerable to a possible French attack. Their volunteers must have been anxious more than anything else to defend their own homes and their own way of life. Even in less exposed parts of Great Britain, the extent of the perceived emergency drove far higher numbers of men into the volunteers than the authorities had asked for or stipulated, despite the fact that these additional volunteers were explicitly told that their service would not exempt them from the militia ballot.

With the bogey of Bonaparte hanging over them, Britons who

69. Thomas Rowlandson, *A Band*.

were poor, more so perhaps even than the prosperous, were drawn into military service not just by apprehension but by the excitement of it all, by a pleasurable sense of risk and imminent drama, by the lure of a free, brightly coloured uniform and by the powerful seduction exerted by martial music. It is easy to forget how limited a range of sound was normally available to the mass of people at this time. Music lessons, concerts and assembly-room orchestras were confined to the affluent few, and most men and women had to make do with the human voice, church bells and perhaps a stray fiddler at fairs and weddings. So when recruiting parties brought their wind instruments, drums and cymbals into small villages, the effect was immediate and powerful. Joseph Mayett, a desperately sad and intelligent farm servant from Buckinghamshire, enlisted in his county's militia in 1803 because he was taken out of himself for once by the recruiting party's brass band, led to his doom by music quite as much as the children who followed the Pied Piper of Hamelin.[60] Suggestively, it was in terms of *sound* that the cartoonist George Cruikshank described the nationwide impact of volunteering in 1806:

> Every town was . . . a sort of garrison – in one place you might hear the 'tattoo' of some youth learning to beat the drum, at another place some march or national air being practised upon

> the fife, and every morning at five o'clock the bugle horn was sounded through the streets, to call the volunteers to a two hours' drill . . . and then you heard the pop, pop, pop, of the single musket, or the heavy sound of the volley, or the distant thunder of the artillery.[61]

Surrounded by loud and exhilarating noises, equipped with brand new uniforms and unfamiliar pikes and muskets, bombarded with tales of French oppression and atrocities in other lands and constantly told that only they could prevent similar evils from befalling their own shores, their own home town or village, some labouring men, it is clear, saw in volunteering a window onto a broader and more vivid existence. To them, coming forward to defend Great Britain offered a brief chance to attempt something big, some slight opportunity to escape drudgery and mundane obligations and become for a time a person who mattered. We do not know how many men thought in these terms. And it seems inherently unlikely that they did so for very long. But such men indubitably did exist at all social levels, and though their voices have been virtually ignored since, they emerge loud and clear from the Defence of the Realm returns, recorded verbatim by the men who compiled them. 'Give me a sword and pistol', urges a carter from Exeter in 1803; 'Will mow down Bonny [*sic*]', boasts one husbandman; 'If Buoneyparte [*sic*] comes will do anything to make him repent', declares another; 'Will crip [*sic*] the wings of the French frog-eaters', says a man who digs gardens for his living; 'Fight sword in hand if the French come', promises a labourer.[62]

The theatricality of such remarks is sad and revealing. In real life, few working men ever had the chance of handling a sword, never mind of learning how to use one. But the nation's emergency clearly gave men like this a chance for fantasy and wishful thinking, an opportunity for drama. For a brief time, they could imagine themselves what so many folklore heroes were – doers of daring deeds, men of destiny, winners not losers. And they relished it. What one working man described as the 'universal pant for glory',[63] the romance of a warrior's life and the prospect of a hero's death, proved as seductive at this social level as it was among contemporary patrician youths in public schools and Oxbridge. And since men at war are rarely entirely rational, why should it not?

THE POLITICS OF POPULAR COMMITMENT

Seen from below, many roads led to the decision to take up arms against the French. Viewed from above, what mattered were not these mainsprings of individual commitment, but the overwhelming success of the call for volunteers. The best way to appreciate the scale of that success is to glance back at the Jacobite invasion of 1745–6, the only other time in this period when the British state was seriously endangered.[64] On that occasion, as we saw, the bulk of Scotland's male population had not actively supported Charles James Stuart, but neither had it endeavoured to resist his progress. Instead, most Scots had stayed at home to await the turn of events; and so had most of the Welsh. In England, resistance to the Young Pretender's invasion had been strong but uneven, more pronounced in the towns and in the acutely threatened north, than in the countryside and in the south. By contrast, what was impressive about the civil defence effort launched some fifty-five years later, was not just its haul in sheer numbers – some half a million civilian volunteers – but the fact that a positive response was forthcoming throughout Great Britain. Not every region responded to the same degree. But every region responded in some degree.

In organisational terms, the contrast between 1745 and 1803 was owing to the increased reach and sophistication of the authorities in London by the latter date, and to the emergence of a more unified British ruling class. If it had not been able to draw on the local knowledge and authority of lords lieutenant, deputy lieutenants and landowners throughout Wales and Scotland as well as in England, London could never have co-ordinated home-defence measures on this scale. There was another vital difference between these two invasion crises. In 1745, Great Britain had skirted perilously near civil war, in the sense that some Highland Scots had taken up arms in the hope of enforcing dynastic change, and Lowland Scottish and English regiments had gone to battle to stop them. But in 1803, the threat proved to be overwhelmingly from without, not from within. Half a million civilians, most of them from the working population, were drawn into civil defence and given arms by the state. The result, argued Henry Addington, who was Prime Minister from 1801 to 1804, was a triumphant renewal of the contract between government and governed:

> A determination on the part of the government to put arms into the hands of a whole people, and a resolution on the part of the people to accept them . . . proved a double security, a double pledge. It was a pledge on the part of the government, that they should never attempt anything hostile to the constitution. It was a pledge on the part of the people that they valued as well as understood its excellence; that they were steadily attached to it, and determined to preserve it.[65]

This was far from being the whole story. But it was the case that by entrusting firearms to men from every part of Great Britain and from all social classes, the authorities had taken a calculated risk. They had abandoned, at least for a while, the repressive attitude towards popular participation adopted in the immediate aftermath of the French Revolution. Even William Pitt, prime author of that repression, was prepared to concede in 1803 that 'There was a time . . . when it would have been dangerous to entrust arms with a great portion of the people of this country . . . *But that time is now past.*'[66] In return, apparently, Britain's volunteers had justified their rulers' confidence. They had not attempted to use their weapons and military training to revolt. They had not even tried to employ them – as the corps of Protestant volunteers formed in Ireland during the American Revolution had done – to extort political concessions from London. That they did neither of these things, while volunteering in such abundant numbers, is the most powerful indication we have that at the end of the day, and in time of extreme danger *from without*, the unreformed British state rested on the active consent of substantial numbers of its inhabitants.

To recognise this is not to deny that large numbers of Britons were opposed to the political ordering of their state, to its fiscal exactions, to its social and economic inequities, and to its involvement in a protracted war. There was massive though uneven discontent at this time. But no more than in other European countries do the bulk of those who were impoverished and/or discontented seem to have viewed a French invasion as an attractive solution to their domestic problems. When such an invasion seemed most likely, Britain's authorities proved able to mobilise volunteers on a scale far greater than they themselves had anticipated. These civilian soldiers were never put to the test, of course. But the speed and unanimity with which militia and volunteer corps in different parts of Great Britain unfailingly assembled during the various false alarms of a French landing suggest that these amateur soldiers and worker patriots would have fought hard and bloodily against Napoleon's legions, if not perhaps particularly successfully. We know now that the French invasions of Spain, Russia and the German states at this time were rarely welcomed with open arms by their inhabitants, but instead encountered fierce popular resistance.[67] There seems little reason to suppose that the mass of Britons, however much they may have disliked their own government, would have reacted any differently – particularly since British wartime propaganda aimed at the masses did not just present the conflict with the French as a struggle to preserve monarchy, or property, or national independence even.

Instead, and quite deliberately, patriotic rhetoric redescribed

70. Anti-invasion propaganda, 1803.

the war as a crusade for freedom against the forces of military tyranny. 'Show yourselves animated by that spirit of liberty and courage which has ever characterised the gallant natives of Wales', the volunteers of Haverford West were told by a visiting major general.[68] 'We fight to preserve the whole earth from the barbarous yoke of military despotism', declared a meeting of Birmingham's volunteers. And from Cumberland and Westmorland at the height of the invasion crisis came a public declaration which suggests how powerful these kinds of appeals were felt to be:

> We abhor monarchical tyranny. We still more abhor republican tyranny . . . Whilst we have life we will not submit to a tyrannical government under any denomination.

It was signed by 19,322 people.[69] Long before 1803, the French had ceased to be viewed, even by many radicals, as liberators and exemplars for the unreformed states of Europe. Under Napoleon, the French reverted in the British imagination to what they had so often seemed in the past: spiritless victims of over-powerful government at home and ferocious exponents of military aggression abroad.[70] Once again, the full barrage of Protestant and libertarian complacency was brought to bear against the traditional enemy across the Channel.

The cumulative impact of these unprecedented civil defence measures was however very far from traditional. The scale and duration of mass arming had a transforming effect upon British society that has hardly begun to be explored. Although the volunteer corps were savagely cut back after 1808, to be replaced by a new Local Militia, there were still some 350,000 men involved in civil defence when the war ended in 1815. In addition, as many as 500,000 men may have been serving in the regular forces in Europe and the empire.[71] In Great Britain, as in other major European powers, it was training in arms under the auspices of the state that was the most common collective working-class experience in the late eighteenth and early nineteenth centuries, not labour in a factory, or membership of a radical political organisation or an illegal trade union. Here, as in Continental Europe, the pressures of war, rather than the experience of work or the example of political revolution, may have had the most obvious potential to change lives, ideas and expectations. Samuel Taylor Coleridge, at this time a radical journalist, with opium and Toryism still largely before him, set out his vision of the state reforged by war in 1800:

> Is the nation in danger? Every man is called into play; every man feels his interest as a *citizen* predominating over his individual interests; the high, and the low, and the middle classes become all alike politicians; the majority carry the day; and Jacobinism is the natural consequence. Let us not be deceived by words. Every state, in which all the inhabitants without distinction of property are roused to the exertion of a public spirit, is for the time a Jacobin state.[72]

Since Napoleon never succeeded in invading Britain, this turned out to be a wildly inflated prophecy. But Coleridge's instinct was still a correct one. Given the extent of mobilisation, some changes in the ideas ordinary Britons held about the state, about the nation and about their own civic importance and identity were inescapable.

In part, this was because those volunteering to defend Britain often experienced far more of it than they ever would have done in peacetime. It terms of how they were organised, volunteer corps were always local rather than national institutions, recruited from a very small area and officered by amateurs from the same neighbourhood. But the authorities tried to ensure that volunteers were brought into contact with wider loyalties than attachment to just one village, or to just one county, or even to just one of the three component parts of Great Britain. Every volunteer was required to take an oath of allegiance, to the king and to the Protestant religion before 1802, to the king only thereafter; and every volunteer was invited by wartime propaganda to see himself as a guardian of British freedoms and to think in terms of Britain as a whole.[73] From 1798, all volunteers had to agree to serve throughout their military district. After August 1803, this was broadened into a requirement that anyone who volunteered did so on the understanding he might be sent to fight in any part of Great Britain. Militia regiments, like regular-army regiments, were always moved around from one part of the island to another, on the grounds that it was easier for men to put down disorder in regions where they had no personal connexions. Thus the authorities took care to dispatch English militia regiments to suppress the anti-militia riots in Scotland in 1797. Many of them were garrisoned around Edinburgh, where the presence of such large numbers of English working men was sufficiently novel to provoke newspaper comment.[74]

As in this case, the movement of men in wartime affected many more individuals than the soldiers themselves. Civilians, particularly those in garrison towns, found themselves suddenly and regularly brought into contact with Britons possessed of different kinds of accents and vocabularies, different cultural backgrounds and leisure practices, and from very different places. The small market town of Woodbridge in Suffolk, for example, played host during the French Revolutionary and Napoleonic wars to no fewer than twenty-two different regiments, including the Gordon Highlanders and regiments from Lincolnshire, Warwickshire and Lancashire.[75] Just what impact this constant movement of men had on the sense of identity of those involved has never been investigated in detail. One can guess that new attachments must have been forged, as soldiers and militiamen married women in towns where they were posted, or simply decided at the end of the wars to make a new start in a new part of Britain rather than return to the place from where they came. And there is some evidence that more thoughtful men found in the geographical mobility of military service a new way of defining who they were. Take the case of poor Joseph Mayett, the Buckinghamshire militia man.[76] We know about him because, extraordinarily, he was literate. He learned to read as a child. And when the militia subsequently taught him how to write, he began to write his autobiography. Through the pages of this exceptional document, we can get some insight into what must have been true for literally hundreds of thousands from this class: namely, mobilisation's capacity utterly to change a man's life and how he saw Britain.

Mayett was no easy, tub-thumping patriot. His militia service proved a grim experience which gave him smallpox, cost him the sight of one eye and left him too unhealthy and rootless ever to settle back into agricultural life when peace came. Yet, for all this, absorption into the war effort was far and away the most exciting and formative experience of his life. Once he enlists, the number of words he allots in his autobiography to each year of his life suddenly zooms up to more than double what it was before. This, for him, was clearly the beginning of a different world. This was when new experiences started for him, when he learned to write, when he obtained access – by means of a sympathetic militia officer who took him under his wing – to books on politics; and this was when he travelled far beyond his own tiny village of Quainton, much further than he could ever have hoped to journey under any other circumstances. His military postings took him all along the south coast into Devon, then through the length of England up to Northumberland, and finally, to Ireland by way of Liverpool. It was on coming home from that country in October 1814, that he finally learnt what he was, pressured into the realisation by contact with what he was not: 'On the 23rd we landed Safe on old England shore.'[77]

I am not suggesting that Mayett's was a typical case, nor that he thought of England very often. His autobiography certainly contains no reference to Great Britain. But the impact of military service on men such as this badly needs intensive and imaginative reconstruction, not least because civilian soldiering, like other forms of soldiering, could serve as a political education in the widest sense.

The British authorities themselves made some sporadic efforts to

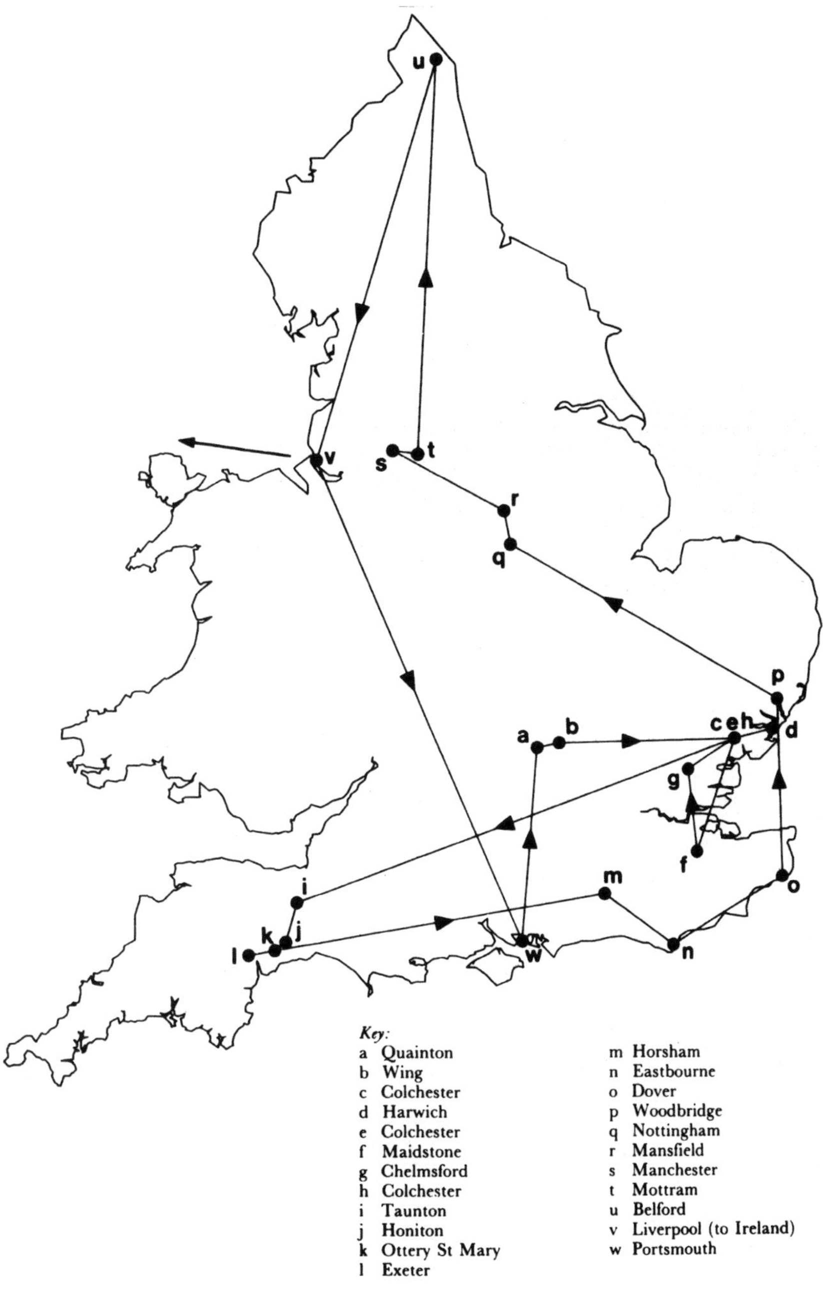

71. Joseph Mayett's militia postings.

politicise the volunteers. Every self-respecting corps had its own banner, emblazoned with emotive provincial and national symbols and presented to it by a local grandee or his wife, amidst much speechifying on the rightness of war and the iniquity of the French. On the king's birthday, and on other patriotic anniversaries, volunteers would march to hear a special sermon at the local church or chapel, or stand to attention in dusty village squares, amidst the giggles of watching children and the adoration of doting wives and girlfriends, listening to a pep talk from the divisional commander or his minions. In 1801, for example, every volunteer-corps commander was sent a printed description of Britain's recent military successes in Egypt and instructed to read it out aloud to his men, 'that all ranks will thereby be inspired with an honourable spirit of emulation, and an eager desire of distinguishing themselves in their country's service'.[78]

Yet, for some of the men, it must have been less these official red-letter days that impressed, than the distinctive comradeship that volunteering and militia service afforded. Unlike professional soldiers, volunteers and militiamen did not spend all their time in total institutions. They were not always in camps and barracks, under the watchful eyes of experienced officers and sergeants, gradually becoming infused with a solid sense of identification with the regiment. At one and the same time, their part-time soldiering taught them group solidarity and allowed them to express it in unpredictable ways. Some volunteer corps set up committees to represent their interests, 'armed parliaments' as one nervous Member of Parliament described them at the time. Other volunteers agitated for the right to elect their own officers.[79] Still more demonstrated their *esprit de corps* by coming to the aid of any of their number who got into trouble. When a Chester volunteer soldier called Daniel Jackson was illegally pressed for the Royal Navy in 1803, his comrades – who made up a fifth of the city's total male population – joined with other citizens to free him by force.[80] Similar incidents continued to occur even after the Volunteers had been run down in favour of the far more disciplined Local Militia. In May 1809, a private serving with the 3rd Western Regiment of Local Militia in Norwich answered a roll call on parade with a bitter 'Here, with an empty belly.' He was promptly slung into the guardhouse from which his entire company just as promptly rescued him.[81]

More worrying for the authorities than these isolated incidents was the fact that on several occasions, volunteers exhibited solidarity not just with each other, but with the local poor. In the north of Scotland, in the Midlands and in the south of England, volunteers joined and in some cases instigated food riots, or simply refused to suppress food riots when called upon to do so. They had enrolled, a spokesman for the Wolverhampton Volunteers told a magistrate, 'to protect their King and Constitution, and that they hold such offers sacred; but that it was never intended by them to give security to the inhuman oppressor, whilst the poor are starving in the midst of plenty'.[82] Some of the volunteer corps in Devon took exactly the same line in 1801, a time of severe food shortage: 'They declare they will fight for their King and Country against the common enemy, but think they have a right to withhold their assistance when called upon to support the civil magistrate in the execution of what they disapprove.'[83] The attitude of these plebeian volunteers was unambiguously clear and entirely logical. As Britons, they would rally to oppose an enemy from without. But they would not necessarily join in suppressing their own countrymen.

The great military historian, Sir John Fortescue, son of a peer, loyal Harrovian, an Honorary Fellow of Trinity College, Cambridge, librarian to King Edward VII, and a Knight Commander of the Victorian Order – not, therefore, an obvious democrat – dismissed such episodes as proof positive that the volunteer corps degenerated very easily into 'an armed rabble'.[84] Army officers and anxious MPs said much the same at the time. And to an extent, they were right. By professional standards, the volunteers were ill-disciplined, much closer to being a crowd than an army. Part-time soldiers, they had to live in the communities they were defending. It was to be predicted, therefore, that some of them would feel compelled to side with the local poor. Without their uniforms, many of them were the poor. Yet these intermittent protests by volunteers cannot just be put down to the fact that they were strictly amateur soldiers. Volunteer protests also happened because of who the volunteers were: namely, a hodge-podge of Britons from all social classes, all religious denominations and all political opinions.

In the face of bitter necessity, the British government had been compelled to call for the support of all Britons – not just Englishmen, or Anglicans, or the propertied, or men of conservative views, but Britons in general. In terms of rallying nationwide support against an invasion from without, this call had proved unexpectedly successful. Among the men who answered it, for example, were many former members of the corresponding societies, those artisan associations of the 1790s which had agitated for manhood suffrage.[85] The largest and most radical of these pressure groups, the London Corresponding Society, was actually debating which volunteer corps its members should join at the moment when the Bow Street

Runners broke up its final meeting in 1798.[86] Volunteer corps and Local Militia regiments also attracted, both as privates and as officers, Protestant non-conformists and Roman Catholics, men who had every reason to want the British state to be reformed, but no reason at all to want to see it invaded by the French.

By summoning men from all classes, all political opinions, all parts of Great Britain and all religious denominations to its defence in this way, by treating them indiscriminately as patriots, the authorities ran an obvious risk of encouraging demands for political change in the future. They ran this risk knowingly, because they recognised they had no choice. A nation where formal political power was concentrated in the hands of the propertied few, and where perhaps only one adult male in fifteen had the vote, had no alternative but to look to the mass of its inhabitants to win its wars and preserve its independence. The prime opponent of the French Revolution had itself to employ revolutionary methods in order to stand a chance of succeeding, and indeed surviving. 'If we employ the mass of the people for our internal defence', a British army officer had written to a member of the government in 1803, 'it will only be recurring to the same expedient for the defence of our independence as a nation, which France has successfully employed during the last ten years.'[87] This was the point precisely. To beat the French, the British had been required to imitate the French, and the challenge this presented to its old order was potentially corrosive.

Reformers recognised this quite as clearly as ministers did. It was Samuel Bamford, a Lancashire weaver and non-conformist turned political radical, who pointed out to William Cobbett that the government's lists of militiamen and volunteers would supply marvellous guides to the number of adult males in each county who might in the near future win the right to vote.[88] For if all adult men were worthy to fight for Great Britain, then surely they had the right to take part in its politics as well? Cobbett certainly thought so. In 1816, he printed a best-selling address 'To the Journeymen and Labourers of England, Wales, Scotland, and Ireland', urging them to rejoice that they belonged to 'the most powerful nation in the world', overflowing with signs of wealth and prosperity:

> Without the journeymen and the labourers none of them could exist . . . It is the same class of men, who must, by their arms, secure its safety and uphold its fame. Titles and immense sums of money have been bestowed upon numerous naval and military commanders. Without calling the justice of these in question, we may assert that the victories were obtained by *you*.[89]

As Cobbett understood, mass arming in Great Britain during the wars against Revolutionary and Napoleonic France had provided irrefutable proof that patriotism – in the sense of an identification with British independence against those foreign forces that threatened it – transcended the divisions between the social classes. But what and when was to be the pay-off? When would those who had demonstrated their willingness to fight receive their due? When would every British patriot come to be a citizen as of right?

72. *The British Atlas, or John Bull supporting the Peace Establishment*, 1816. A radical satire on the costs of peace.

8 *Victories?*

GREAT BATTLES ARE NOT ALWAYS turning-points in history, but Waterloo emphatically was. Although the British might never have won it without their Continental allies, it was they who claimed prime credit, and it was they who reaped the most substantial political and territorial rewards. Waterloo destroyed Napoleon and established Great Britain as indisputably the foremost European power. Moreover, the ensuing division of the spoils at the Congress of Vienna ensured that the British empire emerged from the war the largest the world had ever known. Yet, as far as the home front was concerned, the chauvinistic euphoria that might have been expected from these momentous developments was for a long time strangely absent. 'All the triumphant sensations of national glory', as one writer put it in 1815, 'seem almost obliterated by general depression.'[1]

Some of the reasons for this were obvious enough. These last wars with France had broken out in 1793 – only ten years after the lost American war – and had lasted, virtually without a break, for almost a quarter of a century. Many Britons were simply too worn down and too weary to feel anything more than a dull relief that the strains of conflict were now finally over. And for the poor, and even for the moderately prosperous, there was little in the short term to celebrate. The economy had been geared for so long to war that the outbreak of peace precipitated a severe slump in agriculture, trade and manufacturing which persisted until the early 1820s. The resulting high levels of unemployment and social unrest were made very much worse by the demobilisation of more than a third of a million men. We know extraordinarily little about these veterans, what they thought about coming home and what happened to them when they did. But many of them were clearly angry at returning to poverty and neglect, and even those who were able to find jobs often seem to have found it difficult to settle back into ordinary working life. The alienation – and the military skills – of these hundreds of thousands of men go a long way towards explaining the peculiarly bitter quality of popular protest in Britain in the twenty or even thirty years after Waterloo. As Seymour Drescher writes, during this period 'there was something "extra" behind extra-parliamentary agitation: very tangible reserve armies of violence'.[2]

But neither these short-term economic and social tensions, nor the more protracted impact of a population explosion and industrial expansion is sufficient to account for the high level of post-war malaise and contention. There was also a more profound loss of direction involved. Ever since 1689, England, Wales and Scotland had been caught up in a succession of major wars with the foremost Catholic power in Europe, France. It had been the threat posed by France, and by French support for the Stuart dynasty, that had dictated the Act of Union in 1707 and the formal construction of Great Britain in the first place. Since then, recurrent wars with France had made it possible for the different countries, social classes and ethnic groups contained in Great Britain to have something in common – whether it was fear, or aggression, or a powerful sense of embattled Protestantism. Time and time again, war with an obviously hostile and alien foreign power had forged a semblance of unity and distracted attention from the considerable divisions and tensions within. In a very real sense, war – recurrent, protracted and increasingly demanding war – had been the making of Great Britain. But Waterloo finally slew the dragon; and the immediate reaction among many Britons was less complacency than disorientation. How was Britishness to be defined now that it could no longer rely so absolutely on a sense of beleaguered Protestantism and on regular conflict with the Other in the shape of Catholic France?

Between the outbreak of peace in 1815 and the accession of Queen Victoria in 1837, this profound but generalised uncertainty was given focus by three specific issues, all of which impinged on questions of Britishness. First, and most challenging, were the problems raised by Ireland's incorporation into the United Kingdom by way of the Act of Union of 1800.[3] Even more than the earlier Act of Union with Scotland, the immediate cause of this new political arrangement had been fear of French military intervention. Ireland was annexed to prevent Napoleon from using it as a launching pad for an invasion of the British mainland. But, as intelligent contemporaries recognised, there was not even a possibility of Ireland being permanently reconciled to direct rule from Westminster unless its predominantly Catholic population was granted wider civil rights. Yet, now that Ireland and Great Britain were united in law, how could full citizenship be extended to Irish Catholics without similar concessions also being made to the Catholic minority within Great Britain itself? And how could such an avowedly Protestant nation admit any of its Catholic subjects to a full share in civic life without irredeemably compromising its traditional identity?

The second issue was less emotive but just as intimately bound up with matters of citizenship. Before 1789, the movement for parliamentary reform had aroused only sporadic and minority interest. Thereafter, agitation for an extension of the franchise and for a redistribution of parliamentary seats became more extensive, more consistent, and far more radical. This was due not only to the ideological impact of the revolution in France but also to the imperatives of war. We have already seen how the introduction of mass arming in defence of Britain's territorial integrity allowed radical spokesmen to legitimise their calls for universal manhood suffrage. But the argument that broad participation in the war effort must in justice be rewarded by improved access to civil rights was also used by other groups who felt themselves to be disadvantaged, not least by those who wanted direct representation for the rising industrial and commercial centres and votes for the middling men who dominated them. As a protest meeting in unrepresented Manchester put it in 1815: 'The great importance of trade and manufacture in this country has been fully evinced during the period of the late war, by enabling us to call forth resources impracticable in any state that was merely agricultural.'[4] Having been compelled to draw on the armed service and incomes of unprecedented numbers of its population so as to defeat France, the men who governed Great Britain found themselves under pressure after the peace to change the political system so that all men of property, and all working men, were given access to the vote.

Like parliamentary reform, the third issue had been growing in importance since the 1760s, but the sheer scale of Britain's success in the wars with Revolutionary and Napoleonic France made it very much more urgent. By 1815, the boundaries of the British empire were so extensive that they included one in every five inhabitants of the globe.[5] The question of how these millions of men and women who were manifestly not British, but who had been brought under British rule by armed force should be treated and regarded thus became inescapable. What responsibilities, if any, did the mother country have towards them? Did they have any claim on those vague but valuable freedoms that so many Britons considered to be peculiarly their own? Or could British subjects also be slaves as long as they were black and safely overseas? The argument that they could not, and should not, had triumphed in 1807 to the extent that Parliament had banned British involvement in the slave trade. But Britain's sugar colonies in the West Indies still remained dependent on slave labour. The nationwide campaign to persuade Parliament to free these slaves, a campaign that culminated in the Emancipation Act of 1833–just one year after the first Reform Act remodelled the electoral system, and four years after the achievement of Catholic emancipation in 1829–is often passed over in silence or treated as an exotic diversion by historians of this period. Yet, as its timing suggests, the anti-slavery movement was closely linked with these other agitations over citizenship and the meanings of Britishness.

At peace, with little left to fear from without, and lacking now such an obviously hostile Other across the Channel against which to define themselves, it was scarcely surprising that different groups of Britons should have looked for new ways to establish who they were and what, if anything, made them special and bound them together. Nor was it surprising that this process of adaptation proved divisive and painfully disruptive. For while the struggles over the extension of civil rights to British and Irish Catholics, over the reform of the representative system and over the freeing of black slaves who were also British subjects had many different causes, what was involved in all three of these campaigns was nothing less than a redefinition of the nation.

CATHOLIC EMANCIPATION AND DIVISION

Just after 6 p.m. on 16 October 1834, the Houses of Parliament at Westminster burst into flames. Since 7 o'clock that morning, two workmen had been busy incinerating cartloads of wooden tallies–the dry sticks with which the Exchequer had kept its accounts in the past. They had used the furnaces in the basement of the House of Lords because they were convenient, and because no one had thought to tell them that the chimneys had not been cleaned, or that constantly opening and shutting the furnace doors would cause a fierce draught. It was only in the late afternoon that peers and MPs began to notice that the temperature in their ancient, wooden chambers was rising alarmingly, that faded tapestries were beginning to smoulder, and that crocodiles of tourists were having to peer at the medieval carving through an ever-thickening haze of smoke. By then it was much too late. At 7.30 p.m. the roof of the House of Lords crashed in, at which point the wind veered suddenly north-eastwards, and the House of Commons began to burn furiously. By 11 o'clock that night, it, too, was in ruins. And the largest empire in the world was without a building for its legislature.[6]

The thousands of spectators lining the banks of the Thames seem to have been more delighted than appalled; artists – John Constable and J.M.W. Turner among them – because the brilliance of the conflagration against the night sky gave them ideas for future canvases; conservatives, because the disaster seemed a fit punishment for the passing of the Reform Act in 1832; radicals, because it swept away buildings linked in their minds with centuries of patrician corruption; and the conventionally patriotic, because it opened the way for the making of a new Palace of Westminster fit for a reformed and imperial nation at the height of its power. The subsequent architectural competition was an open one and attracted almost a hundred entries. The winner was the extremely gifted and already well-established London architect, Charles Barry. But he alone was not responsible for what is now far and away the most famous and familiar British skyline. Working with him throughout was a dark, intense and brilliant young man called Augustus Welby Northmore Pugin who would die insane at the age of forty. 'Every visible foot of the Houses of Parliament is the work of Pugin', wrote the late Kenneth Clark, '. . . every panel, every wall-paper, every chair sprang from Pugin's brain, and his last days were spent in designing ink-pots and umbrella stands' for its halls.[7] And why was this significant? Because Pugin was not just the son of a Frenchman, but a convert to Catholicism. The building that most enshrines nineteenth-century Britain's national and imperial pretensions – and was recognised as doing so at the time – was the product of a collaboration between a confirmed Protestant and an ardent Roman Catholic.

What made it possible for Pugin to contribute so much to such a sensitive and symbolic project was not just the passing of the Catholic Emancipation Act in 1829, but also the marked change in attitudes in Great Britain which had preceded it. Toleration of Roman Catholicism and acquiescence in the civic claims of British Catholics had been increasing for some time across the social spectrum. This point needs stressing because it is sometimes suggested that Catholic emancipation occurred when it did only because of the threat of insurrection in Ireland.[8] Yet this is to ignore long-term trends and to concentrate exclusively on short-term causes. The grass-roots campaigning of the Irish Catholic Association which culminated in Daniel O'Connell's election for County Clare in 1828 certainly put the Duke of Wellington's Tory administration and King George IV under enormous pressure and determined the precise timing of the Emancipation Act.[9] But the legislation could never have come to pass without marked shifts of opinion on the British mainland itself.

As far as the governing élite was concerned, the main solvent of traditional Protestant intolerance was war and its demands. Ever since the Reformation, the cage of legislation confining Catholics had been constructed primarily to protect a nervously Protestant state against what was assumed to be a fifth column in its midst. In England and Wales, the chief curbs on Catholic civil rights were the Corporation Act of 1663, which forced local office-holders to take the Anglican sacrament, and the Test Act of 1673, which required all office-holders, whether in local or central government, to take Anglican communion and to repudiate the central Catholic doctrine of transubstantiation. Further acts in 1678 and 1689 specifically excluded Catholics from both Houses of Parliament and from the vote. Similar restrictions operated in Scotland even before the Act of Union in 1707; while in Ireland, the penal laws against Catholics were harsher still. London remained intent on enforcing these restrictions until the mid-eighteenth century primarily for reasons of security. Ministers believed, with some justice, that Catholics retained an attachment to their exiled co-religionists, the princes of the House of Stuart. After the Battle of Culloden had confirmed Jacobitism's insignificance, however, government attitudes towards Catholicism began perceptibly and logically to relax, softened not just by the intellectual impact of the Enlightenment, but also by the strictly practical consideration that the majority of its Catholic subjects lived in Ireland and in the Scottish Highlands, both prime recruiting areas for the British army.[10]

In law, no Catholic from either Britain or Ireland could serve in the armed services. None the less, from the Seven Years War onwards, large numbers of Irish and Scottish Catholics were recruited for active service overseas. In 1764, it was estimated that some 6,000 Scottish Catholics had seen wartime service, most of them in India and the West Indies. Their conduct was so impressive that General Burgoyne urged Parliament in 1770 to relax the penal laws as an aid to future recruitment. This initiative failed. But shortly after, the Dublin Parliament passed legislation allowing Irish Catholics to join the army openly without having to perjure themselves by taking a Protestant oath. Catholic manpower from Ireland, Scotland and North America was drawn on intensively in the War of American Independence, and still more so for both the army and the navy after 1793, when Roman Catholics acquired the right to hold army commissions up to and including the rank of colonel – though only in army units serving in Ireland.[11]

Well before the Act of Union with Ireland in 1800, then, Catholic service in the British military machine at a time of increasingly large and dangerous wars had begun to prise open élite attitudes.

From the 1770s onwards, support for a relaxation of the penal laws had powerful advocates within government circles, and not just among the more advanced members of the Whig opposition like Edmund Burke. More broadly, loyal and substantial Catholic service on the battlefield undermined one of the most longstanding objections to emancipation: namely, that since Catholics owed religious allegiance to a foreign authority in the person of the Pope, their political and patriotic allegiance must necessarily be suspect. In 1816, for example, William Plunket, a brilliant barrister and MP for Dublin University, was able to tear into the Tory Speaker of the House of Commons for congratulating the Duke of Wellington on his victory at Waterloo while, in almost the same breath, championing an exclusively Protestant constitution:

> When you adverted to the splendid victories of our illustrious commander . . . When you spoke of the passage of the Douro, of the battles of Roliça, of Vimeiro, of Talavera, of Salamanca, of Vitoria, the feelings of all who heard you vibrated in unison with your own. Every heart exulted, and every *Irish* heart peculiarly exulted, that Ireland had given birth to such a hero. Was that a well-chosen moment, Sir, to pronounce the irrevocable doom of those who, under their immortal commander, had opened the sluices of their heart's blood in the service of the empire? . . . While you were binding the wreath around the brow of the conqueror, you assured him that his victorious followers must never expect to participate in the fruits of his valour, but that they who had shed their blood in achieving conquests were to be the only persons who were not to share by the profits of success in the rights of citizens.[12]

This kind of language increasingly put the opponents of emancipation on the defensive, making them appear unappreciative of the patriot dead and out of touch with Great Britain's current grandeur and expansiveness. 'England, however considerable, is only a part and not the most flourishing part, of the British empire', argued another Anglo-Irish lawyer coolly:

> The people of Scotland and Ireland have therefore surely a right to protest against any system of general policy, adopted solely with reference to English prejudices and with a view to local establishments with which the Empire has no concern; but especially against a system which was guided principally by attention to the limited notions of clerical residents of an English university.[13]

This was disingenuous in the sense that anti-Catholic prejudice could be even more savage in parts of Scotland and Ireland than it was in England. But the wider argument – that an intolerance forged in the sixteenth century when England was small and vulnerable was inappropriate for the range and power of the British empire three hundred years later – was an important one. It ensured that those Ultra Tory politicians who opposed Catholic emancipation on the grounds that the sanctity of Britain's Protestant constitution must be maintained, were never able to monopolise patriotic language. Instead, they could be presented as championing just one vision of Britain, and a singularly limited vision at that. They seemed to think, one Scottish MP remarked,

> that the great principle of the constitution is the principle of exclusion; but I think, on the contrary, that the great principle of the British constitution is the diffusion to every class of the community of all those blessings which it is so well formed to bestow.[14]

By the early 1820s, in fact, the argument that full inclusion of the Catholic population within the body politic was a wiser and more practical strategy than an already modified exclusion had triumphed as far as the House of Commons and an influential sector of the cabinet were concerned. Whereas 336 MPs had voted against Catholic relief back in 1805 and only 27 per cent had supported it, after 1812 it was rare for the anti-Catholics to secure more than 250 votes. In 1819, a vote in support of relief failed by just two votes; in 1821, another repeal measure succeeded by a slender majority, while a motion two years later to give the franchise to qualified English Catholics passed by more than fifty votes.[15] In other words, as far as the House of Commons was concerned, the gradual but relentless shift of opinion beloved of Whig historians really did take place on this issue and was recognised as doing so at the time. There remained a rump of some 170 Ultra Tory MPs who believed, sincerely and passionately, that to give Catholics full civil rights as distinct from religious toleration would utterly undermine the political settlement established by the Revolution of 1688. But it needs to be stressed that these men were a minority lacking any cabinet spokesman in the Commons except Robert Peel.[16] As far as the Lower House is concerned, then, it is quite wrong to attribute the conversion to emancipation to the Irish crisis of 1828–29. In intellectual terms, a majority of British MPs had accepted that Catholics must be admitted to civil rights several years earlier.

Events in Ireland were crucial, of course, in forcing the Tory administration finally to grasp the nettle. The election in 1828 of the Catholic O'Connell for County Clare, openly campaigning on the Catholic issue, and the likelihood that other Irish constituencies would return Catholic representatives at the next general election, even though such men could not under the existing law take their seats in Westminster, nerved the government to disregard its own Ultra Tory wing and force George IV into accepting an emancipation act.[17] Yet such a sweeping constitutional change would have been impossible if attitudes outside Parliament had not already altered as well. Back in the 1700s, as we have seen, Protestant and Catholic Britons had often lived together peacefully enough. But for the latter there had still been the possibility of physical attack during wartime or in other civil emergencies. Politicians wanting to relax anti-Catholic legislation had still felt restrained by the fear of provoking militant popular Protestantism. By the early nineteenth century, however, mass responses to Catholicism were shifting. Grass-roots reaction to the passing of the Catholic Emancipation Act showed that Protestantism was still a major component of British popular patriotism. But it demonstrated also that the importance of religious zeal and intolerance in the worldview of large numbers of ordinary Britons was shrinking.

Shrinking: but by no means insignificant. In some areas of Great Britain, traditional prejudices had actually become even sharper because of the recent flood of Irish immigrants. Back in the 1780s, the number of Irish men and women living on the mainland was probably little more than 40,000. But by the time of the 1831 census, there were some 580,000 Irish in Britain, close to 5 per cent of the labour force. Although their overall impact on the economy was probably small, since the bulk of them were young adults, disproportionately illiterate and unskilled, they undercut British-born manual labour in those northern and Scottish cities where they were concentrated: Glasgow, Liverpool, Dundee, Manchester and Paisley.[18]

All of these cities petitioned strongly against Catholic emancipation in 1829. Glasgow sent in over twenty-one hostile petitions, bearing 24,000 signatures in all. Manchester's petition, which was not well organised, still picked up 22,000 signatures. Dundee submitted fifty-three petitions, and one newspaper claimed that virtually every Protestant adult in the city signed; while Liverpool's anti-Catholic petition was so enormous that the House of Commons porter could barely lift it. Anti-Irish sentiment may also have been one reason why the Welsh, who had rarely petitioned on any issue before 1829, petitioned so extensively on this one. The Isle of Anglesey, for example, so close physically to Ireland and a stopping-off point for many immigrants bound for the mainland, dispatched more than twenty anti-Catholic petitions to the House of Commons.[19]

Yet anti-Irish sentiment, whether founded on economic grievances or ethnic prejudice, scarcely explains the sheer scale of the agitation against Catholic emancipation. Irish immigrants were concentrated in a small number of predominantly urban areas. Anti-Catholic petitions, by contrast – perhaps as many as 3,000 of them – poured in from almost every county in 1828–9, from the countryside as well as from the towns, from places that had never petitioned Parliament before and would hardly ever petition Parliament again: Troedyraur in Cardiganshire, Llanfihangel Crucornau in Monmouthshire, Ysceifiog in Flintshire, Monks Eleigh in Suffolk, Screveton in Nottinghamshire, Woughton on the Green in Buckinghamshire and Abberwick in Northumberland, tiny villages whose names the London and big provincial newspapers hardly knew how to spell, and where a man from the next county, never mind an Irishman, would have been as rare as a dry summer.[20] It was not anti-Irish sentiment that made the inhabitants of such places carry out the unprecedented act of signing a petition to a distant legislature. Nor, often, was it any direct experience of Roman Catholics or their faith. The protesters acted as they did, as one MP put it, 'not so much from what they knew, *as from what they felt*'.[21] For these men and women, Protestantism was not just a species of religious belief, anymore than Roman Catholicism was. Protestantism was a vital part of who they were now, and the frame through which they looked at the past.

The evidence suggests that many ordinary Britons who signed anti-Catholic petitions in 1828–9 saw themselves, quite consciously, as being part of a native tradition of resistance to Catholicism which stretched back for centuries and which seemed, indeed, to be timeless. In the West Country, where protest was particularly marked, local activists looked back for inspiration to the Monmouth rebellion in 1685, when hundreds of their forbears had taken up arms to oust the Catholic James II and replace him with a Protestant monarch. In Frome, a placard was put up listing the town's twelve 'martyrs' from that occasion, while another in Taunton gave the names of six of its citizens who had been executed for joining the same rebellion. In much the same way, some Scottish parishes opposed to Catholic emancipation pulled out of store the faded banners of the Covenanters who had fought against Charles I's religious policies in the 1630s and '40s, and hung them afresh in their churches.[22]

Most of the crude, printed propaganda spawned by the emancipation crisis has not survived. Cheap and ephemeral, it disappeared into the minds and homes of those kinds of men and women who leave few records behind them for historians. But the extracts from such literature read out in Parliament at the time are sufficient to show just how recent – and just how precarious – the Protestant Reformation still seemed to many of its poorer British champions. In some working-class areas of London, placards appeared showing 'friars and popes, in all attitudes and modes of applying combustible matter to Protestants'. In Surrey, an anti-emancipation tract called *Queen Mary's days* circulated, full of grisly pictures of the burnings at Smithfield. In the West Country, magistrates had to confiscate pictures of 'infants quartered and . . . young girls impaled alive and naked' at the hands of Catholic priests.[23] Even the Lollards, those predominantly plebeian heretics who had been persecuted for challenging Catholic orthodoxy back in the fourteenth century, were not forgotten. A series of letters from 'Wickliff' (a spelling of John Wycliffe's name which suggests that the writer was not particularly well educated) appeared in the *North Wales Chronicle* urging the Welsh to sign anti-Catholic petitions wherever they were available.[24] And some men and women harked back to even further reaches of folk memory. In Kent, for example, a monster anti-Catholic meeting which may have been attended by as many as 60,000 people assembled at Penenden Heath which had been used as a meeting place in time of emergency ever since the Norman Conquest.[25]

Such protests – which were a nationwide phenomenon and have never been properly investigated – confirm yet again just how important Protestantism was in shaping the way that ordinary Britons viewed and made sense of the land they lived in. It was not surprising, therefore, that in many of these demonstrations, anger was expressed at what was seen as a betrayal from above. As on so many occasions in its past, Great Britain was in peril from popery. But this time, many of its own leaders were in open collaboration with the enemy. 'Fellow countrymen', declared a Staffordshire handbill, 'the constitution is betrayed. The citadel is in peril . . . To your tents, O Israel!'[26] When Parliament finally did pass Catholic emancipation in April 1829, the alienation and bewilderment among those below were very great; and this needs to be remembered in any assessment of social and political antagonisms at this time. To many Britons, it seemed that their rulers had palpably failed them – and failed God, history and the nation as well. At first glance, indeed, it is tempting to see the struggle over this issue as just one more example of that withdrawal of the upper classes from their former participation in popular culture which Peter Burke and others have detected in so many European states in the late eighteenth and early nineteenth centuries.[27] Here, apparently, was a clear case of a backward-looking and still rigidly Protestant population being left in the lurch by an élite that had discarded traditional attitudes in favour of newer and more secular imperatives. Yet, on both sides, alignments were in reality far more complex than this.

For not only was Britain's governing élite divided in its support for Catholic emancipation – the king and a vociferous minority of peers and MPs were furious at the concession – but the people below were by no means united in opposing it. The anti-Catholic petitions that emerged from some cities, Glasgow, or Birmingham, or Bristol, for example, contain so many signatures (24,000, 36,000 and 38,000 respectively) that they must have won support from the local middle-class community as well as from the working classes. But in other urban areas, Leicester, or Norwich, or Edinburgh, or London most of all, contemporaries noted that the educated, commercial and professional classes' attitude towards Catholicism was now far more relaxed than it had been in the previous century.[28] It was not so much that these people had become less devout, though some of them had. It was rather that they had ceased to view Catholics as either a religious or a political threat. Even more significant as far as the administration was concerned was the fact that the mass of poorer Britons no longer felt so aggressively on the subject of Catholicism as they had done in the past. They might still dislike it intensely. But the quality of protest in 1829 showed that many of them no longer feared it to the degree that their ancestors had done.

When Parliament had passed a far more anodyne Catholic Relief Act back in 1778, the ensuing protests had led to the Gordon Riots in London, the largest, deadliest and most protracted urban riots in British history; while the opposition in Scotland was so violent that the government was forced to back down from enforcing the legislation there.[29] Nothing like this happened in 1829. There were no major riots on the British mainland on account of the Catholic Emancipation Act. No one seems to have been killed opposing it; and no Catholic chapels were burnt to the ground in retaliation. Toleration was growing. Victory at Waterloo, and the onset of peace with dominance, meant that Britons were less likely to associate the Catholic presence at home with a military threat from abroad. And many of the more ambitious and educated members of the working and middle classes were now investing their hopes and energies in political not religious activism, in the struggle for parliamentary reform.

It was the poorer, more marginal and less literate folk who were

3. A print in favour of Catholic emancipation in 1829 alluding to the opposition from women and 'womanish' politicians).

the most stridently and devotedly anti-Catholic in 1829, the Methodist communities of Devon, Cornwall and North and central Wales, manual workers such as miners, quarrymen, fishermen and farm labourers, and an abundance of women.[30] This was one of the first times in British history when large numbers of women signed petitions to Parliament alongside of men, as distinct from organising their own all-female addresses to the throne as they had done over the Queen Caroline affair. And those women who petitioned appear to have been predominantly working class and to have sided overwhelmingly against Catholic emancipation. Women's prominence in the anti-Catholic camp may have owed something to the fact that they were often more assiduous in their church-going than their menfolk. But women were also, in the main, less formally educated than men, and more dependent on that traditional, largely oral culture in which Protestant intolerance was so deeply embedded. The condescension of one pro-emancipation peer confronted by a piece of crude anti-Catholic propaganda – 'He believed that these tales were handed down by tradition from one old woman to another' – is unattractive, but it probably contained an element of truth.[31]

Whatever its causes, the prominence of women in this agitation was further confirmation that mass Protestantism was ceasing to be the violent and dangerous movement of the eighteenth century and before. In 1829, this was crucial. The Tory administration was able to pass Roman Catholic emancipation and thus defuse the threat of civil war in Ireland, without having to worry that its action would provoke civil commotion on the mainland. Anti-Catholic Britons might feel betrayed, but their frustration was unlikely to be expressed in riot.[32] Of course, some concessions were made to their prejudices. All English, Welsh, Scottish and Irish Catholic males were now citizens in the sense that they could vote, enter Parliament and fill the majority of civil offices if they possessed the necessary economic and social qualifications. But Catholics remained excluded from the throne (as they still are). The ancient universities were still closed to them, and so were the highest legal offices. If appointed to state employment, they still had to swear they would not 'disturb or weaken the Protestant religion or Protestant government in this kingdom'. And, as far as admission to Parliament was concerned, Catholics still had to run the gauntlet of electoral prejudice. No Catholic MP would be returned by a Scottish constituency, for example, until the 1890s.[33] None the less, 1829 was the end of an era.

Before then, as Bruce Lenman has written, Britain's political structure had derived 'its claims to sovereignty directly from the English Reformation under Henry VIII in the sixteenth century, and its claim for popular support on a vague but emphatically Protestant interpretation of freedoms secured by the Glorious Revolution of 1688'.[34] This appeal was bound to be affected by opening civil rights to Roman Catholics. Protestant patriotism remained powerful and widespread, especially among the mass of working men and women. But now that Catholic emancipation had become law, intolerant Protestantism was as likely to divide Britons as it was to unite them. What would emerge as a national cement in its stead?

PARLIAMENTARY REFORM AND COMPROMISE

The accident happened on Wednesday, 15 September 1830. The show train had stopped to take on water at a small quarry mid-way between Liverpool and Manchester, and some of the gentlemen had jumped down onto the line, examining the glittering new machinery, strolling around to admire the view and chatting idly to the musicians who were to play 'God Save the King' when they finally steamed into the station. Those inside stretched their legs discreetly and consulted their watches, wondering how long it would be before the other engine reached them. 'I think you had better get in', called the Duke of Wellington to the loiterers outside. Only then did they see the Rocket bearing down on them fast on the other rails. There was not enough room, they suddenly realised, for them to stand safely on the opposite side of the line, and no space either between the two sets of rails. So men began scrabbling to open the saloon car doors of the stationary train, desperately trying to haul themselves inside, for the carriage was high off the ground and no steps had been provided. The former Secretary of State had already tried to escape the oncoming train by crossing the track. He now ran back in panic and was clutching at one of the doors when the engine caught him and flung him on the rails. Even inside the carriage, Lady Wilton could distinctly hear the crushing of bones, followed by Mrs Huskisson's piercing shriek.[35]

The strange death of William Huskisson has become a set-piece in British history because it seems so easily symbolic. Even at the time, there were suggestions that the reason he had been wandering about the track so carelessly was because he was used to getting out of his own coach whenever it stopped to change horses. Utterly unused to train travel, he had simply and fatally acted as he had always done.[36] Even for contemporaries, then, the accident was interpreted in terms of the old world and its ways suddenly being overwhelmed by the shock of the new. In retrospect, though, the event appears still more portentous. A leading Tory politician, a man whose resignation earlier in 1830 had further weakened a party already badly divided over the passing of Catholic emancipation, had been run down by George Stephenson's most celebrated railway engine at the opening of the first great passenger line between two of Britain's greatest commercial cities. Moreover, it had all happened in the presence of the Tory premier and supreme pillar of the establishment, the Duke of Wellington, who had once predicted that the steam engine would never catch on.[37] Three months after the accident, he in turn would be forced to resign in favour of a Whig administration committed to implementing parliamentary reform. On the large scale, apparently, as on the small, progress and industrial might were bearing down on those who got in their way. Except, of course, it was not quite like that.

Historians have long since retrieved the reputation of Huskisson and his Tory colleagues, and they no longer explain the passing of the Great Reform Act in 1832 in terms of the irresistible advance of economic modernity or a broader democracy.[38] Instead, like so many other large-scale events, this one has been carefully examined and fragmented. We now know that the social texture of the parliamentary reform movement varied in different parts of Britain. We know that the politicians were always divided in what they wanted to achieve, though more or less united in their determination to exclude the mass of working men from the franchise. And we know that those outside Parliament who actively supported reform did so only intermittently and were often at odds over how much the system should be changed. We know so much, in fact, that it is easy to lose sight of the obvious: that the movement for parliamentary reform was nationwide and concerned with restructuring the British electoral system and legislature. As such, debates about the meanings of citizenship and about what was best for the nation were inevitably central to it. And for a variety of reasons, all of its chief proponents made extensive use of the languages of patriotism.

In part this was simply a matter of conviction. One of the reasons Thomas Paine had written his *Rights of Man* (1791) was to shatter the notion that liberty was uniquely first an English, then a British growth, rooted in the Saxon past, and watered successively by Magna Carta, by resistance to Charles I, by the Revolution of 1688, and by the Hanoverian Succession in 1714. There was no ancient and free constitution to reform, he had argued: the vital struggle must be to invent a brand new political order.[39] Yet, for all Paine's impact in general, it is clear that even his more radical readers were reluctant to accept this particular part of his polemic. Too much of their own self-image was bound up with the belief that Britain was historically and in essence the freest nation in the world, however endangered it might now be by the forces of corruption and oligarchy. The most famous of the democratic societies of the 1790s, the London Corresponding Society, had initially contemplated calling itself the Patriotic Club (its imitators in Norwich and Manchester actually did call themselves Patriotic Societies), and the intention in so doing was not just to advertise the radicals' pretensions to full citizenship, but to suggest a more conventional commitment to country. Great Britain must be rescued from its rulers and opened up to new influences so that its pristine and original virtues could shine through: yes. But these original and distinctive virtues were never to be forgotten. As John Thelwall, a leading member of the L.C.S. and perhaps the most original of the radical theorists, declared in 1794: 'There must be something in the constitution of this country which a Briton will ever love and venerate.'[40] By the same token, and paradoxically to modern eyes, this generation of radicals, like their post-war counterparts, and like the Chartists of the 1830s and '40s, berated Parliament for its members' exclusiveness and parasitism on the one hand, while continuing assiduously to petition it on the other. They retained, most of them, a gut belief in the fundamental worth of the institution even as they called for its thoroughgoing reform.[41]

And like earlier British dissidents, they knew that arming themselves with patriotic language and symbols could be a thoroughly pragmatic strategy. At the most rudimentary level, it supplied a way of countering the authorities' condemnation. When 60,000 men, women and children marched on Manchester in 1819 to hear Henry Hunt champion universal manhood suffrage, for instance, the brass bands that accompanied each division of the demonstration cheered them along by playing 'God Save the King' and 'Rule Britannia'. Moreover, and as the magistrates were subsequently told, whenever the strains of the national anthem reached the marchers' ears: 'the people for the most part took off their hats'.[42] Behaving so ostentatiously as loyal Britons was a way of challenging the official description of such activities as seditious. It showed that in the marchers' eyes, at least, what they were doing was legitimate and positively public-spirited. It was they who were the authentic patriots, such actions declared, not their opponents. They were the real Britons, and consequently fully deserving of the vote. As one radical ballad of the time put it:

> As for me, in all weathers, in peace or in war,
> My service my country commands;
> Her rights are at stake and the time is not far
> When her sons shall assert their demands:
> Then, then, my brave Britons, we ne'er shall be slaves,
> Nor shall tyrants rule over this isle:
> See the goddess of freedom her banner high waves,
> And inspires her loved sons with her smile.[43]

Presenting themselves in this patriotic light, rather than identifying with a more sectional ideology, was also a way of attracting wider support. For all strands of the parliamentary reform movement this had to be a vital consideration. Reform ideas had reached the artisanal classes on a large scale for the first time in the 1790s. But even in the big cities, mass enthusiasm for the cause often remained elusive, while government repression kept the movement low-key and fragmented. If all this began to change in the 1810s, it was partly because the radical leadership committed themselves to making reform a national issue in the widest sense. One aspect of this was their acceptance of universal manhood suffrage which became a major part of the radical programme after 1816.[44] But just as important was the much broader degree of co-ordinated activity between reformers in different parts of England, between English and Scottish reformers, and, to a lesser degree, between the English and the Welsh.

Major John Cartwright, that septuagenarian powerhouse of reforming energy, set the trend by embarking on a series of nationwide missionary tours. In 1813, he visited ten counties in the north of England, the Midlands and the West Country. Two years later, he made a thirteen-week progress through Scotland, visiting Edinburgh and Glasgow three times, but also addressing public meetings in Paisley, Dundee, St Andrews, Aberdeen, Kirkcaldy, Dumfermline, Greenock, Stirling and elsewhere. Everywhere he preached the gospel of parliamentary reform as the salve for economic distress as well as for political discontent, urging as many petitions to Parliament as possible signed by as many as possible. He returned home from his Scottish trip with no fewer than six hundred.[45]

Scottish reformers had their own parliamentary reform movement, of course and, as in the 1790s, a minority of them were firmly anti-Unionist.[46] None the less, the fast mail coaches that now connected England with the bulk of Scotland, together with a steady migration of workers between industrial centres on both sides of the border, ensured throughout the reform campaign and after a degree of interchange between the two countries in terms of slogans, symbols, printed propaganda, forms of protest, and personnel that would have astonished (and appalled) the men of John Wilkes's generation. In Sheffield in 1819, an enormous procession of working men in favour of reform thought nothing of marching to the tune of one of the foremost Scottish anthems celebrating a victory over the English, Robert Burns's 'Scots wha hae wi' Wallace bled'.[47] Conversely, when a reform meeting was held later that same year in Rutherglen in the Scottish Lowlands, one of the leading Scottish radical newspapers – called, significantly, *The Spirit of the Union* – reported that the most prominent banners on display bore the message 'Remember Manchester' (a reference to Peterloo) and 'Arise Britons and assert your rights'; and that the proceedings opened with a rendition of 'God Save the King' and 'Rule Britannia', followed by the inevitable 'Scots wha hae'.[48]

Thirteen years later, accounts of the demonstrations that were held in all Scottish towns to celebrate the winning of the Reform Act reveal a very similar amalgam of symbols. At the reformers' procession in Edinburgh, banners displaying images of specifically Scottish heroes – St Andrew, Wallace and Robert Bruce – were raised indiscriminately alongside Union Jacks and flags embroidered with the figure of Britannia. There was even a placard bearing

74. *Staunch Reformers*, 1831. The patriotism of parliamentary reform: the crowd and the crown.

Nelson's order at Trafalgar: 'England expects that every man will do his duty!'[49] On the other side of the border, Thomas Attwood's Political Union in Birmingham refused to hold its own celebration for the passing of the Reform Act for England and Wales, until the separate Reform Act for Scotland had also been passed.[50] This kind of evidence has been too much neglected by those wanting to emphasise the local variations in the reform agitation. These were of course abundant. Yet what is surely far more deserving of attention is the evident extent to which reformers at different levels of the social scale felt that they were part of a single, unitary movement whose scope was Great Britain as a whole.

Even more than the Chartists later, popular radicals in this period simply could not afford to present their appeal in terms of just one country, or just one class, or just one particular section of the labouring population. Instead, they regularly spoke of 'the Nation', using the term in the widest sense, and they spoke of 'the People', meaning whoever would join them in the struggle for reform. In terms of public utterances, at least, the nets were cast

John Bull
REFORM YOURSELVES LEAVE IT NOT FOR ME TO DO.
MY METHOD MAY NOT SUIT YOU.

75. *Reform Yourselves–Leave it not for me to do–My method may not suit you*, 1831. The patriotism of parliamentary reform: the people as John Bull.

as wide and as generously as possible so that the catch of supporters might be adequate to their needs. And this strategy brought with it a further bonus. By describing themselves in broad and British terms, the reformers reduced their opponents rhetorically to a faction. It was they and their supporters who were the freeborn Britons, they implied, men who merited the vote because they bore the heat of the day in peace as in war. By contrast, their opponents were only the borough-mongers, the fund-holders, the sinecurists, the beneficiaries of corruption and monopolisers of political representation, a narrow clique of idlers and parasites at odds with the national interest. This was a style of polemic that brilliantly inverted conventional descriptions of British society, reducing the ultra-privileged few to sinister marginality and promoting the voiceless millions to centre stage as the best of patriots. The people must 'show the atoms of corruption the immense body of freemen which stand before them', a militant tailor called George Petre told a meeting in Leeds.[51] And a similar care in selecting vocabulary so

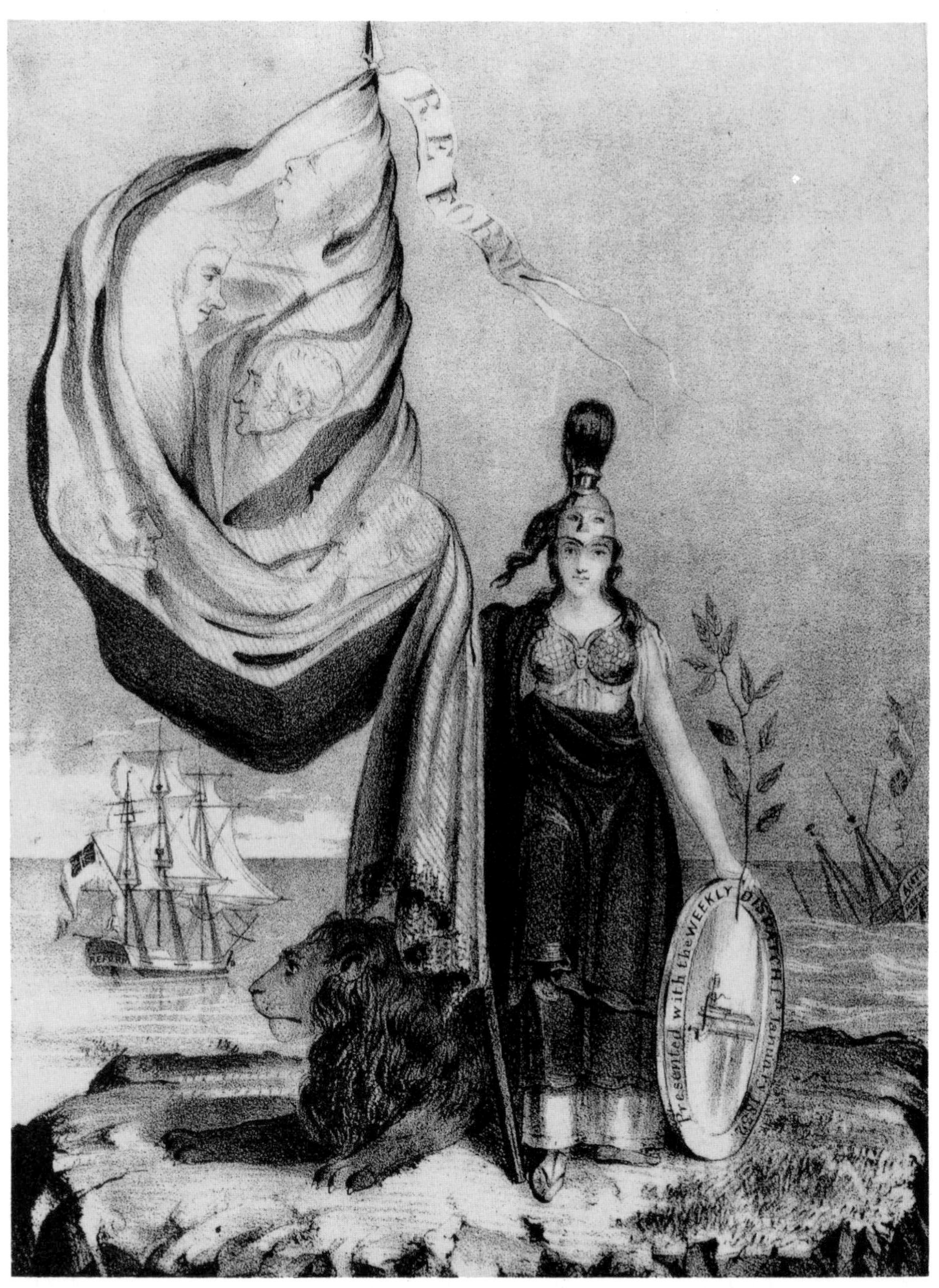

76. *Britannia and the Reform Act*, 1832. A free souvenir given out by the *Weekly Dispatch* newspaper.

as to diminish the opponents of political change can be seen in Bronterre O' Brien's verdict on the Reform Act in 1832:

> Firm, peaceable, and intelligent determination to resist an *odious faction* has been crowned with success, and the *united people* of this country have scared from their prey *the basest and most odious reptiles* the world has ever beheld.[52]

Those more moderate and predominantly middle-class reformers who became increasingly prominent in the 1820s were just as eager to clothe their activities in patriotic rhetoric and symbolism, and for many of the same reasons. They, too, had to confront the same fundamental question that the radicals did: how – as one of them put it – could 'the reformers ever come together, how can those numerous bodies of petitioners be collected, which must take place to have any prospect of success'.[53] They, too, had to find a way of glossing over local variations in support for parliamentary reform, and a way of legitimising their own behaviour and of stigmatising their opponents. But for them, appeals to a free and united British patriotism also served an additional function.

Most middle-class reformers took it for granted that they could make an impression on the parties at Westminster only if they were able to demonstrate mass commitment to parliamentary reform. Yet most of them were also either personally unsympathetic to universal male suffrage, or convinced that it was impractical as an immediate goal. So how – without the lure of votes for all adult males – were they to attract the big battalions of plebeian supporters that would frighten the governing élite into a concessionary mood? One answer was by speaking and writing of reform in terms of what it would achieve for the nation as a whole, rather than embarking on a more detailed and potentially embarrassing analysis of what it might accomplish for the different social classes.

The main weapons employed in the reform agitation, mass open-air meetings held against a background of blaring patriotic music and emotive banners, carefully co-ordinated petitioning campaigns, and the liberal newspaper press, actually aided this kind of conscious or unconscious camouflage. Given the lack of technical aids, most of the people present at the public meetings for reform which were held in almost every substantial British town between 1830 and 1832 can barely have heard even a half of what the speakers said. Questions and objections from the crowd were usually inaudible too; so it was comparatively easy for vaguely worded declarations in support of parliamentary reform to be carried by acclamation. Numerous copies of an already prepared and suitably generalised pro-reform petition would then be left in various nearby shops and offices for people to sign at their leisure, and further copies would be dispatched into the rural villages.[54]

These kinds of tactics, resorted to by both moderate and radical reformers, resulted in over 3,000 petitions being submitted to Parliament between October 1830 and April 1831 alone. The vast majority of these were in favour of parliamentary reform. But a minority explicitly demanded universal manhood suffrage as well as raising other issues: an end to the tithe system, more government intervention to protect wage levels, cheaper bread and so on.[55] Most of the big pro-reform newspapers, however, ignored these dissident voices and instead concentrated on the *fact* of nationwide petitioning.

Take the *Scotsman*, for example, one of the most prestigious papers in the Lowlands, which sold at this time some 2,000 copies every issue, but was read by tens of thousands, particularly among the prosperous and the professional. During the reform crisis, its editor introduced a special column called, deliberately, 'The National Movement'–and the nation referred to was explicitly Great Britain, not Scotland alone. Day after day, the column reproduced snippets of reform gossip from all over the island, extracts from speeches, information about pro-reform souvenirs, reports of which petitions were in progress in the different regions and generous estimates of just how many Britons had signed them.[56] The intention, obviously, was to convey an impression of a relentless and thoroughly unanimous movement:

> A united nation is master of its own destiny; and the people of Britain are now as fully united–are as nearly unanimous in support of this bill, as any nation was in the holiest and ultimately most triumphant cause . . . the Bill is the symbol of unanimity, the pledge of co-operation amongst us: it is the Great Charter, in which our rights are inscribed in terms never to be erased.[57]

Accounts of reform meetings were couched in the same carefully consensual language. The *Scotsman* took enormous care to report the presence of working men at such meetings, while at the same time stressing their eager and peaceful absorption in the whole. Describing a public celebration of reform in Edinburgh in which artisan trade groups were prominent, it noted that the occasion 'gave us treble pleasure, because it blended the rich and poor in a patriotic duty, and sought the interests of *all* in the instrumentality of all'. And it went on to quote a middle-class speaker at a mass meeting in Dalkeith: 'We may well consider ourselves as forming members of one great family of freedom'.[58]

In the eyes of middle-class activists themselves – whether they hailed from Scotland, England or Wales – there was no great hypocrisy involved here. All classes excluded from the representative system, they argued, faced the same enemy: an irresponsible and narrowly constructed Parliament which governed ignorantly, inequitably and expensively. The important task was to unite, across the nation and across the classes, so as to open up and cleanse this torpid system. Then, even if the franchise were to be restricted, all Britons would be bound to benefit. When, after 1832, this was found not to be the case, working-class alienation was extreme. But during the reform agitation itself, it was a line of argument that proved surprisingly effective, if only because those who employed it were themselves frequently convinced. John Fife, a Newcastle doctor who would later take a tough line against the local Chartists, was probably being fundamentally sincere when he told a crowd consisting mainly of miners in October 1831 that:

> We must maintain unanimity of purpose. Although the bill of the present ministry does not go as far as many of us could wish, yet we have seen that it teems with advantages to the people by striking at the very root of that abominable traffic in boroughs which has brought down upon the country such desolation and misery. Now here we count 80,000 reformers, and if every one was employed to frame a bill of reform no two would be alike; but knowing that unanimity alone can promote our great object, each has, like a true patriot, surrendered his own individual opinion for the purpose of obtaining that unanimity.[59]

And if any further justification was needed for taking this line, it was very easily found. Without a revolution, no measure of parliamentary reform was possible unless the Whig party as a whole agreed to sponsor it. This put universal male suffrage and other advanced reforms such as the secret ballot completely out of the question.

The Whigs have had a raw deal from some recent historians, and at a superficial level this can seem justified.[60] Their leading figures were almost all broad-acred patricians concerned to maintain the political supremacy of their own class. If judged by anachronistic standards of democratic rectitude, they naturally emerge badly. And heroic zeal and charisma were hardly for them. On those few occasions when they did aim for the epic during the reform crisis, they tended to come up with farce. 'I warn you, I implore you, on my bended knees, I supplicate you – Reject not this Bill!' declared Lord Brougham, the party's Lord Chancellor (and incidentally, a self-made man), as he flung himself down before his astonished fellow peers in October 1831. He then discovered that his joints had seized up:

> He continued for some time as if in prayer; but his friends, alarmed for him, lest he should be suffering from the effects of the mulled port, picked him up and placed him safely on the woolsack.[61]

Contained within this undignified anecdote, however, is an important and sometimes neglected point: what the Whigs did between their coming to power in November 1830 and the passage of the Reform Act in June 1832 was politically perilous and felt by them and their opponents to be so. Moreover, they very nearly failed to get away with it.[62] Lord Grey and his supporters were, after all, embarking on the first major reconstruction of the British representative system since Oliver Cromwell's rule in the 1650s, not, for most of the ruling élite, a reassuring precedent. The Whigs themselves had only been substantially committed to parliamentary reform since the early 1820s. They possessed minimal experience of government, and their critics inside and outside Parliament were numerous. What upheld them in the struggle was fear of revolution if they failed to act, a natural desire to consolidate their power, and–above all–their own brand of patriotism.

Grey and his fellow Whigs believed that their party had a special and hereditary mission to secure the people's freedom.[63] By this they did not mean, it goes without saying, one man one vote. Rather, the people were to be rescued whenever they fell into the corrupt clutches of an over-powerful executive, and governed by those with sufficient property and intelligence to know what was best for them. It is in the light of this creed that Grey's words to Princess Lieven after the Reform Bill had been introduced to the Lords in March 1831 can be understood: 'I have kept my word with the nation'.[64] He saw himself in this emergency, very much as the sculptor Francis Chantrey would later capture him in marble, as being spiritually at one with those thirteenth-century knights and nobles who had risked death to bring King John to heel and forced him to sign Magna Carta. Now, as then, right-thinking men of substance were acting, not on the people's instructions, *but on the people's behalf.* The Whigs, in their own eyes, were fulfilling the duty traditionally imposed upon them by their wealth, their rank and their political ideology: risking themselves for the sake of an improved but stable liberty and for the public good. Desperately eager to view their actions in this light, they found it enormously helpful that so much of the extra-parliamentary campaign for parliamentary reform had been couched in terms of unanimity,

77. Sir Francis Chantrey, *William IV assenting to the Reform Bill*, at Holkham, Norfolk.

constitutionality and patriotism. Here was surely proof that the work upon which they were embarked was right and good. 'He thought', Lord John Russell told the Commons smoothly in October 1831, 'that the number of those who supported the Reform Bill, compared with the small number of those who opposed it, justified him in stating *that the Reformers were the nation*'.[65] Britons had cried out overwhelmingly for a loyal and responsible liberty, and the Whigs had a positive duty to bestow it.

In the process, they transformed British political and electoral life far more than is usually now granted. The old representative system had been a piecemeal creation, dating back in England to the fourteenth century, in Wales to the sixteenth century, in Scotland to the Union in 1707 and in Ireland to the Union of 1800. It had grown up in response to the demands of particular communities and private interests, and its franchise provisions reflected a bewildering variety of local customs. It was unapologetically a patchwork and emphatically not a seamless garment. The new system, based (loosely) on the census of 1821, was far more uniform. To create it, fifty-six small boroughs which had been very much at the disposal of private patrons lost their representation in Parliament completely, and thirty more had their representation halved. Sixty-four of the seats set free were allocated to the new industrial and commercial centres which were concentrated overwhelmingly in the Midlands and the north, thereby doing something to correct the old system's bias towards the south of England. Roughly the same number of seats was redistributed in favour of the counties, again with the lion's share going to the north and the Midlands.[66]

At the same time, the representative system was made rather less Anglocentric than before. Eight new borough constituencies were created in Scotland. Wales acquired five more MPs, and eight of its existing borough constituencies had their boundaries enlarged to take in more voters.[67] And for the first time, there was a uniform borough franchise throughout Great Britain. Every adult male who occupied a house worth £10 per annum or more now had the vote, providing that he was registered with the authorities. The cumulative effect of all these changes was to quicken the tempo of political life everywhere. But in Wales and Scotland, where landlord influence over the electoral process had previously been suffocatingly close, this was so to a spectacular degree.

For much of the eighteenth century and in the early nineteenth century, the Welsh and Scottish electorates had been little more than stage armies.[68] The respective landowning classes had the bulk of constituencies in these two countries so well sewn up that preselected MPs were more often than not declared elected without a contest being held. So although some 22,000 Welshmen possessed the right to vote in law before the Reform Act of 1832, only 546 of them had actually been able to use their votes in the general election of 1826. The rest had lived in constituencies where no contests occurred, and seen their representatives appointed over their heads by local oligarchies. At the next general election in 1830, Welsh voters fared even worse. No contest occurred in Wales at all that year, so all Welshmen were effectively disenfranchised as far as active participation in their own constituencies was concerned. Scotland's position before the Reform Act had been bleaker still in that here the electorate was less than 5,000 strong. Not one of these men was able to exercise his vote in 1826; and only 239 did so in the elections held four years later.

But the Reform Act created a radically different electoral landscape. Not only did the number of voters increase (in Scotland's case, more than thirteenfold), but with the weakening of patron control, the number of elections that went to a poll also rose sharply. In the first general election held under the new system in 1832, over 43,000 Scots were able to cast their votes. So, at the next elections in 1835, were more than 9,000 Welshmen.[69]

Up to a point, then, a representative system which had been weighted in favour of England, in favour of the south, and in favour of the centrifugal forces of local interests and individual electoral patrons, had been replaced by one more uniformly British, more closely supervised by the state, and considerably more democratic. The most obvious abuses and anomalies had been swept away, and social groups and regions that contributed massively to Britain's wealth but had previously lacked direct representation now gained it. By European standards, the new British electorate of 656,000 was very large indeed, bearing in mind that Austria, Denmark, Russia and Greece still had no popularly elected national legislative assemblies at all. A much bigger proportion of men could now vote in Britain than in France, Spain, Belgium or the Netherlands. In the Europe of 1832, it was only in some of the Scandinavian countries that the boundaries of active citizenship were set wider.[70] To this extent, the Whigs had succeeded in giving British constitutional complacency substance and a fresh lease of life. What they did became a vital part of British patriotic ideology in the nineteenth century, a point that the radical William Cobbett conceded at the time when he predicted that the Reform Act would take its place alongside those other icons, the Protestant Reformation and the Revolution of 1688.[71]

Just as with these two events, however, there were losers and there was unfairness. In the reformed Parliament, England had 468 MPs, whereas Scotland returned 53, and Wales had 32 representatives. As far as Wales was concerned, this allocation of seats accurately reflected its still tiny population–just over 900,000 according to the census of 1831. But Scotland was markedly under-represented in terms of both its wealth and its population. The Whig administration regarded its rural areas as a haven for Tory landlord influence and had therefore been reluctant to increase its county as distinct from its borough seats.[72] But Scotland's lack of parity with the rest of Great Britain stemmed also from the fact that its representative system had been the subject of a separate reform bill, just as Ireland's had. Not until the 1884 Representation of the People Act would all the component parts of the United Kingdom be reformed as a single unit, in accordance with one set of rules. For most Scots, the new franchise provisions which at a stroke increased their electorate from under 5,000 to 65,000 softened any disappointment they might have felt with regard to the number of seats allocated to them. But for many other Britons, it was in this aspect of the Reform Act, its franchise clauses, where the real betrayal lay.

Eighty per cent of adult males had been left without the vote, as, naturally, had all women. No provision had been made for a secret ballot, so landowners and employers were still able to exert pressure on more vulnerable voters.[73] The old system had been cleaned up, rationalised and broadened, but its bias in favour of the propertied had been maintained, as the Whigs had always intended that it should. The degree of anger and bewilderment this provoked can be understood only in the light of how the reform cause had been popularly argued before 1832. Even its more radical proponents, as we have seen, had rarely spoken in terms of winning political rights for working men in defiance of the propertied classes *as a whole*. Instead, reform meetings and printed propaganda had generally been couched in the language of patriotic union. All were to struggle, because all were to benefit. And for an extraordinarily long time this happy prospect had distracted attention from the fissures in the reform movement, and obscured the limitations of the Whigs' Reform Bill.

To be sure, stray radical and conservative opponents of the bill had always been available to warn that it would do nothing directly for the bulk of working men. But popular disbelief remained curiously suspended. Throughout the bill's prolonged progress through Parliament, petitions and meetings in its favour had continued to attract massive support from all classes. Even after the Reform Bill passed, and its exact provisions became known, there was still for a while enormous enthusiasm. The reform jubilees organised throughout Great Britain in the summer and autumn of 1832 were spectacular events, patronised by the newly enfranchised and the still excluded alike.[74] The patriotic language in which the reform campaign had been conducted continued to act as a smokescreen. When it finally dispersed, anger among the excluded was immense. They had been encouraged by the reform agitation to see themselves as part of the political nation and had been led to believe that a reconstructed legislature must lead to better things. Now, the harsh facts of life reminded them that they, the vast majority of Britons, were still without a voice.

Yet, in retrospect, the evident limitations of the Reform Act are less striking than its considerable achievements and the length of time which the system it created endured. For all the fury of the men and women who would go on to attach themselves to the Chartist movement, the fact remained that in 1832 Great Britain was one of the most democratic nations in Europe. But by 1865 – and despite the Chartists – this had ceased to be the case. By then,

Austria, France, Greece, Hungary, Portugal and Switzerland, as well as the Scandinavian nations, all had more generous franchises than the British or the Irish enjoyed. Even after the Reform Acts of 1867 and 1884, neither of which were implemented primarily in response to large-scale public pressure, the United Kingdom remained, right up to the First World War, one of the least democratic states by the standards of eastern as well as western Europe.[75] Why did this happen when the early struggle for the vote had been so vigorous and broad-ranging? Why did Britons in the later nineteenth century not struggle more aggressively and for longer to become fully fledged citizens? At least part of the answer lies in the last of the three great reform campaigns of this era.

SLAVERY, FREEDOM AND CONSENSUS

In 1840, Joseph Mallord William Turner dispatched one of the most sensational even of his paintings to the Royal Academy exhibition. In its background was a tempest-tossed sailing-ship, masts shuddering against the wind, the prow almost hidden by angry spray. But the eye was not meant to linger here. Instead, the reflection of a blood-red sunset would carry it downwards to a vicious sea littered with flailing black limbs. This was no rescue scene, however. The ship was sailing away from the drowning, not towards them. Nor was it a scene of escape, for as one leg flung – almost skittishly – out of the water made clear, those gasping and struggling for life were weighed down with irons. This was a painting of a mass murder. Back in 1783, the *Zong*, a British slave-ship bound for Jamaica, had been hit by an epidemic. Afraid that his stock of water was running low and knowing that his insurance policy only covered slaves lost at sea, not those who perished as a result of unhealthy conditions on board, Captain Collingwood decided to solve both of his problems at one stroke. He ordered 133 sick slaves to be thrown into the sea alive in batches. Realising what was going to happen to them, the last thirty-six resisted. So the captain gave instructions for them to be shackled and then thrown overboard. At which point, ten of the slaves struggled free and jumped into the sea as a final desperate gesture of free will.[76]

Yet *Slave Ship (Slavers throwing overboard the Dead and the Dying, Typhoon coming on)*, which John Ruskin snapped up and then sold because he found it too painful to look at, is both more and less than a representation of a British atrocity. As the title suggests, and as a glance at the brittle, storm-battered slave-ship limping into the blazing sunset confirms, Turner's intention was to commemorate the doom of slavery and not just a handful of its victims. Like other

78. J.M.W. Turner, *Slave Ship (Slavers throwing overboard the Dead and the Dying, Typhoon coming on)*, 1840.

paintings of his at this time – *The Fighting Temeraire*, for instance, where a tall and battered sailing-ship is towed to the breakers' yard by a much less splendid but infinitely faster steamship – *Slavers* was a study of the past giving way before the force of British progress. In 1807, Parliament had abolished the slave trade as far as Britain was concerned, and in 1833, it had provided for the emancipation of three-quarters of a million slaves in its West Indian colonies. Five years later, it completed their liberation. Now, in 1840, London was to host the first International Anti-Slavery Convention, a point of which the publicity-conscious Turner was certainly aware. From being the world's greediest and most successful traders of slaves in the eighteenth century, the British had shifted to being able to preen themselves on being the world's foremost opponents of slavery.[77] This had been an extraordinary revolution in sensibility and ideas, one that revealed as much if not more about how the British thought about themselves, as it did about how they saw black people on the other side of the world.

For most of the 1700s, Britons had seen no inconsistency whatever between trumpeting their freedom at home and buying men, women and children from trading-posts in Africa to sell into slavery abroad. From contributing perhaps 12,000 slaves to the 31,000 shipped annually to North America and the West Indies by the major slave-trading nations in the first decade of the century, the British went on to supply an average of over 23,000 slaves a year over the next eighty years.[78] By the 1790s, when the French had been knocked out of the business by their own revolution and by the slave rebellion in St Domingue, British ships were exporting almost 45,000 blacks annually, which represented perhaps 60 per cent of the total trade. Even on the eve of Britain's withdrawal from the slave trade in 1807, sales were running high and investors in the business could expect to make a 10 per cent profit.[79] As long as it lasted, then, Britain's slave trade was a major contributor to its economy, buttressing its mercantile marine, supplying essential labour for its colonies, providing vital capital for industrialisation and turning Bristol, Glasgow and Liverpool into major ports and splendid cities. Well might Thomas Jefferson (himself, of course, a slave-owner) accuse George III in the Declaration of Independence of a 'cruel war against human nature itself, violating its most sacred rights of life and liberty in the persons of a distant people who never offended him, captivating and carrying them into slavery in another hemisphere'.[80]

Yet it was, in fact, the lost war with America that precipitated not so much a sea-change in British attitudes to the slave trade, as a converting of already existing qualms into positive action. As in the rest of western Europe, there had been ample evidence in the 1760s and '70s of a growing revulsion against the practice of slavery. Samuel Johnson and John Wesley had declared against it; so had Adam Smith and other representatives of the Scottish Enlightenment. And Granville Sharp and other radical and Quaker activists had already launched a campaign to liberate the 9,000 or so black slaves resident in Britain. But until the end of the American war, there had been few signs of mass interest in the slave trade itself. The *Zong* incident, for example, passed almost without notice at the time.[81] Captain Collingwood was not punished. No questions were asked in Parliament. Nor did the newspaper press see fit to comment on Lord Mansfield's statement that dumping slaves was analogous to throwing horses overboard in time of emergency. Those with scruples continued to be at a disadvantage in the face of the argument that slavery, however unfortunate, contributed too much to Britain's prosperity to be dismantled.[82]

With the full realisation of defeat in America, however, came a rise in determination. In 1783, the Quakers presented the first anti-slavery petition to Parliament. Four years later, the Society for

Effecting the Abolition of the Slave Trade was founded in London, with branches in the provinces. And in 1788, Manchester, a rapidly growing industrial town with no representation in Parliament, initiated a mass-petitioning campaign. Perhaps as many as two-thirds of the town's adult males signed a petition demanding an end to the slave trade. Another hundred towns subsequently followed suit, making this the largest petitioning campaign on public matters ever to have been organised in Britain up to this point. The same year saw the first legislation pass regulating the slave-traders' business.[83]

The loss of the American colonies also precipitated a rise in enthusiasm for parliamentary reform, for imperial reform, for religious liberalisation, for the reform of gaols and lunatic asylums: for virtually any change, in fact, that might prevent a similar national humiliation in the future. Yet the new enthusiasm for anti-slavery was bound up with the experience of defeat in a special way. As we have seen, Britons retained a strong belief in Providence. Just as they had attributed their successes in earlier wars to Divine favour for the leading Protestant nation, many of them now sought to explain what appeared an almost inexplicable defeat at the hands of colonists by reference to their own failings in the sight of God. They had been corrupt and presumptuous, and they had warred against fellow Protestants. And they had been duly punished. In this mood, the slave trade, so obviously questionable in moral terms, and so productive of worldly profit and luxury, seemed far more of a liability.

Was it really to be expected that a nation that sold the heathen for selfish gain instead of endeavouring to make them Christians would be allowed to flourish? 'We are all guilty', William Wilberforce would warn the Commons when he launched the first anti-slavery debate there in 1789.[84] And the argument that Great Britain's future progress in secular and not just in moral terms would depend on how it comported itself on this issue became a persistent and powerful one. 'We were a people more favoured by Heaven than any other nation had been from the commencement of time', the Bishop of Durham would tell his fellow peers as they debated the abolition of the slave trade in 1807, '. . . but we should beware how we forfeited the protection of Providence by continual injustice; for if we did we should look in vain hereafter for the glories of the Nile and Trafalgar.'[85] For this overwhelmingly Protestant culture, anti-slavery became a particularly rigorous contract with the Almighty. If Great Britain prospered, then clearly it must persevere with the good work. But if it failed, it must still persevere, in the hope that this might serve as an atonement.

There was another, self-referential reason why the British embraced anti-slavery so vigorously from the 1780s onwards. Doing so was a way of reaffirming their unique commitment to liberty at a time when war with America, and unsuccessful war at that, had called it widely into question. The fact that the newly independent United States of America continued to use slave labour, while Great Britain had already passed laws protecting its own tiny black population and was beginning to turn its face against the slave trade as well, allowed for a welcome restocking of complacency. Even Dr Richard Price, the Welsh Unitarian who had supported the Americans throughout the war, was not above reminding a transatlantic correspondent with regard to slavery that 'on this occasion I can recommend to them the example of my own country – in *Britain*, a negro becomes a freeman the moment he sets his foot on British ground'.[86]

Trumpeting their concern for slave welfare became a standard way for more orthodox Britons to rebut American pretensions to superior freedoms right up to the 1860s and beyond. Identical tactics were used, as we shall see, to put the French in their place after 1789. Anti-slavery became an emblem of national virtue, a means by which the British could impress foreigners with their innate love of liberty and reassure themselves whenever their own faith was in danger of flagging. Was it entirely coincidental, I wonder, that the first mass-petitioning campaign against the slave trade occurred in 1788, the much celebrated centenary of the Glorious Revolution? It seems unlikely. Some Britons, at least, must have seen in the anti-slavery campaign a welcome opportunity to reaffirm their libertarian heritage.

In short, whereas before the loss of the American colonies opposition to the slave trade had seemed to many Britons incompatible with the national interest, however admirable it might be in moral terms, after the American war anti-slavery was increasingly seized on as a means to redeem the nation, as a patriotic act. It had other roots, of course. Humanitarianism, religion, hatred of oppression, a belief in the international brotherhood of men were also important; and, for some, far more important. But these more disinterested motives do not on their own explain the chronology of the anti-slavery movement in Britain, why it became so prominent in the 1780s and not before. Nor are they sufficient to explain why such an extraordinarily large number of people became involved. The petitioning campaign against the slave trade in 1788 was followed four years later by another. This time over 500 petitions were assembled from all over Great Britain. In 1814, the anti-slavery pressure groups mobilised 800 petitions urging the

British government to persuade the restored French monarchy to abandon its slave trade. Three-quarters of a million men and women signed.[87] But this was only the beginning. Before the House of Commons agreed in 1833 to abolish slavery as an institution in the British West Indies, its members were deluged with over 5,000 petitions signed by one and a half million people. In addition, they received a special ladies' petition which stretched for half a mile and bore 187,000 signatures. Five years later, close to half a million women signed another single-sex petition to Parliament, insisting that full liberation should now be given to the slaves.[88]

Mass petitioning, as we have seen, had also been a feature of the agitations over Catholic emancipation and in support of parliamentary reform. But anti-slavery seems to have attracted petitions on an even wider scale. Indeed, no other cause in the nineteenth century was so successful over such a long period of time in eliciting such broad support. And no other cause crossed so many barriers, attracting Anglicans as well as non-conformists, women as well as men, rural as well as urban supporters from all over Great Britain, and enthusiasts from every social class. In part this was a tribute to the sophistication and range of the anti-slavery societies' grass-roots organisation, but it was also a comment on the cause's uniquely uncontroversial and eclectic appeal.

Slaves, unlike the Irish, or the Roman Catholics, or the working class, existed overwhelmingly outside Britain's own geographical and mental boundaries. Its own black population was tiny, little more than 20,000, and concentrated in London and the major ports.[89] Most Britons still lived and died without encountering anyone whose skin colour was different from their own. And although anti-slavery propaganda relayed a great many anecdotes of suffering blacks, it was not concerned with realism. The dominant image continued to be that of Josiah Wedgwood's famous ceramic badge: a black man crying out, 'Am I not a man and a brother?', but doing so from the safe position of his knees. Slaves, in short, did not threaten, at least as far as the British at home were concerned. Bestowing freedom upon them seemed therefore purely an act of humanity and will, an achievement that would be to Great Britain's economic detriment, perhaps, but would have few other domestic consequences. As such, its appeal was enormously wide. Artisans and factory workers could support abolitionism out of fellow-feeling with the oppressed. But so could their employers, on the grounds that slave labour was an affront to free-market economics. Radicals could identify anti-slavery with the wider struggle for the rights of man. But for traditionalists, the movement was still further confirmation that the British political system was peculiarly favourable to freedom:

Hail to Britannia, fair liberty's isle!
Her frown quailed the tyrant, the slave caught her smile;
Fly on the winds to tell Afric the story;
Say to the mother of mourners, "Rejoice!"
Britannia went forth in her beauty, her glory,
And slaves sprang to men at the sound of her voice.[90]

Yet stunning though the breadth of extra-parliamentary support was, it was not by itself sufficient. As it showed in its response to the petitions against Catholic emancipation in 1829 and to those in support of universal manhood suffrage before and after 1832, Parliament was fully capable of disregarding expressions of mass opinion when it wanted to be. Yet with regard to anti-slavery, its receptivity to pressure from without was both remarkable and consistent. The 1788 petitions were followed by an act regulating the slave trade. After the next petitioning campaign in 1792, the House of Commons voted to abolish the trade four years later, a decision aborted owing to procedural difficulties and above all to war. After the 1814 petitions, British ministers made sure that the issue of slavery was discussed when the European powers assembled at the Congress of Vienna the following year. And when one and a half million Britons petitioned for an emancipation act freeing the West Indian slaves in 1833, that, with some modifications, was what Parliament gave them. The Emancipation Act passed that year declared that children under six years old were to be free from 1 August 1834, the 120th anniversary of the Hanoverian Succession. Adult slaves and older children were to become apprentices for up to six years and then be free. Though, as it turned out, full emancipation would be granted to all West Indian slaves from 1 August 1838.

As David Brion Davis has written, 'The question of abolishing slavery was ultimately a question of power.'[91] Why was Britain's governing élite so willing to take up this issue in so determined a fashion? Why, reducing the same question to a symbolic act, was William Wilberforce, the great crusader against slavery, buried in Westminster Abbey in 1834, with a clutch of royal dukes in attendance? Why, in the words of his epitaph, had:

The Peers and Commons of England,
With the Lord Chancellor, and the Speaker, at their head,
Carried him to his fitting place
Among the mighty dead around.[92]

79. Samuel Raven, *Blacks celebrating the Emancipation of Slaves in British dominions August 1834.*

Why had it become positively respectable, indeed indispensable, to advocate the abolition of one of Great Britain's most lucrative trades?

For, as we have already seen, it was not the case that the British pulled out of the slave trade in 1807 because it was ceasing to be profitable. Seymour Drescher is almost certainly right to argue that 'In terms of both capital value and of overseas trade, the slave system was expanding, not declining, at the turn of the nineteenth century.'[93] Nor did the British dismantle slavery in their West Indian colonies after 1833 because it had become uneconomic, or out of nervousness because the incidence of slave rebellions was increasing. As they showed in so many other parts of the world, the British were perfectly willing to maintain their economic and territorial interests by way of military force when necessary. The British governing élite was not compelled to take up anti-slavery by events beyond its control. Nor did it succumb helplessly to the momentum of public pressure at home, though extra-parliamentary agitation certainly had some impact. Britain's rulers ended the slave trade and freed the West Indian slaves primarily because they wanted to.

In part, their motives were the same as those experienced by lesser Britons. There was a large evangelical contingent in both Houses of Parliament, deeply responsive to Wilberforce's argument that anti-slavery was a necessary act of national atonement.[94] Other politicians, including William Pitt the Younger, shared Adam Smith's opinion that slavery was the most uneconomic form of labour as well as a blight on humanity. And there was a widespread view among ministers and MPs that rescuing slaves confirmed Great Britain's appetite for freedom in a most satisfactory and convenient way. This was particularly the case after Napoleon reintroduced slavery into the French empire in 1802. Before then, some British conservatives had held back, fearing that the cause of anti-slavery was too closely connected with Jacobinism and the rights of man. Thereafter, supporting the cause of the slaves became a means to uphold the reputation of the existing order against both radicals at home and the French enemy. Parliament's debates on the abolition of the slave trade in 1807 are as riddled with national pride and complacency as they are with genuine humanity. Ending the trade, the Lord Chancellor declared,

> was our duty to God, and to our country which was the morning star that enlightened Europe, and whose boast and glory was to grant liberty and life, and administer humanity and justice to all nations.

While Samuel Romilly, a reforming Whig, contrasted Wilberforce's fame with Napoleon's notoriety, the former sleeping soundly at night having saved 'so many millions of his fellow creatures', the latter still wading 'through slaughter and oppression' to his doom.[95] The clear implication, which other MPs were quite happy to spell out, was that British dominion, by contrast with that of the French, was benign and a boon to civilisation.

Anti-slavery supplied the British with an epic stage upon which they could strut in an overwhelmingly attractive guise. Acknowledging that this was so does not detract from what was achieved. Not all great powers are so anxious to redeem past oppressions, or so eager for the world's good opinion. Thousands of lives were saved because of the acts of 1807 and 1833; many more benefited because of the Royal Navy's campaign against other nations' slave-traders later in the nineteenth century. And the financial cost of these efforts to Britain in terms of loss of trade, compensation to the West Indian planters and naval patrols must be counted in millions of pounds.[96] On the other hand, the psychic and political gains were enormous. At exactly the same time as Great Britain established itself as unquestionably the foremost European and imperial power, it had acquired, through its anti-slavery campaigns, a reputation for moral integrity that even the most cynical foreign observer was likely to pay some tribute to. Successful abolitionism became one of the vital underpinnings of British supremacy in the Victorian era, offering – as it seemed to do – irrefutible proof that British power was founded on religion, on freedom and on moral calibre, not just on a superior stock of armaments and capital.

Politically, those who benefited most from this propaganda coup were Britain's governing class. At the time, the anti-slavery campaign had not been a conservative force, far from it. It had given millions of Britons from all classes, including large numbers of women, an opportunity to express their own opinions. And it had made them think more carefully about the meanings of oppression. There must have been many who moved from contemplating the fate of black slave labour, to seeing in the fields, mines and factories at home in Britain a problem approaching white slavery.[97] None the less, as almost all of the major spokesmen for mass radicalism had come to realise by the 1830s, the success of the anti-slavery movement had an overwhelmingly conservative impact.

A conservative impact, first of all, because it supplied the British with a powerful legitimation for their claims to be the arbiters of the civilised and the uncivilised world. In 1846, when Lord

Palmerston was informed of slave-trade atrocities in Zanzibar, his immediate response was to instruct the local British consul to 'take every opportunity of impressing upon the Arabs that the nations of Europe are destined to put an end to the African slave trade *and that Great Britain is the main instrument in the hands of the Providence for the accomplishment of this purpose*'.[98] For Palmerston, as for many of his countrymen, nineteenth-century Great Britain was still Israel, and its crusade against slavery was just one more vital proof and guarantee of its supremacy among the nations. British gun-boats sailed under God's protection because they carried out God's work.

Moreover, in acting against slavery, the British élite demonstrated once again its ability to take a popular and patriotic line without giving up very much in the way of authority. By eradicating the slave trade as far as Britain was concerned, by abolishing slavery in the West Indies and by continuing thereafter to harass alien slave-traders, its members displayed their public spirit, their moral idealism, their disinterestedness and their receptivity to responsible expressions of public opinion. As Lord Stanley told the Commons in May 1833: 'The nation have now loudly, and for a length of time declared that the disgrace of slavery should not be suffered to remain part of our national system.'[99] And, on this issue, the nation was to be obeyed.

Whether consciously or not, responding to public pressure over slavery helped to deflect attention from the élite's refusal to give way to public opinion on other matters rather nearer to home, such as the Chartists' demands for a broader franchise and extensive social reform. On a small scale, anti-slavery did what Britain's long succession of wars with France had done so extensively in the past: distract people's attention from domestic affairs and encourage them to contrast their own position favourably with that of less fortunate peoples abroad. Freeing the slaves made large numbers of Britons feel important, benign and above all, patrons and possessors of liberty. It reassured them that their country was worthy of their attachment and of other nations' envy: that it was still God Land, to use the nicely provocative term coined by Conor Cruise O'Brien.[100] This self-congratulatory conviction was scarcely enough to offset domestic unrest in the bitter 1830s and '40s. But when political and economic conditions improved in the mid-nineteenth century, the memory and mythology of the anti-slavery campaign – in which so many Britons had so satisfactorily taken part – became an important part of the Victorian culture of complacency in which matters of domestic reform were allowed to slide. It was a case of the good getting in the way of the best.

A NATION REDEFINED AND UNDEFINED

Yet to end on that note would be too downbeat. In terms of the forging of British national consciousness, the changes that had been effected in the years after Waterloo were extremely important. By passing Catholic emancipation in 1829, Britain's rulers unavoidably compromised Protestantism's value as a national cement and a rallying cry. But the Reform Act of 1832, together with the freeing of the slaves one year later, supplied them and every other conventional British patriot with ample compensation. They helped to ensure that if Britons could no longer posture so confidently as being exclusively and uniquely Protestant, they could still see themselves as being different and better than their European neighbours and even their one-time American colonists. Peaceful and orderly constitutional reform and pioneering and successful abolitionism would serve for many as further and conclusive proofs of the superior quality of British freedom.

And beneath the bogus complacency, there was some real substance. Looked at in retrospect–*and in tandem with each other*–the struggles for Catholic emancipation, parliamentary reform and the abolition of slavery were, in some respects, both successful and transforming. Roman Catholics, marginalised and disadvantaged since the sixteenth century, won full citizenship on almost the same terms as Protestant Britons. The representative system was extensively remodelled, so that for a time active citizenship was more widespread in Wales and in Scotland, as well as in England, than in almost any other part of Europe. Finally, Parliament and the people together determined that British subjects abroad–like Britons at home–never, never, never would be slaves. In practice, slavery persisted in parts of the British empire–and especially in India–long after the legislation of 1833 and 1838. None the less, it was worth something that the institution had been declared to be unacceptable by statute, and that for the rest of the nineteenth century British military and diplomatic pressure was more often than not exerted against those who still practised it.

These were substantial achievements. No such sudden quantum leaps in terms of rights and citizenship would occur again in Great Britain until the wars of the twentieth century. The fact that votes for women and universal manhood suffrage had to wait until 1918, and that a welfare state was fully implemented only in the aftermath of the Second World War, confirmed what the post-Waterloo period also demonstrated: that in Great Britain, a nation forged more than anything else through military endeavour, the winning of radical constitutional and social change was also intimately

80. *The Battle of the Petitions, a Farce now performing with great applause at both Houses*. A satire on the scale of popular petitioning in 1829.

bound up with the impact of war. Yet in one vital respect the reformism that followed the war against Napoleon proved unique. Universal suffrage and the welfare state happened in Britain primarily because that was what the men at Westminister decided was to happen. Britons at large were not unmoved by these changes. But neither in the wake of lethal and exhausting world wars were they very actively involved in securing them. By contrast, the years between Waterloo and the accession of Queen Victoria – and especially the late 1820s and early 1830s – were arguably the only period in modern British history in which people power – as we have seen it operate in parts of eastern Europe in the late twentieth century – played a prominent and pervasive role in effecting significant political change.

The sheer numbers of men and women from all social classes, and from all parts of Great Britain, who took part in marches, in demonstrations and in petitions during these years were astonishing. Still more so was the fact that the 3,000 plus petitions submitted against or in favour of Catholic emancipation in 1828–9, like the 3,000 petitions on parliamentary reform that flooded in after the Whigs came to power in 1830, and like the 5,000 petitions urging the abolition of slavery in 1833, were not loftily ignored by Parliament. Nor were they simply waved away with a formal order that they be printed in advance of being forgotten (the fate of most public petitions in Great Britain from the mid-1830s onwards).[101] As the pages of *Hansard* reveal, peers and MPs discussed the content, the validity and the meaning of these public petitions closely and contentiously for months on end. 'It is mainly in attention to petitions', one observer reported without exaggeration in 1829, 'that the parliamentary session has passed away'. During the anti-slavery debates four years later, an MP could complain – again quite legitimately – that 'There had not been a petition upon which there had not been a long debate.'[102]

I am not suggesting, of course, that Great Britain in these years had anything approaching government by plebiscite. Quite obviously, it did not. But it was the case that a unitary political discourse was able to emerge to a quite extraordinary degree. On the one hand, the rapid expansion of the newspaper press, together with large-scale reporting of parliamentary debates, meant that Britons outside Parliament were made aware of the language of those inside it as never before. On the other, successive waves of petitions weighed down with signatures – and Parliament's close attention to them – familiarised MPs and peers with the opinions and language of at least some of the men and women they strove to govern.

This extrordinary interplay between the voices of Britons outside the walls of Westminster and the deliberations of those closeted grandly within is one reason why the period between Waterloo and the end of the Hanoverian dynasty in 1837 is so illuminating with regard to questions of patriotism and British identity. Not only did the foremost political controversies of this era impinge directly on questions of citizenship: they also brought together both sexes, every social level and all parts of the nation, not in a consensus to be sure, but in an instructive and revealing debate. So often interpreted only in sectional terms, as the product of class, or localist, or partisan pressures, Catholic emancipation, parliamentary reform and the campaign against slavery have to be understood as well in terms of nationwide mobilisation and in the light of different ideas about what constituted Britishness.

Mass involvement in the last and greatest of Britain's wars against France had been followed by mass excursions into post-war politics. The victories won in the process were broadly fought and important. Yet they were also manifestly incomplete. At the time of Victoria's accession in 1837, only a fraction of Britain's population had achieved formal political rights. The vast majority of Britons were still not citizens. To what extent, then, was it plausible to view Great Britain as a nation by this time? That is what we must now finally consider.

Conclusions

WHEN THE EIGHTEEN-YEAR-OLD GIRL named Alexandrina Victoria emerged from her suffocatingly sheltered background in June 1837, to become Queen of Great Britain, Ireland and the empire beyond the seas, one of her first acts was to confirm Sir David Wilkie as Principal Painter to the Crown.[1] Wilkie was a Scot, a minister's son from Fifeshire. Since his arrival on the London art scene back in the early 1800s, his reputation for genre and history painting had been a commanding one, but he was now well past his artistic prime. And although the new monarch's relationship with Scotland was to be a close – if sentimental – one, this particular Scottish connexion proved a bitter disappointment on both sides. Victoria found Wilkie's conscientious attempts at royal portraiture unflattering, while none of the epic canvases he turned out in the early years of her reign came close to matching the impact of his much earlier and still most famous historical work: *Chelsea Pensioners Reading the Gazette of the Battle of Waterloo*.

This had caused a sensation when it was first exhibited at the Royal Academy in 1822. Thousands of men and women had queued for hours to see it, crowds had clustered around it from morning to night, and special barriers had been erected in front of it so as to keep it safe. Even today, it remains an extraordinarily audacious work, as well as a many-layered one. The date, the artist tells us, is Thursday, 22 June 1815, and the first official confirmation has just been released of the British and Allied victory at Waterloo. The scene is a long-since demolished street in Chelsea called Jew's Row, lined with old, low-storeyed taverns, cheap lodging houses, pawn-brokers and rag shops, but close, none the less to Chelsea Hospital, a home for invalid and retired soldiers since the late seventeenth century. And it is a miscellaneous crowd of soldiers, veterans, womenfolk and shabbily dressed workers that is shown reacting to the news. A Scottish Highlander plunges into a celebratory tune on the bagpipes, and women are being drawn into a dance. A sergeant tosses his baby into the air, the child fizzing with excitement at the colour and the noise. His companion pauses in

31. Sir David Wilkie, *Chelsea Pensioners Reading the Gazette of the Battle of Waterloo*, 1822.

arranging her hair, her arms raised motionless above her head as she listens pensively to the account of the battle. Just as entranced is an elderly oyster-seller who has stopped in the very act of slitting open an oyster and is grinning toothlessly as her imagination catches fire. Girls wave handkerchiefs, men strain out of windows to catch the news. Everywhere, there is music, laughter, abundant beer, good-humoured flirtation, intense interest and something far more significant.

Explicit in this strictly imaginary scene is the existence of a mass British patriotism transcending the boundaries of class, ethnicity, occupation, sex and age. But the key to the painting which Wilkie published at the time shows that he wanted to convey something more than this.[2] *Chelsea Pensioners Reading the Gazette of the Battle of Waterloo* is, in fact, one man's very perceptive interpretation of both the variety and the roots of Britishness. The horseman shown bringing the news of the victory is from a Welsh regiment; the soldiers gathering around him include Scotsmen, Englishmen, an Irishman and even a black military bandsman. The Chelsea pensioner reading aloud from the closely printed pages of the *Gazette* is a veteran of the battle for Quebec in 1759. And hanging above the row of taverns are inn signs bearing witness to yet more battles, yet more wars. There is 'The Duke of York', in memory

82a. Detail of pl. 81.

of Britain's war with Revolutionary France. There is 'The Snow Shoes', a relic from the War of American Independence. And there is even a sign commemorating the Marquess of Granby, hero of the Battle of Culloden in 1746 and of the Seven Years War. More than anything else, Wilkie seems to be suggesting, it is the experience of recurrent wars that has brought these diverse peoples together. Conflict with a dangerous and hostile Other has glossed over internal divisions and fostered union of a kind, making it possible for him, a Scot, to paint a London street scene in celebration of a

82b. Detail of pl. 81.

victory won by an Anglo-Irishman, Arthur Wellesley, Duke of Wellington. War, this picture contends and proclaims, has been the making of Great Britain.

As this book has endeavoured to show, this was true – but it was not the whole truth. War played a vital part in the invention of a British nation after 1707, but it could never have been so influential without other factors, and in particular without the impact of religion. It was their common investment in Protestantism that first allowed the English, the Welsh and the Scots to become fused together, and to remain so, despite their many cultural divergences. And it was Protestantism that helped to make Britain's successive wars against France after 1689 so significant in terms of national formation. A powerful and persistently threatening France became the haunting embodiment of that Catholic Other which Britons had been taught to fear since the Reformation in the sixteenth century. Confronting it encouraged them to bury their internal differences in the struggle for survival, victory and booty. 'There is no more effective way of bonding together the disparate sections of restless peoples', as Eric Hobsbawm has written, 'than to unite them against outsiders.'[3] Imagining the French as their vile opposites, as Hyde to their Jekyll, became a way for Britons – particularly the poorer and less privileged – to contrive for themselves a converse and flattering identity. The French wallowed in superstition: therefore, the British, by contrast, must enjoy true religion. The French were oppressed by a bloated army and by absolute monarchy: consequently, the British were manifestly free. The French tramped through life in wooden shoes, whereas the British – as Adam Smith pointed out – were shod in supple leather and, therefore, clearly more prosperous.[4]

That many of these assumptions about French disadvantages and British benefits were wrong was immaterial. Britons clung to them so as to give themselves worth, and as a way of reassuring themselves, when times were hard, that they had drawn the long straw in life. As late as the 1940s, a Methodist grocer in Grantham, Lincolnshire, called Alfred Roberts, would give it as his opinion that the French as a nation were 'corrupt from top to bottom'.[5] As a self-made man who had clawed his way to his town's aldermanic bench, he instinctively felt the need to refer to the old enemy in dismissive terms so as to throw into still greater relief his own conspicuously puritan morality, spartan lifestyle and commitment to duty. By vilifying France, he vaunted Britain's virtue, and by inference his own. Just how much of this slanted perspective on the people across the Channel, one must wonder, did he pass on to his deeply serious and adoring elder daughter, the future Margaret Thatcher?

As this example shows, the Protestant worldview which allowed so many Britons to see themselves as a distinct and chosen people persisted long after the Battle of Waterloo, and long after the passing of the Catholic Emancipation Act in 1829 as well. For most Victorians, the massive overseas empire which was the fruit of so much successful warfare represented final and conclusive proof of Great Britain's providential destiny. God had entrusted Britons with empire, they believed, so as to further the worldwide spread of the Gospel and as a testimony to their status as the Protestant Israel.[6] And this complacency proved persistent. Well into the twentieth century, contact with and dominion over manifestly alien peoples nourished Britons' sense of superior difference. They could contrast their law, their treatment of women, their wealth, power, political stability and religion with societies they only imperfectly understood, but usually perceived as inferior.[7] Empire corroborated Britain's blessings, as well as what the Scottish socialist Keir Hardie called 'the indomitable pluck and energy of the British people'.[8]

In this broad sense, then, Protestantism lay at the core of British national identity, and this was only to be expected. Religion was the crucial unifying force in most nations within Europe as outside it. Sweden and Holland, for instance, owed their initial self-definition to Protestantism quite as much as Great Britain did, and so, later on, did the newly independent United States of America.[9] It was the pull of the Orthodox Church that gave even the poorest of its inhabitants an attachment to 'Holy Russia' as early as the sixteenth century, if not before.[10] And men and women in early modern France appear to have felt united and distinguished by their overwhelming Catholicism, even though the majority of them had still to learn how to speak or write the French language. Here, as in so many other countries, it was religion that first converted peasants into patriots, long before the onset of modernisation in the shape of railroads, mass education, advanced press networks and democracy.[11]

Of course, this does not mean that other agencies played an insignificant part in nation-building. Great Britain's position as a compact island, held together even in the early eighteenth century by a relatively advanced system of canals and roads, the free trade that flourished within its boundaries so much earlier than in other European nation states, the precocity and ubiquity of its newspaper and periodical press, and the fact that England and Scotland were the most swiftly urbanising parts of Europe in the 1700s: all of these economic conditions undoubtedly contributed towards the coming together and the continuing together of this essentially invented nation. Men and women living in or near towns with some access to print, and particularly those caught up in the mesh of the nation's internal and foreign trade, seem always to have been among the busiest and most reliable of patriots. They might not approve of the men in power in London, but they still had a stake in the nation's security and were acutely sensitive to its dangers. The economic peculiarities of the British aided their cohesion, then, but it was the coincidence of the island's pan-Protestantism and its successive wars with a Catholic state that did most to give it what Eugen Weber calls 'a true political personality'.[12]

Their recurrent experience of Protestant warfare after 1707 affected different Britons in different ways, though almost all of them were obliged to react and change in some way. As far as the Hanoverian kings were concerned, the threat of France – which, initially at least, imperilled their dynasty's survival – led, slowly and unevenly, to the emergence of a more consciously patriotic and even popularist royal style. Though it was only after George III's accession and a decline in the crown's political intrusiveness, that a really successful formula for a nationalist monarchy was worked out. Royal visits to every part of the kingdom, carefully choreographed and synchronised royal celebrations in which all classes and both sexes were encouraged to participate, an ostentatious royal patronage of British culture: all of these became evident as never before in the wake of the lost war with America and in the face of the near quarter-century of war with Revolutionary and Napoleonic France.

The making of a more authentically British ruling class was also, as we have seen, powerfully assisted by the demands of war. The growing need to raise taxes and cannon-fodder from the island as a whole (and from that other island across the Irish Sea) forced those élite Englishmen who initially monopolised civilian power in London to accept a quota of Scots, Anglo-Irish and Welshmen into their ranks. Moreover, the elastic empire that resulted from the wars with France increasingly depended on Britons who were not English for government, exploration and exploitation – a dependence that persisted into the twentieth century. As more Anglo-Irish, Scottish and Welsh dynasts and careerists entered imperial service or London employments, it became far more common for them to socialise and intermarry with their English counterparts. And though this could savour of a selling-out to English values, the behaviour of these onetime Celtic outsiders can just as appropriately be interpreted as a purchasing into what were then the substantial profits of being British.

Unprecedentedly large-scale and recurrent warfare also transformed Britain's rulers in the sense that it obliged them to demand far more from the people below. Before 1700, the mass of men and women had generally been expected to be orderly, obedient *and above all, passive* in the face of those set in authority over them. Active citizenship was viewed as the prerogative of the propertied and of the male. 'The poorer and meaner people', the Duke of Albemarle wrote with splendid hauteur in the 1670s, could have 'no interest in the commonwealth but the use of breath'.[13] Successive wars with France rendered this kind of disdain increasingly impracticable. Higher and more rigorous wartime taxation fostered political awareness among the mass of ordinary Britons, just as it did among the inhabitants of the American colonies after 1760. And the recurrent threat of a French invasion of the British mainland meant that active loyalty had regularly to be incited on a wider scale, and at a lower social level, than in earlier centuries. After 1793, even women were being called upon to play a part in the war effort, raising money, organising comforts for the soldiery, taking a role in patriotic festivals and inciting their menfolk to fight. Resignation in the face of authority was no longer enough: subjects of all kinds now had to become Britons in deed.

As this book has sought to show, impressive numbers of Britons did make the step from a passive awareness of nation to an energetic participation on its behalf. But they did so in the main not just because patriotism was recommended from above, but also because they expected to profit from it in some way. Men and women became British patriots in order to advertise their prominence in the community, or out of ambition for state or imperial employment, or because they believed that a wider British empire would benefit them commercially, or out of fear that a French victory would damage their security and livelihoods, or from a desire for excitement and an escape from the humdrum, or because they felt that their religious identity was at stake, or – in some cases – because being an active patriot seemed an important step towards winning admission to full citizenship, a means of coming closer to the vote and to a say in the running of the state. Nor was this last group mistaken. The rate of political change in Britain in the two decades after Waterloo suggests that there *is* a relationship – albeit a complex one – between mass involvement in a war effort and the widening of political rights and participation.[14] One may wonder, indeed, whether the comparatively slow rate of political reform in Great Britain after the 1830s was due in part to the absence until 1914 of major wars demanding popular mobilisation on a large scale. Did the fact that there was never a compelling need to summon ordinary Victorian Britons to defend the nation state mean that their rulers could more easily ignore their demands? It seems probable.

What is abundantly clear is that in Great Britain in this period, as in all nations at all times, patriotism had many roots and was as much a rational as it was an irrational response. Coming to terms with the complexity and depth of patriotism is vital if we are to understand the British past – and indeed the British present. So many historians have written so extensively and so well on riots, on Jacobitism, on Jacobinism and on the various manifestations of class conflict in eighteenth- and nineteenth-century Britain, that it can sometimes appear that protest of some kind made up the whole sum of popular political behaviour; that it was only through oppositional activity that men and women outside the governing élite advanced their claims for recognition, reform and a broader citizenship. Yet this is quite wrong. The growing involvement in politics of men and women from the middling and working classes that characterised British society at this time was expressed as much if not more in support for the nation state, as it was in opposition to the men who governed it. Becoming a patriot was a political act, and often a multi-faceted and dynamic one. We need to stop confusing patriotism with simple conservatism, or smothering it with damning and dismissive references to chauvinism and jingoism. Quite as much as any other human activity, the patriotism of the past requires flexible, sensitive and above all, imaginative reconstruction.[15]

Acknowledging that all sorts of men and women found good and powerful reasons to identify themselves as Britons in this period, is not, of course, to say that *all* men and women did so. Nor is it to say that those who supported the nation against attacks from without invariably gave uncritical support as well to the existing order at home. Nor, emphatically, is it the case that a growing sense of Britishness after 1707 completely displaced and crowded out other loyalties. Particularly in the more rural and remote parts of Britain, in the Scottish Highlands, in central Wales, in Cornwall, East Anglia and much of the North Country, intense localism remained the norm, at least until the coming of the railways, if not until the more violent intrusion of conscription in the First World War. 'There is no post office in the village', wrote an exasperated Richard Cobden in 1850 of Heyshott in Sussex – a parish with fewer than 400 souls, situated some fifty miles from London:

> Every morning an old man, aged about seventy, goes into Midhurst for the letters. He charges a penny for every dispatch he carries . . . His letter-bag for the whole village contains on an average from two to three letters daily, including newspapers. The only newspapers which enter the parish are two copies of *Bell's Weekly Messenger*, a sound old Tory Protectionist much patronised by drowsy farmers.[16]

Far more nineteenth-century Britons than is usually recognised lived in places exactly like Heyshott, little worlds to themselves, cut off for most of the time by custom, poverty, ignorance and apathy.

Welshness, Scottishness and Englishness also remained powerful divides – though not perhaps as powerful as regionalism and localism. 'Britain is an invented nation', wrote Peter Scott recently, 'not so much older than the United States'.[17] And because Great Britain was invented only in 1707, it was inevitably superimposed on much older allegiances. For a half-century or more after the Union, as we have seen, the relationship between Scotland and the rest of Britain was marred by suspicion and hatred, as was the relationship between Lowland Scotland and the Highlands. Thereafter, growing prosperity and a common investment in Protestant warfare and lucrative imperial adventure – as well as the passage of years – worked to make these internal fractures conspicuously less violent, though they never faded away completely. By 1837, Scotland still retained many of the characteristics of a distinct nation, but it was comfortably contained within a bigger nation. It was British as well as Scottish.[18] By contrast, Wales was rather more distinct. Possessed of its own unifying language, less urbanised than Scotland and England, and – crucially – less addicted to military and imperial endeavour, it could still strike observers from outside its boundaries as being resolutely peculiar to itself. 'If nothing can please him but what is *foreign*', an English writer on tourism declared with some exaggeration in 1831, 'he will find the language, manners, and dress of the inhabitants [of Wales], except in the inns, as completely foreign as those of France or Switzerland.'[19]

It would be wrong, then, to interpret the growth of British national consciousness in this period in terms of a new cultural and political uniformity being resolutely imposed on the peripheries of the island by its centre. For many poorer and less literate Britons, Scotland, Wales and England remained more potent rallying calls than Great Britain, except in times of danger from abroad. And even among the politically educated, it was common to think in terms of dual nationalities, not a single national identity. Iolo Morgannwg, for example, one of the most radical of Welsh writers at the end of the eighteenth century, routinely referred to Welsh and English as being his two *native* languages. He was binational just as he was bilingual.[20] By the same token, Sir John Sinclair, a Caithness Scot who became the first President of the Board of Agriculture in 1793, saw no inconsistency whatsoever between his enthusiastic membership of the British political establishment on the one hand, and his devotion to the Highland Society and all things Scottish on the other:

> National peculiarities are of great use in exciting a spirit of manly emulation . . . It is in the interest of the United Kingdom to keep alive those national, *or what, perhaps, may now more properly be called local distinctions* of English, Scotch, Irish and Welsh.[21]

Sinclair's uncertainty as to what to call the United Kingdom, Great Britain and the component parts of Great Britain has been followed by many later commentators. Yet this agonising over definitions is necessary only if one remains wedded to an unrealistically narrow view of what constitutes nationhood. Few nations since the world began have been culturally and ethnically homogeneous; and dual nationalities are common enough. Great Britain, as it emerged in the years between the Act of Union and the accession of Queen Victoria, and as it exists today, must be seen both as one relatively new nation, and as three much older nations – with the precise relationship between these old and new alignments still changing and becoming more fiercely debated even as I write.

Since virtually every major European state is currently under pressure from a resurgence of small nationalities which once acquiesced in being a component part of a greater whole, today's increasingly strident calls for a break-up of Britain should not be attributed exclusively to this island's own peculiar development.[22] But we can understand the nature of the present crisis only if we recognise that the factors that provided for the forging of a British nation in the past have largely ceased to operate. Protestantism, that once vital cement, has now a limited influence on British culture, as indeed has Christianity itself. Recurrent wars with the states of Continental Europe have in all likelihood come to an end, so different kinds of Britons no longer feel the same compulsion as before to remain united in the face of the enemy from without. And, crucially, both commercial supremacy and imperial hegemony have gone. No more can Britons reassure themselves of their distinct and privileged identity by contrasting themselves with impoverished Europeans (real or imaginary), or by exercising authority over manifestly alien peoples. God has ceased to be British, and Providence no longer smiles.

The resulting doubt and disarray have taken many forms. On the one hand, now that so many of the components of Britishness have faded, there have been predictable calls for a revival of other, older loyalties – a return to Englishness, or Scottishness, or Welshness. The Scots, in particular, who became British after 1707 in part because it paid such enormous commercial and imperial dividends, are now increasingly inclined to see partial or complete independence plus membership of a federal Europe as the most profitable strategy for the future. On the other hand, even among those who want to remain British, there has been a marked rise of controversy about just what this does and should entail. The validity and appropriateness of many of the patriotic icons discussed in this book – the Royal Family, Parliament and even fox-hunting – are now being anxiously and incessantly debated as never before. But national uncertainty is most evident, perhaps, in the apprehension with which so many Britons regard increasing assimilation into a united Europe. Whereas the Germans and the French, who are more confident about their unique identity, see a Europe without frontiers in terms of opportunity, the British are far more inclined to view it as a threat. This is partly because they have so often fought against Continental European states in the past; but their apparent insularity is to be explained also by their growing doubts about who they are in the present. Consciously or unconsciously, they fear assuming a new identity in case it obliterates entirely the already insecure identity they currently possess.

How all this will resolve itself – whether Great Britain will break down into separate Welsh, Scottish and English states, or whether, as is more likely, a more federal Britain will emerge as part of an increasingly federal Europe – remains to be seen. What seems indisputable is that a substantial rethinking of what it means to be British can no longer be evaded.

Even in the eighteenth and early nineteenth centuries, there were those who feared that British identity was too dependent on recurrent Protestant wars, commercial success and imperial conquest, and that more thought and attention should be devoted to consolidating a deeper sense of citizenship on the home front. 'Foreign commerce is a fine thing, so is my bright India', wrote a Scottish pro-consul called Sir John Macpherson in the 1790s:

> But the world is under the hand of great changes and violent revolutions and the rising genius of other nations and their detestation of our monopolies will divest us some day of these eastern and western wings. We must then look at home, and if we have not turned our commercial and asiatic sovereignty to the real improvement of our own island and to the domestic union of the three kingdoms . . . we have abused the inheritance which the spirit and minds of our forefathers have acquired for our enjoyment and improvement.[23]

But Sir John was a well-known eccentric. No one paid any attention.

Appendix 1: The Geography of Loyalty in 1745

In July 1745, Charles Edward Stuart landed in the north of Scotland with the aim of restoring his dynasty's rule over Great Britain, Ireland and the British colonies. Three months later, he crossed the border into England with an army of over 5,000 men. Between September and mid-December, when the prince retreated back to Scotland and defeat, over 200 places in England, Wales and Scotland dispatched loyal addresses to the ruling monarch, George II, and over 50 raised subscriptions or private armies to defend themselves against the Jacobite invasion.

Many other towns and counties demonstrated their allegiance to the Hanoverian dynasty *after* the Stuart prince had begun his retreat. But, by then, the danger was over and loyalty cost nothing. By contrast, the places shown on this map made their views known when there was still a marginal chance that the Stuart claimant might succeed. Those of their citizens who signed loyal addresses and – still more – those who volunteered money or their own military service in support of the existing order were therefore taking something of a calculated risk. As such, their behaviour should be taken seriously.

This map is based on reports in the government paper, the *London Gazette*, and on information in P.R.O. S.P. 36. There were many other, less formal acts of citizen mobilisation against the invasion which never reached the administration. So this is only an indication of where active loyalty was to be found at this time. It is not comprehensive.

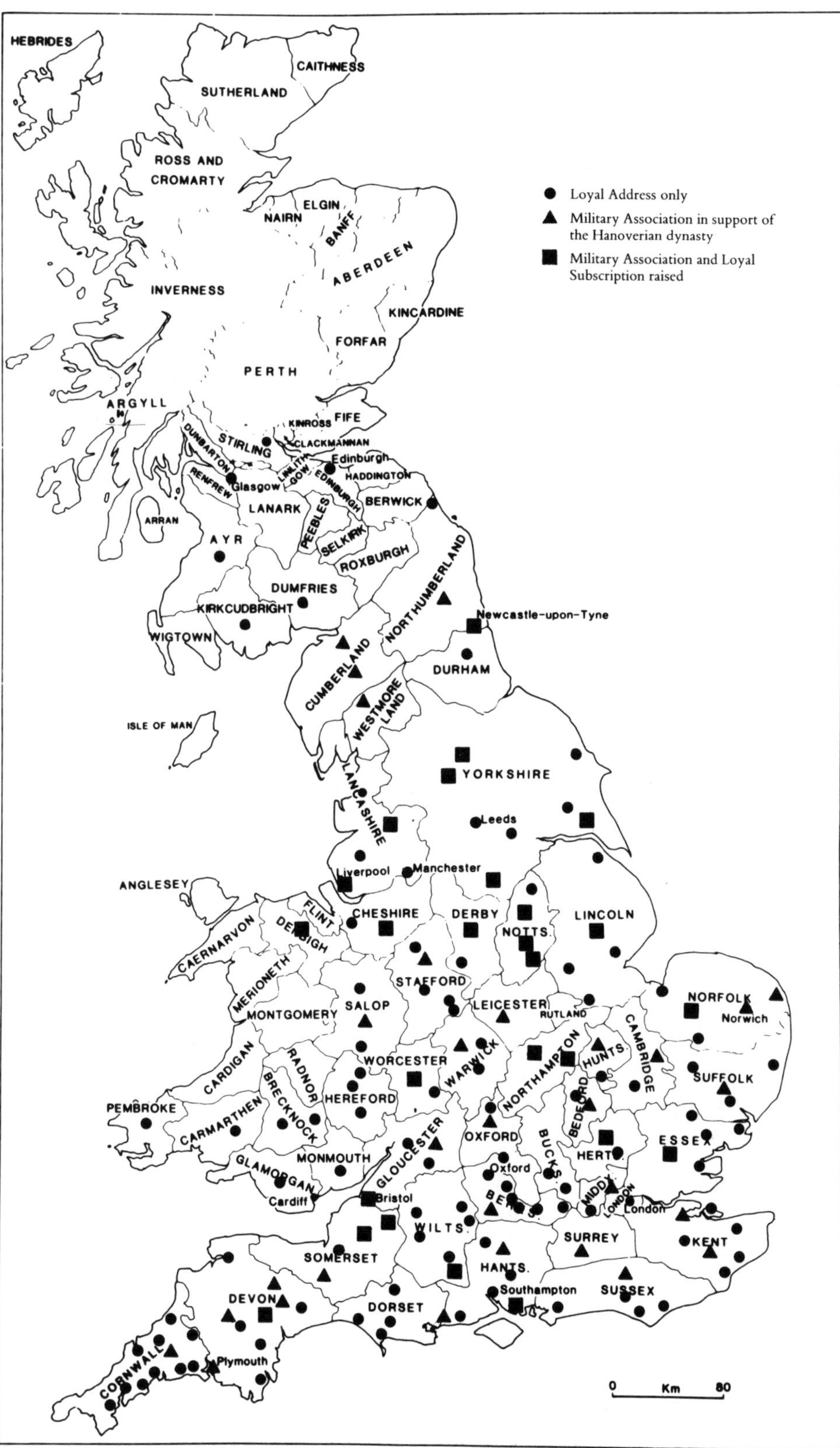
Loyal Address only
Military Association in support of the Hanoverian dynasty
Military Association and Loyal Subscription raised
HEBRIDES
CAITHNESS
SUTHERLAND
ROSS AND CROMARTY
ELGIN
NAIRN
BANFF
ABERDEEN
INVERNESS
KINCARDINE
FORFAR
PERTH
ARGYLL
KINROSS
FIFE
STIRLING
CLACKMANNAN
DUNBARTON
Edinburgh
LINLITHGOW
HADDINGTON
RENFREW
Glasgow
EDINBURGH
BERWICK
LANARK
ARRAN
PEEBLES
SELKIRK
AYR
ROXBURGH
NORTHUMBERLAND
DUMFRIES
KIRKCUDBRIGHT
Newcastle-upon-Tyne
WIGTOWN
CUMBERLAND
DURHAM
WESTMORELAND
ISLE OF MAN
YORKSHIRE
LANCASHIRE
Leeds
Liverpool
Manchester
ANGLESEY
FLINT
CHESHIRE
DERBY
LINCOLN
DENBIGH
NOTTS.
CAERNARVON
MERIONETH
STAFFORD
SALOP
LEICESTER
NORFOLK
RUTLAND
Norwich
MONTGOMERY
CAMBRIDGE
NORTHAMPTON
HUNTS.
CARDIGAN
RADNOR
WORCESTER
WARWICK
SUFFOLK
BRECKNOCK
HEREFORD
BEDFORD
PEMBROKE
CARMARTHEN
OXFORD
BUCKS.
GLOUCESTER
ESSEX
HERTS.
MONMOUTH
GLAMORGAN
Oxford
Cardiff
Bristol
BERKS.
MIDDX.
LONDON
London
WILTS.
SURREY
KENT
SOMERSET
HANTS.
Southampton
SUSSEX
DEVON
DORSET
CORNWALL
Plymouth
0 Km 80

Appendix 2: Men at Arms throughout Great Britain, May 1804

FOLLOWING ON THE HOME DEFENCE legislation passed in 1803, every county in Great Britain was required to establish how many male inhabitants it contained between the ages of seventeen and fifty-five, how many of these would be willing to take up arms and join volunteer corps, and how many were already enrolled in the militia, in the fencible regiments in the case of Scotland, and in existing volunteer corps. These estimates which were sent first to the respective Lords Lieutenant and then abstracted for London's benefit are not complete. Nor, it should go without saying, are they likely to be entirely accurate given the speed with which they were compiled and early nineteenth-century transport and clerical conditions. But they still provide an unparalleled guide to civilian responses in wartime.

	A Number of men aged 17–55	B Number of volunteers	C Number of men already in uniform	B and C as % of A
ENGLAND				
County				
Bedfordshire*	10997	5814	unknown	—
Berkshire	19418	2457	734	16%
Bucks.	18141	6034	1893	44%
Cambs.*	17109	unknown	1404	—
Cheshire	34799	7211	2641	28%
Cornwall	33440	3213	4354	23%
Cumberland	19683	1615	76	9%
Derbyshire	27947	14985	319	55%
Devonshire	51101	15919	10312	51%
Dorset	20066	4353	2306	33%
Durham	23523	1101	6325	32%
Essex	36243	3391	3926	20%
Glos.	35220	17440	390	51%
Hants and Isle of Wight	36229	19680	4847	68%
Herefordsh.	13561	3494	502	29%

Herts.	18261	6618	447	39%
Hunts.	6900	753	133	13%
Kent	37929	4233	14373	49%
Lancs.	131535	27728	13846	32%
Leics.	20815	8755	918	46%
Lincs.	32948	5122	4968	31%
Middsx and London*		Figures imperfect		
Norfolk	49325	15458	3019	37%
Northants.	21260	5494	562	28%
Northld.	15222	6916	4649	76%
Notts.	24841	3079	1916	20%
Oxfordsh.*	19369	8184	unknown	—
Rutland	3089	1269	182	47%
Salop.	29796	3981	2971	23%
Somerset	39878	9035	8249	43%
Staffs.	41951	18497	780	46%
Suffolk	37452	11217	2195	36%
Surrey	39411	1846	10337	31%
Sussex	27838	9510	3109	45%
Warwks.	35703	11644	213	33%
Westld.	4609	2702	3?	59%
Wilts.	29317	12334	909	45%
Worcs.	14195	3739	216	28%
Yorkshire:				
North Riding	25398	7642	1356	35%
East Riding	22386	2584	803	15%
West Riding	102527	9980	1396	11%
Cinque Ports	10205	445	4998	53%

WALES

County				
Anglesey	5553	1729	1729	62%
Brecon*	6659	1295	unknown	—
Cardigan	5899	489	618	19%
Carmarthen	10609	531	371	8%
Carnarfon	5939	632	1394	34%
Denbigh	9426	518	1?	5%
Flint	6420	718	2561	51%
Glamorgan	14758	4441	234	32%
Merioneth	4292	396	260	15%
Monmouth*	10254	1457	unknown	—
Montgomery*	8374	1867	unknown	—
Pembroke*	8215	unknown	737	—
Radnor*	3691	unknown	unknown	—

SCOTLAND

County				
Aberdeen	19279	2585	3162	30%
Argyll	13404	10989	1280	91%
Ayr*	13197	4458	unknown	—
Banff	3982	1108	902	50%
Berwick	4883	1471	337	37%
Bute*	2056	unknown	480	—
Caithness*	3113	unknown	925	—
Clackmannan*	1360	unknown	unknown	—
Cromarty	1041	180	209	37%
Dumbarton	3795	716	554	33%
Dumfries*	8370	unknown	unknown	—
Elgin*	4081	unknown	717	—
Fife	12278	3673	3035	55%
Forfar	14936	1021	1238	15%
Inverness	9629	830	716	16%
Kincardine	4148	1397	266	40%
Kinross*	1112	unknown	18	—
Kircudbright*	3166	unknown	906	—
Lanark*	28617	7356	unknown	—
Linlithgow	2300	541	450	43%
Lothian	17955	3048	3038	34%
Nairn*	Figures imperfect			
Orkney	Figures unknown			
Peebles	1696	315	460	46%
Perth	20166	8694	814	47%
Renfrew*	10653	unknown	247	—
Ross	6574	4289	394	71%
Roxburgh	5850	3507	100	62%
Selkirk	959	464	150	64%
Stirling	7869	2135	421	32%
Sutherland*	3433	unknown	1080	—
Wigtown	4252	1417	137	36%

* Although the counties marked with an asterisk did not submit complete returns in May 1804, they did send in returns of the number of their rank-and-file volunteers in December 1803. At that time, Bedfordshire had 1,978 men serving in volunteer units; Cambridgeshire had 2,500; London, Westminster, Tower Hamlets and Middlesex together had 35,256; Oxfordshire had 3,516, Brecon, 1,196; Monmouthshire, 1,656; Montgomeryshire, 1,680; Pembrokeshire, 2,701; Radnor, 1,000; Ayrshire, 2,691; Bute, 90; Caithness, 1,320; Clackmannanshire, 336; Dumfrieshire, 1879; Elgin, 784; Kinross, 280; Kircudbright, 946; Lanarkshire, 4,513;

Nairn, 320; Renfrew, 2,414; Sutherland, 1,092. How many of these men were still serving in 1804 is unknown, but presumably many of them were.

Sources: Abstracts of the Subdivision Rolls in Great Britain, 7 May 1804, *Hansard*, 1st series, 2 (1804) lxii-lxiii, checked against the originals in P.R.O., 30/8/240, fol. 97. The December 1803 returns are in *Hansard*, 1st series, 1 (1803–4), p. 1902.

Appendix 3: Volunteers and their Chosen Sphere of Action in 1798

During the invasion crisis of autumn 1798, the British government ordered a survey of the total number of infantry and cavalry volunteer corps in existence throughout the island. It also attempted to establish how many of these essentially private defence bodies were willing to serve a) throughout the military district of which their county was a part, or b) only within their own home county, or c) only within a radius of twenty miles or less from their town of village, or d) whether the territorial scope of their duties was still unknown. The results are tabulated below:

	Number of Volunteers	Percentage of men willing to serve in a) Military District	b) Home County only	c) 20 miles radius only	d) unknown
ENGLAND					
County					
Beds.	346	54%	—	46%	—
Berks.	1422	4%	11%	71%	14%
Bucks			unknown		
Cambs.	313	16%	—	84%	—
Cheshire	1230	31%	29%	40%	—
Cornwall	4415	49%	9%	25%	17%
Cumbld.			unknown		
Derbysh.	460	54%	33%	13%	—
Devon	8800	66%	1%	22%	11%
Dorset	2265	69%	—	26%	6%
Durham	1945	33%	—	52%	15%
Essex	2362	12%	2%	83%	3%
Glos.	2350	20%	—	80%	—
Hants. and I. of Wight	6326	65%	1%	18%	16%
Herefsh.	450	40%	—	60%	—
Herts.	1150	29%	9%	62%	—
Hunts.	160	62%	—	38%	—
Kent	5276	66%	2%	19%	13%
Lancs.	7050	35%	1%	55%	9%
Leics.	980	59%	—	35%	6%
Lincs.	1440	54%	15%	31%	—
Middsx.			unknown		
Norfolk	2921	38%	3%	59%	—

Northants.	1030	44%	—	56%	—
Northld.	2350	70%	6%	16%	8%
Notts.	1270	33%	—	12%	55%
Oxon.	600	18%	—	82%	—
Rutland	570	90%	—	10%	—
Salop.	820	72%	—	28%	—
Somerset	4806	44%	1%	29%	26%
Staffs.	2340	13%	—	73%	14%
Suffolk	2120	48%	3%	35%	14%
Surrey	2740	20%	—	64%	16%
Sussex	1000	52%	6%	12%	30%
Warwks.	1245	30%	—	47%	23%
Westld.			unknown		
Wilts.	2270	56%	—	44%	—
Worcs.	920	25%	—	75%	—
Yorkshire:					
North Riding	1620	52%	4%	14%	30%
East Riding	1450	88%	—	12%	—
West Riding	3950	70%	—	30%	—
Cinque Ports	1430	100%	—	—	—

WALES

County

Anglesey	440	45%	55%	—	—
Brecon	60	100%	—	—	—
Cardigan	970	77%	—	—	23%
Carmarthen	260	100%	—	—	—
Carnarfon	340	—	53%	35%	12%
Denbigh	560	21%	27%	52%	—
Flint	230	74%	—	26%	—
Glamorgan	2240	73%	10%	7%	10%
Merioneth	110	—	—	—	100%
Monmouth	976	5%	66%	29%	—
Montgomery			not known		
Pembroke	1246	87%	5%	—	8%
Radnor			not known		

SCOTLAND

County

Aberdeen	1070	65%	35%	—	—
Argyll	1352	100%	—	—	—
Ayr	1389	48%	15%	12%	25%
Banff	1230	100%	—	—	—
Berwick	516	100%	—	—	—
Bute	290	65%	35%	—	—
Caithness	600	100%	—	—	—
Clackmannan	560	21%	—	—	79%
Cromarty	310	58%	—	—	42%

Dumbarton	660	100%	—	—	—
Dumfries	150	100%	—	—	—
Elgin	360	100%	—	—	—
Fife	1875	89%	8%	—	3%
Forfar	1313	91%	—	9%	—
Inverness	2407	93%	—	5%	2%
Kincardine	210	—	—	—	—
Kinross			unknown		
Kircudbr't	180	67%	—	23%	—
Lanark	1270	90%	—	10%	—
Linlithgow	300	100%	—	—	—
Lothian	3460	100%	—	—	—
Nairn	220	100%	—	—	—
Orkney			unknown		
Peebles	120	100%	—	—	—
Perth	2730	100%	—	—	—
Renfrew	1580	100%	—	—	—
Ross	760	100%	—	—	—
Roxburgh	366	66%	16%	18%	—
Selkirk	90	33%	—	67%	—
Stirling	360	100%	—	—	—
Sutherland	600	100%	—	—	—
Wigton	290	100%	—	—	—

SUMMARY

Total number of volunteers in England:	84,762	(35 counties only)
Total number of volunteers in Wales:	7,432	(11 counties only)
Total number of volunteers in Scotland:	26,618	(30 counties only)
	118,812	

Source: P.R.O., 30/8/244, fol. 237

Notes

Since the references to each chapter make up what is in effect a running bibliography, I have dispensed with a separate list of further reading. Throughout, references are given in full at the first citation in each chapter and are abbreviated thereafter. The place of publication of the edition used in the text is London unless otherwise stated. When quoting from manuscript sources, I have modernised the spelling whenever it seemed necessary.

The following abbreviations are used in the notes:

Add. MS	Additional Manuscript
B.L.	British Library, British Museum
Hansard	*Hansard's Parliamentary Debates*
H.M.C.	Reports of the Royal Commission on Historical Manuscripts
H.O.	Home Office
Political and Personal Satires	Frederick George Stephens and Mary Dorothy George, *Catalogue of Prints and Drawings in the British Museum: Political and Personal Satires* (11 vols, 1870–1954).
Parl. Hist.	W. Cobbett, *The Parliamentary History of England from the Earliest Period to 1803* (36 vols, 1816).
P.R.O.	Public Record Office, London
S.P.	State Papers

INTRODUCTION

1. Paul Kennedy, *The Rise and Fall of the Great Powers* (1988), p. 160.
2. See, for example, John Lough's, *France Observed in the Seventeenth Century by British Travellers* (Stocksfield, 1985), and his *France on the Eve of Revolution: British Travellers Observations 1763–1788* (1987).
3. P.G.M. Dickson, *The Financial Revolution in England* (1967); John Brewer, *The Sinews of Power: War, Money and the English State, 1688–1783* (1989).
4. For example, only two books to my knowledge have been published in the last few decades surveying domestic responses to Britain's epic wars with Revolutionary and Napoleonic France, even though, as Asa Briggs wrote, 'The way into the nineteenth century led across the battlefield as well as through the cotton mill and the iron foundry.' *The Age of Improvement 1783–1867* (1979 edn), p. 129. Contrast this poor showing with the unceasing torrent of books and articles on the impact of industrialisation on Britain.
5. See, for example, Paul Kleber Monod,

Jacobitism and the English People, 1688–1788 (Cambridge, 1989); James E. Bradley, *Popular Politics and the American Revolution in England* (Macon, Georgia, 1986); J.E. Cookson, *The Friends of Peace: Anti-War Liberalism in England, 1793–1815* (Cambridge, 1982); Roger Wells, *Insurrection: The British Experience 1795–1803* (Gloucester, 1983).

6. Benedict Anderson, *Imagined Communities: Reflections on the Origin and Spread of Nationalism* (1991 edn), p. 6. See also Eric Hobsbawm, *Nations and Nationalism since 1780: Programme, Myth, Reality* (Cambridge, 1990). Both of these books are invaluable in demonstrating the unsoundness of any single platonic notion of what constitutes nationalism and nationhood.
7. Peter Sahlins, *Boundaries: The Making of France and Spain in the Pyrenees* (Berkeley and Los Angeles 1989), p. 271.
8. See my 'Britishness and Otherness: an argument', *Journal of British Studies* 31 (1992).
9. On the 'blending' of Britain, see Keith Robbins, *Nineteenth-century Britain: Integration and Diversity* (Oxford, 1988), and for the most developed expression of the theory that Britain was forged by an imperialistic English core which 'gradually replaced' local and regional cultures and established 'one national culture', see Michael Hechter, *Internal Colonialism: The Celtic Fringe in British National Development, 1536–1966* (Berkeley and Los Angeles, 1975). It should go without saying that both of these books contain much that is of value, but I dissent from what seems to be their shared assumption that Great Britain could come into being only through the creation of some kind of cultural uniformity.
10. R.F. Foster, *Modern Ireland 1600–1972* (1988), p. 163. Philip Yorke, a future Lord Chancellor, set out London's attitude to Ireland with unusual candour in 1721: 'The subjects of Ireland were to be considered in two respects, as English and Irish . . . the Irish were a conquered people and the English a colony transplanted hither, and are a colony subject to the law of the mother country', *ibid.*, p. 248. This was very different from the metropolitan stance on Wales and Scotland.
11. *The Times*, 22 November 1991.

1 PROTESTANTS

1. *The Complete Poetical Works of James Thomson*, ed. J. Logie Robertson (Oxford, 1908), p. 420. The figure of Britannia dates from the time when much of Britain was a Roman province. She seems first to have appeared on English coins in 1665, though she acquired her familiar trident only in 1797 in the wake of a succession of naval victories against the French. In 1821, Britannia became an even more martial icon and appeared on British coins equipped with a helmet: see C. Wilson Peck, *English Copper, Tin and Bronze Coins in the British Museum 1558–1958* (2nd edn, 1964), pp. 110, 288, 295. For how she was used to represent Great Britain as a whole in eighteenth-century prints, see Herbert M. Atherton, *Political Prints in the Age of Hogarth* (Oxford, 1974), pp. 89–97.
2. On the making of the Union, see Bruce Galloway, *The Union of England and Scotland, 1603–1608* (Edinburgh, 1986); T.I. Rae (ed.), *The Union of 1707: Its Impact on Scotland* (1974); P.W.J. Riley, *The Union of England and Scotland: A Study in Anglo-Scottish Politics in the 18th Century* (Manchester, 1978). Denys Hays, 'The use of the term 'Great Britain' in the Middle Ages', *Proceedings of the Society of Antiquaries of Scotland* 89 (1955–56).
3. Rosalind Mitchison, *Lordship to Patronage: Scotland 1603–1745* (1983), pp. 1–129; T.M. Devine, 'The Union of 1707 and Scottish development', *Scottish Economic and Social History* 5 (1985), p. 26.
4. Brian P. Levack, *The Formation of the British state: England, Scotland, and the Union 1603–1707* (Oxford, 1987); Alexander Murdoch, *The People Above: Politics and Administration in Mid-18th Century Scotland* (Edinburgh, 1980).
5. For a particularly paranoid complaint on this score, see John Free, *Seasonable Reflections upon the Importance of the Name of England* (1755).
6. Timothy J. McCann (ed.), *The Correspondence of the Dukes of Richmond and Newcastle 1724–1750*, Sussex Record Society, 73 (Trowbridge, 1984), pp. 204 and 236.
7. Kenneth O. Morgan, *Rebirth of a Nation:*

Wales 1880–1980 (Oxford, 1981), p. 20.

8. W.T.R. Pryce, 'Wales as a culture region: patterns of change 1750–1971', *Transactions of the Honourable Society of Cymmrodorion* (1978).
9. John Evans, *The Christian Soldier . . . a Sermon Preached before the Most Honourable and Loyal Society of Ancient Britons* (1751), p. 25.
10. See Richard Rose, *Understanding the United Kingdom: The Territorial Dimension in Government* (1982), pp. 15 *et seq.* As Rose cautions, the implication that there is a monolithic Celtic identity is one of the problems in Michael Hechter's otherwise interesting *Internal Colonialism: The Celtic Fringe in British National Development, 1536–1966* (Berkeley and Los Angeles, 1975).
11. *The Break-Up of Britain: Crisis and Neo-Nationalism* (2nd edn, 1981), p. 147. On the different regional cultures throughout Great Britain, see Hugh Kearney, *The British Isles: A History of Four Nations* (Cambridge, 1989).
12. See, for instance, the views of Patrick Sellar, the Countess of Sutherland's factor, in T.C. Smout and Sydney Wood, *Scottish Voices, 1745–1960* (1990), pp. 292–3. Sir Walter Scott's determination to turn George IV's famous visit to Scotland in 1822 into a celebration of all things Highland profoundly offended many Scottish Lowlanders. 'A great mistake was made by the stage managers', wrote Elizabeth Grant at the time: 'one that offended all the southron Scots; the King wore at the Levee the highland dress. I daresay he thought the country all highland, expected no fertile plains, did not know the difference between the Saxon and the Celt', *Memoirs of a Highland lady* (2 vols, Edinburgh, 1988), II, pp. 165–6.
13. Philip Jenkins, *The Making of a Ruling Class: The Glamorgan Gentry 1640–1790* (Cambridge, 1983), p. 11.
14. Quoted in Benedict Anderson, *Imagined Communities: Reflections on the Origin and Spread of Nationalism* (1991 edn), p. x.
15. See R.A. Houston, *Scottish Literacy and the Scottish Identity* (Cambridge, 1985).
16. D.J. Withrington and I.R. Grant (eds), *The Statistical Account of Scotland 1791–1799* (20 vols, Ilkley, 1975–83), III, p. 491.
17. G.L. Gomme (ed.), *The Gentleman's Magazine Library* (30 vols, 1883–1905), I, p. 20.
18. *John Clare's Autobiographical Writings*, ed. Eric Robinson (Oxford, 1983), p. 58.
19. Peter Sahlins, 'National frontiers revisited: France's boundaries since the seventeenth century', *American Historical Review* 95 (1990), p. 1435.
20. Quoted in Peter Furtado, 'National pride in seventeenth-century England', in Raphael Samuel (ed.), *Patriotism: The Making and Unmaking of British National Identity* (3 vols, 1989), I, p. 50.
21. See John Bossy, *The English Catholic Community, 1570–1850* (1975), an excellent survey which fails, however, to come to grips with the extent of anti-Catholicism. On Welsh anti-Catholicism, see Geraint H. Jenkins, *Literature, Religion and Society in Wales, 1660–1730* (Cardiff, 1978). As yet, little work has been done on the very similar prejudices existing in Scotland, but see Robert Kent Donovan, *No Popery and Radicalism: Opposition to Roman Catholic Relief in Scotland, 1778–1782* (New York, 1987).
22. Geoffrey Holmes, *The Trial of Doctor Sacheverell* (1973), p. 35.
23. See David Cressy, *Bonfires and Bells: National Memory and the Protestant Calendar in Elizabethan and Stuart England* (1989). Despite its title, this book also contains references to Wales. My research student, James Caudle, is currently writing his dissertation on the importance of the Protestant calendar of commemoration throughout Great Britain as a whole in the eighteenth century.
24. William Keeling, *Liturgiae Britannicae* (Cambridge, 1851), p. 398.
25. Quoted in E.J. Hobsbawm, *Nations and Nationalism since 1780: Programme, Myth, Reality* (Cambridge, 1990), p. 12.
26. This and the next paragraph are based on Bernard Capp, *Astrology and the Popular Press: English Almanacs 1500–1800* (1979).
27. *Ibid.*, p. 245.
28. *Literature, Religion and Society in Wales*, p. 47.
29. On this, see Colin Haydon, 'Anti-Catholicism in eighteenth century England c.1714–c.1780', Oxford University D.Phil. dissertation, 1985.
30. See, for example, Defoe's comments on the easy-going relationship between Protestants and Catholics in Holy-well

in Flintshire in the 1720s, *A Tour Through the Whole Island of Great Britain*, ed. P.N. Furbank, W.R. Owens and A.J. Coulson (New Haven and London, 1991), p. 199.

31. For a graphic example of this kind of wartime persecution, see Haydon, 'Anti-Catholicism in eighteenth century England', p. 199.
32. *Ibid.*, p. 55.
33. 'Religion and national identity in nineteenth-century Wales and Scotland', in Stuart Mews (ed.), *Religion and National Identity* (Oxford, 1992), p. 502.
34. William J. Callahan and David Higgs (eds), *Church and Society in Catholic Europe of the Eighteenth Century* (Cambridge, 1979).
35. Quoted in Jeremy Black, 'The challenge of autocracy: the British press in the 1730's, *Studi Settecenteschi* (1982–3), p. 113.
36. Samuel Chandler, *Plain Reasons for Being a Protestant* (1735), pp. 63–4. The most lucid survey of the Jacobite threat is Bruce Lenman, *The Jacobite Risings in Britain 1689–1746* (1980).
37. See Kenneth Bourne, *The Foreign Policy of Victorian England* (1970).
38. Gerald Newman, *The Rise of English Nationalism: A Cultural History 1740–1830* (1987).
39. On this, Katharine R. Firth, *The Apocalyptic Tradition in Reformation Britain 1530–1645* (Oxford, 1979) should be read alongside William Haller's dated but still valuable *The Elect Nation: The Meaning and Relevance of Foxe's Book of Martyrs* (New York, 1963).
40. *The Book of Martyrs: containing an account of the sufferings and death of the Protestants in the reign of Queen Mary the first* (1732), preface.
41. *Ibid.*, pp. 723–4.
42. *The Pilgrim's Progress from this World to that which is to come*, ed. J.B. Wharey and R. Sharrock (Oxford, 1960), p. 65.
43. Christopher Hill, *A Turbulent, Seditious, and Factious People: John Bunyan and his Church* (Oxford, 1988); E.P. Thompson, *The Making of the English Working Class* (1965), pp. 26–54.
44. See Paul Fussell, *The Great War and Modern Memory* (Oxford, 1975), pp. 137–44. There were also more strident expressions of Protestant identity on the British side during the First World War. Some of the Ulster regiments reputedly went into battle against the Germans to the cry of 'Death to the Pope'.
45. On Dunkirk and its legend, see Nicholas Harman, *Dunkirk, the Patriotic Myth* (New York, 1980); Russell Plummer, *The Ships that Saved an Army: A Comprehensive Record of the 1300 'little ships' of Dunkirk* (Wellingborough, 1990).
46. For Protestant nationalism in Sweden and Holland, see Michael Roberts, 'The Swedish church', *Sweden's Age of Greatness* (1973); Simon Schama, *The Embarrassment of Riches: An Interpretation of Dutch Culture in the Golden Age* (Berkeley and Los Angeles, 1988), pp. 1–125. See also the very similar coming together of religion and identity across the Atlantic: Nathan O. Hatch, *The Sacred Cause of Liberty: Republican Thought and the Millenium in Revolutionary New England* (New Haven and London, 1977).
47. *Blake: The Complete Poems*, ed. W.H. Stevenson (2nd edn, 1989), pp. 491–2. Firth, *Apocalyptic Tradition*, pp. 109 *et seq*.
48. Quoted in William Donaldson, *The Jacobite Song: Political Myth and National Identity* (Aberdeen, 1988), p. 45 (my emphasis); Bonamy Dobree, 'The theme of patriotism in the poetry of the early eighteenth century', *Proceedings of the British Academy* xxxv (1949), p. 52.
49. Adam Ferguson, *A Sermon Preached in the Erse Language to His Majesty's First Highland Regiment of Foot* (1746); Alexander Webster, *The Substance of Two Sermons* (1746). I owe these references to the assiduous researches of James Caudle.
50. Haydon, 'Anti-Catholicism in eighteenth century England', p. 199.
51. I owe much of the following paragraph to the work of Robert Forbes of Yale University.
52. Christopher Hogwood, *Handel* (1984), p. 251 and *passim*.
53. *Tour Through the Whole Island of Great Britain*, p. 157.
54. For this interpretation, from two very different political perspectives, see Edward Thompson's *Whigs and Hunters: The Origin of the Black Act* (1975) and J.C.D. Clark, *English Society 1688–1832* (1985), pp. 42–118.

55. Ronald Paulson, *Hogarth: His Life, Art and Times* (2 vols, New Haven and London, 1971), II, pp. 75–8.
56. Quoted in Black, 'Challenge of autocracy', p. 107.
57. Ralph A. Griffin in *This Royal Throne of Kings, this Sceptr'd Isle: The English Realm and Nation in the Later Middle Ages* (Swansea, 1983) detects similar *English* prejudices during the Hundred Years War.
58. Quoted in Jeremy Black, *The British and the Grand Tour* (1985), p. 174; for the Bristol slogan: Linda Colley, *In Defiance of Oligarchy: The Tory Party 1714–60* (1982), p. 155.
59. Quoted in Black, *British and the Grand Tour*, pp. 193–4.
60. E.g., Clark, *English Society*, *passim*. Using the term '*ancien régime*' to describe even Continental Europe before 1789 is anachronistic, since it was applied in this sense only retrospectively by Alexis de Tocqueville and others. Since – as Simon Schama comments – it carries a 'heavy semantic freight of obsolescence' and is therefore increasingly being discarded by historians of pre-Revolutionary France, it is not clear why British historians should want to adopt it.
61. Fernand Braudel, *The Identity of France*. II: *People and Production* (New York, 1990), pp. 371–84. For the position in Britain, see K.E. Wrightson, 'Kindred adjoining kingdoms: an English perspective on the social and economic history of early modern Scotland', in R.A. Houston and I.D. Whyte (eds), *Scottish Society 1500–1800* (Cambridge, 1989), p. 255. But cf. Roger Wells, *Wretched Faces: Famine in Wartime England 1793–1801* (Gloucester, 1988).
62. I am indebted for this point to an unpublished paper by E.A. Wrigley, 'Society and the economy in the eighteenth century'.
63. See Eric Pawson, *Transport and Economy: The Turnpike Roads of Eighteenth-Century Britain* (1977), pp. 134–69.
64. T. Hunter (ed.), *Extracts from the Records of the Convention of the Royal Burghs of Scotland 1738–59* (Edinburgh, 1915), p. 256; *Bibliography Lindesiana: Catalogue of English Broadsides 1505–1897* (Aberdeen, 1898), p. 302.
65. Jan de Vries, *European Urbanization, 1500–1800* (1984).
66. P.J. Corfield, *The Impact of English Towns 1700–1800* (Oxford, 1982); Peter Clark (ed.), *The Transformation of English Provincial Towns* (1984); Ian H. Adam, *The Making of Urban Scotland* (1978).
66. Wrigley, 'Society and the economy'; R. Houston, 'Geographical mobility in Scotland, 1652–1811: the evidence of testimonials', *Journal of Historical Geography* 11 (1985).
68. John Chamberlayne, *Magnae Britanniae Notitia: or, the present state of Great Britain* (1716), p. 362.
69. I am grateful to A.D. Sterenberg of the Eighteenth Century Short Title Catalogue for this information.
70. G.A. Cranfield, *The Development of the Provincial Newspaper* (Oxford, 1962); M.E. Craig, *The Scottish Periodical Press, 1750–89* (Edinburgh, 1931). Much more work needs to be done on the Scottish newspaper, periodical and religious press which has been neglected in favour of the far less widely distributed works of the luminaries of the Scottish Enlightenment.
71. E.g., *Scots Magazine* 1 (1739), pp. 76–8, 486, 603.
72. Colley, *In Defiance of Oligarchy*, p. 325n. 80.
73. *Literature, Religion and Society in Wales*, p. 54.
74. *Scotland's Opposition to the Popish Bill: A Collection of All the Declarations and Resolutions* (Edinburgh, 1780), p. 191; John and Dorothea Teague, *Where Duty Calls Me: The Experiences of William Green of Lutterworth in the Napoleonic Wars* (West Wickham, 1975), p. 47.
75. Quoted in *The Collected Essays of Asa Briggs*. II: *Images, Problems, Standpoints, Forecasts* (Brighton, 1985), p. v.
76. Percy A. Scholes, *God Save the Queen! The History and Romance of the World's First National Anthem* (1954).
77. See *infra*, p. 209.
78. Paulson, *Hogarth*, II, p. 90.
79. E.N. Williams, *The Eighteenth-Century Constitution* (Cambridge, 1960), p. 56.
80. Graham C. Gibbs, 'English attitudes towards Hanover and the Hanoverian Succession in the first half of the eighteenth century', in Adolf M. Birke and Kurt Kluxen (eds.), *England und Hannover* (Munich, 1986), p. 37; and see Ragnhild Hatton, *George I. Elector and*

King (1978).

81. He went on to add: 'As well might we say that a ship is built, and loaded, and manned for the sake of any particular pilot, instead of acknowledging that the pilot is made for the sake of the ship, her lading, and her crew, who are always the owners in the political vessel; as to say that kingdoms were instituted for kings, not kings for kingdoms', *The Works of Lord Bolingbroke* (4 vols, Philadelphia, 1841), II, p. 380.
82. Richard Willis, *The Way to Stable and Quiet Times: A Sermon Preached before the King* (1715), p. 25.
83. On this, see Donaldson, *The Jacobite Song*, and Paul Kleber Monod, *Jacobitism and the English People, 1688–1788* (Cambridge, 1989).
84. I am indebted here to an unpublished paper by Professor Lois G. Schwoerer.
85. L.G. Wickham Legg, *English Coronation Records* (1901), p. xxx.
86. I am indebted here to the work of James Caudle.
87. John James Caesar, *A Thanksgiving Sermon Preached the First Sunday after the Landing of his Majesty* (1714), p. 6.
88. On England and Wales, the classic account is W.A. Speck's *Tory and Whig: The Struggle in the Constituencies, 1701–15* (1970). The eighteenth-century Scottish electoral system was much narrower and still perplexes historians.
89. See my *Namier* (1989), p. 86.
90. *Ibid.*, p. 87.
91. A.R. Myers, *Parliaments and Estates in Europe to 1789* (1975), *passim*.
92. W. Charles Townsend, *Memoirs of the House of Commons, from the Convention Parliament of 1688–9 to 1832* (2 vols, 1844), II, p. 87; T.I. Jeffreys Jones, *Acts of Parliament concerning Wales 1714–1901* (Cardiff, 1959).
93. *The Public General Statutes Affecting Scotland 1707–1847* (3 vols, Edinburgh, 1987).
94. Frank O'Gorman, *Voters, Patrons and Parties: The Unreformed Electorate of Hanoverian England, 1734–1832* (Oxford, 1989), p. 182.
95. *Ibid.*, *passim*.
96. Jacob M. Price, 'The excise affair revisited' in Stephen Baxter (ed.), *England's Rise to Greatness 1660–1773* (1983), p. 293.
97. David Neave, 'Anti-militia riots in Lincolnshire, 1757 and 1796', *Lincolnshire History and Archaeology* 11 (1976), p. 26 (my emphasis).
98. John Brewer, *The Sinews of Power: War, Money and the English State, 1688–1783* (1989), pp. 7–14.

2 PROFITS

1. Miroslav Hroch, *Social Preconditions of National Revival in Europe*, trans. Ben Fowkes (Cambridge, 1985), p. 12.
2. Jeremy Black, *Culloden and the '45* (Stroud, Glos., 1990), preface.
3. Thompson, *Whigs and Hunters: The Origin of the Black Act* (1975), *passim*; Bruce Lenman, *Jacobite Risings in Britain 1689–1746* (1980), p. 231.
4. F.J. McLynn, *France and the Jacobite Rising of 1745* (Edinburgh, 1981), p. 6.
5. E.g., Ian and Kathleen Whyte, *On the Trail of the Jacobites* (1990).
6. Julian Hoppit, *Risk and Failure in English Business, 1700–1800* (Cambridge, 1987), p. 4. We know much more about the higher echelons of the trading community in Scotland and England at this time than about their far more numerous poorer brethren or about Welsh commercial life in general. See, for instance, the following excellent studies: Paul Langford, *A Polite and Commercial People: England 1727–1783* (Oxford, 1989); Peter Earle, *The Making of the English Middle Class: Business, Society and Family Life in London 1660–1730* (1989); T.M. Devine, *The Tobacco Lords: A Study of the Tobacco Merchants of Glasgow and their Trading Activities, c.1740–90* (Edinburgh, 1990 edn).
7. Ruth McClure, *Coram's Children* (New Haven and London, 1981); for the significance of this painting, see Ellis Waterhouse, *Painting in Britain 1530 to 1790* (4th edn, 1978), p. 174.
8. Ronald Paulson, *Hogarth: His Life, Art and Times* (2 vols, New Haven and London, 1971), II, pp. 35–42.
9. R.M. Nichols and F.A. Wray, *A History of the Foundling Hospital* (1935), pp. 249–64.
10. *Magnae Britanniae Notitia: Or, the Present State of Great Britain* (1718), p. 33; *ibid.* (1755), p. 42.
11. John McVeagh, *Tradefull Merchants* (1981), p. 65.
12. *Parl. Hist.*, XI, pp. 7, 19.

13. T.K. Meier, *Defoe and the Defense of Commerce* (Victoria, B.C., 1987), p. 15.
14. Preface to the first volume; J.R. Raven, 'English popular literature and the image of business 1760–1790', Cambridge University Ph.D. dissertation, 1985, (2 vols), II, unpaginated.
15. W.D. Rubinstein, *Men of Property* (New Brunswick, 1981).
16. Lawrence Stone and Jeanne C. Fawtier Stone, *An Open Elite?: England 1540–1880* (Oxford, 1984), pp. 211–55.
17. Marie Peters, *Pitt and Popularity* (Oxford, 1980), p. 111.
18. David Cannadine, *The Decline and Fall of the British Aristocracy* (New Haven and London, 1990), pp. 8–25.
19. Neil McKendrick, '"Gentlemen and players" revisited: the gentlemanly ideal, the business ideal and the professional ideal in English literary culture', in N. McKendrick and R.B. Outhwaite (eds), *Business Life and Public Policy* (1986); and see McVeagh, *Tradefull Merchants*, pp. 80 *et seq.*
20. J.G. Links, *Canaletto and his Patrons* (1977).
21. E.A. Wrigley, 'A simple model of London's importance in changing English society and economy, 1650–1750', *Past & Present* 37 (1967); and Earle, *Making of the English Middle Class*, *passim*.
22. Paul Langford, *Public Life and the Propertied Englishman, 1689–1798* (Oxford, 1991), p. 194.
23. The best description is still Defoe's; see his *Tour Through the Whole Island of Great Britain*, pp. 133–65.
24. P.G.M. Dickson, *The Financial Revolution in England* (1967), *passim*.
25. J.V. Beckett and Michael Turner, 'Taxation and economic growth in eighteenth-century England', *Economic History Review*, 2nd series, 43 (1990).
26. John Brewer, *The Sinews of Power: War, Money and the English State, 1688–1783* (1989), pp. 29–63.
27. Quoted in P.K. O'Brien and S.L. Engerman, 'Exports and the growth of the British economy from the Glorious Revolution to the Peace of Amiens', in B. Solow and S.L. Engerman (eds), *Slavery and the Rise of the Atlantic System* (Cambridge, 1991). I am indebted to Professor O'Brien for being able to see this splendid piece of re-revisionism before it was published. N.A.M. Rodger, *The Wooden World: An Anatomy of the Georgian Navy* (1986), pp. 145–82.
28. On this, see Kathleen Wilson, 'Empire, trade and popular politics in mid-Hanoverian Britain: The case of Admiral Vernon', *Past & Present* 121 (1988); Nicholas Rogers, *Whigs and Cities: Popular Politics in the Age of Walpole and Pitt* (Oxford, 1989).
29. Julian Hoppit, 'The use and abuse of credit in eighteenth-century England', in McKendrick and Outhwaite, *Business Life and Public Policy*. The use of credit in Wales and Scotland has been much less investigated, but see Charles Munn's suggestion that in the latter country there was a 'large, and as yet unresearched, area of private credit between individuals': *The Scottish Provincial Banking Companies* (Edinburgh, 1981), p. 5.
30. Earle, *Making of the English Middle Class*, p. 412.
31. Brewer, *Sinews of Power*, p. 186.
32. Quoted in Dickson, *Financial Revolution*, p. xxi.
33. See, for example, the papers of Thomas Carew, a quite unimportant Tory MP, in the Somerset Record Office.
34. T. Hunter (ed.), *Extracts from the Records of the Convention of the Royal Burghs of Scotland 1738–59* (Edinburgh, 1915), *passim*.
35. This and the next two paragraphs are heavily indebted to O'Brien and Engerman, 'Exports and the growth of the British economy'.
36. Denys Forrest, *Tea for the British: The Social and Economic History of a Famous Trade* (1973), p. 284.
37. Patrick Crowhurst, *The Defence of British Trade 1689–1815* (1977), p. 157.
38. Jacob M. Price, 'What did merchants do? Reflections on British overseas trade, 1660–1790', *Journal of Economic History* 49 (1989), p. 276.
39. Forrest, *Tea for the British*, pp. 55–8.
40. Quoted in Virginia C. Kenny, *The Country House Ethos in English Literature 1688–1750: Themes of Personal Retreat and National Expansion* (New York, 1984), p. 68.
41. The quotation is from Burke's memorial to Pitt the Elder, Peters, *Pitt and Popularity*, p. vi.
42. Crowhurst, *Defence of British Trade*,

pp. 15–80.

43. Benjamin Newton, *Another Dissertation on the Mutual Support of Trade and Civil Liberty* (1756), p. 13. For the European-wide debate at this time on commerce and public spirit, see Albert O. Hirschman, *The Passions and the Interests: Political Arguments for Capitalism before its Triumph* (Princeton, 1977).
44. See Lenman, *Jacobite Risings in Britain.*
45. In the sense that many of the keenest chroniclers of Jacobitism in the twentieth century have come from firmly Scottish Nationalist, Roman Catholic or High Tory backgrounds. This is scarcely surprising since anti-Unionist Scots, Catholics, and High Tories – not Tories in general – were at the heart of active Jacobitism in the eighteenth century.
46. J.C.D. Clark, *English Society 1688–1832* (1985), p. 173.
47. John Childs, *The Army, James II and the Glorious Revolution* (Manchester, 1980), p. 175, and his *The British Army of William III, 1689–1702* (Manchester, 1987), p. 6.
48. Brewer, *Sinews of Power*, pp. 29–63; J.A. Houlding, *Fit for Service: The Training of the British Army 1715–1795* (Oxford, 1981).
49. See the guidebook *House of Dun: Tour of the House and History*, published by the National Trust for Scotland; but, better still, visit the house.
50. I am indebted for this estimate to my colleague at Yale, David Underdown.
51. Quoted in Paul Kleber Monod, *Jacobitism and the English People, 1688–1788* (Cambridge, 1989), p. 266. Though overly sympathetic to the Stuart cause, this book provides a learned and imaginative reconstruction of what might be styled 'passive' Jacobitism. No such work yet exists for Scotland, but Walter Scott gives a fictional version of the same kind of reluctant quietism in *Waverley* (1814) where the eponymous hero rejects (at least initially) the temptation to revolt: 'Whatever were the original rights of the Stuarts, calm reflection told him that . . . since that period [1688] four monarchs had ruled in peace and glory over Britain, sustaining and exalting the character of the nation abroad, and its liberties at home. *Reason asked, was it worth while to disturb a government so long settled and established, and to plunge a kingdom into the miseries of civil war . . . ?*' (my italics). The first part of this quotation reflects Scott's own politics, but the last sentence captures a much more widespread response in Scotland, especially by 1745. I owe this reference to Cyrus Vakil of Yale University.
52. For this, see Monod, *Jacobitism and the English People*, and William Donaldson, *The Jacobite Song: Political Myth and National Identity* (Aberdeen, 1988).
53. *A Collection of State Songs, Poems etc. that have been published since the Rebellion* (1716), p. 137.
54. Olwen H. Hufton, *The Poor of Eighteenth-Century France 1750–1789* (Oxford, 1974), p. 367.
55. When a Stockport man did fire at and kill a Jacobite soldier, the Highlanders burned his cowhouse and barn, killed his cattle and seized his father in retaliation: F.J. McLynn, *The Jacobite Army in England, 1745* (Edinburgh, 1983), p. 147.
56. *Ibid.*, p. 145.
57. McLynn, *France and the Jacobite Rising of 1745.*
58. For French commercial strength at this time, see Ralph Davis, *Aleppo and Devonshire Square* (1967), p. 28; K.N. Chaudhuri, *The Trading World of Asia and the English East India Company 1660–1760* (Cambridge, 1978), pp. 223–5; William Doyle, *The Old European Order 1660–1800* (Oxford, 1978), pp. 62–70; James C. Riley, *The Seven Years War and the Old Regime in France* (Princeton, 1986), pp. 105–10.
59. Jeremy Black, *Natural and Necessary Enemies: Anglo-French Relations in the Eighteenth Century* (1986), pp. 146–7.
60. F.J. McLynn, *Charles Edward Stuart* (1988).
61. W.A. Speck, *The Butcher: The Duke of Cumberland and the Suppression of the '45* (Oxford, 1981), pp. 27–52.
62. *Ibid.*, p. 62; P.R.O., S.P. 36/74/3.
63. See A. Livingstone, C.W.H. Aikman, and B.S. Hart (eds), *Muster Roll of Prince Charles Edward Stuart's Army 1745–46* (Aberdeen, 1984).
64. R. Garnett, 'Correspondence of Archbishop Herring and Lord Hardwicke during the rebellion of 1745', *English Historical Review* 19 (1904),

p. 542.
65. See Appendix 1.
66. Speck, *The Butcher*, pp. 72 and 211.
67. P.R.O., S.P. 36/74/24.
68. *Report from the Committee of the Guildhall Subscription Towards the Relief, Support, and Encouragement of the Soldiers Employed in Suppressing the Rebellion* (1747), p. 3.
69. Monod, *Jacobitism and the English People*, pp. 336–41.
70. Vanessa S. Doe (ed.), *The Diary of James Clegg of Chapel en le Frith 1708–55* (3 vols, Derby, 1978–81), II, p. 559.
71. P.R.O., S.P. 36/71/17; S.P. 36/74, Part II, fol. 57.
72. Lenman, *Jacobite Risings in Britain*, p. 257.
73. *Ibid.*, Garnett, 'Correspondence of Archbishop Herring', p. 729.
74. T.C. Smout, 'The burgh of Montrose and the Union of 1707: a document', *Scottish Historical Review* 182 (1987), pp. 103–4; and see Speck, *The Butcher*, p. 185.
75. Lenman, *Jacobite Risings in Britain*, pp. 101–2, 216–18; I am also indebted here to information from Paul Monod.
76. All historians agree that by the 1740s, the Union was paying economic dividends as far as Scotland was concerned: Christopher A. Whatley, 'Economic causes and consequences of the Union of 1707: a survey', *Scottish Historical Review* 68 (1989).
77. P.R.O., S.P. 36/70/107.
78. *Boswell's Life of Johnson*, ed. G.B. Hill and L.F. Powell (6 vols, Oxford, 1934), III, pp. 156–7. I owe this reference to James Caudle.
79. A.J. Youngson, *The Prince and the Pretender: A Study in the Writing of History* (1985), p. 115.
80. See McLynn, *France and the Jacobite Rising*.
81. See, for example, Rosalind Mitchison (ed.), *The Roots of Nationalism: Studies in Northern Europe* (Edinburgh, 1980); C. Prignitz, *Vaterlandsliebe und Freiheit. Deutscher Patriotismus von 1750 bis 1850* (Wiesbaden, 1981); and the essays in Otto Dann and John Dinwiddy (eds), *Nationalism in the Age of the French Revolution* (1988). For the Ossian phenomenon, see Fiona J. Stafford, 'The sublime savage: a study of James Macpherson and the poems of Ossian in relation to the cultural context in Scotland in the 1750s and 1760s', Oxford University D.Phil. dissertation, 1986.
82. Paulson, *Hogarth*, II, pp. 90–2.
83. David Owen, *English Philanthropy 1660–1960* (1965), p. 50; James Stephen Taylor, 'Philanthropy and empire: Jonas Hanway and the infant poor of London', *Eighteenth-Century Studies* 12 (1978–9).
84. John Brown, *An Estimate of the Manners and Principles of the Times* (2nd edn, 1757), p. 111.
85. T.D. Kendrick, *The Lisbon Earthquake* (1956).
86. Brown, *Estimate of the Manners*, p. 92; and see my 'The apotheosis of George III: loyalty, royalty and the British nation 1760–1820', *Past & Present* 102 (1984), p. 99.
87. Gerald Newman, *The Rise of English Nationalism: A Cultural History 1740–1830* (1987), especially pp. 63–122.
88. *Ibid.*, p. 71.
89. For this, see John Brewer, 'Clubs, commercialization and politics', in Neil McKendrick, John Brewer and J.H. Plumb, *The Birth of a Consumer Society: The Commercialization of Eighteenth-Century England* (1982), pp. 231–62; and Kathleen Wilson, 'Urban culture and political activism in Hanoverian England: the emergence of voluntary hospitals', in Eckhart Hellmuth (ed.), *The Transformation of Political Culture: England and Germany in the Late Eighteenth Century* (Oxford, 1990), pp. 165–84.
90. See Isaac Hunt, 'Some account of the laudable institution of the society of Antigallicans', in *Sermons on Public Occasions* (1781).
91. John Free, *A Sermon preached at St. John's, in Southwark . . . before the laudable and loyal associations of Anti-Gallicans* (1756), pp. 18 *et seq.*, and see his *An Essay Towards an History of the English Tongue* (1749), and *The Danger Attending an Enlightened and Free People* (1753), where he makes similar claims for a common Saxon ethnicity.
92. John Butley, *A Sermon preached at the church of Greenwich . . . before the laudable association of Antigallicans* (1754), pp. 17–18.
93. D.G.C. Allan, *William Shipley: Founder of the Royal Society of Arts* (1979 repr.);

Derek Hudson and Kenneth W. Luckhurst, *The Royal Society of Arts 1754–1954* (1954).

94. Hudson and Luckhurst, *Royal Society of Arts*, pp. 1–89.
95. *Ibid.*, p. 87.
96. Iain Pears, *The Discovery of Painting: The Growth of Interest in the Arts in England, 1680–1768* (New Haven and London, 1988), pp. 127–9.
97. Allan, *William Shipley*, pp. 6–7.
98. James Stephen Taylor, *Jonas Hanway: Founder of the Marine Society* (1985), pp. 67–102.
99. Jonas Hanway, *Letter to the Marine Society* (2nd edn, 1758), p. 4.
100. Taylor, *Jonas Hanway*, p. 75.
101. This is very much Gerald Newman's argument in *The Rise of English Nationalism, passim.* Much earlier, Jürgen Habermas made the same point with regard to social developments in Western Europe as a whole at this time. I have found an unpublished paper by Geoff Eley, 'Nations, publics, and political cultures: placing Habermas in the nineteenth century', of great value here.
102. William Thornton, *The Counterpoise. Being Thoughts on a Militia and a Standing Army* (1752), preface.
103. Hanway, *Letter to the Marine Society*.
104. D.G.C. Allan, 'The Society of Arts and government, 1754–1800', *Eighteenth-Century Studies* 7 (1973–4).
105. J.B. Harley, 'The Society of Arts and the surveys of English counties 1759–1809', *Journal of the Royal Society of Arts* 112 (1963–4).
106. 'A dissertation on the progress of agriculture, arts and commerce in that part of Great Britain called England', Royal Society of Arts, MS A5/7.
107. Hanway, *Letter to the Marine Society*, p. iv.
108. Allan, *William Shipley*, p. 44.
109. D.G.C. Allan, 'The Society for the Encouragement of Arts, Manufactures and Commerce: organization, membership and objectives in the first three decades 1755–84', London University Ph.D. dissertation, 1979, p. 282; *A List of the Subscribers for the Benefit of the British Troops* (1760).
110. Allan, 'Society for the Encouragement of Arts', p. 290.
111. *List of the Subscribers for the Benefit of the British Troops* compared with *A Complete Guide to All Persons who have any Trade or Concern with the City of London* (1757).
112. Helena Hayward, *Thomas Johnson and the English Rococo* (1964), pp. 23–5.
113. *Rococo: Art and Design in Hogarth's England*, catalogue of an exhibition at the Victoria and Albert Museum, 1984, pp. 48–9.
114. *List of the Subscribers for the Benefit of the British Troops*, p. 47.
115. Taylor, *Jonas Hanway, passim.*
116. Jonas Hanway, *Letter to the Encouragers of Practical Public-Love* (1758), p. 57.
117. Taylor, *Jonas Hanway*, p. 72.
118. *Monitor*, 11 September 1762.
119. Brewer, 'Clubs, commercialization and politics', p. 232.

3 PERIPHERIES

1. *Parl. Hist.*, XVII, p. 147; Ronald Hyam, 'Imperial interests and the Peace of Paris', in Hyam and Ged Martin (eds) *Reappraisals in British Imperial History* (1975).
2. Patricia B. Craddock, *Young Edward Gibbon: Gentleman of Letters* (1982), pp. 198 *et seq.*
3. Jack P. Greene, *Peripheries and Center: Constitutional Development in the Extended Polities of the British Empire and the United States, 1607–1788* (1986), pp. 2–3. And see P.J. Marshall, *A Free Though Conquering People: Britain and Asia in the Eighteenth Century* (1981).
4. Quoted in J.P. Thomas, 'The British empire and the press, 1763–1774', Oxford University D.Phil. dissertation, 1982, pp. 321–2.
5. Though there were schemes for a French invasion which proved abortive, see Eveline Cruickshanks (ed.), *Ideology and Conspiracy: Aspects of Jacobitism, 1689–1759* (Edinburgh, 1982).
6. Basil Williams, *Life of William Pitt* (2 vols, 1913), I, p. 294. Limited numbers of Highlanders had been recruited before 1745 to serve in the Black Watch regiment.
7. See *Scots Magazine* 25 (1763), pp. 473–86, 533.
8. See *Political and Personal Satires*, IV, print no. 4071.
9. See Alexander Murdoch, 'Lord Bute, James Stuart Mackenzie, and the government of Scotland', in Karl

W. Schweizer (ed.), *Lord Bute: Essays in Reinterpretation* (Leicester, 1988), p. 139.

10. A new biography of Wilkes is badly needed. Raymond Postgate's, *That Devil Wilkes* (1930) is the best of the old accounts, while George Rudé, *Wilkes and Liberty* (Oxford, 1962) and John Brewer, *Party Ideology and Popular Politics at the Accession of George III* (Cambridge, 1976) provide splendid analyses of his supporters and tactics.
11. V.E. Lloyd Hart, *John Wilkes and the Foundling Hospital at Aylesbury, 1759–1768* (Aylesbury, 1979).
12. *The Speeches of John Wilkes* (2 vols, 1777), I, pp. 57–67.
13. Election manifesto in 1784, B.L., Add. MS. 30866, fol. 54.
14. Rudé, *Wilkes and Liberty*, p. 44.
15. *Memoirs of the Life of Sir Samuel Romilly*, (3 vols, 1840), I, p. 84; John Wilkes, *The History of England from the Revolution to the Accession of the Brunswick Line* (1768).
16. See Hugh Cunningham, 'The language of patriotism', in Raphael Samuel, *Patriotism: The Making and Unmaking of British National Identity* (3 vols, 1989), I, pp. 57–89.
17. See my *In Defiance of Oligarchy: The Tory Party 1714–60* (Cambridge, 1982); Brewer, *Party Ideology and Popular Politics*, p. 23–136.
18. Eg. *Political and Personal Satires*, IV, print no. 4063.
19. Rudé, *Wilkes and Liberty*, p. 69; Brewer, *Party Ideology and Popular Politics*, p. 175.
20. Rudé, *Wilkes and Liberty*, pp. 136–7.
21. Brewer, *Party Ideology and Popular Politics*, p. 190.
22. I am indebted for this information to Gareth Stedman Jones.
23. *Political and Personal Satires*, IV, print no. 4028.
24. *Ibid.*, print nos 4020, 4033.
25. *North Briton*, 5 June 1762; Alexander Stephens, *Memoirs of John Horne Tooke* (2 vols, 1813), I, p. 61.
26. *North Briton*, 25 June 1763.
27. *Freeholder's Magazine*, October 1769; *London Evening Post*, 23/25 May 1780.
28. *The Literary Life of the Late Thomas Pennant, Esq., By Himself* (1793), p. 13.
29. See William Grant and David D. Murison (eds), *The Scottish National Dictionary* (10 vols, 1931–76), VIII, p. 236.
30. This and the next paragraph are based on Alexander Murdoch, '"Beating the Lieges": The military riot at Ravenshaugh toll on 5 October 1760', *Transactions of the East Lothian Antiquarian and Field Naturalists' Society* 17 (1982).
31. See Byron Frank Jewell, 'The legislation relating to Scotland after the Forty-Five', University of North Carolina Ph.D. dissertation, 1975.
32. See Annette M. Smith, *Jacobite Estates of the Forty Five* (Edinburgh, 1982).
33. *Parl. Hist.*, XIV, p. 728.
34. *H.M.C.* Polwarth V, pp. 236–7.
35. *A Prophecy of Famine* (1763). This was a fiercely anti-Scottish piece by John Wilkes's ally Charles Churchill.
36. The belief that Scottish Highlanders were unusually well endowed sexually was an old one in the Lowlands and in England, reflecting the fact that – like blacks in the American south – they were seen as both threatening and primitive.
37. See, for example, *Political and Personal Satires*, IV, prints nos 3825, 3848, 3852, and 3939.
38. *Ibid.*, print no. 3849.
39. J.O. Bartley, *Teague, Shenkin and Sawney: Being an Historical Study of the Earliest Irish, Welsh and Scottish Characters in English Plays* (Cork, 1954) p. 228.
40. 'Scotland in the 17th and 18th centuries – a satellite economy?', in Ståle Dyrvik, Knut Mykland and Jan Oldervoll (eds), *The Satellite State in the 17th and 18th Centuries* (Bergen, Norway, 1979), p. 18.
41. See R.A. Houston and I.D. Whyte (eds), *Scottish Society, 1500–1800* (Cambridge, 1989); and T.C. Smout's classic *A History of the Scottish People 1560–1830* (2nd edn, 1970).
42. A.J. Youngson, *The Making of Classical Edinburgh 1750–1840* (Edinburgh, 1966), *passim*.
43. Manuscript comment by John Wilkes in the margins of his copy of *The History of the Late Minority* (1766), B.L., G. 13453.
44. Derek A. Dow, *The Influence of Scottish Medicine: An Historical Assessment of Its International Impact* (Carnforth, 1988), p. 39.
45. See Janet Adam Smith 'Some eighteenth-century ideas of Scotland', in N.T. Phillipson and R. Mitchison (eds), *Scotland in the Age of Improvement* (Edinburgh, 1970); Gerald Newman, *The Rise of English Nationalism: A*

Cultural History 1740–1830 (New York, 1987), p. 153.
46. The table is based on the biographies in Lewis Namier and John Brooke (eds), *The History of Parliament: The House of Commons, 1754–1790* (3 vols, 1964).
47. *Ibid.*, II, pp. 229–30.
48. *Ibid.*, III, pp. 618–20.
49. *Ibid.*, III, pp. 237–40.
50. James Hayes, 'Scottish officers in the British army 1714–63', *Scottish Historical Review* 37 (1958).
51. *Dictionary of National Biography*, III, p. 828.
52. 'Our gentry are both poor and proud . . . and we can neither submit to the putting our sons to trades, nor afford to place them in the genteeler walk of commerce, nor to buy them commissions, so we send them to fight for their bread': *Scotch Modesty Displayed* (1778), p. 19. Scott is quoted in Janet Adam Smith, *John Buchan: A Biography* (Oxford, 1985), p. 13.
53. Bruce Lenman, *The Jacobite Clans of the Great Glen 1650–1784* (1984), pp. 177–212.
54. I owe this information to Alexander Murdoch.
55. P.E. Razzell, 'Social origins of officers in the Indian and British home army, 1758–1962', *British Journal of Sociology* 14 (1963); James G. Parker, 'Scottish enterprise in India, 1750–1914', in R.A. Cage (ed.), *The Scots Abroad: Labour, Capital, Enterprise, 1750–1914* (1985).
56. John Reddy, 'Warren Hastings: Scotland's benefactor', in Geoffrey Carnall and Colin Nicholson (eds), *The Impeachment of Warren Hastings* (Edinburgh, 1989).
57. See Clements R. Markham, *Narratives of the Mission of George Bogle to Tibet* (1876).
58. *Ibid.*
59. C. Duncan Rice, 'Archibald Dalzel, the Scottish intelligentsia and the problem of slavery', *Scottish Historical Review* 62 (1983), p. 124 and *passim*.
60. See Murdoch, 'Lord Bute, James Stuart Mackenzie, and the government of Scotland', in Schweizer, *Lord Bute*, for an illuminating discussion of this point.
61. Carnall and Nicholson, *Impeachment of Hastings*, p. 33.
62. The words of Wilkes's ally John Sawbridge, *Parl. Hist.*, XVIII, p. 1236.
63. Lenman, *The Jacobite Clans*, p. 204.
64. Namier and Brooke, *House of Commons*, II, p. 511; Carnall and Nicholson, *Impeachment of Hastings*, p. 54.
65. See Iris Butler, *The Eldest Brother: The Marquess Wellesley* (1973).
66. John Le Carré, *Smiley's People* (1980), p. 43.
67. See Kingsley Amis, *The James Bond Dossier* (1965).
68. I am indebted for this information to my colleague at Yale, Jules Prown.
69. David Fischer. *Albion's Seed: Four British Folkways in America* (Oxford, 1989).
70. See R.L. Schuyler, 'The rise of anti-imperialism in England', *Political Science Quarterly* 37 (1922).
71. See Robert W. Tucker and David C. Hendrickson, *The Fall of the First British Empire* (London, 1982).
72. I have benefited here from an unpublished paper by John Elliott, 'The role of the state in British and Spanish colonial America'.
73. Printed in Frederick Madden and David Fieldhouse (eds), *The Classical Period of the First British Empire 1689–1783* (1985), p. 270; Edmund Morgan, *Inventing the People: The Rise of Popular Sovereignty in England and America* (New York, 1988), pp. 122–48, 239–62.
74. See H.G. Koenigsberger, 'Composite states and representative institutions', *Historical Research* LXII (1989), pp. 147–53.
75. John Brooke, *King George III* (1972), p. 175.
76. See, for example, Peter Marshall, *Bristol and the American War of Independence* (Bristol, 1977); John Sainsbury, *Disaffected Patriots: London Supporters of Revolutionary America 1769–1782* (Gloucester, 1987).
77. Preface to *Annual Register* (1775).
78. These are printed in the *London Gazette* from 12/16 September 1775 to 9/12 March 1776.
79. The anti-war petitions are discussed most fully in James E. Bradley, *Popular Politics and the American Revolution in England* (Macon, Georgia, 1986); and see Sainsbury, *Disaffected Patriots*.
80. Fischer, *Albion's Seed*, pp. 13–205.
81. Bradley, *Popular Politics*, pp. 76, 204.
82. Fischer, *Albion's Seed*, pp. 219, 436–8.
83. *Middlesex Journal*, 29 April 1769.
84. See Owen Dudley Edwards and George Shepperson (eds), *Scotland, Europe and the American Revolution* (Edinburgh,

1976), p. 69 and *passim*.

85. Bernard Bailyn, *Voyagers to the West: A Passage in the Peopling of America on the Eve of the Revolution* (1987), p. 26; G. Murray Logan, *Scottish Highlanders and the American Revolution* (Halifax, Nova Scotia, 1976).
86. *London Gazette*, 21/25 November 1775.
87. *Ibid.*, 14/18 November 1775.
88. *Ibid.*, 16/20 January 1776, 14/18 November 1775.
89. 'Lord Bute, James Stuart Mackenzie, and the government of Scotland', in Schweizer, *Lord Bute*, p. 140.
90. *Speeches of John Wilkes*, II, p. 41.
91. See, for instance, the *Leeds Intelligencer*, 16 December 1777.
92. *The Analysis of Patriotism: or, an enquiry whether opposition to government, in the present state of affairs is consistent with the principles of a* PATRIOT (1778), pp. 36–7.
93. See my 'Radical patriotism in eighteenth-century England', in Samuel, *Patriotism*, I, pp. 169–87.
94. Common Hall, Book 8, entry for 6 December 1782, Corporation of London Record Office.
95. Notes by Vicar of Hanbury, 1 January 1779, Staffordshire Record Office, D 1528/1/4.
96. Though low-key criticism of Scottish ambition and success did continue, see *Political and Personal Satires*, VI, prints nos 7125, 7130, 7152, 7139 and 7280.
97. Frederick Madden and David Fieldhouse (eds), *Imperial Reconstruction, 1763–1840* (1987), p. 1.

4 DOMINANCE

1. *Annual Register* (1778), pp. 264–70.
2. Maurice Keen, *Chivalry* (New Haven and London, 1984), p. 237. For the cultural background to this neo-chivalry, see Mark Girouard, *The Return to Camelot: Chivalry and the English Gentleman* (New Haven and London, 1981).
3. Thomas Gray's 'Elegy written in a country churchyard', from Roger Lonsdale (ed.), *The Poems of Thomas Gray, William Collins, Oliver Goldsmith* (1969), pp. 123–4.
4. Paul Kennedy, *The Rise and Fall of the Great Powers* (1988), p. 105.
5. George Fasel, *Edmund Burke* (Boston, 1983), p. 82; Harvey C. Mansfield (ed.), *Selected Letters of Edmund Burke*, (1984), p. 331.
6. Quoted in John Cannon, *Aristocratic Century: The Peerage of Eighteenth-century England* (Cambridge, 1984), p. 166.
7. R.G. Thorne (ed.), *The History of Parliament: The House of Commons 1790–1820* (5 vols, 1986), I, p. 334.
8. *Ibid.*, III, p. 404.
9. *Ibid.*, I, pp. 331–2.
10. John Wade, 'The aristocracy', *The Extraordinary Black Book* (1832 edn.), p. 260.
11. Charles Pigott, *A Political Dictionary, Explaining the Meaning of Words* (1795), p. 71; Thomas Paine, *Rights of Man*, ed. Henry Collins (1969), p. 102.
12. Hannah More, *Thoughts on the Importance of the Manners of the Great to General Society* (9th edn, 1799), p. 116; Paul Langford, *Public Life and the Propertied Englishman, 1689–1798* (Oxford, 1991), p. 548.
13. See, for example, Thorne, *House of Commons*, I, pp. 290, 318–25.
14. Cannon, *Aristocratic Century*, p. 33; Gregory W. Pedlow, *The Survival of the Hessian Nobility 1770–1870* (Princeton, N.J., 1988), p. 17.
15. John Burke, *A Geneological and Heraldic History of the Commoners of Great Britain and Ireland* (4 vols, 1977 repr.), I, pp. xi-xiviii.
16. Thorne, *House of Commons*, I, pp. 280–9.
17. James J. Sacks, 'The House of Lords and parliamentary patronage in Great Britain, 1802–1832', *Historical Journal* 23 (1980), p. 919.
18. Quoted in Frank O'Gorman, *Edmund Burke: His Political Philosophy* (1973), p. 121.
19. Ronald Syme, *Colonial Elites: Rome, Spain and the Americas* (1958), pp. 4 and 13.
20. Vicary Gibbs (ed.), *The Complete Peerage of England, Scotland, Ireland, Great Britain and the United Kingdom* (13 vols, 1912), II, p. 294; X, pp. 696–8.
21. For Merioneth, see Peter R. Roberts, 'The decline of the Welsh squires in the eighteenth century', *National Library of Wales Journal* 13 (1963–4); Philip Jenkins, *The Making of a Ruling Class: The Glamorgan Gentry 1640–1790* (Cambridge, 1983), pp. xxi–xxvi, 1–42; and his 'The demographic decline of the landed gentry in the

eighteenth century', *Welsh Historical Review* 11 (1982).

22. J.V. Beckett, *The Aristocracy in England 1660–1914* (1986), pp. 96–7.
23. I owe this reference to David Cannadine whose work has been of enormous assistance in helping me to understand the economic and demographic transformation of the British landowning class during this period.
24. Philip Jenkins, 'The creation of an "ancient gentry": Glamorgan, 1760–1840', *Welsh History Review* 12 (1984).
25. H.J. Habakkuk, 'Marriage and the Ownership of Land', in R.R. Davies *et al.* (eds), *Welsh Society and Nationhood: Historical Essays presented to Glanmor Williams* (Cardiff, 1984), p. 194.
26. F.M.L. Thompson, *English Landed Society in the Nineteenth Century*, (1963), pp. 212–25; T.C. Smout, 'Scottish landowners and economic growth, 1650–1850', *Scottish Journal of Political Economy* 11 (1964).
27. I owe the information in this paragraph to Andrew McKenzie.
28. Patricia C. Otto, 'Daughters of the British aristocracy: their marriages in the 18th and 19th centuries with particular reference to the Scottish peerage', Stanford Ph.D. dissertation, 1974, p. 395.
29. See introduction to R.J. Adam, *Papers on Sutherland Estate Management, 1802–1816*, 2 vols, (Scottish Historical Society, Edinburgh, 1972).
30. A.P.W. Malcomson, *The Pursuit of the Heiress: Aristocratic Marriage in Ireland 1750–1820* (Ulster Historical Foundation, 1982).
31. See my *In Defiance of Oligarchy: The Tory Party 1714–60* (Cambridge, 1982), p. 76.
32. Thorne, *House of Commons*, v, 596.
33. *Catalogue of Works on the Peerage and Baronetage of England, Scotland, and Ireland* (privately printed in 1827).
34. For example, Jenkins, *Making of a Ruling Class*, pp. 213–16.
35. *Hansard*, 1st series, 4 (1805), p. 365.
36. H.J. Hanham, 'Mid-century Scottish nationalism: romantic and radical', in R. Robson (ed.), *Ideas and Institutions in Victorian Britain* (1967).
37. Muriel Chamberlain, *Lord Aberdeen: A Political Biography* (1983), pp. 5 and 187.
38. Information from Andrew McKenzie.
39. Thorne, *House of Commons*, v, 596.
40. *Ibid.*, IV, 246.
41. [John Hay Beith], *The Oppressed English* (New York, 1917), p. 30.
42. Richard Rush, *A Residence at the Court of London* (1987 edn), p. 34.
43. Philip Mansel, 'Monarchy, uniform and the rise of the *frac* 1760–1830', *Past & Present* 96 (1982), pp. 104–6.
44. Jeremy Black, *The British and the Grand Tour* (1985), *passim*.
45. Iain Pears, *The Discovery of Painting: the Growth of Interest in the Arts in England, 1680–1768* (New Haven and London, 1988), p. 228.
46. Douglas Hay, 'Property, authority and the criminal law', in Hay *et al.*, *Albion's Fatal Tree* (1975), p. 34.
47. See *infra*, pp. 87–92.
48. Lord Holland, *Memoirs of the Whig Party* (2 vols, 1852), I, p. 3.
49. John Cannon, *Aristocratic Century*, p. 48.
50. T.W. Bamford, 'Public schools and social class, 1801–1850', *British Journal of Sociology* 12 (1961), pp. 224–35.
51. Cannon, *Aristocratic Century*, p. 48.
52. George Robert Chinnery, 'The statue of the dying gladiator', *Oxford Prize Poems* (Oxford, 1831), p. 134. Maurice Bowra made the point well: 'The classical education was created by men who believed in an aristocratic ideal and was intended primarily for those who were free from pecuniary anxiety . . . It was an elegance, a luxury, a pride', quoted in Iris Butler, *The Eldest Brother: The Marquis Wellesley* (1973), p.87.
53. Essays by, respectively, Reginald Heber, Edward Garrard Marsh, Charles P. Burney and William Attfield.
54. See Richard Jenkyns, *The Victorians and Ancient Greece* (Oxford, 1980).
55. Quoted in P.J. Marshall, 'Empire and authority in the later eighteenth century', *Journal of Imperial and Commonwealth History* 25 (1987), p. 107; and see Frank M. Turner, 'British politics and the demise of the Roman republic: 1700–1939', *Historical Journal* 29 (1986).
56. Catalogue of the exhibition of the Eton leaving portraits, Tate Gallery, London, 1951. See also *Leaving Portraits from Eton College*, Dulwich Picture

Gallery, 1991.

57. H.C. Maxwell Lyte, *A History of Eton College* (1911), pp. 497–511.
58. Charles Henry Cooper, *Annals of Cambridge* (4 vols, 1852), IV, pp. 481–2.
59. Quoted in John Chandos, *Boys Together. English Public Schools 1800–1864* (1984), p. 26.
60. *The Times*, 18 July 1803.
61. Cooper, *Annals of Cambridge* IV, p. 499.
62. Thompson, *English Landed Society in the Nineteenth Century*, p. 145.
63. William Leeke, *The History of Lord Seaton's Regiment at the Battle of Waterloo* (2 vols, 1866), I, 197.
64. David C. Itzkowitz, *Peculiar Privilege: A Social History of English Foxhunting 1753–1885* (1977), p. 20.
65. Malcolm Andrews, *The Search for the Picturesque: Landscape Aesthetics and Tourism in Britain, 1760–1800* (Aldershot, 1989), p. 112 and *passim*.
66. Christopher Smout, 'Tours in the Scottish Highlands from the eighteenth to the twentieth centuries', *Northern Scotland* 5 (1983), p. 110.
67. See Andrews, *Search for the Picturesque*, *passim*. And compare David Solkin, *Richard Wilson: The Landscape of Reaction* (1982), p. 57.
68. *The Novels of Jane Austen* (5 vols, Oxford, 1987 edn), V, p. 111.
69. S.H.A. Bruntjen, *John Boydell, 1719–1804: A Study of Art Patronage and Publishing in Georgian London* (New York, 1985).
70. Quoted in Francis Haskell, 'The British as Collectors', in Gervase Jackson-Stops (ed.), *The Treasure Houses of Britain: Four Hundred Years of Private Patronage and Art Collecting* (Washington, 1986), p. 51.
71. *Ibid.*, pp. 50–9; Margaret Greaves, *Regency Patron: Sir George Beaumont* (1966); Felicity Owen and David Blayney Brown, *Collector of Genius: A Life of Sir George Beaumont* (New Haven and London, 1988); Stephen Deuchar, *Paintings, Politics and Porter: Samuel Whitbread II* (1984).
72. St John Gore, 'Three centuries of discrimination', *Apollo* 105 (1977); Evelyn Joll, 'Painter and patron: Turner and the third earl of Egremont', *Apollo* 105 (1977).
73. A. Tintiswood, *A History of Country House Visiting* (Oxford, 1989), *passim*.
74. Gervas Huxley, *Lady Elizabeth and the Grosvenors: Life in a Whig Family 1822–1839* (Oxford, 1965), p. 6; on Lord Stafford's art collection, see Eric Richards, *The Leviathan of Wealth: The Sutherland Fortune in the Industrial Revolution* (1973), p. 14, and the references cited there.
75. Peter Fullerton, 'Patronage and pedagogy: the British Institution in the early nineteenth century', *Art History* 5 (1982).
76. Sir Egerton Brydges, *Collins's Peerage of England* (9 vols, 1812), I, p. x (my italics).
77. Rush, *A Residence at the Court of London*, p. 46.
78. For the most recent analysis, see Simon Schama, *Dead Certainties (Unwarranted Speculations)* (1991), pp. 3–70.
79. Ann Uhry Abrams, *The Valiant Hero: Benjamin West and Grand-Style History Painting* (Washington, 1985), pp. 165–82.
80. For the popularity of patriotic prints at this time, see David Alexander and Richard T. Godfrey, *Painters and Engraving: The Reproductive Print from Hogarth to Wilkie* (New Haven, 1980).
81. Alison Yarrington, *The Commemoration of the Hero 1800–64: Monuments to the British Victors of the Napoleonic Wars* (1988).
82. Robin Reilly, *Pitt the Younger 1759–1806* (1978), p. 345.
83. A.D. Harvey, *Britain in the Early Nineteenth Century* (1978), p. 217.
84. Tom Pocock, *Horatio Nelson* (1987), p. 20.
85. *Ibid.*, p. 161.
86. *Ibid.*, p. 181.
87. Michael Lewis, *The Navy in Transition 1814–1864: A Social History* (1965), p. 22.
88. Philip Mansel, *Pillars of Monarchy: An Outline of the Political and Social History of Royal Guards 1400–1984* (1984), p. 78.
89. Thorne, *House of Commons*, I, pp. 306–17.
90. *The Whole Art of Dress! or, the road to elegance and fashion at the enormous saving of thirty per cent* (1830), p. 83.
91. N.P. Dawnay, 'The staff uniform of the British army 1767–1855', *Journal of the Society foı Army Historical Research* 30–1 (1952–3); Mansel, 'Monarchy, Uniform and the *frac*', pp. 117–23.

92. Alan Mansfield, *Ceremonial Costume* (1980), pp. 171, 220–1.
93. Jean Starobinski, 'Reflections on some symbols of the Revolution', *Yale French Studies* 40 (1968), p. 50.
94. Aileen Ribeiro and Valerie Cumming, *The Visual History of Costume* (1989), pp. 31–2.
95. See, for instance, *The Whole Art of Dress!*, pp. 13–14; Ribeiro and Cumming, *The Visual History of Costume*, p. 32.
96. W.D. Rubinstein, 'The end of "Old Corruption" in Britain 1780–1860', *Past & Present* 101 (1983), pp. 55–86.
97. Lord Lansdowne to Lady Londonderry, 12 October 1809, History of Parliament Trust, Camden MSS transcripts.
98. John Rosselli, 'An Indian Governor in the Norfolk Marshland: Lord William Bentinck as improver, 1809–27', *Agricultural History Review* 19 (1971), pp. 46–7 and *passim*.
99. J.N. McCord, Jr, 'Lord Holland and the Politics of the Whig Aristocracy (1807–1827): A Study in Aristocratic Liberalism', Johns Hopkins University Ph.D. dissertation, 1968, p. 396.
100. George T. Kenyon, *The Life of Lloyd, First Lord Kenyon* (1873), p. 223. On the élite and evangelicalism, see Ford K. Brown, *Fathers of the Victorians: The Age of Wilberforce* (Cambridge, 1961).
101. I am not suggesting that all British politicians in office lived impeccable private lives at this time: only that they were more conscious of the need to seem to be doing so.
102. Derek Jarrett, *Pitt the Younger* (1974), p. 112.
103. From the minutes of the Pitt Club which are in the Osborn collection of manuscripts at the Beinecke Library, Yale University, New Haven.
104. Michael W. McCahill, 'Peerage creations and the changing character of the British nobility, 1750–1830', *English Historical Review* 96 (1981), pp. 269–74.
105. *Memoirs of the life of Sir Samuel Romilly, written by himself* (3 vols, 1840), II, p. 136.
106. Peter J. Jupp, 'The landed elite and political authority in Britain, 1760–1850', *Journal of British Studies* 29 (1990), pp. 78–9.
107. See David Cannadine, *The Decline and Fall of the British Aristocracy* (New Haven and London, 1990), pp. 8–23.
108. See, for example, Beckett, *The Aristocracy in England*; and Lawrence Stone and Jeanne C. Fawtier Stone, *An Open Elite?: England 1540–1880* (Oxford, 1984).
109. Quoted in G.L. Gomme, *The Gentleman's Magazine Library* (30 vols, 1883–1905), I, p. 17.

5 MAJESTY

1. Lewis Namier, 'George III speaks out', *In the Margin* (1939), p. 137. Ida Macalpine and Richard Hunter argue in *George III and the Mad-Business* (1969) that the king's real ailment was porphyria, a rare blood disease.
2. Roy Porter, *A Social History of Madness: The World Through the Eyes of the Insane* (1987), p. 51.
3. Macalpine and Hunter, *George III*, p. xii.
4. Accounts of royal power in eighteenth-century Britain are thin on the ground, and those that exist sometimes supply too static a picture, based on legal writings and clerical propaganda which describe how the monarchy was supposed to function, rather than how it functioned in fact over time. Two interpretations that avoid this error are B.W. Hill, 'Executive monarchy and the challenge of parties, 1689–1832: two concepts of government and two historiographical interpretations', *Historical Journal* 13 (1970); and Richard Pares, *King George the Third and the Politicians* (1953).
5. H.M. Colvin *et al.*, *The History of the King's Works* (6 vols, 1963–1982), IV (part 2), p. 28.
6. *Ibid.*, p. 39.
7. John M. Beattie, *The English Court in the Reign of George I* (Cambridge, 1967), pp. 106–12; E.A. Reitan, 'The civil list in eighteenth-century politics: parliamentary supremacy versus the independence of the crown', *Historical Journal* 9 (1966).
8. John Brooke, *George III* (1972), p. 108.
9. Colvin, *History of King's Works*, V, p. 127.
10. *Ibid.*; Ragnhild Hatton, *George I. Elector and King* (1978), pp. 262–4.
11. See Norbert Elias, *The Court Society*

(New York, 1983); and for a more historically sensitive intepretation, Orest Ranum, 'The court and capital of Louis XIV', in J.C. Rule, *Louis XIV and the Craft of Kingship* (Columbus, Ohio, 1969).

12. Beattie, *English Court in the Reign of George I*; for the monarchy's reliance on the London theatres, see Peggy Ellen Daub, 'Music at the court of George II', Cornell University Ph.D. dissertation, 1985, *passim*.
13. John, Lord Hervey, *Some Materials Towards Memoirs of the Reign of King George II*, ed. Romney Sedgwick (3 vols, 1931), I, pp. 98–9.
14. *Weekly Journal or British Gazetteer*, 3 August 1723.
15. *London Gazette* 23/7 July 1723. One of the few historians to have noticed this extraordinary measure (which was certainly implemented in parts of Britain), is Edward Thompson: *Whigs and Hunters: The Origin of the Black Act* (1975), pp. 199–200.
16. 'Thoughts on the coronation of his present Majesty King George the Third', in Donald J. Greene, *Samuel Johnson: Political Writings* (New Haven and London,1977), p. 293.
17. For the first two Hanoverian monarchs and the politicians, see Hatton, *George I* and Beattie, *English Court in the Reign of George I*. No adequate political biography of George II exists, but see my *In Defiance of Oligarchy: The Tory Party 1714–60* (Cambridge, 1982), and John Owen, 'George II reconsidered', in Anne Whiteman, J.S. Bromley and P.G.M. Dickson (eds), *Statesmen, Scholars and Merchants* (1973), pp. 113–34.
18. Arthur Byron, *London Statues: A Guide to London's Outdoor Statues and Sculpture* (1981), pp. 121–5.
19. Hatton, *George I*, pp. 260–3.
20. Simon Schama, 'The domestication of majesty: royal family portraiture, 1500–1850', *Journal of Interdisciplinary History* 17 (1986), p. 170.
21. See my *Namier* (1989), pp. 50–7.
22. See A.N. Newman (ed.), 'Leicester House politics, 1750–60', *Camden Miscellany* 23 (1969).
23. Kimerly Rorschach, 'Frederick, Prince of Wales (1707–51) as a patron of the visual arts: princely patriotism and political propaganda', Yale University Ph.D. dissertation, 1985; Christopher Lloyd, *The Queen's Pictures: Royal Collectors Through the Centuries* (1991), pp. 117–42.
24. Brooke, *George III*, p. 65.
25. Schama, 'Domestication of majesty', pp. 170–1.
26. Walther Hubatsch, *Frederick the Great of Prussia: absolutism and administration* (1975), p. 123; and see T.C.W. Blanning, *Joseph II and Enlightened Despotism* (1970). These accounts should be compared with Pares, *George III and the Politicians*.
27. *Memoirs of the Life of Sir Samuel Romilly, written by himself*, (3 vols, 1840), II, pp. 299–301 (my emphasis).
28. Quoted in J.C.D. Clark, *English Society 1688–1832* (1985), p. 236. I cannot agree with Paul Langford's assertion in *Public Life and the Propertied Englishman 1689–1798* (Oxford, 1991), p. 508, that celebration of George III as father of his people was 'commonplace in the 1760s and 1770s'. The king was certainly more well liked from his accession than his two predecessors had been, but most informed contemporaries agreed that it was only from the 1780s that the really *sustained* rise in his popularity–and in his patriotic significance–began.
29. Ben Ross Schneider, *Index to the London Stage, 1660–1800* (Carbondale, Ill., 1979), p. 358.
30. See, for instance, *Political and Personal Satires*, IV, print nos 4021, 4303, 4374, 4376; V, print nos 4859, 5105, 5288, 5544, 5675; and *ibid.*, VI, p. xxv, print no. 6608.
31. *Ibid.*, VI, print nos 6918, 7355, 7645, 8074; VII, print nos 8346, 9542; VIII, print nos 10013, 10424, 10436, 10738. Jeannine Surel, 'La première image de John Bull, bourgeois radical, anglais loyaliste, 1779–1815', *Mouvement Social* 106 (1979), p. 79n.
32. For the king's political coup in the aftermath of American defeat, see John Cannon, *The Fox-North Coalition: Crisis of the Constitution 1782–4* (Cambridge, 1969).
33. Colvin, *History of the King's Works*, VI, pp. 354–6, 375; *Report from the Commissioners of Inquiry into the Conduct of Business in the Office of Works*, Parliamentary Papers, 1812–13 (258), V, pp. 321–525.
34. David Watkin, *The Royal Interiors of*

Regency England (1984), p. 100. See, too, *Carlton House: The Past Glories of George IV's Palace*, catalogue of an exhibition at The Queen's Gallery, Buckingham Palace, 1991.

35. *Benjamin West: American Painter at the English Court* (Baltimore, 1989), p. 68.
36. For the political background to the gothic revival, see Mark Girouard, *The Return to Camelot: Chivalry and the English Gentleman* (New Haven and London, 1984), especially pp. 19–25.
37. Christopher Hibbert, *George IV* (2 vols, 1972–3), II, p. 345; and see *George IV and the Arts of France*, catalogue of an exhibition at the Queen's Gallery, Buckingham Palace.
38. Quoted in Helen Rosenau, *Social Purpose in Architecture: Paris and London Compared, 1760–1800* (1970), p. 41.
39. For the French revolutionary festivals, see Marie-Louise Biver, *Fêtes révolutionnaires à Paris* (Paris, 1979); Mona Ozouf, *Festivals and the French Revolution* (Cambridge, Mass., 1988) and D.L. Dowd, *Pageant-master of the Republic: Jacques-Louis David and the French Revolution* (Lincoln, Neb., 1948). David had visited London and enjoyed close ties with its resident artists and polite society before the Revolution.
40. The extract from the *Morning Chronicle* is in a book of newspaper cuttings: B.L., Add. MS 6307, fol. 57; and see the comments on the Naval Thanksgiving of the *Anti-Jacobin*, 11, 18, and 25 December 1797.
41. *Bath Chronicle*, 19 October 1809.
42. See *Account of the National Jubilee in August 1814* (1814).
43. Lord Holland's description of the king's attitude, quoted in A. Aspinall (ed.), *The Later Correspondence of George III* (5 vols, Cambridge, 1966–70), IV, p. 365n; *Gentleman's Magazine* 75 (1805), p. 375.
44. Windham is quoted in Joseph Taylor, *Relics of Royalty: Or, Anecdotes, Amusements and Conversations of the Late Most Gracious Majesty George III* (1820), p. 154.
45. *The Times*, 24 April 1805.
46. See N.G. Cox, 'Aspects of English radicalism: the suppression and re-emergence of the constitutional democratic tradition, 1795–1809', Cambridge University Ph.D. dissertation, 1971, pp. 340–62.
47. Mrs R.C. Biggs to the Earl of Dartmouth, 14 October 1809, Staffordshire Record Office, D (W) 1778/I/ii/1737; Henry Wollaston, *British Official Medals for Coronations and Jubilees* (Nottingham, 1978), pp. 93–6.
48. Mrs Biggs to Dartmouth, 14 October 1809, *loc. cit.*
49. The best description of the festivities – compiled interestingly enough by a woman – is *An Account of the Celebration of the Jubilee . . . of George the Third* (Birmingham, 1809).
50. For an extended discussion of this point, see *infra*, pp. 268–73.
51. The *Scotsman*, quoted in Charles Maclaren, *Railways compared with Canals and Common Roads, and their Uses and Advantages explained* (1825), p. 81.
52. G. Boyce, J. Curran, and P. Wingate, *Newspaper History from the Seventeenth Century to the Present Day* (1978), p. 99; Joan P.S. Ferguson, *Directory of Scottish newspapers* (Edinburgh, 1984).
53. K.G. Burton, *The Early Newspaper Press in Berkshire* (Reading, 1954), p. 33.
54. Arthur Aspinall, *Politics and the Press, c.1780–1850* (Brighton, 1973 repr.), pp. 88–9, 206–14. For the pressure this kind of incitement of royal celebration could put on individuals, see Thomas MacCrie, *Free Thoughts on the Late Religious Celebration of the Funeral of . . . Princess Charlotte* (Edinburgh, 1817); *A Letter to the Rev. Andrew Thomson* (Edinburgh, 1817), *passim.*
55. See *infra*, pp. 270–3.
56. One landowner wrote that he thought the Jubilee should have 'been left alone, *but as there seemed such an universal disposition to notice the day*, it would have been difficult to have avoided taking some share in it', B.L., Add. MS 35648, fols. 198–9 (my emphasis).
57. See for example *Chester Chronicle*, 25 August–10 November 1809.
58. *Felix Farley's Bristol Journal*, 14, 21, 28 October 1809.
59. See *Hull Packet*, 24 October 1809; John Sykes, *An Account of the Rejoicings, Illuminations etc. that have taken place in Newcastle* (Newcastle-upon-Tyne, 1821), p. 4; *An Account of the Celebration of the Jubilee*, pp. 132, 137, 187.
60. *Ibid.*, p. xiii.
61. Cited in *Notes and Queries*, 9th series, 10 (1902), p. 493.
62. Mark Harrison, *Crowds and History: Mass Phenomena in English Towns, 1790–1835* (Cambridge, 1988), pp. 53, 60–1,

255–6.
63. *London Gazette*, 31 October/4 November 1809.
64. Broadsheet in Liverpool City Record Office, 731 GEO 4.
65. Harrison, *Crowds and History*, p. 254.
66. *An Account of the Celebration of the Jubilee*, p. 52.
67. W. Branch Johnson (ed.), *Memorandums for . . . the Diary Between 1798 and 1810 of John Carrington* (1973), p. 91.
68. Elizabeth Longford, *Victoria R.I.* (1966), p. 624.
69. See T.W. Laqueur, *Religion and Respectability: Sunday Schools and Working Class Culture 1780–1850* (New Haven, 1976).
70. *Gentleman's Magazine* 83 (1813), pp. 630–2.
71. For Lancaster's coronation procession, Liverpool City Record Office, 942 HOL vol. 5, fol. 266; for medals, see Manchester City Library, F 942 7389 M1, fol. 60.
72. See *infra*, Chapter 6.
73. *Grand Lodge, 1717–1967* (Oxford, 1967); Chris Cook and John Stevenson, *British Political Facts, 1760–1830* (1980), pp. 194–5.
74. Harrison, *Crowds and History*, pp. 245–58.
75. *Ibid., passim.*
76. Lynn Hunt, *Politics, Culture and Class in the French Revolution* (Berkeley, 1984), p. 72.
77. Edward Thompson, *The Making of the English Working Class* (1965), pp. 679–80.
78. *Gentleman's Magazine*, 32 (1762), p. 551.
79. Quoted in J.C.D. Clark (ed.), *The Memoirs & Speeches of James, 2nd Earl Waldegrave 1742–1763* (Cambridge, 1988), p. 89. If nothing else did, this blatant disrespect for George II's funeral rites would seem to cast doubt on Dr Clark's contention that eighteenth-century Britain was a 'court society' on the French model.
80. *The Castle and the Tomb . . . or, A Visit to Windsor on Occasion of the Funeral Procession of George III* (1820).
81. See David Cannadine, 'The context, performance and meaning of ritual: the British monarchy and the "Invention of Tradition", c.1820–1977', in Eric Hobsbawm and Terence Ranger (eds), *The Invention of Tradition* (Cambridge, 1983).
82. See Richard Williams, 'Public discussion of the British monarchy 1837–1887', Cambridge University Ph.D. dissertation, 1988.
83. Cannadine, 'The British monarchy and the "Invention of Tradition"', in Hobsbawm and Ranger, *Invention of Tradition*, pp. 101–64.
84. See, for example, Manchester City Record Office, M 22/7/2, fols 40–96; and Thomas Hallack, *Origin and Progress of the Proceedings which Ultimately led to the Coronation Dinner* (Cambridge, 1838), p. 2.
85. *The Times*, 25 October 1809; *Day*, 17 October 1809.
86. Roger Fulford, *Royal Dukes: The Father and Uncles of Queen Victoria* (1933), p. 292.
87. See Crook and Port, *History of the King's Works*, VI, pp. 96–651; Donald J. Olsen, *Town Planning in London: The Eighteenth and Nineteenth Centuries* (New Haven and London, 1982).
88. Corporation of London Record Office, MS 88.6 (1789 Thanksgiving); *ibid.*, MS 23.29 (Naval Thanksgiving); *An Account of the Expences of the Entertainments Given in the Guildhall . . . 9 July 1814* (1814), p. 8.
89. *Reflections on the Revolution in France by Edmund Burke & The Rights of Man by Thomas Paine* (New York, 1973), p. 91.
90. *The Times*, 17 November 1820 (my emphasis).
91. Quoted in Macalpine and Hunter, *George III*, p.11.
92. Details of these royal visits are scattered throughout the newspapers of the period, especially the London *Times*.
93. See, for example, the quasi-informal quality of Prince William of Gloucester's visit to Liverpool: *The Times*, 9 September 1803.
94. *Letters to Sir Walter Scott, Bt. on the Moral and Political Character and Effects of the Visit to Scotland* (Edinburgh, 1822), pp. 51–2. For the significance of this, the first visit by a ruling monarch to Scotland since the early seventeenth century, see Gerald Finley, *Turner and George the Fourth in Edinburgh 1822* (1981). and John Prebble, *The King's Jaunt: George IV in Scotland, August 1822* (1988).
95. Quoted in Marquess of Anglesey, *One-leg: The Life and Letters of Henry William Paget, First Marquis of Anglesey* (New York, 1961), pp. 227–9.

6 WOMANPOWER

1. *Taunton Courier*, 30 June 1814.
2. See the example cited in Maurice Agulhon, *Marianne into Battle: Republican Imagery and Symbolism in France 1789–1880* (Cambridge, 1981), p. 14.
3. *Magnae Britanniae Notitia: Or, the Present State of Great Britain* (1716), pp. 192–3; *The Laws Respecting Women as they Regard their Natural Rights* (1777), p. 65.
4. Rosalind K. Marshall, *Virgins and Viragos: A History of Women in Scotland from 1080 to 1980* (1983), p. 87; and see R.A. Houston, 'Women in the economy and society of Scotland, 1500–1800', in Houston and I.D. Whyte (eds), *Scottish Society 1500–1800* (Cambridge, 1989).
5. William Alexander, *The History of Women, from the Earliest Antiquity to the Present Time* (2 vols, 1779), II, p. 336.
6. Jean-Jacques Rousseau, 'Émile, ou de l'éducation', in *Oeuvres Complètes* (5 vols, Paris, 1969), IV, p. 768.
7. *Vindication of the Rights of Woman*, ed. Miriam Kramnick (1975), p. 258.
8. See, for example, the highly influential piece by William Cadogan, *An Essay upon Nursing* (1748).
9. P.J. Corfield, *The Impact of English Towns 1700–1800* (Oxford, 1982), pp. 99–106.
10. Marshall, *Virgins and Viragos*, p. 209.
11. James Fordyce, *The Character and Conduct of the Female Sex* (1776), p. 19; *Lady's Magazine* (1784), p. 375.
12. Paul Langford, *A Polite and Commercial People: England 1727–1783* (Oxford, 1989), p. 109.
13. *Edinburgh Magazine* (1820), p. 339; A.J. Youngson, *The Making of Classical Edinburgh 1750–1840* (Edinburgh, 1966), pp. 250–3.
14. Roy Porter, in his otherwise splendid 'Seeing the past', *Past & Present* 118 (1988), p. 204.
15. Georgiana's obituary is in *Gentleman's Magazine* 76 (1806), p. 386. The best if still limited biography is Brian Masters, *Georgiana, Duchess of Devonshire* (1981).
16. See Karl von den Steinen, 'The discovery of women in eighteenth-century English political life', in Barbara Kanner (ed.), *The Women of England* (Hamden, Conn., 1979).
17. See L.G. Mitchell, *Charles James Fox and the Disintegration of the Whig Party* (Oxford, 1971); and Loren Reid, *Charles James Fox: A Man for the People* (1969).
18. Earl of Bessborough (ed.), *Georgiana: Extracts from the Correspondence of Georgiana, Duchess of Devonshire* (1955), pp. 74–5 (my emphasis).
19. *History of the Westminster Election* (1784), p. 314.
20. Bessborough, *Georgiana*, p. 82.
21. Edward Porritt, *The Unreformed House of Commons: Parliamentary Representation before 1832* (2 vols, 1963 edn), I, p. 581; H.J. Hanham, *The Nineteenth-Century Constitution 1815–1914* (Cambridge, 1969), pp. 264–5.
22. *Lady's Magazine* (1784), p. 205.
23. Such arguments have been advanced particularly by historians of Revolutionary and Napoleonic France but are often applied more broadly: see Michelle Perrot (ed.), *A History of Private Life: From the Fires of the Revolution to the Great War* (1990). I don't at all dissent from the view that separate-spheres ideology was pushed more intensively and self-consciously in the Revolutionary era. The fact remains, however, that the scope of female activity in nineteenth-century Britain (and, indeed, in nineteenth-century France) seems in general to have been wider than it was in the eighteenth century.
24. John Andrews, *Remarks on the French and English Ladies* (1783), p. 4; Mary Wollstonecraft, 'A vindication of the rights of women', in *The Works of Mary Wollstonecraft*, ed. Janet Todd and Marilyn Butler (7 vols, 1989), VI, pp. 124–5.
25. Thomas Gisborne, *An Enquiry into the Duties of the Female Sex* (1796), p. 266.
26. *Ibid.*, pp. 324–5.
27. For the Jacobin critique of pre-Revolutionary womanpower, see Lynn Hunt, 'The many bodies of Marie Antoinette: political pornography and the problem of the feminine in the French Revolution', in her *Eroticism and the Body Politic* (1991).
28. Fordyce, *Character and Conduct of the Female Sex*, p. 27; Andrews, *Remarks on the French and English Ladies*, p. 245.
29. B.W. Hill (ed.), *Edmund Burke: On Government, Politics and Society* (1975), pp. 337–44.
30. Joan W. Scott, *Gender and the Politics of History* (Cambridge, 1988), p. 48.

31. For this, see Leonora Davidoff and Catherine Hall, *Family Fortunes: Men and Women of the English Middle Class 1780–1850* (1987), *passim*.
32. *The Unsex'd Females* (1798), p. 16.
33. *Gentleman's Magazine* 65 (1795), p. 103; Gisborne, *Enquiry into the Duties of the Female Sex*, pp. 213–16.
34. Houston and Whyte, *Scottish Society*, pp. 137–8.
35. *Hansard*, 1st series, 2 (1804), pp. 501–2.
36. See, for example, the stories of female fortitude in the face of the guillotine in the *Lady's Monthly Magazine* 11 (1803), pp. 373 *et seq*.
37. Wollstonecraft, 'An historical and moral view of the origins and progress of the French Revolution', in Todd and Butler, *Works*, VI, p. 209 (my emphasis).
38. Bessborough, *Georgiana*, p. 204; *The Yale Edition of Horace Walpole's Correspondence*, ed. W.S. Lewis *et al*. (48 vols, 1937–83), XII, p. 52.
39. William Roberts, *Memoirs of the Life and Correspondence of Mrs Hannah More* (4 vols, 1834), II, p. 385.
40. On the sentimentality that surrounded the French Royal Family *after its fall*, see David Bindman, *The Shadow of the Guillotine: Britain and the French Revolution* (1989), pp. 129–43, 150–4.
41. Joan Landes, *Women and the Public Sphere in the Age of the French Revolution* (1988), *passim*.
42. Quoted in Mary Poovey, *The Proper Lady and the Woman Writer: Ideology as Style in the Works of Mary Wollstonecraft, Mary Shelley and Jane Austen* (1984), p. 33.
43. H.F.B. Wheeler and A.M. Broadley, *Napoleon and the Invasion of England* (2 vols, 1908), I, p. 65.
44. A. Temple Patterson, *Radical Leicester: A History of Leicester 1780–1850* (Leicester, 1954), p. 80.
45. Diary of William Rowbottom, 1787–1830, Oldham Local Interest Library, e.g., 10 March 1809.
46. Rebecca Fraser, *The Brontës: Charlotte Brontë and Her Family* (1988), pp. 33–69 *passim*.
47. Marie F. Busco, 'The "Achilles" in Hyde Park', *Burlington Magazine* 130 (1988), p. 922 and *passim*.
48. J.W. Fortescue, *A History of the British Army* (13 vols, 1899–1930), IV, pp. 900–1.
49. From a list drawn up by Sarah Banks in B.L., LR 301.h.6, fols 55–64.
50. D.G. Vaisey, 'The pledge of patriotism: Staffordshire and the voluntary contribution, 1798', in M.W. Greenslade (ed.), *Essays in Staffordshire History* (Staffordshire Record Society, 1970), p. 213.
51. List of the subscribers for clothing the volunteers of the county, National Library of Wales, Tredegar MS 1064; *Report of the Committee for Managing the Patriotic Fund Established at Lloyds Coffee House* (1804).
52. Cf. Roger Chickering, '"Casting their gaze more broadly": women's patriotic activism in imperial Germany', *Past & Present* 118 (1988).
53. *Life and Correspondence of Mrs Hannah More*, II, p. 415.
54. *Report of the Committee for Managing the Patriotic Fund*, *passim*.
55. Perrot, *A History of Private Life*, p. 44.
56. B.L., LR 301.h.6, fol. 64.
57. See Donald Read, *Peterloo: The Massacre and its Background* (Manchester, 1958); Robert Reid, *The Peterloo Massacre* (1989).

T.W. Laqueur, 'The Queen Caroline affair: politics as art in the reign of George IV', *Journal of Modern History* 54 (1982).

59. *The Times*, 14 July and 18 September 1820.
60. Quoted in Davidoff and Hall, *Family Fortunes*, p. 152 (my emphasis).
61. *Ibid.*, p. 151.
62. *The Queen and Magna Carta, or the thing that John signed. Dedicated to the Ladies of Great Britain* (1820), pp. 17–18.
63. *The Times*, 25 September 1820.
64. Laqueur, 'Queen Caroline affair', p. 442.
65. Classically, in Davidoff and Hall, *Family Fortunes*, *passim*.
66. See my 'The apotheosis of George III: loyalty, royalty and the British nation 1760–1820', *Past & Present* 102 (1984), p. 125.
67. *Ibid.* An intelligent biography that will place Princess Charlotte in a wider context of nineteenth-century attitudes towards women and the monarchy would be invaluable.
68. N.B. Penny, 'English church monuments to women who died in childbed between 1780 and 1835', *Journal of the Warburg and Courtauld Institutes*, 38 (1975).
69. *Gentleman's Magazine* 87 (1817), p. 610.

70. Jean Bethke Elshtain, *Public Man, Private Woman*, (1981), pp. 164–5; and see Joel Schwartz, *The Sexual Politics of Jean-Jacques Rousseau* (Chicago, 1984).
71. *Vindication*, p. 86.
72. M.G. Jones, *Hannah More* (New York, 1968 edn); and see Mitzi Meyers, 'Reform or Ruin: "A Revolution in Female Manners"', *Studies in Eighteenth-Century Culture* 11 (1982).
73. *Life and Correspondence of Mrs Hannah More*, II, p. 371.
74. Poovey, *The Proper Lady*, pp. 33–4.
75. *Strictures on the Modern System of Female Education* (2 vols, 1799), I, p. 5 and *passim*.
76. *Females of the Present Day, Considered as to their Influence on Society by a Country Lady* (1831), pp. 1–37.
77. Quoted in J.T. Williams, 'Bearers of moral and spiritual values: the social roles of clergymen and women in British society, c.1790–c.1880, as mirrored in attitudes to them as fox-hunters', Oxford University D.Phil. dissertation, 1987, p. 171.
78. Quoted in Ruth and Edmund Frow, *Political Women, 1800–50* (1989), p. 13.
79. James Epstein, 'Understanding the cap of liberty: symbolic practice and social conflict in early nineteenth century England', *Past & Present* 122 (1989), pp. 100–1.
80. *Ibid.* William Cobbett claimed that the idea of plebeian women awarding liberty caps to their male 'champions' derived from the practice of affluent women presenting banners to the volunteer corps.
81. Louis Billington and Rosamund Billington, '"A burning zeal for righteousness": women in the British anti-slavery movement, 1820–1860', in Jane Rendall (ed.), *Equal or Different: Women's Politics 1800–1914* (Oxford, 1987).
82. *Ibid.*; and see F.K. Prochaska, *Women and Philanthropy in Nineteenth-Century England* (Oxford, 1980).
83. Seymour Drescher, *Capitalism and Antislavery: British Mobilization in Comparative Perspective* (1986), p. 85.
84. *Hansard*, 2nd series, 20 (1829), p. 572.
85. *Ibid.*, p. 1324.
86. *Ibid.*, 3rd series, 8 (1831), p. 916.
87. *Ibid.*, 2nd series, 20 (1829), p. 373.
88. *Ibid.*, 3rd series, 18 (1833), p. 309.
89. Alex Tyrrell, '"Women's mission" and pressure group politics in Britain (1825–60)', *Bulletin of the John Rylands University Library* 63 (1980–1), p. 205.

7 MANPOWER

1. None of the many brilliant graphic artists at work in Britain at this time, Isaac Cruickshank, Thomas Rowlandson, George Woodward, Charles Williams or Gillray himself, was able to forge a convincing and uncondescending image of the plebeian patriot. The reasons for this were aesthetic as well as political: see John Barrell, *The Dark Side of the Landscape: The Rural Poor in English Painting 1730–1840* (Cambridge, 1980); and cf. Matthew Paul Lalumia *Realism and Politics in Victorian Art of the Crimean War* (Epping, 1984), pp. 1–38.
2. Quoted in Geoffrey Best, *War and Society in Revolutionary Europe 1770–1870* (1982), p. 63.
3. See, for example, Alan Forrest, *Conscripts and Deserters: The Army and French Society During the Revolution and Empire* (New York, 1989); and his *The Soldiers of the French Revolution* (Durham, N.C., 1990); Charles J. Esdaile, *The Spanish Army in the Peninsular War* (Manchester, 1988); T.C.W. Blanning, *The French Revolution in Germany: Occupation and Resistance in the Rhineland 1792–1802* (Oxford, 1983).
4. *Insurrection: the British Experience 1795–1803* (Gloucester, 1983), p. 262.
5. John Brewer, *The Sinews of Power: War, Money and the English State, 1688–1783*, (1989), p. 30.
6. Paul Kennedy, *The Rise and Fall of the Great Powers* (1988), pp. 156–80.
7. See Clive Emsley, *British Society and the French Wars 1793–1815* (1979), *passim*.
8. In March 1805, Lord Hawkesbury told his fellow peers that 810,000 men were serving within the United Kingdom alone: 'That was nearly one in four of the whole male population of this country capable of bearing arms... greater than any other country on the globe has now', *Hansard*, 1st series, 3 (1805), p. 808.
9. J.R. Western, *The English Militia in the Eighteenth Century: The Story of a Political Issue* (1965), pp. 127–54.
10. See I.F.W. Beckett, 'Buckinghamshire

militia lists for 1759: a social analysis', *Records of Buckinghamshire*, 20 (1977).

11. See the nationwide militia return dated 13 August 1796, P.R.O., 30/8/244, fol. 92.
12. Western, *English Militia* pp. 219–24; and see his 'The Formation of the Scottish militia in 1797', *Scottish Historical Review* 117 (1955).
13. *A View of the Establishment of the Royal Edinburgh Volunteers* (Edinburgh, 1797); I am grateful to Professor J.E. Cookson for allowing me to consult his 'Patriotism and social structure: the Ely volunteers, 1798–1808' in advance of publication.
14. Ann Hudson, 'Volunteer soldiers in Sussex during the Revolutionary and Napoleonic Wars, 1793–1815', *Sussex Archaeological Collections* 122 (1984), p. 179.
15. The debate on the feasibility of revolution in Britain during the 1790s and after has been sharp and – naturally enough since the question is hypothetical – inconclusive. For two well-documented interpretations from opposite ends of the political spectrum see Wells, *Insurrection: The British Experience*, and Ian R. Christie, *Stress and Stability in Late Eighteenth-Century Britain* (Oxford, 1984). My own view is that alienation and discontent were more savage than Professor Christie suggests, but that to discuss these strains *primarily* in terms of the potential for revolution is unhelpful.
16. D.V. Glass, *Numbering the People: The 18th Century Population Controversy and the Development of Census and Vital Statistics in Britain* (1978), p. 107.
17. Richard Cobb, *The People's Armies*, trans. Marianne Elliott (New Haven and London, 1987), p. 10. For a list of many of the extant returns from English and Welsh counties, see I.F.W. Beckett (ed.), *The Buckinghamshire Posse Comitatus 1798* (Aylesbury, 1985), pp. 363–6. No exhaustive list exists because the research necessary has never been done.
18. See Appendix 2.
19. Defence of the Realm return for Crickadarn parish, National Library of Wales, Maybery MSS 6941–64.
20. *Sussex Militia List, Pevensey Rape 1803 Northern Division* (Eastbourne, 1988), under East Grinstead.
21. W.G. Hoskins (ed.), *Exeter Militia List 1803* (Chichester, 1972), pp. 52 and 74.
22. Quoted in J.R. Dinwiddy, 'Parliamentary reform as an issue in English politics, 1800–1810', London University Ph.D. dissertation, 1971, pp. 56–7.
23. Return of volunteers in Sharnbrook, Bedfordshire Record Office, HA 15/1–4; Litcham parish association list, Norfolk Record Office, Townshend MS 5 B 6.
24. See Appendices 2 and 3; Western, *English Militia*, pp. 447–8.
25. Nicholas Mansfield, 'Volunteers and recruiting', in G. Gliddon (ed.), *Norfolk and Suffolk in the Great War* (Norwich, 1988), p. 19. Coastal, as distinct from inland East Anglia – and especially Norfolk – did have a strong naval tradition: but I suspect that in many cases the prime objects of desire were the sea and its opportunities, rather than the land and its rulers.
26. J.W. Fortescue, *The County Lieutenancies and the Army 1803–14* (1909), pp. 32–7.
27. In December 1803, the House of Commons was told that 217,196 firearms had been distributed among volunteer corps: *Hansard*, 1st series, 1 (1803–4), pp. 381–2.
28. For the kind of pressure Scottish grandees were able to exert in recruitment, see Eric R. Crageen, *Argyll Estate Instructions: Mull, Morevern, Tiree 1771–1805* (Edinburgh, 1964), p. 195.
29. *Hansard*, 1st series, 1 (1803–4), p. 1902.
30. See Appendix 2.
31. Quoted in Hudson, 'Volunteer soldiers in Sussex', p. 169.
32. Lord Advocate to Lord Pelham, 6 August 1803, P.R.O., H.O. 102, vol. 18, Part 2, R.H. 2/4/88, fol. 244.
33. Western, 'Formation of the Scottish militia', p. 8.
34. See the arguments of William Withering to Henry Dundas, 26 April 1798, Scottish Record Office, GD 51/1/931.
35. Defence of the Realm returns for Basingstoke hundreds 1798, Hampshire Record Office, B/XVIIa/5/3.
36. Defence of the Realm returns for Barford, Stodden and Willey hundreds, Bedfordshire R.O. HA 15/1–4.
37. M.Y. Ashcroft, *To Escape the Monster's Clutches: notes and documents illustrating the preparations in North Yorkshire to repel the invasion threatened by the French from 1793*, North Yorkshire County Record

Office Publications, no. 15 (1977), p. 75.
38. Information on Provence from a lecture by Alan Forrest: 'Conscription, desertion, and the rural community in France, 1792–1814'.
39. Western, *English Militia*, pp. 258–9.
40. These calculations are based on a comparison of the 1804 returns analysed in Appendix 2 with the abstract of the 1801 census.
41. Forrest, *Conscripts and Deserters*, pp. 79–81.
42. *Edinburgh Review* 5 (1803), pp. 10–11.
43. On unemployment and enlistment, see Clive Emsley, 'The impact of war and military participation on Britain and France 1792–1815', in his and James Walvin (eds) *Artisans, Peasants and Proletarians 1760–1860: Essays presented to Gwyn A. Williams* (1985), pp. 71–2.
44. Fortescue, *County Lieutenancies*, p. 111.
45. Defence of the Realm return for Edinburgh county, 30 April 1798, Scottish Record Office, GD 224/628/3/18.
46. Letter dated 7 August 1803 included in the Defence of the Realm return for Riseley, Bedfordshire Record Office, HA 15/2.
47. Autobiography of Peter Laurie, Guildhall Library, London, MS 20,334, fol. 17.
48. The rest of this paragraph is based on James Brown's *The Rise, Progress and Military Improvement of the Bristol Volunteers* (1798).
49. E.A. Wrigley and R.S. Schofield, *The Population History of England, 1541–1871* (Cambridge, 1981), p. 529. In Scotland, over 60 per cent of the population was under thirty in 1821, T.C. Smout, *A History of the Scottish People 1560–1830* (Glasgow, 1972), p. 262.
50. 'The Pitman's Revenege [*sic*] against Buonaparte', in *A Collection of New Songs* (Newcastle, n.d.).
51. K.J. Logue, *Popular Disturbances in Scotland 1780–1815* (Edinburgh, 1979), p. 103 (my emphasis).
52. David Neave, 'Anti-Militia riots in Lincolnshire, 1757 and 1796', *Lincolnshire History and Archaeology* 11 (1976), p. 25.
53. National Library of Wales, Tredegar MS 405.
54. See Fortescue, *County Lieutenancies*, pp. 198 *et seq*.
55. Printed letter from John Trevor to parish superintendants, 4 August 1803, Bedfordshire Record Office, HA 15/4/2.
56. Richard Fothergill to Charles Morgan, 6 May 1797, National Library of Wales, Tredegar MS 396 (my emphasis).
57. J.W. and Anne Tibble (eds), *The Prose of John Clare* (1951), p. 47. For one nightmare caused by the invasion panic, see *The Diary of Joseph Farington*, ed. Kenneth Garlick, Angus Macintyre and Kathryn Cave (16 vols, New Haven and London, 1978–84), VI, pp. 2082–3.
58. Pamela Horn, *The Rural World 1780–1850: Social Change in the English Countryside* (1980), p. 63.
59. See Appendix 2.
60. Ann Kussmaul (ed.), *The Autobiography of Joseph Mayett of Quainton 1783–1839*, Buckinghamshire Record Society, no. 23 (Cambridge, 1986), p. 23.
61. Quoted in Hudson, 'Volunteer soldiers in Sussex', p. 180.
62. All responses recorded in Hoskins, *Exeter Militia List*, pp. 51, 53, 54, 59.
63. William Rowbottom, an Oldham weaver, quoted in G.A. Steppler, 'The common soldier in the reign of George III, 1760–1793', Oxford University D.Phil. dissertation, 1984, p. 30.
64. See *infra*, pp. 80–5.
65. Reference untraced at time of going to press.
66. *The Times*, 19 July 1803.
67. See, for example, Blanning, *French Revolution in Germany*.
68. David Salmon, 'The French invasion of Pembrokeshire in 1797', *West Wales Historical Records* 14 (1929), p. 202.
69. C.J. Hart, *The History of the 1st volunteer Battalion, the Royal Warwickshire Regiment* (Birmingham, 1906), p. 57; P.R.O., H.O. 42/72/174–6.
70. A *popular* cult of Napoleon only emerged in Britain after Waterloo.
71. In 1815, the economist Patrick Colquhoun calculated that the total military and naval strength of the British empire was over one million men, an estimate that included the East India Company's armed forces: C.A. Bayly, *Imperial Meridian: The British Empire and the World 1780–1830* (1989), p. 3.
72. Quoted in John Barrell, *The Political Theory of Painting from Reynolds to Hazlitt* (New Haven and London, 1986), p. 139.

73. See *A Digest of the Whole Law now in Force Relating to Volunteer Corps in Great Britain* (6th edn, 1804), p. 7.
74. *Scots Magazine* 59 (1797), p. 705. And see Sir John Dalrymple's speech in Edinburgh the following year congratulating the volunteer regiments on connecting the different parts of Great Britain more closely together: *ibid* 60 (1798), p. 788.
75. Information from the local history museum at Woodbridge, Suffolk.
76. This and the next paragraph are based on Kussmaul, *Autobiography of Joseph Mayett.*
77. *Ibid.*, p. 58.
78. Printed general order, 16 May 1801, Staffordshire Record Office, D (W) 1788, parcel 1, bundle 4. For a selection of addresses to volunteers, see Thomas Preston, *Patriots in Arms* (1881).
79. See my 'Whose nation? Class and national consciousness in Britain 1750–1830', *Past & Present* 113 (1986), pp. 114–15.
80. P.R.O., H.O. 42/69/238, 42/78/269.
81. J.R. Harvey, 'A History of the Military Forces of the county of Norfolk', typescript in Norfolk Record Office, IV, p. 641.
82. Quoted in Clive Emsley, 'The military and popular disorder in England, 1790–1801', *Journal of the Society for Army Historical Research* 61 (1983), p. 106.
83. John Bohstedt, *Riots and Community Politics in England and Wales 1790–1810* (Cambridge, 1983), p. 51.
84. Fortescue, *County Lieutenancies*, p. 200.
85. See, for example, the secret information from 'J. Notary', 19 January 1804, P.R.O., H.O. 42/78/216–19.
86. Edward Thompson, *The Making of the English Working Class* (1965), p. 171.
87. Proposals from J.G. at Royal Military College, May 1803, P.R.O., 30/8/245, fols 21–3.
88. *The Autobiography of Samuel Bamford*, ed. W.H. Chaloner, (2 vols, 1967 edn), II, p. 19.
89. G.D.H. and M. Cole, *The Opinions of William Cobbett* (1944), p. 207.

8 VICTORIES?

1. Quoted in N. Gash, 'After Waterloo: British society and the legacy of the Napoleonic Wars', *Transactions of the Royal Historical Society* 28 (1978), p. 146.
2. Seymour Drescher, *Capitalism and Antislavery: British Mobilization in Comparative Perspective* (1986), p. 96; for the problems of the post-war British economy, see Boyd Hilton, *Corn, Cash, Commerce: The Economic Policies of the Tory Government 1815–1830* (Oxford, 1977).
3. For this: G.C. Bolton, *The Passing of the Irish Act of Union* (Oxford, 1966); R.B. McDowell, *Ireland in the Age of Imperialism and Revolution 1760–1801* (Oxford, 1979).
4. Archibald Prentice, *Historical Sketches and Personal Recollections of Manchester* (1970 edn), p. 70.
5. C.A. Bayly, *Imperial Meridian: The British Empire and the World 1780–1830* (1989), p. 3. Professor Bayly suggests that as much as 26 per cent of the world's population may have been included within the empire by 1820.
6. Katherine Solender, *Dreadful fire! Burning of the Houses of Parliament* (Cleveland, Ohio, 1984), pp. 27–41.
7. Kenneth Clark, *The Gothic Revival* (1962 edn), pp. 130–3; but see also M.H. Port (ed.), *The Houses of Parliament* (New Haven and London, 1976), pp. 53–72, 122–141.
8. For example, in G.I.T. Machin's classic *The Catholic Question in English Politics 1820 to 1830* (Oxford, 1964), p. 194, but see also p. 8.
9. Oliver MacDonagh, *The Hereditary Bondsman: Daniel O'Connell 1775–1829* (1988).
10. Colin Haydon, 'Anti-Catholicism in eighteenth century England c.1714–c.1780', Oxford University D.Phil. dissertation, 1985, *passim.*
11. Robert Kent Donovan, 'The military origins of the Roman Catholic relief programme of 1778', *Historical Journal* 28 (1985); Christine Johnson, 'Developments in the Roman Catholic church in Scotland, 1789–1829', Edinburgh University Ph.D. dissertation, 1981, pp. 31–2.
12. Quoted in Edward Porritt, *The Unreformed House of Commons: Parliamentary Representation Before 1832* (2 vols., 1963 edn.), II, p. 468.
13. B. Aspinwall, 'Was O'Connell necessary? Sir Joseph Dillon, Scotland and the movement for Catholic emanci-

pation', in David Loades (ed.), *The End of Strife* (Edinburgh, 1984).

14. *Hansard*, 2nd series, 20 (1829), p. 795.
15. R.G. Thorne (ed.), *The History of Parliament: The House of Commons 1790–1820* (5 vols, 1986), I, pp. 141–225.
16. Too many tears and–by now–too much ink has been spent on the Ultra Tories: see D.G.S. Simes, 'The Ultra Tories in British politics 1824–1834', Oxford University D.Phil. dissertation, 1974; G.F.A. Best, 'The Protestant constitution and its supporters, 1800–1829', *Transactions of the Royal Historical Society* 8 (1958).
17. See Machin, *The Catholic Question*, pp. 65–178.
18. Jeffrey Williamson, 'The impact of the Irish on British labour markets during the Industrial Revolution', in Roger Swift and Sheridan Gilley (eds), *The Irish in Britain 1815–1939* (1989).
19. Information on the anti-Catholic petitions is taken throughout from the High Tory newspaper *John Bull*.
20. By contrast, the repeal of the Test and Corporation Acts in 1828 and the formal extension of full civil rights to British Protestant dissenters provoked only twenty-eight hostile petitions. As always, the divisions within the Protestant community proved far less flammable than the Protestant-Catholic divide. See G.I.T. Machin, 'Resistance to repeal of the Test and Corporation Acts, 1828', *Historical Journal* 22 (1979).
21. Quoted in the *Taunton Courier*, 4 March 1829 (my emphasis).
22. *Hansard*, 2nd series, 20 (1829), pp. 644 and 905 (Taunton and Frome); *John Bull*, 22 March 1829.
23. *Hansard*, 2nd series, 20 (1829), pp. 905, 1062.
24. G.I.T. Machin, 'Catholic emancipation as an issue in North Welsh politics 1825–1829', *Transactions of the Honourable Society of Cymmrodorion* (1962), p. 89.
25. Machin, *The Catholic Question*, p. 140.
26. *Hansard*, 2nd series, 20 (1829), p. 808.
27. See Peter Burke, *Popular Culture in Early Modern Europe* (1978), pp. 270–86.
28. *Hansard*, 2nd series, 20 (1829), pp. 358, 422, 580.
29. J.P. de Castro, *The Gordon Riots* (Oxford, 1926); Robert Kent Donovan, *No Popery and Radicalism: Opposition to Roman Catholic Relief in Scotland, 1778–1782* (New York, 1987).
30. MPs and peers regularly drew attention to the 'marginality' of the protesters: *Hansard*, 2nd series, 20 (1829), pp. 316, 372–3, 572, 610, 1324; *ibid.* 21 (1829), p. 659.
31. *Ibid.* 20 (1829), p. 604.
32. A point well made in J.R. Wolfe, 'Protestant societies and Anti-Catholic agitation in Great Britain 1829–1860', Oxford University D.Phil. dissertation, 1984, pp. 184 and 353.
33. On the continuing strength of anti-Catholicism throughout Great Britain after 1829, see Wolfe, 'Protestant societies'; W.L. Arnstein, *Protestant versus Catholic in mid-Victorian England* (1982); Geoffrey Best, 'Popular Protestantism in Victorian Great Britain' in R. Robson (ed.), *Ideas and Institutions of Victorian Britain* (1967).
34. Bruce Lenman, *Integration, Enlightenment, and Industrialization: Scotland 1746–1832* (1981), p. 159.
35. This account is based on C.R. Fay, *Huskisson and His Age* (1951), pp. 1–11; and Frances Ann Kemble, *Record of a Girlhood* (3 vols, 1878), II, pp. 187–90.
36. I owe this information to my graduate student Stephanie Barczewski.
37. *Geoffrey Madan's Notebooks*, ed. J.A. Gere and John Sparrow (1981), p. 117.
38. The most recent detailed account is M. Brock, *The Great Reform Act* (1973); and see Eric J. Evans, *Britain before the Reform Act: Politics and Society 1815–1832* (1989).
39. For Paine's iconoclasm: Edward Thompson, *The Making of the English Working Class* (1965), pp. 83–101.
40. *The Times*, 6 December 1794.
41. See T.M. Parssinen, 'Association Convention and Anti-Parliament in British radical politics, 1771–1848', *English Historical Review* 87 (1973); and Gareth Stedman Jones, 'Rethinking Chartism', in his *Languages of Class* (Cambridge, 1983).
42. Prentice, *Historical Sketches*, p. 188.
43. Included in *The Radical Reformers' New Song Book: being a choice collection of patriotic songs* (Newcastle, n.d., but after 1819).
44. J.R. Dinwiddy, *From Luddism to the First Reform Bill* (1986), pp. 24–30.
45. W.M. Roach, 'Radical reform move-

ments in Scotland from 1815 to 1822', Glasgow University Ph.D. dissertation, 1970, pp. 18–21.

46. See J.D. Brims, 'The Scottish "Jacobins", Scottish nationalism and British union', in Roger A. Mason (ed.), *Scotland and England 1286–1815* (Edinburgh, 1987); and his 'The Scottish Democratic Movement in the Age of the French Revolution', Edinburgh University Ph.D. dissertation, 1983.
47. Thompson, *Making of the English Working Class*, p. 693.
48. Roach, 'Radical reform movements in Scotland', pp. 163–4.
49. See the anonymous pamphlet *Order of the Procession* (Edinburgh, n.d., but 1832), National Library of Scotland.
50. *Scotsman*, 2 and 13 June 1832.
51. J. Belchem, 'Henry Hunt and the evolution of the mass platform', *English Historical Review* 93 (1978), p. 755.
52. Quoted in Dorothy Thompson, *The Chartists* (1984), p. 13 (my emphasis).
53. J.R. Dinwiddy, *Christopher Wyvill and Reform 1790–1820*, Borthwick Papers, no. 39 (York, 1971), p. 23.
54. See Joseph Hamburger, *James Mill and the Art of Revolution* (New Haven, 1963), pp. 75–136; Peter Fraser, 'Public petitioning and Parliament before 1832', *History* 158 (1961).
55. John Cannon, *Parliamentary Reform 1640–1832* (Cambridge, 1973), p. 214n.; *Hansard*, 3rd series, 3 (1831), pp. 1201–2.
56. For example, the issue for 5 October 1831.
57. *Scotsman*, 10 September 1831.
58. *Ibid.*, 13 June 1832 (Dalkeith meeting); 25 April 1832.
59. *Ibid.*, 22 October 1831.
60. See, for instance, Paul Johnson, *The Birth of the Modern* (1991), pp. 995–7.
61. G.M. Trevelyan, *Lord Grey of the Reform Bill* (1920), pp. 308–9.
62. The best account is Cannon, *Parliamentary Reform*, pp. 204–63.
63. See E.A. Smith, *Lord Grey 1764–1845* (Oxford, 1990).
64. Trevelyan, *Lord Grey*, p. 285.
65. *Hansard*, 3rd series, 8 (1831), p. 599 (my emphasis).
66. See Brock, *Great Reform Act*, pp. 310–13.
67. David A. Wager, 'Welsh politics and parliamentary reform, 1780–1832', *Welsh History Review* 7 (1975); Michael Dyer, '"Mere detail and machinery": The great Reform Act and the effects of re-distribution in Scottish representation, 1832–1868', *Scottish Historical Review* 62 (1983).
68. This and the next paragraph draw heavily on Derek Beales's excellent essay 'The electorate before and after 1832: the right to vote, and the opportunity', which I was allowed to consult before its publication.
69. The Reform Act's impact on England was less startling, but still striking. In 1826, 104,558 men were able to cast their votes in the English constituencies out of a possible total of over 340,000. In 1830, only 88,216 voted. But in the first general election under the new system, 381,375 English voters were able to use their votes.
70. I use here the estimates supplied in Robert J. Goldstein, *Political Repression in 19th Century Europe* (1983), pp. 4–5. The relative generosity of the 1832 franchise emerges even more starkly if one looks at the electorate in England, Wales and Scotland alone, rather than in the United Kingdom as a whole as Goldstein does.
71. John Belchem, *Orator Hunt: Henry Hunt and English Working Class Radicalism*, (Oxford, 1985), p. 222.
72. For complaints by Scottish MPs about this: *Hansard*, 3rd series, 9 (1831–2), pp. 187 and 632 *et seq.*; *ibid.*, 10 (1832), pp. 1080–97. Since most of them were staunch Tories, they were hampered by the fact that they were bound to oppose the Reform Act in general, and so were scarcely in a position to demand more generous terms for Scotland in particular.
73. See Dyer, '"Mere detail and machinery"'; N. Gash, *Reaction and Reconstruction in English Politics, 1832–1853* (Oxford, 1965).
74. See the illustration '"The Gathering of the Unions" on Newhall Hill, 7 May 1832', in *The Collected Essays of Asa Briggs*. I: *Words, Numbers, Places, People* (Brighton, 1985), pp. 60–1.
75. Goldstein, *Political repression*, pp. 4–5.
76. Albert Boime, *The Art of Exclusion: Representing Blacks in the Nineteenth Century* (1990), pp. 67–70.
77. The most useful survey is James

Walvin, *England, Slaves, and Freedom, 1776–1838* (Jackson, Miss., 1986). Despite its title, this book does not in fact confine itself to England.

78. Seymour Drescher, *Econocide: British Slavery in the Era of Abolition* (Pittsburgh, 1977), p. 27.
79. *Ibid.*, pp. 28–30. Cf. Paul Lovejoy, 'The volume of the Atlantic slave trade', *Journal of African History* (1982).
80. Quoted in David Brion Davis, *The Problem of Slavery in the Age of Revolution, 1770–1823* (1975) p. 24.
81. *Ibid.*, pp. 45–9; Drescher, *Capitalism and Antislavery*, p. 60.
82. Roger Anstey, *The Atlantic Slave Trade and British Abolition 1760–1810* (1975), p. 239.
83. Drescher, *Capitalism and Antislavery*, pp. 70–3.
84. John Pollock, *Wilberforce* (1977), p. 89.
85. *Hansard*, 1st series, 8 (1806–7), pp. 670–1.
86. Quoted in Davis, *The Problem of Slavery*, p. 379.
87. Drescher, *Capitalism and Antislavery*, pp. 59, 74–94.
88. *Ibid.*, p. 85; Alex Tyrrell, 'The moral radical party and the Anglo-Jamaican campaign for the abolition of the negro apprenticeship system', *English Historical Review* 99 (1984), p. 492.
89. Folarin Shyllon, *Black People in Britain 1555–1833* (1977).
90. *The Bow in the Cloud; Or, the Negro's Memorial* (1834), p. 405. This collection of amateur verses by different Britons on the emancipation of the West Indian slaves is an invaluable text for the more complacent brand of patriotism at this time.
91. Davis, *The Problem of Slavery*, p. 49.
92. Robin Furneaux, *William Wilberforce* (1974), pp. 455–6.
93. *Econocide*, p. 16. Drescher is rebutting here, to my mind successfully, the argument of Eric Williams's classic, *Capitalism and Slavery* (1944).
94. See Boyd Hilton, *The Age of Atonement: The Influence of Evangelicalism on Social and Economic Thought 1795–1865* (Oxford, 1988), *passim*.
95. *Hansard*, 1st series, 7 (1806), p. 807; *ibid.*, 8 (1806–7), pp. 978–9.
96. Drescher, *Econocide*, *passim*. In economic, as in moral terms, Britain's record on slavery was mixed. After 1838, its sugar was produced by free men, but its cotton textile industry continued to draw over 70 per cent of its raw material from the slave states of America: David Brion Davis, *Slavery and Human Progress* (New York, 1984), pp. 208–9.
97. See Seymour Drescher, 'Cart whip and billy roller: or Anti-Slavery and reform symbolism in industrializing Britain', *Journal of Social History* 15 (1981).
98. Davis, *Slavery and Human Progress*, p. xviii (my emphasis). My debt to this remarkable book in the interpretation offered here will be obvious.
99. *Hansard*, 3rd series, 15 (1833), p. 1197.
100. See Conor Cruise O'Brien, *God Land: Reflections on Religion and Nationalism* (Cambridge, Mass., 1987).
101. For Parliament's refusal to debate petitions after the mid-1830s, a decision prompted in part by the determination to cut down opportunities for popular pressure on the legislature, see Fraser, 'Public petitioning', pp. 209–11.
102. *Hansard*, 3rd series, 16 (1833), p. 1201; Fraser, 'Public petitioning', p. 207.

CONCLUSIONS

1. This and the next paragraph draw heavily on H.A.D. Miles and David Blayney Brown, *Sir David Wilkie of Scotland* (Raleigh, N.C., 1987).
2. See Allan Cunningham, *The Life of Sir David Wilkie* (3 vols, 1843), II, pp. 71–7.
3. E.J. Hobsbawm, *Nations and Nationalism since 1780* (Cambridge, 1990), p. 91.
4. John Lough, *France on the Eve of Revolution: British Travellers' Observations 1763–1788* (1987), p. 61.
5. Hugo Young, *The Iron Lady: A Biography of Margaret Thatcher* (New York, 1989), p. 9.
6. See Brian Stanley, *The Bible and the Flag: Protestant Missions and British Imperialism in the Nineteenth and Twentieth Centuries* (1990).
7. For this tendency, see Edward W. Said, *Orientalism* (New York, 1978): for example, pp. 33–4.
8. F. Reid, *Keir Hardie: The Making of a Socialist* (1978), p. 124.
9. See Simon Schama, *The Embarrassment of Riches: An Interpretation of Dutch Culture in the Golden Age* (Berkeley and Los Angeles, 1988); Michael Roberts, 'The Swedish Church', in his edited

volume, *Sweden's Age of Greatness* (1973).

10. Paul Bushkovitch, 'The formation of a national consciousness in early modern Russia', *Harvard Ukrainian Studies* 10, no. 3/4 (1986).
11. I am emboldened to make this criticism of Eugen Weber's remarkable *Peasants into Frenchmen: The Modernization of Rural France, 1870–1914* (Stanford, Ca., 1976), by the work of my colleague David Bell.
12. *Ibid.*, p. 112.
13. Quoted in Christopher Hill, *Collected Essays.* III: *People and Ideas in 17th Century England* (1986), p. 249.
14. Cf. Arthur Marwick, *The Deluge: British Society and the First World War* (1965).
15. This is beginning to happen. See, for instance, the essays in Raphael Samuel, ed., *Patriotism: The Making and Unmaking of British National Identity* (3 vols, 1989).
16. Quoted in John Morley, *The Life of Richard Cobden* (Boston, Mass., 1881), p. 313.
17. Peter Scott, *Knowledge and Nation* (Edinburgh, 1990), p. 168.
18. See R.J. Morris, 'Scotland, 1830–1914: The Making of a Nation within a Nation', in R.J. Morris and W.H. Fraser, eds., *People and Society in Scotland.* II: *1830–1914* (Edinburgh, 1990). James Bryce made the point well in 1887: 'An Englishman has but one patriotism, because England and the United Kingdom are to him practically the same thing. A Scotchman has two, but he is sensible of no opposition between them', *Mr. Gladstone and the Nationalities of the United Kingdom: A Series of Letters to the 'Times'* (1887), p. 15.
19. *Gentleman's Magazine* 101 (1831), pp. 438–9.
20. Glanmor Williams, *Religion, Language and Nationality in Wales* (Cardiff, 1979), pp. 143–4.
21. Sir John Sinclair, *An Account of the Highland Society of London* (1813), pp. 27 and 35.
22. Tom Nairn's Scottish Nationalist classic *The Break-Up of Britain: Crisis and Neo-Nationalism* (2nd edn, 1981) has been followed by a succession of similar studies. But anyone who wants a sense of just how urgent and widespread this debate has now become need only glance at the daily newspaper press in Britain.
23. Sir John Macpherson to Sir John Sinclair, 9 November 1798, History of Parliament Trust, Sinclair transcripts.

Index

Photograph Acknowledgements

1, 2, 6, 9, 16, 17, 24, 27, 28, 36, 43, 58, 60, 65, 66, 68, 72, 73, 74, 75, 76, 80 courtesy of the Trustees of the British Museum; 3, 69 courtesy of the Henry E. Huntington Library and Art Gallery; 4, 18, 19 courtesy of Cambridge University Library; 5, 61 courtesy of the Beinecke Rare Book and Manuscript Library, Yale University; 7, 14, 15, 22, 23, 25, 26, 30, 50, 52, 53, 54, 55, 56, 57, 59 courtesy of the Print Collection, Lewis Walpole Library, Yale University; 10 courtesy of the Thomas Coram Foundation for Children; 11, 34 courtesy of the Trustees of the Tate Gallery; 12: India Office Collection (photo: Paul Mellon Centre for Studies in British Art); 13a and b courtesy of the National Trust for Scotland; 19, 67, 70 courtesy of the Director, National Army Museum London; 29, 32, 37, 38, 40, 41, 45, 46, 47, 49, 63 courtesy of the Yale Center for British Art, Paul Mellon Collection; 31 by permission of the Provost and Fellows of Eton College and the Governors of Dulwich Picture Gallery; 33 courtesy of the National Gallery of Canada, Ottawa; 35 courtesy of the National Maritime Museum London; 39: Windsor Castle, Royal Library © 1991. Her Majesty Queen Elizabeth II; 42, 62: Royal Collection, St James's Palace © 1991. Her Majesty Queen Elizabeth II; 48 courtesy of the Guildhall Library, London; 64 by permission of the Dean and Canons of Windsor; 71 reproduced from Ann Kussmaul, *The Autobiography of Joseph Mayett of Quainton 1783–1839*, Buckinghamshire Record Society, No. 23, 1986, by permission of the Buckinghamshire Record Society; 77: Viscount Coke and the Trustees of the Holkham Estate (photo: Courtauld Institute of Art, University of London); 78: Henry Lillie Pierce Fund. Courtesy Museum of Fine Arts, Boston; 79 courtesy of the Menil Collection, Houston, Texas (photo: Janet Woodward); 81 courtesy of the Trustees of the Victoria and Albert Museum; map, Appendix 1, based on a map in Andrew Charlesworth, ed., *An Atlas of Rural Protest in Britain 1548–1900*, Croom Helm: London and Canberra, 1983, by permission of the publishers.